Jesus and the Missional Movement in Galilee

Jesus and the Missional Movement in Galilee

Markan Spatial Presentation
and Its Hermeneutical Significance

SUN WOOK KIM

☙PICKWICK *Publications* • Eugene, Oregon

JESUS AND THE MISSIONAL MOVEMENT IN GALILEE
Markan Spatial Presentation and Its Hermeneutical Significance

Copyright © 2019 Sun Wook Kim. All rights reserved. Except for brief quotations in critical publications or reviews, no part of this book may be reproduced in any manner without prior written permission from the publisher. Write: Permissions, Wipf and Stock Publishers, 199 W. 8th Ave., Suite 3, Eugene, OR 97401.

Pickwick Publications
An Imprint of Wipf and Stock Publishers
199 W. 8th Ave., Suite 3
Eugene, OR 97401

www.wipfandstock.com

PAPERBACK ISBN: 978-1-4982-0295-4
HARDCOVER ISBN: 978-1-4982-0297-8
EBOOK ISBN: 978-1-4982-0296-1

Cataloging-in-Publication data:

Names: Kim, Sun Wook, author.

Title: Jesus and the missional movement in Galilee : Markan spatial presentation and its hermeneutical significance / by Sun Wook Kim.

Description: Eugene, OR : Pickwick Publications, 2019 | Includes bibliographical references and index(es).

Identifiers: ISBN 978-1-4982-0295-4 (paperback) | ISBN 978-1-4982-0297-8 (hardcover) | ISBN 978-1-4982-0296-1 (ebook)

Subjects: LCSH: Bible. Mark—Criticism, interpretation, etc. | Hermeneutics.

Classification: LCC BS2585.52 K45 2019 (print) | LCC BS2585.52 (ebook)

Manufactured in the U.S.A.   07/10/19

To my father, Son Joong Kim, and my mother, Jeong Ho Kim,
with love, gratitude, and respect

Contents

Preface | ix
Abbreviations | xi

chapter 1
Introduction | 1
   Issues Raised | 1
   Methodological Considerations | 10
   Study Plan | 55

chapter 2
Social Space: The Social World of Galilee and Markan Spatial Presentation | 58
   Previous Studies on Markan Spatial Presentation | 58
   Social Circumstances of Galilee and Markan Presentation | 79

chapter 3
Geographical Space: Structural Analysis of Mark 4:35—8:21 | 101
   Survey of Previous Structural Analyses of Mark 4–8 | 101
   The Narrative Structure of a Cyclic Pattern in Mark 4:35—8:21 Based on Geographical Arrangement, Literary Parallelism, and Boat and Bread Motifs | 125
   Conclusion | 159

chapter 4
Allusive Space: Spatial Allusions of Exodus Imagery in the Sea and the Wilderness | 161
   Intertextual Relationship between Ps 78(77):12–32 and Mark 4:35—8:21 | 163
   The Sea and the Wilderness as the Spatial Settings of the New Exodus | 175
   Conclusion | 229

chapter 5
Conclusion | 232
   Summary | 232
   Theological Implications | 238

Bibliography | 241
Author Index | 257

Preface

THE PURPOSE OF THIS work is to explore Jesus' missional movement in Mark 4:35—8:21 through the use of spatial analysis. Space is not simply an inert container or static backdrop where events take place, but rather plays a key role in revealing themes and purposes in a narrative. Exploring Mark's narrative from the perspective of spatial analysis will provide a fresh hermeneutical lens through which to understand Jesus' life and ministry.

In this study, I divide space into three categories, "social," "geographical," and "allusive," and I examine Jesus' missional movement in terms of each kind of space. First, a study of social space deals with how Mark presents the social world of Galilee in his narrative. Galilean society, which was influenced by, but also in conflict with, Jewish religious authorities, was open and ready to accept a new order and value system that differed from those of the temple and Jerusalem. Galilee provided good soil where Jesus' missional movement could take root and grow toward success.

Second, looking at geographical space allows us to trace the route of Jesus' geographical movement in his missional journey in and beyond Galilee. My structural analysis of 4:35—8:21 is based on the geographical arrangement of Jesus' ministry as portrayed through Mark's rhetorical devices. This structure presents a cyclic pattern consisting of two cycles (4:35—6:44 and 6:45—8:10) and a conclusion (8:11–21); one cycle focuses on Jesus' mission to the Jews, the other on his mission to the Gentiles. Markan geographical description consequently shows the theological purpose of Jesus' journey, namely his missions to both the Jews and the Gentiles.

Third, a study of allusive space explores how Markan space evokes memories of the history of Israel. Space contains historical traces, symbolic meanings, and ideological or theological significance. The sea and the wilderness in Jesus' sea and feeding miracles (4:35–41; 6:31–44; 6:45–52; 8:1–10) not only serve as spatial settings that allude to the exodus events of the victory at the sea and the provision of manna in the wilderness, but also carry cosmological and eschatological implications that prompt us to interpret Jesus' missional movement in the light of the new exodus.

This book is a slightly revised version of my doctoral dissertation accepted at Trinity Evangelical Divinity School in 2013. With God's grace, love, and guidance, I could complete the dissertation. I could also finish my writing with many people's prayers, encouragements, and supports. To begin, I give sincere thanks to Dr. Grant R. Osborne who is my dissertation mentor. He has always shown me warm-hearted kindness and consistently encouraged me to write a dissertation. Even when he was in a hospital after heart surgery, he read my papers and gave me precious comments. In his consistent concerns and instructions, I could continue my research. I also want to express my thanks to Dr. David W. Pao (my second reader) who evaluated my paper with valuable advice; and to Dr. Richard E. Averbeck (my program's director).

My deep gratitude goes to my family members and church community members. With their love, encouragements, supports, and prayers, I could continue to study in this long journey of scholarship. I am also grateful to the faculty, staff, and colleagues in Trinity Evangelical Divinity School, with whose instructions and encouragements I could advance my theological study in the doctoral program.

In Memory of Dr. Grant R. Osborne (1942–2018)

Last year, I heard the news of the passing of Dr. Grant R. Osborne who was my mentor during the doctoral program. He was a prominent scholar in the academic circle, a sincere servant of God in church ministry, and a gracious teacher in the school. He showed a deep love and commitment to the Scripture and guided his students with a pastoral mind. To me, he is remembered as the man of God who stood firm on God's Word. He had promised to write a foreword for this book, unfortunately the book now stands without it. However, I believe he will be delighted for its publication in heaven. I will always remember his encouragement, kindness, and grace to me. My gratitude to him is immeasurable.

Abbreviations

AAAG	*Annals of the Association of American Geographers*
AB	Anchor Bible
ABD	*Anchor Bible Dictionary*
ABRL	Anchor Bible Reference Library
AnBib	Analecta biblica
AR	*Archiv für Religionswissenschaft*
ATJ	*Ashland Theological Journal*
BCOTWP	Baker Commentary on the Old Testament Wisdom and Psalms
BDAG	Bauer, W., F. W. Danker, W. F. Arndt, and F. W. Gingrich. *Greek-English Lexicon of the New Testament and Other Early Christian Literature*
BDF	Blass, F., A. Debrunner, and R. W. Funk. *A Greek Grammar of the New Testament and Other Early Christian Literature*
BECNT	Baker Exegetical Commentary on the New Testament
BETL	*Bibliotheca ephemeridum theologicarum lovaniensium*
Bib	*Biblica*
BibOr	Biblica et orientalia
BNTC	Black's New Testament Commentaries
BSac	*Bibliotheca Sacra*
BT	*Baptistic Theologies*
BTB	*Biblical Theology Bulletin*
BZAW	Beihefte zur Zeitschrift für die alttestamentliche Wissenschaft

BZNW	Beihefte zur Zeitschrift fur die neutestamentliche Wissenschaft die Kunde der *älteren* Kirche
CBET	Contributions to Biblical Exegesis and Theology
CBQ	*Catholic Biblical Quarterly*
CBQMS	*Catholic Biblical Quarterly Monograph Series*
CBRA	Collectanea Biblica et Religiosa Antiqua
CCSS	Catholic Commentary on Sacred Scripture
DJG	*Dictionary of Jesus and the Gospels*
DNTB	*Dictionary of New Testament Background*
DPL	*Dictionary of Paul and His Letters*
DTIB	*Dictionary for Theological Interpretation of the Bible*
EBC	Expositor's Bible Commentary
ECC	Eerdmans Critical Commentary
EDB	*Eerdmans Dictionary of the Bible*
EKKNT	Evangelisch-Katholischer Kommentar zum Neuen Testament
ETL	*Ephemerides theologicae lovanienses*
FAT	Forschungen zum Alten Testament
FRLANT	Forschungen zur Religion und Literatur des Alten und Neuen Testaments
GBS	Guides to Biblical Scholarship
Hermeneia	Hermeneia—A Critical and Historical Commentary on the Bible
HKAT	Handkommentar zum Alten Testament
HNT	Handbuch zum Neuen Testament
HNTC	Harper's New Testament Commentaries
HSM	Harvard Semitic Monographs
HTKNT	Herders theologischer Kommentar zum Neuen Testament
HTR	*Harvard Theological Review*
IBC	Interpretation: A Bible Commentary for Teaching and Preaching
Int	*Interpretation*

IVPDNT	*The IVP Dictionary of the New Testament*
JAAR	*Journal of the American Academy of Religion*
JAF	*Journal of American Folklore*
JBL	*Journal of Biblical Literature*
JLCRS	Jordan Lectures in Comparative Religion Series
JR	*Journal of Religion*
JSNT	*Journal for the Study of the New Testament*
JSNTSup	Journal for the Study of the New Testament: Supplement Series
JSS	*Journal of Semitic Studies*
KEK	Kritisch-exegetischer Kommentar über das Neue Testament
LNTS	Library of New Testament Studies
NAC	New American Commentary
NCB	New Century Bible
NCBC	New Cambridge Bible Commentary
NDT	*New Dictionary of Theology*
NIBCOT	New International Biblical Commentary on the Old Testament
NICNT	New International Commentary on the New Testament
NICOT	New International Commentary on the Old Testament
NIDB	*New Interpreter's Dictionary of the Bible*
NIGTC	New International Greek Testament Commentary
NIVAC	NIV Application Commentary
NovTSup	Supplements to Novum Testamentum
NTL	New Testament Library
NTS	*New Testament Studies*
OTL	Old Testament Library
PIBA	*Proceedings of the Irish Biblical Association*
PNTC	Pillar New Testament Commentary
Proof	*Prooftexts: A Journal of Jewish Literary History*
PRSt	*Perspectives in Religious Studies*

ResQ	*Restoration Quarterly*
SBLDS	Society of Biblical Literature Dissertation Series
SBT	Studies in Biblical Theology
ScEccl	*Sciences ecclésiastiques*
SHS	Scripture and Hermeneutics Series
SJOTSup	Journal for the Study of the Old Testament: Supplement Series
SJT	*Scottish Journal of Theology*
SNTSMS	Society for New Testament Studies Monograph Series
SNTW	Studies of the New Testament and Its World
SP	Sacra Pagina
StPB	Studia post-Biblica
SUNT	Studien zur Umwelt des Neuen Testaments
SwJT	*Southwestern Journal of Theology*
TDNT	*Theological Dictionary of the New Testament*
TDOT	*Theological Dictionary of the Old Testament*
TJ	*Trinity Journal*
TZ	*Theologische Zeitschrift*
TNTL	Tyndale New Testament Lecture
TS	*Theological Studies*
VT	*Vetus Testamentum*
VTSup	Supplements to Vetus Testamentum
WBC	Word Biblical Commentary
WC	Westminster Commentaries
WUNT	Wissenschaftliche Untersuchungen zum Neuen Testament
ZDPV	*Zeitschrift des deutschen Palästina-Vereins*
ZNW	*Zeitschrift für die neutestamentliche Wissenschaft und die Kunde der älteren Kirche*

chapter 1

Introduction

Issues Raised

IN NEW TESTAMENT (NT) scholarship, the study of space has been somewhat underrepresented in comparison with the study of time, and Markan scholarship offers no exception to this tendency. Stewart comments on this imbalance:

> Nowhere is the privileging of time over space more apparent than in New Testament studies. The major questions surrounding historical Jesus research for much of its history have been related to Jesus and eschatology. *When* Jesus expected the kingdom of God has been the dominant question. This preoccupation with eschatology and apocalypticism has dominated the study of the Gospels as well. The relative paucity of studies addressing the question of space in the Gospel of Mark attests to that fact.[1]

Stewart argues that the lack of attention to space is caused, in large part, by the use of the historical-critical interpretive approach which deals primarily with historical questions in relation to time.[2] Thus NT scholarship has examined "the historical Jesus and the coming of the kingdom of God" with respect to eschatology, focusing on time.[3] Stewart goes on to call for

---

1. Stewart, *Gathered around Jesus*, 41–42.
2. Stewart, *Gathered around Jesus*, 42.
3. Stewart, *Gathered around Jesus*, 1. According to Stewart, "the study of first-century Jesus movements has long focused largely on temporal questions. This is seen most clearly, perhaps, in the debate regarding the historical Jesus and the coming of the

more attention to the study of space in biblical scholarship; he suggests that a social-scientific approach might play a significant role in explorations of space[4]—space here referring to the production of human social activities.[5] In recent years, the study of the social space of first-century Palestine, especially Galilee, has been increasingly employed to understand Jesus' life and ministry.[6]

The study of space has also been disregarded to some degree in literary approaches to biblical interpretation. The narrative approach, one of various literary methodologies, has largely focused on the study of characterization and plot while devoting little attention to the significance of spatial settings. According to Bland, "the role and technique of background description has been somewhat neglected" in more general literary studies.[7] One of

---

kingdom of God. *When* Jesus expected the kingdom has been a crucial question to biblical scholars for more than a century. This focus on temporal matters has been matched by a substantial lack of focus on issues of spatiality in first-century Jesus movements."

4. Stewart, *Gathered around Jesus*, 32–42. In general, a historical-critical approach is performed in a diachronic dimension, while a social-critical approach is carried out in a synchronic dimension. The former is related to time and the latter to space. While historians highlight its "differences" and "changes" in the process of history, sociologists emphasize the "organization" and "patterns of social activity." Consequently, there exists a gap or conflict between historical and sociological approaches. Despite these methodological clashes, however, it is essential to examine historical events and social phenomenon using both historical and sociological approaches

5. See Lefebvre, *Production of Space*.

6. Though the Third Quest for the Historical Jesus encompasses diverse views, Moxnes argues that the Third Quest's fresh study of the historical Jesus presents "a general trend in historical and religious studies towards social and local contexts" (Moxnes, "Construction of Galilee—Part II," 64). Sociological approaches have been applied especially to investigate the social space of Galilee, the area where Jesus was born, grew up, and began and successfully carried out his missional movement. We can interpret historical texts such as the Gospels in terms of social models, in which a structure of social space (geography) is constructed in the text. Jesus' life and ministry may be examined in this structure. Sack, however, pointed out that we need to pay attention to the "difference between the particularistic approaches of historical geography and the generalizing approaches of social geography" (Sack, *Human Territoriality*, 2). Considering this difference, we should use both historical and social approaches to interpret a text—we should not adopt one (social) while excluding the other (historical), or vice versa. The synchronic approach of social geography may make the mistake of generalization, ignoring the particular situations of historical geography. Therefore, when we examine social space in a text, we must also consider the diachronic approach of historical geography. Using the term "social history," Rhoads explains the combination of social and historical approaches as follows: "Social historians seek to understand the broad sweep of change in history. This approach applies a comprehensive knowledge of social description through time to produce a social history of the period" (Rhoads, "Social Criticism," 147–48).

7. Bland, "Endangering the Reader's Neck," 313.

the reasons for this lack of scholarly attention to spatial settings (or "background description," as Bland calls it) is that settings are often understood "without relevance to the totality" of narrative: they are simply interpreted in themselves.[8] This is problematic because spatial settings are not independent in themselves; rather, they should be identified and explicated in relation to characters and plot.[9] Spatial settings do not function only as stages for characters' action; they also convey particular meanings in interaction with characters and plot. Recent narrative studies have increasingly recognized the significance of spatial settings in terms of their relationships to characters, events, plot, and theme.[10] Smith, for example, notes that "despite the frequent observation that Mark is full of vivid detail, the evangelist uses hardly a word in his settings which is not directly relevant to either characterization, plot or theology."[11]

Despite these developments, however, spatial presentation has not been truly recognized in Markan scholarship. One of the reasons for this is the idea that Mark's description is vague and inaccurate in its geographical designations or arrangements. Commentators have generally agreed that Mark was confused and ignorant of the geography of Palestine and its vicinity, that his description of place-names and routes of Jesus' travel is clumsy and erroneous, and that the geographical information in Mark therefore has little value as a historical record.[12] However, several questions may be

---

8. Bland, "Endangering the Reader's Neck," 314. Bland explains the indifference to the study of background description in the novel as follows: "One reason for this neglect is that description—of a sort—is so easy to do, and so frequently done for its own sake, without relevance to the totality of the novel, that the critic avoids so obvious a field for adverse comment."

9. Bland, "Endangering the Reader's Neck," 314. According to Bland, "scene is only justified in the novel where it can be shown, or at least felt, to act upon action or character."

10. Smith says that literary critics' interest in spatial settings has increased in the time since Bland's comments on their neglect: "it has been increasingly recognized that in the better novels spatial setting (or background description) is not merely an elaboration which could easily be discarded without any fear of doing violence to the work, but is often indispensable to character or plot" (Smith, *Lion with Wings*, 150–52).

11. Smith, *Lion with Wings*, 153.

12. Malbon, *Narrative Space*, 15. For the reason of Mark's inaccurate geographical description, Wrede argues that Mark does not show a well-organized arrangement in geographical description, because he simply connected his historical traditions in order to express his "dogmatic or semi-dogmatic ideas" (Wrede, *Messianic Secret*, 129–32). In the story of Jesus and his disciples' voyage toward Bethsaida in Mark 6:45–52, for example, Rawlinson claims that "the geography is vague. . . . It is possible that the Evangelist himself had no clear picture of the locality in his mind; to him, as to his readers, the various places he mentions may have been little more than names in the tradition" (Rawlinson, *St. Mark*, 89). For a similar opinion that Mark was confused or ignorant of

raised against this argument regarding Markan geographical mistakes. Can we legitimately say that Mark's geographical description contains "vagueness" and "errors"?[13] Are we evaluating Mark's geographical description on the basis of modern methods and standards of cartographical accuracy?[14] Do we ignore Mark's literary choices and theological intentions in arranging Jesus' geographical movement in his narrative?[15] Have we been negligent in failing to study the spatial understanding of first-century Mediterranean

---

Palestinian geography, Nineham maintains that the geographical vagueness and inaccuracy in Mark were caused by Mark's lack of direct acquaintance with Palestine (e.g., Nineham, *Gospel of St. Mark*, 40, 180, 186). See also Theissen, *Gospels in Context*, 237. Regarding the description of Jesus' geographical movement in northern Palestine in 7:31, Cranfield asserts that "this verse reflects a certain vagueness on Mark's part about the geography of northern Palestine" (Cranfield, *Gospel according to Saint Mark*, 250). Chapman introduces five verses in which Mark seems to have made mistakes in the geographical description of Palestine and its vicinity because of his unfamiliarity with these areas: "(1) Mark's placement of Gerasa on the shore of the Sea of Galilee (5:1); (2) Jesus' itinerary from Tyre, through Sidon, to the Sea of Galilee (7:31a); (3) Mark's locating the Sea of Galilee 'in the midst of' the Decapolis (7:31b); (4) the apparent lumping together of Judea and Beyond the Jordan (10:1); and (5) the sequence of Bethphage and Bethany on the approach to Jerusalem (11:1)" (Chapman, "Locating the Gospel of Mark," 24).

13. According to Chapman, "focus on these 'mistakes' has obscured the larger question: how does one account for the abundance, accurate placement, and even correct sequence of geographical data in Mark's Gospel?" (Chapman, "Locating the Gospel of Mark," 24).

14. Though an unknown place-name, Dalmanutha, is mentioned in Mark, for example, we cannot conclude that it is an incorrect geographical designation. Jenkins argues that the place-name of Dalmanutha in 8:10 is a "memory-corruption of Gennesaret" in 6:35, because Dalmanutha is a cryptic and unfamiliar name—no other material records this name (Jenkins, "Marcan Doublet," 103). Gundry, however, refutes the idea that the place-name Dalmanutha is not historical, arguing that Mark had no reason to insert a mysterious name in this context instead of a familiar one. The name Dalmanutha might have been used among people in some areas at one time, but disappeared later. We might also note that Dalmanutha was not necessarily an official name such as an administrative district, but a name used by local people at that time. Use of an unofficial place-name does not equate to inaccuracy of geographical description. See Gundry, *Mark*, 403.

15. Even historians cannot be completely objective in recording historical events; rather, they collect, choose, and arrange events in order to compose a historical record reflecting their own style and perspective. Mark, who wrote his gospel as a narrative, describes and arranges Jesus' ministry and geographical movement according to his own theological view and literary techniques. In relation to this study, for example, though Mark's geographical description of 4:35—8:21 seems to be inaccurate and clumsy, it actually forms a cyclic pattern (two cycles), a structure that Mark deliberately chose as a literary technique to express his theological purposes. One cycle is concerned with Jesus' mission to the Jews; the other is concerned with his mission to the Gentiles. I will demonstrate this in chapter 3.

people and consider the implications for Markan space?[16] Have we forgotten that space is not simply a place where events take place, but in fact contains historical, ideological, and symbolic implications that lead us to recollect the past or anticipate the future?[17] These questions open deep and broad prospects for improving our understanding of Markan space. Markan space (geography) is described with historical accuracy, arranged according to Mark's literary techniques, and rich with allusion that advances his theological purpose.

To further the present study I will introduce three important discussions relating to Markan space. Mark was written in a narrative form that includes historical records and is intended for theological purposes. Mark's narrative thus has historical, literary, and theological characteristics. Likewise, Markan space has various traits, which may be classified into different kinds of space: social, geographical, and allusive. In this study of Jesus' missional movement in Mark 4:35—8:21, I will analyze Markan space in terms of these three kinds of space, all of which contribute to an integrative and comprehensive understanding of the subject.[18] The three discussions that follow are associated with the three kinds of space.

16. Chapman argues that the so-called "geographical mistakes" in Mark's narrative come from "a paradigmatic difference between twentieth-century Western culture and that of the first-century Mediterranean" (Chapman, "Locating the Gospel of Mark," 24).

17. In Mark's narrative, space is not simply an inert container or backdrop for events. Rather, Markan space serves to recollect past events with theological implications. Mark describes the places Jesus visited on his missional journey with attention to Mark's own historical and theological perspective, cosmological and eschatological implications, and events of Israel's history. See Rhoads et al., *Mark as Story*, 69–70. For example, the Sea of Galilee is, strictly speaking, not a "sea" (θάλασσα), but a "lake" (λίμνη). Mark should have employed the geographical accurate term "lake" instead of "sea." However, we cannot say that this implies Mark's error of geographical description. The "Sea" of Galilee, where Jesus' miracles were performed, may reflect the Red "Sea," where the Israelites escaped from the Egyptian army in the exodus. In the expression "Sea" of Galilee, the word "sea" contains the images of threat or chaos, allowing Jesus' miracles to be interpreted in a cosmological or eschatological aspect. See Malbon, "Jesus of Mark and the Sea of Galilee," 376.

18. Since space may be examined in diverse categories, it is important to define the limits of a spatial study. This study will deal with space as presented or produced by a text, exploring Markan space in three categories—social, geographical, and allusive. Other types and categories of space in a text may also be found and investigated. Malbon identifies three types of space: topographical, geopolitical, and architectural (Malbon, *Narrative Space*, 15–140). Further, Powell discusses the spatial significance of "props" and "furniture" in narrative (Powell, *What Is Narrative Criticism?*, 70). Though architectural space is important for an investigation of how human beings create, use, and are influenced by space, and though props and furniture play a significant role in narrative settings, I will exclude these aspects of space from the present study in order to focus attention to Jesus' missional movement in and beyond Galilee. Topographical

First, when it comes to social space—especially Galilean society as regards this study—discussions about the spatial relationship between Jerusalem and Galilee have proceeded in Markan scholarship since the early twentieth century. Some scholars have used historical-critical[19] or redactional approaches[20] to argue that Jerusalem and Galilee were situated in rivalry or confrontation. Others have explored their relationship by assuming a bipolar structure based on Lévi-Strauss's structuralism,[21] or by positing a "geography of restoration" based on a social model of lateral and vertical ethnicity.[22] The relationship between the two regions is the key to understanding the social space of Galilee, because Galilee was influenced by Jerusalem: knowing to what extent and in what ways Jerusalem influenced Galilee helps clarify the characteristics of Galilean society.

Markan scholarship has also seen discussions about how strongly the Jewish society of Galilee was influenced by the Gentiles and their culture. Regarding the balance between Jewish and Gentile characteristics in Galilean society, three views have been suggested: "Galileans as Israelites," "a pagan Galilee," and "a Jewish Galilee."[23] The exploration of Jewish and Gentile

and geopolitical space will be addressed as appropriate. Looking at Mark's narrative in particular, Roads, Dewey, and Michie highlights the significance of "the cosmic depiction of space" and "humanly constructed space," which refer to "cosmic settings" and "political-cultural settings." "Cosmic space" is discussed in the present study as an aspect of allusive space, while "political-cultural space" corresponds to social space (Roads et al., *Mark as Story*, 63–66). In the following pages, I will explain the nature and functions of the spatial types that I categorize, and demonstrate how Jesus' missional movement can be interpreted in the light of these kinds of space.

19. E.g., Lohmeyer, *Galiläa und Jerusalem*; Lightfoot, *Locality and Doctrine*; Elliott-Binns, *Galilean Christianity*.

20. E.g., Marxsen, *Mark the Evangelist*; Kelber, *Kingdom in Mark*.

21. Malbon explores Mark's narrative with the aid of Lévi-Strauss's studies of myth, suggesting a bipolar structure of Jerusalem versus Galilee (Malbon, *Narrative Space*). See also Lévi-Strauss, "Structural Study of Myth," 428–44.

22. Freyne suggests the lateral and vertical ethnicity models in order to understand Jesus' ministry in Galilee and Jerusalem. The former model implies territorial expansion for the greater Israel, while the latter model indicates the establishment of identity by making boundaries to distinguish the Jews from the Gentiles. Freyne newly applied these two models to Mark's narrative of Jesus' ministries in Galilee and Jerusalem. Mark presents Jesus' ministry in Galilee in the light of the lateral ethnicity model, suggesting the expansion of ethnic diversity—in other words, those who follow Jesus become the people of God regardless of their ethnicity. Mark describes Jesus' ministry in Jerusalem, on the other hand, in the light of the vertical ethnicity model, suggesting the renewal of ethnic identity—in other words, the question of who is true Israel does not depend on blood, but on the faith of God. See Freyne, "Geography of Restoration," 289–311.

23. Freyne, "Geography of Restoration," 297–304. Freyne introduces these three views of Galilean society, explaining the characteristics of Galilee posited by each view and mentioning scholars who support each option. I will consider these views in detail

characteristics in Galilee may contribute to our understanding of the social circumstances of Galilean society. The social space of Galilee is significant for the interpretation of Mark 4:35—8:21 because Jesus' missional movement originated in Galilee. In this study I will examine the social space of Galilee as the matrix in which Jesus' missional movement successfully developed and went on to break the ethnic boundaries between the Jews and the Gentiles.

Second, when we consider geographical space, we find that the geographical description in Mark 4:35—8:21 was not assembled carelessly but organized intentionally through the use of rhetorical devices designed to serve Mark's theological purpose. Many stories about Jesus' miracles are collected in this section (4:35—8:21). Indeed, the section consists entirely of miracle episodes with the exception of six units — a prophet without honor (6:1-6a); Jesus' sending out the Twelve (6:6b-13, 30); the execution of John the Baptist (6:14-29); instructions on clean and unclean (7:1-23); the Pharisees' seeking a sign (8:11-12); and the discussion about bread (8:13-21). The section contains two sea miracles (Jesus' calming the storm [4:35-41] and walking on the water [6:45-52]), six healing miracles (a Gerasene demoniac [5:1-20], Jairus's daughter [5:21-24, 35-43], a woman with a hemorrhage [5:25-34], a summary of Jesus' healing ministry [6:53-56], a Syrophoenician woman's daughter [7:24-30], and a deaf and mute man [7:31-37]), and two feeding miracles (Jesus' feeding of the five thousand [6:31-44] and the four thousand [8:1-10]).

In contrast to the well-organized structure of Mark's passion narrative (chs. 14-16), this section (4:35—8:21) seems to be loose in its arrangement of episodes and questionable in its geographical accuracy. The transition into Herod's execution of John the Baptist in the middle of the story about Jesus' sending of the Twelve, the presence of two feeding miracles where one would likely have been sufficient, the apparent ignorance of the geography of Palestine and its vicinity (e.g., 7:31), and the inconsistent description of Jesus' route (e.g., the abrupt change from the voyage toward Bethsaida to the arrival at Gennesaret in 6:45-53) all suggest a clumsy arrangement of miracles and sayings in Mark 4:35—8:21. Close examination, however, reveals that the awkward arrangement, repetition of episodes, and inconsistent geography are caused not by Mark's arbitrary collection methods but by his own literary techniques and theological purposes.[24]

---

in ch. 2.

24. Mark's geographical description presents the historical route of Jesus' travel. At the same time, Mark's arrangement of episodes according to geography is carefully designed to express his theological intention. Markan geographical space thus plays a role not only in providing historical information about Jesus' journey but also in

There have been many attempts to explicate the literary structure of Mark 4–8 by presenting a cyclic pattern. Some scholars have performed structural analysis on the basis of assumed pre-Markan sources,[25] while others have examined the section's structural frame using compositional or narrative approaches.[26] Studying the narrative structure of 4:35—8:21 with the help of geographical analysis may provide a fresh hermeneutical framework for understanding this section.[27] As Grant R. Osborne says, "the movements of peoples and topography of the land can add marvelous insight to the study of a passage."[28] I will explore Mark's geographical arrangement of Jesus' movement in terms of his literary use of a cyclic pattern in which his theological purpose may be discovered. For this study, I will analyze the narrative structure of this section by dividing it into two cycles (4:35—6:44; 6:45—8:10)—the former focused on the Jews and the latter on the Gentiles—and a conclusion (8:11–21).

Third, we can look at allusive space because Markan space contains historical traces, ideological significance, or symbolic meanings. I employ the term "allusive space" to this kind of space—space that alludes to prior texts or historical events, presents an ideological vision, or carries eschatological and cosmological implications. Some spaces in Mark's narrative, such as the river, the sea, the wilderness, and the mountains, may evoke memories of important events in the history of Israel.[29] The most significant

communicating Mark's theological purpose. This will be discussed in detail in ch. 3.

25. See Van Oyen's well-summarized introduction to the history of structural analyses of Mark 4–8, especially those based on the two feeding miracles (6:33–44; 8:1–9) (Van Oyen, *Interpretation of the Feeding Miracles*). See also Weizsäcker, *Untersuchungen über die evangelische Geschichte*, 43; Soden, "Das Interesse des apostolischen Zeitalters," 111–69; Meyer, *Ursprung und Anfänge des Christentums*, 131–32; Jenkins, "Marcan Doublet," 87–111; Schmid, *Das Evangelium nach Markus*, 147–48; Pesch, *Das Markusevangelium 8:27–16:20*, 277–81; Kuhn, *Ältere Sammlungen in Markusevangelium*; Achtemeier, "Toward the Isolation of Pre-Markan Miracle Catenae," 265–91.

26. For a compositional approach, see Petersen, "Composition of Mark 4:1–8:26," 185–217; Phelan, "Rhetoric and Meaning in Mark 6:30–8:10," 196–228. For a narrative approach, see Malbon, "Echoes and Foreshadowings in Mark 4–8," 211–30.

27. Mark's geographical description in this section is significant for its depiction of Jesus' attempts to travel into Gentile territory and of Galilee as the outpost of the Gentile mission. See Marxsen, *Mark the Evangelist*, 66–75; Kümmel, *Introduction to the New Testament*, 86–89.

28. Osborne, *Hermeneutical Spiral*, 161.

29. Swartley argues that the Synoptic Gospels (Matthew, Mark, and Luke) share a similar pattern or structure regarding the ways in which God dealt with Israel in the past. The stories of the Old Testament (OT), especially the exodus, exerted the "formative influence" on the Synoptic Gospels. He suggests the following structural pattern, which shows the four main streams of the OT traditions: (1) "exodus and Sinai traditions on the synoptic Galilean narrative"; (2) "the way-conquest (and exodus)

historical event in Israel's thinking may have been the exodus, the story of which had been retold through the ages and reinterpreted to reflect changes in historical contexts or invoke eschatological and cosmological implications. The exodus story may serve as the ground not only for the faith that God has the power to redeem his people in the light of his past actions and also for the anticipation that he will deliver his people in the future.

Swartley asserts that the description of Jesus' Galilean ministry in the Synoptic Gospels was influenced by the exodus and Sinai traditions in terms of "the structural design and the theological emphases."[30] Settings such as the sea and the wilderness serve to connect Jesus' miracles and the exodus events. The sea and the wilderness where Jesus performed miracles in Mark 4:35—8:21 may allude to the places where the exodus events took place as described in the book of Exodus. These places may also have eschatological and cosmological implications, as later Pentateuchal literature such as the Psalms and the Prophets reinterpreted and elevated the exodus story while anticipating a new exodus—in this sense, they belong to allusive space. Though the sea and the wilderness are geographical locations, I will discuss these places in terms of allusive space if they have historical, ideological, eschatological, or cosmological implications. Many scholars have attempted to discover exodus imagery in Mark's narrative,[31] and I will search for it in spatial allusions. In this way, Jesus' missional movement in and beyond Galilee (4:35—8:21) will be interpreted in the light of the new exodus.

---

traditions on the synoptic journey narrative"; (3) "temple traditions on the synoptic pre-passion (and passion) narrative"; (4) "kingship traditions on the synoptic passion narrative." In relation to space, he notes that the repeated mentions of "the wilderness" in Mark 6 recall the exodus story. See Swartley, *Israel's Scripture Traditions and the Synoptic Gospels*, 44–251. Refer also to Rhoads et al., *Mark as Story*, 69–70; Smith, *Lion with Wings*, 152–56.

30. Swartley, *Israel's Scripture Traditions*, 254.

31. Refer to the well-summarized survey of studies of the "OT influence on Mark's literary/theological structure," or "Mark's overall attitude to the OT" in Watts, *Isaiah's New Exodus and Mark*, 9–28. I will introduce studies about the exodus imageries in Mark with the aid of Watts's survey. See Farrer, *Study in St. Mark*, Hobbs, "Gospel of Mark and the Exodus"; Piper, "Unchanging Promises," 3–22; Nixon, *Exodus in the New Testament*; Suhl, *Die Funktion der alttestamentlichen Zitate und Anspielungen im Markusevangelium*; Bowman, *Gospel of Mark*; Hooker, "Mark," 220–30; Hatina, *In Search of a Context*; and Perkins, "Kingdom, Messianic Authority, and the Re-Constituting of God's People,*"* 100–15. For studies focusing on the exodus pattern and structure in Mark, see Swartley, "Study in Markan Structure"; Swartley, *Israel's Scripture Traditions*; Fisher, "New and Greater Exodus," 69–79; Derrett, *Making of Mark*. For studies focusing on Isaianic new exodus in Mark, see Marcus, *Way of the Lord*; Schneck, *Isaiah in the Gospel of Mark I–VIII*; Watts, *Isaiah's New Exodus and Mark*; Hooker, "Isaiah in Mark's Gospel," 35–49; Johnston, "Mark 2:1–3:6 and the Sequence of Isaiah's New Exodus."

The three discussions mentioned above will be applied to the study of Markan spatial presentation in 4:35—8:21. The three kinds of space, "social," "geographical," and "allusive," will function as a framework for exploring Jesus' missional movement. In the following section, I will introduce methodological approaches to investigating these three kinds of spaces.

Methodological Considerations

This study will use an integrative method that combines diverse approaches to understanding a text. When only one specific method is used, a reader is likely to fail to perceive the nature of a text that should be examined in multiple dimensions. The biblical writings contain historical, literary, and theological features. According to Hatina, explorations of the Gospels have gradually "moved away from the polarization of methods to a more pluralistic approach" because "no single method can adequately treat and appreciate the complexity of the Gospels."[32] Various methods serve as interpretive tools, each with its own peculiar angle on how to read a text, and a combination of diverse methods has increasingly been required to achieve more integrative and comprehensive understanding. DeSilva argues that "exegesis is not fully engaged simply by performing one or two of these methods; rather, the fruits of the application of a good number of these skills must be combined and integrated before the interpreter can truly claim to have mined the text and unearthed its message and significance."[33]

In general, scholars have taken three approaches to the interpretation of the Gospels: historical, literary, and theological.[34] To obtain the best possible understanding of a text, these approaches must be considered together, not in isolation. Overreliance on a historical approach may lead to the neglect of the literary characteristics of a text,[35] while exclusive attention to a text's literary aspect may cause the reader to overlook the significance of the historical facts contained in the text.[36] As Osborne notes, "in reality the

---

32. Hatina, *In Search of a Context*, 49.

33. DeSilva, *Introduction to the New Testament*, 23.

34. According to Bartholomew, many scholars—such as M. Sternberg, N. T. Wright, and A. C. Thiselton—insist on "a careful integration of the historical and literary dimensions of the Bible, as well as the ideological or theological" (Bartholomew, "Introduction," 7).

35. Bartholomew, "Introduction," 6. Bartholomew criticizes the historical-critical method for neglecting "the literary shape of the text itself."

36. Osborne points out the risk of a "dehistoricizing tendency" in narrative criticism that mainly deals with literary characteristics of a text: "many others also have denied the historical background behind the text. Indeed, the Bible has been cast adrift

literary and historical exist side by side and are interdependent. As a literal representation of event and its significance, both text and its background are essential components of meaning."[37] Pao explains the literary analysis of ancient texts within their historical backgrounds as follows: "A literary analysis of ancient documents must also be 'historical' in the sense that only after fully understanding the documents in their historical and cultural contexts can the texts be examined in literary terms."[38] The literary characteristics of the text should therefore be examined on the basis of the investigation of the text's historical background.

A theological hermeneutic that had been neglected in biblical interpretation during the modern and postmodern periods is gradually being restored.[39] Bartholomew identifies three interpretive turns in biblical studies—historical, literary, and postmodern—and observes that a new theological turn is now underway.[40] He evaluates Childs's contribution of a theological hermeneutic as follows:

> Childs has long argued that the goal of the interpretation of Christian Scripture must be to understand both Testaments as witness to the self-same divine reality, namely the God and Father of Jesus Christ. Although this theological turn is now gathering momentum in response to the pluralism and nihilistic direction of (some) postmodernism, Childs's extensive corpus has played a major role in the twentieth century in laying the foundation for a theological, canonical hermeneutic in biblical studies.[41]

Bartholomew mentions two characteristics of this theological turn: a way of "reading the Bible theologically," especially in connection to "the church and Christian doctrine," and the establishment of "a theology of

---

from its moorings and left to float on a sea of modern relativity" (Osborne, *Hermeneutical Spiral*, 213–14).

37. Osborne, *Hermeneutical Spiral*, 213–14. Powell says the following about the combined use of narrative and historical methods to interpret a text: "In fact, a symbiotic relationship exists between narrative and historical approaches to texts. Although the two methods cannot be used simultaneously, they can be used side by side in a supplementary fashion. They might even be viewed as necessary complements, each providing information that is beneficial to the exercise of each other" (Powell, *What Is Narrative Criticism?*, 98).

38. Pao, *Acts and the Isaianic New Exodus*, 18.

39. Bartholomew, "Introduction," 10.

40. Bartholomew, "Introduction," 2–12.

41. Bartholomew, "Introduction," 10.

history (and literature, etc.) to fund biblical interpretation."[42] The interpretation of biblical texts is ultimately theological because these texts speak about God's actions upon human history through various forms of literature which must be read to edify the church community. Consequently, the biblical texts contain all three aspects—historical, literary, and theological—and should be interpreted with consideration for all these dimensions.[43]

In the present study, I will undertake an integrative exploration of Jesus' missional movement in Mark 4:35—8:21, considering historical, literary, and theological elements in the text. Three major methodological approaches will be employed for this study. First, I will employ a (social) spatial theory to examine the social space of first-century Galilee. Social space is produced through human social activities and interactions and is represented by individuals or communities' imagination, ideology, or visions. With the aid of spatial theory, I will examine the social world of first-century Galilee in its social, cultural, economic, political, ethnic, and religious aspects, and show how Mark represents the social world of Galilee as the matrix for Jesus' missional movement in his own narrative world.

Second, I will take a narrative approach to the exploration of geographical space. The structure of Mark 4:35—8:21 will be constructed on the basis of the narrative analysis of Jesus' geographical movement. This narrative structure serves as a hermeneutical framework for understanding Mark's theological intention in reporting Jesus' missional movement. The narrative analysis will involve examining temporal, spatial, and social settings. Though this study focuses primarily on spatial (geographical) setting, I will investigate all three elements of setting for an integrative understanding of the narrative. In addition, the structural analysis of this section will be performed by considering Mark's rhetorical devices. The repetitive (cyclic) pattern of Jesus' geographical movement can be explained by Mark's literary techniques, especially repetition.

Third, I will examine intertextuality and allusion to gain an understanding of allusive space. Jesus' ministry reflects Israel's history, and the places where Jesus worked promote the recollection of historical events. Markan space thus has the function of alluding to Israel's past. The concept

---

42. Bartholomew, "Introduction," 11.

43. In his explanation of socio-rhetorical criticism, Robbins says that a text that is placed under diverse situations must be examined in terms of the text's multiple textures. He suggests five textures of a text: "(a) inner texture; (b) intertexture; (c) social and cultural texture; (d) ideological texture; and (e) sacred texture." Since the meanings in a text are interrelated with other meanings and defined by their relationship, the interpretation of a text must be performed in complex but systematic ways to explicate the integral meanings in a diverse milieu. See Robbins, *Exploring the Texture of Texts*, 3–4.

of intertextuality is significant for an understanding of allusive space in that the images of Markan space do not simply correspond to images produced by a single earlier text, but rather contain the intertextual images produced and cumulated by many antecedent texts. For the study of the allusive space, I will introduce intertextuality as a concept and explain allusion as a methodology. The application of intertextuality and allusion to the study of Markan space will lead us to understand Jesus' ministry in the light of Israel's past, especially the exodus events.

Methodologically, therefore, I will investigate Jesus' missional movement in Mark 4:35—8:21 using a spatial theory for social space, a narrative approach for geographical space, and allusion for allusive space. Social space provides a background study of the social circumstances of Jesus' missional movement. Geographical space shows the purpose of Jesus' journey in and beyond Galilee by tracing Jesus' travel routes as seen through Markan rhetorical devices. Allusive space reveals the theological implications of Jesus' ministry in the sea and the wilderness as the new exodus.[44]

Spatial Theory

Space is not simply perceived as an inert container or neutrally presented as a static room.[45] Rather, space is a product of societies that is interpreted socially, culturally, and politically by individuals and communities.[46] Space is constructed though various kinds of relations in society. According to Tilley, "space has no substantial essence in itself, but only has a relational significance, created through relations between peoples and places."[47] Space also gains special meaning, influence, or power through relations caused by

---

44. This spatial study proceeds from external to internal or explicit to implicit aspects of space, considering the social environment of Galilee (social space), the geographical route of Jesus' journey (geographical space), and the theological implications of the sea and the wilderness (allusive space) in turn.

45. In general, there are two ways to recognize space: one is generic and biological, and the other is social, cultural, and political. The former is a deterministic view that sees space as the environment to which humans must accustom themselves. On the other hand, the latter sees space as an object to be controlled and produced by human social behaviors. Another division of spatial types distinguishes between physical, mental, and social space. For spatial theories and territoriality, see Sack, *Human Territoriality*; Lefebvre, *Production of Space*; Harvey, *Condition of Postmodernity*; Johnston, *Question of Place*; Tilley, *Phenomenology of Landscape*; Storey, *Territory*.

46. For a detailed explanation of social space as a social product, see Lefebvre, *Production of Space*, 26–27, 68–168.

47. Tilley, *Phenomenology of Landscape*, 11.

human social activities. Using the term "territoriality,"[48] Sack explains the relationship between space and society as follows:

> Territoriality for humans is a powerful geographical strategy to control people and things by controlling area. Political territories and private ownership of land may be the most familiar forms but territoriality occurs to varying degrees in numerous social contexts. It is used in everyday relationships and in complex organizations. Territoriality is a primary geographical express of power. It is the means by which space and society are interrelated. Territoriality is embedded in social relations.[49]

In terms of territoriality, space is understood as the object of a human strategy to control human behaviors by governing space. Sack suggests three steps involved in making space into territory or obtaining territoriality: "classification, communication, and enforcement."[50] First, space is classified according to the areas to which one belongs: one space is perceived by distinguishing it from other spaces.[51] If someone argues that the things in a room are his or her possessions, those things are accepted as "his," "hers," or "not yours" on the ground of the area that he or she occupies.[52] Second, classified space creates a boundary that generates communication. "The territorial boundary may be the only symbolic form that combines direction in space and a statement about possession or exclusion."[53] Setting a boundary in area may create a "marker or sign," which consequently enables communication with others.[54] Third, classified and communicated space has the ability to enforce and control behavior, which is the most significant

---

48. Sack defines "territoriality" as "the attempt by an individual or group (x) to influence, affect, or control objects, people, and relationships (y) by delimiting and asserting control over a geographic area" (Sack, "Human Territoriality," 56).

49. Sack, *Human Territoriality*, 5.

50. Sack, *Human Territoriality*, 31–42. Sack suggests ten tendencies of territoriality: "classification, communication, enforcement of access, reification symbol, displacement, impersonal relations, neutral place-clearing, mold, conceptually empty space, and multiplication of territories." The first three tendencies are logically prior to the remaining seven that are derivative from the first three.

51. Sack, *Human Territoriality*, 21. Sack notes that, according to Jean Piaget, space may be classified into two major forms: "type" and "area." Though territoriality can use both of them, it always uses area. See also Piaget and Inhelder, *Child's Conception of Space*. Sack argues that territoriality mainly deals with classification of space according to area rather than type (Sack, "Human Territoriality," 58).

52. Sack, *Human Territoriality*, 21.

53. Sack, *Human Territoriality*, 21.

54. Sack, *Human Territoriality*, 21.

characteristic of territoriality.⁵⁵ When others intrude into a person's area without permission, he or she can exercise force to expel them.

Sack's basic three steps of territoriality focus on the aspect of area in examining space. Because space is also categorized by type, however, the same three steps can be applied to analyze spatial type.⁵⁶ For example,⁵⁷ first, in terms of classification, if one enters a temple area, he or she recognizes that place to be holy by separating it from other places that are labeled as secular. Second, in terms of communication, a temple is regarded as the place where one prays or worships. People come to know that their actions within the boundary of a temple should be quiet and pious. Third, in terms of enforcement, someone who makes noise or creates a disturbance is forcibly controlled or expelled from the temple area due to his or her performance of actions that are not permitted in that place.

In the episode of the cleansing of the temple (Mark 11:15–17), Jesus' actions express the territoriality of the temple. First, the temple is classified as the holy place that is "a house of prayer for all the nations" (v. 17). Second, while visitors' behaviors should be limited to prayer and worship of God in the temple, some people undertook inappropriate commercial activities in the temple space (e.g., exchanging money and selling doves; v. 15). Third, Jesus exerted force to expel those people on account of their improper actions (vv. 15–17).

Sack describes the relationship between (social) space and power in human society as follows:

> People do not just interact in space and move through space like billiard balls. Rather, human interaction, movement and contact are also matters of transmitting energy and information in order to affect, influence, and control the ideas and actions of others and their access to resources. Human spatial relations are the results of influence and power. Territoriality is the primary spatial form power takes.⁵⁸

Chapman, who adopts Sack's spatial theory of territoriality to interpret Mark's geographical description, says that "all the geographical references

---

55. Sack, *Human Territoriality*, 22.

56. Area and type of space can also be considered together at the same time.

57. I devise this example related to the space of the temple on the basis of Sack's spatial theory of territoriality. Sack introduces territoriality of the church in primitive Christianity, the early Roman Catholic Church, the early Middle Ages, the late Middle Ages and Renaissance, and the Reformation and after. See Sack, *Human Territoriality*, 92–126.

58. Sack, *Human Territoriality*, 26.

in his Gospel [Mark] were part of his geography of meaning. For a peasant community, this would mean that such references were more associative than locative."[59] Mark's geographical description of Jesus' journey from place to place does not simply show a route of travel, but rather implies that Jesus was establishing his "place": in other words, "it is his *territory*."[60] Chapman argues that for Mark, Jesus' geographical movement indicates a "physical expression of the confession, 'Jesus is Lord.'"[61] "In a peasant culture, such a confession must be understood literally, i.e., 'Jesus rules my (physical) world.'"[62] In relation to the present study, Jesus' missional journey in and beyond Galilee (4:35—8:21) takes a cyclic pattern with one cycle (4:35—6:44) focused on Jesus' travels in Jewish territory and the other cycle (6:45—8:10) on his travels in Gentile territory. In the light of territoriality, Jesus' geographical movement in this section demonstrates his lordship over Jewish territory and Gentile territory, indicating that they are both ultimately God's territory. In this way, Jesus is manifested as the Lord not only of the Jews, but also of the Gentiles. His geographical movement also breaks the boundary of spatial type between Jewish territory and Gentile territory, showing that the kingdom of God has come not only to Jewish land but also to Gentile land.

Another important spatial theory for this study is concerned with how space is represented. In order to examine the shift "from *things in space* to the actual *production of space*," Lefebvre introduced three concepts of space: "spatial practice" ("pratique spatiale"), "representations of space" ("représentations de l'espace"), and "representational space" ("espaces de représentation").[63] First, spatial practice is related to actual space as a physical environment where social activities are made from social interactions; in this process, social spaces are produced and reproduced.[64] Spatial practice, therefore, refers to the "experienced" space. Second, representations of

---

59. According to Chapman, in a primitive society geographical description is related to social significance rather than geographical sites: "For instance, Tyre and Sidon received their location from their social significance, not vice versa" (Chapman, "Locating the Gospel of Mark," 35).

60. Chapman, "Locating the Gospel of Mark," 35.

61. Chapman, "Locating the Gospel of Mark," 35.

62. Chapman, "Locating the Gospel of Mark," 35.

63. According to Lefebvre, "if space is a product, our knowledge of it must be expected to reproduce and expound the process of production" (Lefebvre, *Production of Space*, 37–39). Harvey interprets Lefebvre's three concepts of space as "the experienced," "the perceived," and "the imagined" (Harvey, *Condition of Postmodernity*, 219).

64. Lefebvre, *Production of Space*, 38.

space are related to "conceptualized" space,[65] which scientists or planners think about, systemize, and design. They are abstract in that they consist of signs and codes. Social relations are generated and established in representations of space: maps, models, and plans are applied to this concept of space.[66] Third, representational spaces imply "space as directly *lived* through its associated images and symbols."[67] They are the spaces that "the imagination seeks to change and appropriate."[68] Representational spaces have "their source in history," and the changes of history show how they are expressed.[69] This space is related to imagination, ideology, and visions, which may produce social movements.

We can find an example of "representational space" in the episode of the dispute on clean and unclean in Mark 7:1–23, which is a significant turning point of Jesus' misssional movement. The religious leaders from Jerusalem criticized the disciples' behavior of eating food without washing their hands. In the system of Jewish purity rules, the Jews should keep the rule of eating with washed hands because this serves as a sign of the people of God or a boundary to separate them with the Gentiles. Jesus, however, rejected this purity system based on the tradition of Jewish elders and declared that all food are clean (v. 19), which implies that anyone can belong to the people of God, regardless his or her ethnicity. Jesus' proclamation provides a new spatial configuration (representational space) by breaking down the barrier between the Jews and the Gentiles, as is demonstrated by his repeated geographical movement between Jewish territory and Gentile territory. After making this proclamation in Jewish territory, Jesus ventured northeast into Gentile territory (v. 24).

When one uses space as a resource, space comes to have different values and political tendencies.[70] Space is differently interpreted, accepted, and exploited according to changes of societies and generations. Tilley lists the following differences between the characteristics of "Western and capitalist 'spaces' and non-Western and pre-capitalist 'spaces'" as follows:

---

65. Lefebvre, *Production of Space*, 41.
66. Lefebvre, *Production of Space*, 33.
67. Lefebvre, *Production of Space*, 39.
68. Lefebvre, *Production of Space*, 39.
69. Lefebvre, *Production of Space*, 41.
70. Tilley, *Phenomenology of Landscape*, 20.

Capitalist/Western space	Pre-capitalist/Non-Western Space
infinitely open	different densities
desanctified	sanctified
control	sensuousness
surveillance/partitioning	ritualized/anthropomorphic
economic	cosmological
'useful' to act	'useful' to think
architectural forms resemble each other in 'disciplinary' space	architecture an embodiment of myth and cosmology
landscape as backdrop to action	landscape as sedimented ritual form
time linear and divorced from space	time constitutive of rhythms of social action in space-time[A]

A. Tilley, *Phenomenology of Landscape*, 20–21.

In a human society, space is not given *per se*, but socially produced. Social space is created from cultural, religious, economic, and political interactions among classes and regions, and the power structure in a society is established in this process. Every society produces "its own space" with its own manner of interpreting space.[71] Social spaces are therefore different according to the difference among societies. Likewise, presentations of social space differ from person to person because different individuals understand and experience it in different ways. "Space becomes detotalized by virtue of its relational construction and because, being differently understood and produced by different individuals, collectivities and societies, it can have no universal essence. What space is depends on who is experiencing it and how."[72]

In the present study, I will explore the social space of Galilee by examining its relations with other social spaces in first-century Palestine. First, the social space of Galilee can be explored by investigating the relationship between Galilee and Jerusalem in terms of conflict, control, resistance, submission, expansion, and so on. Since Jerusalem exercised power and control over Galilee, Galilean society might contain the social factors of conflict against Jerusalem.[73] In addition, the social space of

71. Lefebvre, *Production of Space*, 31.

72. Tilley, *Phenomenology of Landscape*, 11.

73. While the Romans resided in Caesarea (Maritima), the location of the headquarters of the Roman governors, they exerted political power in Galilee and Jerusalem. In a political sense, the major force of Rome in Galilee controlled Jerusalem. Inasmuch as Galilean society was placed under the Jewish religious and cultural ethos, however, Jerusalem exercised strong influence upon Galilee. For example, the religious leaders from Jerusalem evaluated and criticized the sayings and deeds of Jesus and his disciples, who ministered in Galilee (e.g., Mark 3:22; 7:1). This study will focus on the

Galilee can be explored by investigating the spatial interactions between cities and villages within Galilean society or those between Galilee and the neighboring Gentile regions.

In order to study Markan spatial presentation in 4:35—8:21, two steps are needed. The first step is to explore the social environments of first-century Galilee, which, as mentioned above, can be discovered by investigating the interactions between social spaces. The second step is to examine how Mark represents the social space of Galilee in his own narrative world. Since representational spaces (the imagined space) are disclosed in dialectic interactions with spatial practices (the experienced space), Markan spatial presentation of Galilee should be understood in comparison with its historical and social realities. Exploring how Mark represents spaces in relation to Jesus' geographical movement (4:35—8:21) will help us discover Mark's theological purpose or ideological vision. This study will be presented in chapter 2.

Narrative Settings and Rhetorical Devices

Osborne explains the significance of the "story" format of biblical narratives, which has the function of delivering and representing the meaning of the text, as follows:

> The biblical narratives contain both history and theology, and I would add that these are brought together via a "story" format. The historical basis for the stories is crucial, but the representation of that story in the text is the actual object of interpretation. While I believe that background is critical in biblical study, it must be controlled by the text and not vice versa. Our task is to decipher the meaning of the historical-theological text in biblical narrative, not to reconstruct the original event.[74]

In biblical narratives, the realities in the text are expressed in a narrative form and the meaning of the text is discovered by looking at how they are represented. The description of events in biblical narratives is not simply the record of historical facts; it also carries theological implications about how and why God has done certain things. Narrative is a crucial means for conveying history and theology in the two Testaments. In addition,

---

strength of Jerusalem's religious and cultural influence on Galilean society.

74. Osborne, *Hermeneutical Spiral*, 200.

narrative is a "*form of representation*," and the goal of a narrative approach is to explore how the biblical narratives are represented.[75]

Chatman explains the concept of narrative by distinguishing between story and discourse: story corresponds to the "what" of a narrative and discourse corresponds to the "how."[76] While story refers to the content of the narrative, discourse refers to the rhetoric of the narrative, "the means by which the content is communicated."[77] Story is the interaction of narrative elements such as characters, events, settings, and plot; discourse, on the other hand, focuses on how the story is told and includes features such as a point of view, symbolism, irony and so on. Even stories that contain the same basic elements of characters, events, and settings may be created as different narratives by telling them in different ways.[78] Story and discourse are not divided, however. As Chatman says, they should be considered in an integrative way as "the story-as-discoursed."[79]

In general, narrative approaches to a text deal with implied author, implied reader, characters, events, settings, plot, and rhetoric.[80] The pres-

---

75. According to Berlin, interpretation of the biblical narratives requires "knowledge about narrative in general and about the linguistic and literary structures of the biblical text" (Berlin, *Poetics and Interpretation of Biblical Narrative*, 13–15).

76. Chatman, *Story and Discourse*, 15–42. Osborne explains the "how" and the "what" in narrative analysis as follows: "The interpretation of narrative has two aspects: poetics, which studies the artistic dimension of the way the text is constructed by the author; and meaning, which recreates the message that the author is communicating. The 'how' (poetics) leads to the 'what' (meaning)" (Osborne, *Hermeneutical Spiral*, 203).

77. Chatman, *Story and Discourse*, 19.

78. Powell says that a typical example of the conceptual difference between story and discourse is discovered in the four Gospels (Powell, *What Is Narrative Criticism?*, 23). According to Malbon, "the four canonical Gospels, for example, share a similar (although not identical) story of Jesus, but the discourse of each Gospel is distinctive. The story is where the characters interact; the discourse is where the implied author and implied reader interact" (Malbon, "Narrative Criticism," 32).

79. Chatman, *Story and Discourse*, 3.

80. The implied author, the implied reader, the narrator, and the narratee are crucial concepts which distinguish narrative criticism from other methodologies. We can make a diagram based on "the communication model of sender-message-receiver" in narrative as follows: real author → implied author → narrator → story → narratee → implied reader → real reader. See Malbon, "Narrative Criticism," 33; Powell, *What Is Narrative Criticism?*, 27; Chatman, *Story and Discourse*, 151. Powell explains narrator and narratee in distinction with the implied author and the implied reader as follows: "The narrator and the narratee are not identical with the implied author and the implied reader. They are rhetorical devices, created by the implied author. They are part of the narrative itself, part of the discourse though which the story is told" (Powell, *What Is Narrative Criticism?*, 27). Malbon defines the implied author and the implied reader as follows: "The implied author is a hypothetical construction based on the requirements

ent study will focus on the nature and functions of settings in a narrative. Settings consist of time, space, and social circumstances, and spatial settings play a significant role in forming the structure of Mark 4:35—8:21. In addition to introducing these three elements of setting, I will explain the rhetorical devices Mark used to develop a literary pattern and compose his narrative.

Rhoads explains the functions of settings in a narrative as follows: "Settings provide a narrative with a context where events take place and characters act. They are not incidental backdrops. They provide the conditions—the possibilities and the limitations—for the events in the story to take place."[81] Settings are closely related to characters and events because settings establish the time, space, and social circumstances in which characters work and events occur. Regarding the close relationship between characters and settings, Chatman notes that the demarcation between them is "not a simple line" but a "continuum."[82] At times, characters who are active in a narrative can simply become a part of the background: for instance, the crowd in the Gospels is sometime treated as background.[83] The reverse is also possible: settings can be "characterized."[84] Paying attention to the traits of settings, Powell argues that "settings may be 'characterized' as possessing certain descriptive qualities."[85] When settings are characterized, they

---

of knowledge and belief presupposed in the narrative. The same is true of the implied reader" (Malbon, "Narrative Criticism," 33). According to Osborne, "the implied reader is a figure that enables a person to detect the original intended message of a text rather than an elusive entity that allows one to play with multiple meanings in the text" (Osborne, *Hermeneutical Spiral*, 211). On the rest see Malbon, "Narrative Criticism," 32.

81. Rhoads, "Narrative Criticism," 110. Drawing a comparison with English sentence structure, Powell explains settings as follows: "Events correspond roughly to verbs, for in them the story's action is expressed. Characters are like nouns, for they perform these actions or, perhaps, are acted upon. Character traits may be likened to adjectives since they describe the characters involved in the action. And settings? Settings are the adverbs of literary structure: they designate when, where, and how the action occurs." See Powell, *What Is Narrative Criticism?*, 69.

82. Chatman, *Story and Discourse*, 141.

83. The distinction between characters and settings depends on whether entities have a point of view or not. If they have a point of view, they are characters; if they do not, they are settings. Powell, *What Is Narrative Criticism?*, 69–70, 118.

84. Powell, *What Is Narrative Criticism?*, 69–70.

85. Powell, *What Is Narrative Criticism?*, 69–70. Powell gives the example of the sea of *Moby Dick* in explaining the character-likeness of settings as follows: "The sea in *Moby Dick* is 'hostile.' To the extent that such traits are ascribed to settings, the latter may seem 'character-like.' The ascription of traits, however, is only one part of the process of characterization. There is no thought in Moby Dick that the sea actually evinces a hostile attitude towards the characters. If it did (as it sometimes does in fairy tales, for example) it would cross the line and become a character itself."

are active much as characters are active—they become "character-like."[86] In relation to the present study, for instance, the sea is sometimes described as chaos or a threat in the Bible, and the storm-swept sea in Mark 4:35–41 is portrayed as an object, namely chaos, to be rebuked and subjugated by Jesus. It would be controversial to regard this hostile sea as a character because it is not clear that the sea itself is represented as adopting a specific point of view,[87] but the stormy sea clearly does not remain as an inert background, but takes an active role, interacting with other characters. The furious chaos-sea threatens the disciples with fear; Jesus rebukes the sea and calms it down; and the disciples are amazed, saying that the sea obeys Jesus (Mark 4:35–41)—in all these ways the sea shows character-likeness.

Settings are not simply limited to the subordinate function of providing a context where characters take action; sometimes they have their own autonomous significance, possessing "a life of their own" much as characters do.[88] Powell notes the ability of settings to generate images in themselves as follows:

> Settings resemble characters in one other respect. They too are not limited to the functional role they serve in the story but have the capacity to transcend that role. Some settings (such as Camelot, the Garden of Eden, or the Land of Oz) become so clearly entrenched in the mind of the reader that they, like memorable characters, take on a life of their own. The reader can easily imagine events not reported in the narrative occurring within these settings.[89]

If a certain setting is strongly stamped on the memory of readers, it has its own independent capacity to interpret a narrative by imposing a particular meaning onto the events. For instance, spatial settings such as the sea, the wilderness, and the mountain where the exodus events took place cause readers to connect the Gospel events that occur in those settings with the exodus events and interpret the Gospel events as a new exodus.

Rhoads explains the diverse functions of settings with examples from the Gospels as follows:

---

86. Powell, *What Is Narrative Criticism?*, 69–70. Though a setting may possess a certain trait, this does not mean that the setting become a character. In the case of possessing a point of view, a setting can be a character.

87. In Mark 4:35–41, the stormy sea is personified in that Jesus rebuked the sea and the disciples were astonished, saying that even the sea obeys Jesus. It is also true that the sea is hostile to Jesus and his disciples. It is not certain, however, that the sea itself has its own point of view as a character toward Jesus and his disciples in Mark's narrative.

88. Powell, *What Is Narrative Criticism?*, 69–70.

89. Powell, *What Is Narrative Criticism?*, 70.

They [settings] provide themes and motifs, such as mountains in Matthew and "the way" in Mark. They can serve to generate atmosphere (hostility in Jerusalem), create suspense, drive an episode (storm at sea), provide the reason for a conflict (Sabbath), reveal traits of characters as they interact with the settings (such as a lack of bread in a desert), and provide public and private space for events and interactions.[90]

Settings may play a role in the thematic development of a narrative, generate atmosphere, or offer cause for conflict.[91] In addition, they may provide a structural framework for a narrative.[92] Just as changes in the scenery on stage divide a play into acts, changes of setting give structure to a narrative.[93] In this study I will explore changes of settings, especially in regard to space (Jesus' geographical movement), as part of my structural analysis of Mark 4:35—8:21.

Settings largely consist of three elements: time, space, and social-cultural circumstances.[94] Though all three elements of setting should be considered together in narrative analysis, spatial settings play a key role in providing structure to Mark's narrative. Mark is explicitly divided into three parts according to Jesus' geographical movement: ministry in Galilee and its vicinity (1:1—8:21), journey to Jerusalem (8:22—10:52), and final events in Jerusalem (11:1—16:8). However, the detailed structures of each part differ in terms of time and space: while the events of 11:1—16:8—from Jesus' entrance of Jerusalem to his resurrection—are organized chronologically,[95]

90. Rhoads, "Narrative Criticism," 110.

91. Resseguie explains the functions of settings as follows: "Setting may develop a character's mental, emotional, or spiritual landscape; it may be symbolic choices to be made; it provides structure to the story and may develop the central conflict in a narrative" (Resseguie, *Narrative Criticism*, 88).

92. Kort, *Narrative Elements and Religious Meanings*, 20–29. Rhoads argues that Mark's settings are "almost never irrelevant" to the construction of narrative. See Rhoads, *Reading Mark*, 13.

93. Though thematic changes also provide structure for a narrative, Mark composed his narrative according to the changes of settings. In particular, spatial settings play a key role in the structural analysis of Mark's narrative.

94. See Abrams and Harpham, *Glossary of Literary Terms*, 330; Smith, *Lion with Wings*, 124.

95. In Mark 11:1—16:8, Mark describes Jesus' ministry according to date and time. As for date, e.g., "on the following day" (τῇ ἐπαύριον, 11:12); "when the evening came" (ὅταν ὀψὲ ἐγένετο, 11:19); "in the morning" (πρωΐ, 11:20); "on the first day of Unleavened Bread" (τῇ πρώτῃ ἡμέρᾳ τῶν ἀζύμων, 14:20); "when it was evening" (ὀψίας γενομένης, 14:17); "as soon as it was morning" (εὐθὺς πρωΐ, 15:1); "when evening had come, and because it was the day of Preparation, that is, the day before the Sabbath" (καὶ ἤδη ὀψίας γενομένης, ἐπεὶ ἦν παρασκευὴ ὅ ἐστιν προσάββατον, 15:42); "when

the events of 1:1—10:52 are arranged geographically. Since the structure of 4:35—8:21 is based on spatial settings, this study will closely examine the depiction of Jesus' geographical movement in the light of spatial settings while considering Mark's literary techniques. In the following pages, I will first introduce the nature and functions of the three elements of setting—time, space, and social circumstances—and then explain the rhetorical devices that form the narrative patterns and structures in this section of Mark.

Time

Time can generally be understood in two ways. One approach is philosophical: "What is the nature of time? How do we experience it?"[96] The other, literary, approach examines the meaning and functions of "time in the text."[97] Since our concern in the present study is "time in the text," we need to examine time as a setting in literature.

According to Powell, temporal settings are distinguished into two types: "*chronological* and *typological.*"[98] The chronological type of time is subdivided into two kinds: "*locative* or *durative*." While locative time indicates "the particular point in time in which a given action takes place," durative time refers to "an interval of time."[99] In Mark's narrative, for example, locative time is used to describe the moment of Jesus' crucifixion ("it was the third hour," 15:25), while durative time is employed to explain that the hemorrhaging woman had been bleeding for "twelve years" (5:25).[100] The typological type of time refers to "the kind of time within which an action transpires."[101] This type is seen in the episode of Jesus' walking on the sea (6:45–52):[102] "About the fourth watch of the night" (περὶ τετάρτην φυλακὴν

---

the Sabbath was over" (διαγενομένου τοῦ σαββάτου, 16:1); "and very early on the first day of the week, when the sun had risen" (καὶ λίαν πρωΐ τῇ μιᾷ τῶν σαββάτων . . . ἀνατείλαντος τοῦ ἡλίου,16:2). As for time, e.g., "it was the third hour" (ἦν δὲ ὥρα τρίτη, 15:25); "when it was sixth hour . . . until the ninth hour" (γενομένης ὥρας ἕκτης . . . ἕως ὥρας ἐνάτης, 15:33).

96. Smith, *Lion with Wings*, 124.
97. Smith, *Lion with Wings*, 124.
98. Powell, *What Is Narrative Criticism?*, 72.
99. Powell, *What Is Narrative Criticism?*, 72.
100. Powell, *What Is Narrative Criticism?*, 72-73.
101. Powell, *What Is Narrative Criticism?*, 73.
102. Smith considers "night" as a typological type of temporal setting in Mark. "Night is a time of trouble or danger. The disciples find themselves beset by high winds on the Sea of Galilee in the middle of the night (6:45-51). It is a time of anguish for Jesus in the Garden of Gethsemane (14:32-42), and the time of his betrayal, arrest

τῆς νυκτός, v. 48), when the disciples were straining at the oars against an adverse wind, Jesus came towards them, walking on the sea. Though this time (the fourth watch), which means "at dawn," may be understood as locative time, it also has a typological significance as "the time when God's help is especially needed."[103] This kind of time is also "allusive or symbolic."[104] When Jesus was tested in the wilderness for forty days (1:13), this time not only indicates the duration of the testing but also alludes to the Israel's forty years of testing in the wilderness during the exodus.[105]

Osborne describes the significance of narrative time in comparison with chronological time as follows: "Narrative time is distinct because it has to do with literary arrangement rather than with historical sequence."[106] In particular, if we compare the four Gospels, all of which describe the life and ministry of Jesus, we can find differences in the sequence of events in terms of time and space. This leads us to concentrate on the reasons why the authors arranged the events of Jesus' life in different orders and the purposes they intended to accomplish by doing so.[107] It is therefore necessary to understand the nature and roles of narrative time in the story.

In *Narrative Discourse: An Essay in Method*, Genette explores the characteristics and functions of time in a narrative text.[108] Following Ger-

---

(14:43–52), trial before the High Priest (14:55–65) and denial by Peter (14:54–55, 66–72). It is to be noted that Jesus taught in the Temple day after day (14:49) but was never arrested then; his opponents had to wait until darkness, the time of evil." See Smith, *Lion with Wings*, 146.

103. Donahue and Harrington, *Gospel of Mark*, 213; Marcus, *Mark 1–8*, 423. Time often shows both functions of the two types together. Here, "at dawn" is both chronological (locative) and typological time. In other words, it is both historical and symbolic (allusive).

104. According to Malbon, "some temporal references are clearly allusive and symbolic" (Malbon, "Narrative Criticism," 37). Though Malbon does not explain allusive or symbolic characteristics of temporal references in the category of typological type of time, those characteristics belong to the typological type of temporal setting.

105. Malbon, "Narrative Criticism," 37. Donahue and Harrington argue that "the 'forty days' more likely alludes to the fast of Moses (Deut 9:18) in the wilderness of Sinai and that of Elijah near Mount Horeb (see 1 Kgs 19:8)" (Donahue and Harrington, *Gospel of Mark*, 66). However, the forty days of Jesus' testing in the wilderness uses the exodus imagery of Israel's wilderness wanderings for forty years (Deut 8:2) because the setting of the wilderness and the theme of testing are common between the two stories, which also share similar temporal settings, forty days and forty years.

106. For example, the period of Jesus' public ministry is different between the Synoptics (Matthew, Mark, and Luke) and John: while the Synoptics describe a one-year ministry by mentioning one Passover, John portrays a two- or three-year ministry by referring to three Passovers (2:13; 6:4; 11:55). See Osborne, *Hermeneutical Spiral*, 206.

107. Stein, "Interpreting the Synoptic Gospels," 352–53.

108. Genette, *Narrative Discourse*.

man literary theorists' understanding of "temporal duality,"[109] he classifies time into two categories: "*erzählte Zeit* (story time) and *Erzählzeit* (narrative time)."[110] Story time is related to the order of events that a text itself shows; in other words, it refers to the sequence of events that appear as a reader progresses through the text. Story time is linear because it follows the progression that a narrative develops. Narrative time, on the other hand, is concerned with how events are arranged in plotted time and how time is expressed in a narrative.[111] Genette discovers three basic principles from the relationship between the time of story and the time of narrative: "*order*," "*duration*," and "*frequency*."[112]

In the "*order*" of narrative discourse, anachronies may occur. Anachrony refers to "all forms of discordance between the two temporal orders of story and discourse."[113] This discordance is categorized into two types: "*prolepsis*" (foreshadowing) and "*analepsis*" (flashback).[114] In relation to the present study, for example, analepsis is found in the episode of the execution of John the Baptist in Mark 6:17–29.[115] This episode is furtively inserted in the middle of a story about Jesus' sending of the Twelve with mission instructions (6:6b–13, 30). Readers might expect the story of John's death to be told at the point of time when John was arrested (1:14), but the episode is delayed until a time when Jesus' name had become well known and questions about his identity arose (6:14–16).[116] Faced with rumors about Jesus' identity as John the Baptist, Elijah, or one of the prophets, Herod believed that Jesus was John the Baptist, raised again after his beheading. At this

---

109. Genette gives as an example Gunther, "Erzählzeit und erzählte Zeit," 195–212.

110. Genette, *Narrative Discourse*, 33–35.

111. Scholars use terms referring to time in different ways. As story and discourse are distinguished in narrative, it is proper to distinguish between "story-time" and "discourse-time" in order to define the nature of time in narrative: "narrative-time" may be used to refer to the relations between story-time and discourse-time. Using narrative-time as equivalent to discourse-time, however, Genette examines the relationship between story-time and narrative-time.

112. Genette, *Narrative Discourse*, 35.

113. Genette, *Narrative Discourse*, 35–47. For example, if the order of events is 1–2–3–4–5 in the time of story, their order is changed into 2–1–4–3–5 in the time of narrative (discourse).

114. Genette, *Narrative Discourse*, 40. Genette defines prolepsis as "any narrative maneuver that consists of narrating or evoking in advance an event that will take place later" and analepsis as "any evocation after the fact of an event that took place earlier than the point in the story where we are at any given moment." For detailed discussions of analepsis and prolepsis, see Gennette, *Narrative Discourse*, 48–67 and 67–79 respectively.

115. Smith, *Lion with Wings*, 138.

116. Smith, *Lion with Wings*, 138.

point, Mark explains how John had been executed by Herod (6:17–29). According to Smith, "the effect of the intercalation of the story here is to separate the sending out of the Twelve from their return, and thus to present the illusion of the passing of time."[117] Inserting John's execution in the middle of Jesus' sending his disciples also functions to show "what John's death means for discipleship and mission with Jesus."[118]

"*Duration*" focuses on the discursive speed of time in a narrative, which originates in the difference between the time of story and the time of narrative (discourse).[119] While the former is fixed (isochrony: consistency in speed), the latter is flexible (anisochrony: variation in speed).[120] Genette suggests four elements of duration, labeled as "the four narrative movements": "summary," "ellipsis," "pause," and "scene."[121] Consequently, duration deals with narrative pace, the acceleration and deceleration of narrative development.[122] Smith describes narrative pace in Mark as follows: "Mark begins his narrative at breakneck speed, and ends it at a virtual standstill."[123] While Mark 1–10 progresses with the same fast tempo, a deceleration occurs in chapters 11–16. Though chapters 11–16 make up one third of Mark's length, they cover only one week of Jesus' life; even further, Mark 14:12—15:39 describes the twenty-four hours before Jesus' crucifixion.[124] Overall, Mark's narrative pace decreases until the Passion and crucifixion are described by the hour.

"*Frequency*" is examined in the relationship between the number of times an event actually occurred in life and the number of times an event is described in a narrative.[125] Genette suggests three types of frequency:

---

117. Smith, *Lion with Wings*, 139.

118. Edwards, *Gospel according to Mark*, 177.

119. Genette, *Narrative Discourse*, 86–88. Genette regards narrative (discourse) time as "the pseudo-time, or conventional time, of the narrative" (Genette, *Narrative Discourse*, 94).

120. Genette, *Narrative Discourse*, 88. Genette says the significance of anisochrony as the prerequisite essential in narrative discourse as follows: "a narrative can do without anachronies, but not without *anisochronies*."

121. Genette, *Narrative Discourse*, 94–112. Genette explains the concept of scene and summary in terms of tempo as follows: "Scene . . . realizes conventionally the equality of time between narrative and story; *summary*—a form with variable tempo (whereas the tempo of the other three [scene, pause, and ellipse] is fixed, at least in principle), which with great flexibility of pace covers the entire rage included between scene and ellipse."

122. Smith, *Lion with Wings*, 142–43.

123. Smith, *Lion with Wings*, 143.

124. Smith, *Lion with Wings*, 143.

125. Genette, *Narrative Discourse*, 113–17. Genette defines frequency as "relations

"*singulative*" ("narrating once what happened once" or "narrating *n* times what happened *n* times"), "*repeating*" ("narrating *n* times what happened once"), and "*iterative*" (narrating one time what happened *n* times).[126] For example, repetition is found in Jesus' discussion with his disciples in a boat (8:19–21), in which Jesus refers again to the two feeding miracles that took place earlier.[127]

In order to understand time in the NT, it is necessary to study the concept and characteristics of time in the primitive Christian community of the first century. Cullmann argues that the concept of time in the NT is distinguished by the words καιρός ("a point of time") and αἰών ("age").[128] While καιρός implies a "definite *point of time*," αἰών indicates a "*duration*" of time.[129] Καιρός refers to the decisive moment at which God's works are and will be accomplished. Αἰών, on the other hand, refers to a certain period that contains not only "an exactly defined period of time" but also "an undefined and incalculable duration," which means eternity.[130] Αἰών is particularly employed to present "the division of divine time into this present age (αἰὼν οὗτος or ἐνεστώς) and the coming age (αἰὼν μέλλων)."[131] In view of redemptive and revelatory history, time is conceived in a linear way that differs from the Hellenistic understanding of time as circular.[132] According to Cullmann, "on the one side, time does not stand in contrast to God's eternity; on the other side, it is thought of as a straight line, not as a circle. Mention is made of a 'beginning' (ἀρχή) and an 'end' (τέλος)."[133]

The word καιρός, which refers to the decisive moment of God's intervention, appears in Mark 1:15.[134] When the coming of the kingdom of God was announced, Jesus proclaimed that "the time is fulfilled" (πεπλήρωται ὁ καιρὸς). Καιρός here refers to a critical moment with eschatological sig-

---

between the repetitive capacities of the story and those of the narrative" (Genette, *Narrative Discourse*, 35).

126. Genette, *Narrative Discourse*, 114–16.

127. Smith, *Lion with Wings*, 145.

128. Cullmann, *Christ and Time*, 37–50.

129. Cullmann, *Christ and Time*, 39.

130. Cullmann, *Christ and Time*, 45.

131. Cullmann, *Christ and Time*, 47.

132. Cullmann, *Christ and Time*, 51–60. Cullmann argues that "the symbol of time for Primitive Christianity as well as for Biblical Judaism and the Iranian religion is the line, while in Hellenism it is the circle."

133. Cullmann, *Christ and Time*, 51.

134. For the use of καιρὸς in reference to a decisive moment, see Mark 12:2; 13:33. Καιρὸς is also used to refer to a span of time, as in 10:30; 11:13. See Marcus, *Mark 1–8*, 172.

nificance, the appointed time when the prophetic expectation of messianic redemption is accomplished with the advent of Jesus.[135] Αἰών, which refers to the age to come and eternity, appears in 10:30,[136] where those who are persecuted for the sake of Jesus and the gospel are promised eternal life (ζωὴν αἰώνιον) in the age to come (ἐν τῷ αἰῶνι τῷ ἐρχομένῳ).

Another useful division of the concept of time is suggested by Malina.[137] He explores how time was perceived by members of first-century peasant societies in the Mediterranean, a group that includes the NT writers. He separates time into two categories: experienced time and imaginary time. Experienced time refers to the time when a person experiences reality in the present. The present does not refer to a punctual or definite time, but the time in which the past and the future are involved with an on-going significance: "The present, then, is a single context of meaning that often is of long duration, depending on the process or event involved."[138] Imaginary time, on the other hand, refers to time beyond the experienced world—in other words, imaginary time incorporates everything that does not take place in the present.[139] Past and future belong to imaginary time, which looks to "all that happened earlier than any living witness in fact experienced, as well as all the possibilities wrapped up in the modalities of what actually does not exist."[140] For example, imaginary time appears in Mark 13:32: "No one knows about that day or hour, not even the angels in heaven, nor the Son, but only the Father."[141]

---

135. France, *Gospel of Mark*, 91; Guelich, *Mark 1–8:26*, 43; Edwards, *Gospel according to Mark*, 47.

136. For the use of αἰών as the age to come or eternity, see Mark 3:29; 11:14. In 4:19, however, αἰών refers to this present age. France, *Gospel of Mark*, 206.

137. Malina, "Christ and Time," 1–31. Malina criticizes Cullman's discussion of time conception because "Cullmann's methods were typically eisegesis rather than exegesis, and his *Christ and Time* revealed contemporary hope rather than past biblical belief" (Malina, "Christ and Time," 1).

138. Malina, "Christ and Time," 12.

139. Malina, "Christ and Time," 14.

140. Malina, "Christ and Time," 14.

141. Malina, "Christ and Time," 15. Malina argues that even a future event may sometimes be classified as experienced time. The time in Rev 1:7 is considered as experienced time because "'everyone who pierced him' was still available": "Look! He is coming with the clouds; every eye will see him, even those who pierced him; and all the tribes of the earth will mourn because of him."

Space

According to Powell, spatial settings contain "the physical environment in which the characters of the story live as well as the 'props' and the 'furniture' that make up that environment."[142] Spatial settings play the role of activity room for the characters. As time is classified into two types, *chronological* and *typological*, space is also categorized largely into two types, *physical* and *typological*. Physical space is subdivided into three kinds: *topographical*, *geopolitical*, and *architectural*.[143] Topographical space refers to the portrayal of the physical features of a region that might be "observed from an aerial photograph," such as wilderness, way, river, sea, village, mountain, etc.[144] Geopolitical space refers to areas by "human-made boundaries of civic or governmental units," which have specific place-names such as Nazareth, Capernaum, Tyre, Sidon, Jerusalem, the Jordan River, the Sea of Galilee, the Mount of Olives, etc.[145] Architectural space refers to "artificially enclosed space" such as a house, tomb, room, temple, courtyard, etc.[146]

Typological space refers to the kind of space that imposes a special meaning on characters' actions and events. This kind of space, like typological time, is allusive or symbolic. The wilderness, for example, is a topographical space where events take place, but from the perspective of Israel's history it also connotes diverse meanings in relation to the exodus from Egypt, allowing it to be identified as a place of testing, punishment, discipline, revelation, provision, etc. The spatial implications of the wilderness in the exodus are discovered in Jesus' ministries in the wilderness. For example, Jesus was tested in the wilderness for forty days (Mark 1:14) and fed the crowds in the wilderness (6:31–44; 8:1–10), which recollect wilderness events from the exodus, namely the Israelites' forty years wandering and God's provision of manna in the wilderness.

In addition to physical and typological spaces, another spatial setting, *cosmic* space, may be considered in the Gospel narratives. According to Rhoads, Dewey, and Michie, "the larger setting of Mark's story is the 'creation that God created'": "This world is inhabited by God and angels,

---

142. Powell, *What Is Narrative Criticism?*, 70.

143. Though I refer to Malbon's division of narrative space, I do not follow her approach to analyzing space, which focuses on a mythic structure based on Lévi-Straus's structuralism. I simply divide narrative space in physical sides. See Malbon, *Narrative Space*.

144. Malbon, *Narrative Space*, 51.

145. Malbon, *Narrative Space*, 15.

146. Malbon, *Narrative Space*, 107.

Satan and demons, unclean and clean animals, as well as humans."[147] In a cosmic dimension, the histories of humans and nature in the created world are united: warfare takes place together with earthquakes and famine (Mark 13:8); a darkened sun, an eclipsed moon, falling stars, and shaking heavenly bodies declare the coming of the Son of Man with glory (v. 24).[148] Cosmic space is divided into two kinds, pure and impure, with reference to sacredness, and this creates a line of demarcation: thus the Jews are separated from the Gentiles (e.g., 7:24–30); religious leaders are separated from demon-possessed persons, lepers, and a bleeding woman (e.g., 1:21–28, 40–45; 5:1–20; 25–34); and cleanness is separated from uncleanness by the religious purity system (e.g., 7:1–23).[149]

Buchholz and Jahn classify narrative space, where characters live and move and events take place, by four factors: "(1) by boundaries that separate it from coordinate, superordinate, and subordinate spaces, (2) by the objects which it contains, (3) by the living conditions which it provides, and (4) by the temporal dimension to which it is bound."[150] These factors help divide narrative space according to its characteristics. This classification of narrative space is concerned not only with landscapes but also with favorable or hostile conditions.[151]

We also need to study how spaces are arranged, connected, and highlighted in a narrative. Chatman distinguishes story-space from discourse-space as he separates story-time from discourse-time.[152] Story-space refers to

---

147. Rhoads et al., *Mark as Story*, 64.

148. Rhoads et al., *Mark as Story*, 64.

149. Rhoads, Dewey, and Michie describe the changes of cosmic space through the coming of the kingdom of God, which is realized by Jesus, as follows: "The beginning of [Mark's] story proclaims that the whole cosmic setting is changing. Into the midst of this bounded world gone awry, God opens the heavens and sends the spirit upon Jesus, who announces that 'the rule of God has arrived.' The arrival of God's rule changes cosmic space, because the power of God from above is now available on earth for healing and exorcism. The power of God's rule breaks out of local, national, and natural boundaries to make all space into God's space. After the execution and resurrection of Jesus, followers are to spread the holy power of the rule of God outward from Israel to the limits of the earth." See Rhoads et al., *Mark as Story*, 64–65. For a study of sacred space in Mark and Matthew, see Riches, *Conflicting Mythologies*.

150. Buchholz and Jahn, "Space in Narrative," 552. In relation to "spatial organization" in a narrative world, Buchholz and Jahn categorized three kinds of spaces as follows: "(1) texts containing contiguous subspaces, where characters freely move from one space to the next, (2) texts with discontinuous, ontologically distinct spaces that allow communication in exceptional circumstances only, (3) texts with ontologically distinct spaces that do not allow communication, except through metalepsis."

151. Buchholz and Jahn, "Space in Narrative," 552.

152. Chatman, *Story and Discourse*, 96. Chatman's distinction between story-time

the spatial framework which is filled with existents (characters and settings), "the entities that perform and are affected" by events.[153] Discourse-space, on the other hand, refers to the "focus of spatial attention": "It is the framed area to which the implied audience's attention is directed by the discourse, that portion of the total story-space that is 'remarked'" through a narrator's eyes.[154] While characters can only see the space that the story produces, namely story-space, a narrator's eyes may observe how the spatial sceneries change and characters move from one point to the other in discourse-space.[155] For example, in Mark 4:35—8:21, while story-space refers to the places where Jesus visited in and beyond Galilee, discourse-space indicates how Jesus' geographical movement is arranged, presenting a cyclic pattern (two cycles: 4:35—6:44; 6:45—8:10) that communicates Mark's theological implications.[156] Because the structural pattern of Jesus' geographical movement comes from Mark's literary technique, discourse-space may be discovered through an exploration of Markan rhetorical devices. Discourse-space should therefore be studied in concord with rhetorical devices in narrative analysis.

Social Circumstances

Social circumstances as narrative settings can be examined in two ways. One way is to investigate how an author and his or her literary works were affected by the surrounding socio-cultural environments. The other way is to discover how the author projected social circumstances into his or

---

and discourse-time generally agrees with that of most literary theorists and is similar to that of Genette (the time of story vs. the time of narrative), which I already introduced. I will therefore omit the explanation about the difference between story-time and discourse-time that Chatman argues.

153. Chatman distinguishes between events and existents. While events refer to the narrative units in the dynamic state such as actions and happenings, existents refer to the actual constituents of the story such as characters and settings. See Chatman's diagram in *Story and Discourse*, 26.

154. Chatman, *Story and Discourse*, 102. Buchholz and Jahn explain the concept of Chatman's "discourse-space" as follows: "Discourse space denotes the narrator's current environment (more globally also all environments framing the narrator's activities, including the act of storytelling or writing itself)." Buchholz and Jahn, "Space in Narrative," 552.

155. Chatman, *Story and Discourse*, 101–7.

156. The present study will deal with the narrative structure of 4:35—8:21 on the basis of Mark's geographical description—how Mark arranges space. Structural analysis will therefore be accompanied by consideration of Mark's literary techniques, which are consequently related to the study of discourse-space.

her literary works. While the former approach focuses on real-life situations of the society that surrounded the author and audience, the latter looks at the point of view from which the author interpreted social circumstances and produced his or her own social world in literary works.

The first way of exploring social circumstances is to learn about the actual (real-life) social world in which a literary work was written (or the actual social world that forms the background of the literary work) from all available sources, including "literature, archeological excavation, art, coins, inscriptions, and so on."[157] Analyzed, classified, and organized, this information facilitates the interpretation of social settings in literature. Literary works are inevitably conditioned by the social conventions, cultural customs, religious tendencies, class structures, economic systems, political organizations, and power interactions prevalent at the time of writing.[158] Reconstructing the actual social world should therefore be a precedent study for interpreting a literary work.

Since Mark was written against the background of first-century Palestine and its neighboring regions, we need to reconstruct its actual social world by collecting and organizing the information we have from that time and use this to further interpretations of Mark's narrative. For example, the woman with a hemorrhage in Mark 5:25–34 was isolated from Jewish society because Jewish religious laws regarded menstruating women as unclean and impure. The Syrophoenician woman in 7:24–30 was compared to a dog because the Jews separated themselves from the Gentiles by disregarding them as dogs. Studying the background of the actual social world of first-century Palestine and its vicinity helps us to understand why these women in Mark's narrative were isolated and treated with contempt.

The second way of examining social circumstances is required as the next step toward understanding how an author creates and constructs the social world in his own narrative. Social environments in a narrative do not always exist neutrally; rather, they are expressed through the lens of the author. The social world of a narrative is represented by the author, who delineates the narrative world with his or her own point of view. According

---

157. Rhoads suggests five approaches for the social study of the NT: "(1) social description, (2) social history, (3) the sociology of knowledge, (4) the use of models from the social sciences, particularly cultural anthropology, and (5) the identification of social location." Among the five approaches of social criticism, the first three are useful as the background study of social circumstances. Social description refers to "the information that we have from the ancient world: literature, archeological excavations, art, coins, inscriptions, and so on." Social history deals with "the broad sweep of change in history." Sociology of knowledge provides "the insight that different cultural worldviews support different social systems." See Rhoads, "Social Criticism," 145–56.

158. Abrams and Harpham, *Glossary of Literary Terms*, 334.

to Rhoads, "the author has not simply collected traditions, organized them, made connections between them, and added summaries; the author has told a story, a dramatic story, with characters whose lives we follow to the various places they travel and through the various events in which they are caught up."[159] In a narrative, characters and events are not presented directly but retold in the social world, which the author experienced and expressed through his or her worldview.

After first enriching our sociological knowledge of a literary work, we must then examine the social world produced by the narrative, which may lead us to grasp the author's intentions. Mark portrays both a real world and a represented world. Though he delivers a real description of the actual social circumstances of first-century Palestine, he also shows us a represented social world defined by what he includes in his narrative and how he presents his material.[160] For example, among diverse social conflicts in first-century Palestine, Mark focuses on religious conflicts regarding the keeping of laws between Jesus and Jewish religious leaders (e.g., 2:23–28; 3:1–6; 7:1–23). Further, Mark shows that Jewish religious systems (such as Sabbath-keeping and ritual distinction between cleanness and uncleanness) are re-evaluated by Jesus, through whom "God's point of view" is expressed.[161] In this study I will first examine the social circumstances of first-century Palestine and then investigate how Mark presents its social world in his own narrative.

Rhetorical Devices

My primary concern in this study is to interpret Mark 4:35—8:21 on the basis of spatial analysis. Since the episodes in Mark's narrative are arranged according to Jesus' geographical movement, the exploration of spatial settings is especially important. In order to understand how the episodes are organized and arranged in given spatial settings, however, we need to investigate Mark's literary techniques, namely rhetorical devices. Time, space, and social circumstances should be examined in the light of "the rhetoric

---

159. Rhoads, "Narrative Criticism and the Gospel of Mark," 413.

160. See Petersen's study of the differences between a narrative world and a real world in Luke-Acts (Petersen, *Literary Criticism for New Testament Critics*, 81–92).

161. When point of view has the characteristic of evaluation, we call it the "evaluative point of view." This implies "the norms, values, and general world view that the implied author establishes as operative for the story." In the four Gospels, the evaluative point of view is "God's point of view," and this may be expressed through godly persons, angels, miracles, dreams, and so on. Of course, God's point of view is most explicitly expressed through Jesus. See Powell, *What Is Narrative Criticism?*, 23–24.

of the narrative."[162] According to Powell, "stories concerning the same basic events, characters, and settings can be told in ways that produce very different narratives."[163] Spatial settings do not simply exist as fixed backdrops, but are diversely expressed through the use of different rhetorical devices.[164] I will here introduce Mark's rhetorical devices, which play a key role in my analysis of narrative structure based on spatial settings.

Malbon observes Mark's rhetorical devices in the light of "juxtaposition"—"placing scene over against scene in order to elicit comparison, contrast, and insight."[165] She suggests six kinds of juxtaposition as Mark's major rhetorical devices: "repetition, intercalation, framing, foreshadowing and echoing, symbolism and irony."[166] Repetition refers to re-

---

162. Powell, *What Is Narrative Criticism?*, 23–34. Powell regards "discourse" as "the rhetoric of the narrative," which is distinguished from "story" as "the content of the narrative." Like Chatman, Powell understands narrative as "story-as-discoursed" and suggests several "devices intrinsic to the process of storytelling" that the implied author may use to guide the reader. These include "point of view," "narration," "symbolism and irony," and "narrative patterns."

163. Powell, *What Is Narrative Criticism?*, 23.

164. Discourse space in a narrative is created through the author's rhetorical devices. In relation to rhetorical devices or narrative patterns, Bauer suggests the following fifteen categories of "compositional relationship," which are used to divide a narrative into units and to show the connections between these units. (1) *Repetition* (*recurrence*): "the repetition or re-occurrence of the same or similar terms." (2) *Contrast*: "the association of opposites or of things which are dissimilar." (3) *Comparison*: "the association or juxtaposition of things which are alike or at least essentially similar." (4) *Causation* and *substantiation*: "causation represents the movement from cause to effect"; "substantiation involves the movement from effect to cause." (5) *Climax*: "the movement from the lesser to the greater to the greatest." (6) *Pivot*: "a radical reversal or turning around—a change of direction—of the movement of the material." (7) *Particularization* and *generalization*: "particularization involves a movement from the general to the particular"; "generalization designates the movement from the particular to the general." (8) *Statement of purpose*: "the movement from means to end." (9) *Preparation* (*introduction*): "the inclusion of background or setting for events or ideas." (10) *Summarization*: "an abridgement or compendium (summing up) of a unit of material." (11) *Interrogation*: "employment of a question or problem followed by its answer or solution." (12) *Inclusio*: "the repetition of features, words, phrases, and so on at the beginning and the ending of a unit, thus having a 'bracket' function." (13) *Interchange*: "the exchanging or alternation of certain elements (a, b, a, b, a)." (14) *Chiasm*: "the repetition of elements in inverted order (a, b, b', a')." (15) *Intercalation*: "the insertion of one literary unit in the midst of another literary unit (a, b, a)." See Bauer, *Structure of Matthew's Gospel*, 13–19.

165. Malbon, "Narrative Criticism," 39.

166. Malbon, "Narrative Criticism," 39–40. Dewey offers the following list of Mark's literary techniques: "inclusio, hook words, key words, anticipation and retrospection, repetition for rhetorical effect, lack of word repetition, chiasm, ring composition, extended concentric structure, interposition, and frame." See Dewey, *Markan Public Debate*, 31–34.

curring words, phrases, and scenes; duality is Mark's most favorite manner of repetition. Intercalation frequently appears in Mark's narrative, serving to disclose the central theme by inserting one episode into the other. Framing involves placing similar stories at the beginning and end of a certain section. Foreshadowing and echoing can occur in words, phrases, and events that reveal "intratextual (within the text) or intertextual (between texts)" relationships.[167] Symbolism associates "a literal meaning" with "a metaphorical one."[168] Irony turns "an apparent or expected meaning" into "a deeper or surprising one."[169] Malbon identifies these six rhetorical devices as Mark's narrative discourse, by which Mark tells the story according to his intention.[170]

Repetition is here the most significant the rhetorical devices deployed in Mark to reveal its narrative patterns. A number of episodes in Mark's narrative are linked by "various forms of repetition" rather than by "linear progression."[171] Repetition serves as the basic element of other rhetorical devices and produces diverse narrative patterns with its variations. For example, though inclusio, interchange, chiasm, and intercalation include repetition, they create different patterns through different arrangements of repetition. According to Rhoads, Dewey, and Michie, "the Markan episodes are intertwined with each other by the repetition of words and phrases, the occurrence of foreshadowing and retrospections, similarities of scenes and situations, and the clustering of episodes in concentric or parallel patterns."[172] Resseguie explains the significance and functions of repetition as follows:

> Repetition is a stylistic device that reiterates words, phrases, themes, patterns, situations, and actions for emphasis. When repetition is employed intentionally, it "adds force and clarity to a statement" or motif. It is commonplace in biblical literature and helps identify the norms, values, beliefs, and point of view that the narrator considers important. Repetition is also important for identifying narrative structure and design. A repeated word or thought may divide a narrative passage into smaller

---

167. Malbon states that "the intertextual echoes heard in Mark's Gospel reverberate with the Septuagint" (Malbon, "Narrative Criticism," 40).

168. Malbon, "Narrative Criticism," 40.

169. Malbon, "Narrative Criticism," 40.

170. Malbon, "Narrative Criticism," 40.

171. Supposing that Mark was intended to be heard orally, Rhoads, Dewey, and Michie argue that the repetitive characteristics made it easier for the listening audience to understand the highly episodic story. See Rhoads et al., *Mark as Story*, 47.

172. Rhoads et al., *Mark as Story*, 47.

units. Repetition occurs in small units such as a repeated word at the beginning of consecutive phrases or sentences, or it occurs in very large units such as narrative type-scenes that have a set pattern of repeated events.[173]

Mark uses many and various forms of repetition in order to emphasize themes and develop plot with variations by repeatedly highlighting the important characteristics of episodes.[174] In relation to the present study, I will briefly introduce the rhetorical devices that present the diverse repetitive patterns of Mark's narrative.[175]

First, the simplest form of repetition is the use of "key words." Key words, which appear repeatedly in episodes, help build a structure, disclose the central themes or *Leitmotifs*, and connect one episode to the others.[176] "Boats," for example, are repeatedly featured in Mark 4–8 as the means of Jesus' travel across the Sea of Galilee, forming a *Leitmotif* that provides a structural framework for Mark 4–8. In another instance, the repetition of "bread" in the episodes of the two feeding miracles (6:31–44; 8:1–10) and the discussion between Jesus and his disciples on the sea (8:13–21) serves to reveal the central themes of Christology and discipleship in Mark 4–8.

Second, "intercalation"—also known as a "sandwich technique"—is Mark's favorite rhetorical device for emphasizing central themes.[177] This literary technique involves inserting one episode in the middle of another

---

173. Resseguie, *Narrative Criticism*, 42. Williams summarizes four functions of repetition: (1) to "emphasize matters" that are essential to the right appreciation of the story; (2) to "highlight variations" that disclose the differences between similar episodes; (3) to "signal new developments" in which character and plot take fresh forms; and (4) to "create expectation" of an anticipated outcome in a repeated pattern. See Williams, *Other Followers of Jesus*, 52–54.

174. Rhoads et al., *Mark as Story*, 47.

175. Emphasizing the significance of repetition in Mark' narrative, Rhoads, Dewey, and Michie explains the characteristics of Mark's repetitive patterns in storytelling as follows: "By design, this repetition is not simple or exact, but is repetition with variation. The different patterns of repetition overlap and interweave in so many complex ways that it is really not possible to make a linear outline of Mark's story. Awareness of these narrative patterns sensitizes the reader to the interconnections of various episodes that on the surface are only loosely related. The rich variety in repetition serves also to develop character, advance the plot, and amplify themes in Mark's narrative design." They also list the following rhetorical devices that show repetitive patterns in Mark: verbal threads, foreshadowing and retrospection, two-step progressions, type scenes, sandwiched episodes, framing episodes, and episodes in a concentric pattern. See Rhoads et al., *Mark as Story*, 47–61.

176. Rhoads et al., *Mark as Story*, 47–48; Dewey, *Markan Public Debate*, 32.

177. Edwards, *Gospel According to Mark*, 11–12. See also Fowler, *Let the Reader Understand*, 143–44.

episode (a, b, a) so that the inserted episode (b) serves as the theological key to the bracket episode (a).[178] For example, the episode of the woman with a hemorrhage (5:25–34) is sandwiched within the episode of Jairus's daughter (5:21–24, 35–43), and the woman's faith becomes an example to Jairus, who needs faith. Edwards identifies nine sandwich episodes in Mark's narrative: 3:20–35; 4:1–20; 5:21–43; 6:7–30; 11:12–21; 14:1–11; 14:17–31; 14:53–72; 15:40—16:8.[179]

Third, "framing" refers to a bracket structure in which two similar episodes are positioned at the beginning and end of a large section, but do not belong to the section itself.[180] For example, the two similar episodes in which Jesus heals blind men—the blind man at Bethsaida (8:22–26) and blind Bartimaeus (10:46–52)—serve as the frame of the section describing Jesus' journey to Jerusalem (8:22—10:52) and help reveal the main theme of this section as discipleship is symbolically understood as gaining sight after blindness. Some scholars consider framing to be identical with "inclusio,"[181] but others distinguish framing from inclusio by limiting inclusio to words or phrases. Dewey defines inclusio as "the repetition of the same word or phrase at or near the beginning and ending of some unit, a sentence, a pericope, or a larger section."[182]

Fourth, "type-scenes" refer to patterned stories in that similar episodes are repeated with variation.[183] According to Alter, type-scenes are the literary convention of the Hebrew Bible: parallel episodes appear recurrently in fixed situations, and their variations guide the development of a narrative according to motifs.[184] Type-scenes have the functions of "characterization,

---

178. Edwards, *Gospel According to Mark*, 11. Rhoads, Dewey, and Michie explain the functions of intercalation as follows: "The two paired episodes often repeat a common theme, one episode illuminating the theme by comparison or contrast with the other episode" (Rhoads et al., *Mark as Story*, 52).

179. Edwards, *Gospel According to Mark*, 11.

180. Dewey explains the difference between "frame" and "extended concentric structure" as follows: "For example, the two healings of blind men constitute a frame for Mark 8:27–10:45, but the two miracle-controversies beginning and ending Mark 2:1–3:6 are not a frame because they themselves are part of the controversy section." The former example illustrates a "frame," while the latter represents an "extended concentric structure." See Dewey, *Markan Public Debate*, 34.

181. E.g., Hooker notes that some exegetes regard the two healing episodes of blind men (8:22–26; 10:46–52) as an "inclusio" of Mark 8:22—10:52. See Hooker, *Gospel according to Saint Mark*, 197.

182. Dewey, *Markan Public Debate*, 31.

183. Rhoads et al., *Mark as Story*, 51. See also Teugels, *Bible and Midrash*, 51.

184. Alter, *Art of Biblical Narrative*, 55–78.

plot development, and thematic amplification."¹⁸⁵ For example, the two parallel feeding miracles (6:31–44; 8:1–10) are described in terms of similar situations (e.g., both take place in the wilderness) with some variations (e.g., the five thousand and twelve baskets; the four thousand and seven baskets), indicating that one feeding miracle is for the Jews, and the other is for the Gentiles. The two miracles are also connected by a bread motif, which discloses the themes of Christology and discipleship in the discussion about bread on the sea (8:13–21) by revealing who Jesus is and how ignorant the disciples are.

Fifth, "anticipation and retrospection" are important patterns of repetition in Mark's narrative. While anticipation is used to foreshadow later events, retrospection is used to recollect earlier events.¹⁸⁶ Since anticipation and retrospection connect the whole story forward and backward, they give the narrative "a sense of unity."¹⁸⁷ Typical cases include Jesus' prediction of Peter's denial (14:27–31) as anticipation, and Peter's reminiscence of Jesus' word to him (v. 72) as retrospection. Anticipation and retrospection take place not only within the text, but also between texts.¹⁸⁸ For example, Jesus' feeding miracles in the wilderness recollect the manna event in the exodus story.

Sixth, "chiasm" denotes repetition in which the order of words, phrases, or pericopes is inverted (a, b, b', a'; a, b, c, b', a').¹⁸⁹ According to Dewey, chiastic elements may be included in an "extended concentric structure"—"the symmetrical arrangement or inverted parallelism of four, five or more pericopes or items of narrative" (a, b, c, b', a'; a, b, c, c', b', a').¹⁹⁰ An extended concentric structure, which shows a symmetrical pattern, uses numerous corresponding parallelisms in words, contents, forms, etc.¹⁹¹ Dewey provides the following example of an extended concentric structure: "A—2:1-12 The healing of the paralytic; B—2:13-17 The calling of Levi/eating with sinners;

185. Rhoads et al., *Mark as Story*, 51.
186. Rhoads et al., *Mark as Story*, 48.
187. Dewey, *Markan Public Debate*, 32.
188. Malbon, "Narrative Criticism," 40.
189. Dewey, *Markan Public Debate*, 32–33. There is also "syntactical chiasm": "subject, verb: verb, subject."
190. Dewey, *Markan Public Debate*, 33. Dewey explains that "an extended concentric pattern may often contain chiastic elements, and it may often be grouped or collapsed into a ring composition, e.g., (a b) c (b' a')."
191. Dewey, *Markan Public Debate*, 33, 37. Dewey lists the following possible functions of concentric structure: (1) "to emphasize its central element"; (2) "to hold opposite ideas in tension with one another for the audience"; (3) "to interrelate ideas in a more complex fashion than permitted in a non-symmetrical structure"; and (4) "to integrate additional dimensions or emphases into a chronological or linear narrative."

C—2:18-22 The sayings on fasting and on the old and the new; B'—2:23-27 Plucking grain on the sabbath; A'—3:1-6 The healing on the sabbath."[192] Another pattern similar to chiasm is "ring composition," which refers to a circular technique (a, b, a).[193] Though its simplest form may be regarded as inclusio, ring composition is more similar to chiasm in that it is based on repeated content rather than repeated words.[194]

Seventh, "two-step and three-step progressions" exist where similar or connected phrases, sentences, and episodes appear repeatedly and progress a narrative by way of two steps or three steps.[195] For example, a two-step progression is discovered in Mark's introduction of Jesus as "Christ, the son of God" (1:1), a designation that is demonstrated in two steps. Jesus is manifested first as the Christ and then as the son of God: in the middle of Mark, Peter recognizes Jesus as the Christ (8:27) and in the end of Mark, the centurion confesses Jesus as the son of God (15:39).[196] A three-step progression explicitly appears in a number of important parts of Mark's narrative. Among many episodes of a three-step progression,[197] a typical example is Jesus' three predictions of his death and resurrection (8:31; 9:31; 10:33-34) connected by a way motif. Likewise, three episodes of Jesus and the disciples in a boat—two sea miracles (4:35-41; 6:45-52) and a discussion between Jesus and the disciples in a boat (8:13-21)—show a three-step progression unified by a boat motif, while two feeding miracles (6:31-44; 8:1-10) and a discussion in a boat (8:13-21) also present a three-step progression linked by a bread motif.[198]

---

192. Dewey, *Markan Public Debate*, 110. See also Dewey, "Literary Structure of the Controversy Stories in Mark 2:1—3:6," 141-51. Witherington identifies this structure as chiasm. An extended concentric structure belongs to the category of chiasm as its extended form (Witherington, *Gospel of Mark*, 36).

193. Dewey, *Markan Public Debate*, 33.

194. Dewey, *Markan Public Debate*, 33.

195. Rhoads et al., *Mark as Story*, 49-50, 54-55.

196. Rhoads et al., *Mark as Story*, 50. The main function of two-step progression is to generate "suspense by maintaining readers' desire to see what is yet to come, for the recurrence of this pattern conditions readers to wait for the second step, for further clarifications." Another example of a two-step progression is the healing of a blind man at Bethsaida (8:22-26). Here Jesus touches the eyes of the blind man two times: at Jesus' first touch, the blind man did not see clearly, but at his second touch, the blind man could see everything clearly.

197. Rhoads et al., *Mark as Story*, 54. E.g., Jesus prays three times (14:32-42); Peter denies Jesus three times (14:66-72); Pilate asks the crowd how to judge Jesus three times (15:6-15); and Jesus' crucifixion is described three times with three-hour intervals (the third, the sixth, and the ninth hour: 15:25-39).

198. Rhoads et al., *Mark as Story*, 54.

My structural analysis in this study is also based on Mark's rhetorical device of repetition. Jesus' journeys in and beyond Galilee in Mark 4:35—8:21 show a repetitive pattern consisting of two identifiable cycles (4:35—6:44; 6:45—8:10) and a conclusion (8:11-21). Though my proposed structure is basically built on Jesus' geographical movement, the locations and routes of Jesus' journey are arranged according to Mark's literary pattern of repetition. In each of the two cycles, Jesus' ministry begins at the sea with sea miracles (4:35–41; 6:45-52) and ends at the wilderness with feeding miracles (6:31-44; 8:1-10). The sea and the wilderness here play the role of a framework. The structural framework, which functions to bracket the two cycles, may be presented as a, b, a', b'. In the concluding section, Jesus' discussion about bread with his disciples in a boat (8:13–21, c) is connected with his two previous sea and feeding miracles by its use of boat and bread motifs, presenting a three-step progression. In conclusion, Mark's repetitive pattern in a geographical arrangement demonstrates the following structure (a, b, a', b', c):

    A—Jesus calming the roaring sea (4:35–41)
    (An overland journey, 5:1—6:30)
      B—The feeding of five thousand (6:31-44)
    A'—Jesus walking on the sea (6:45-52)
    (An overland journey, 6:53—7:37)
      B'—The feeding of four thousand (8:1-10)
        C—Jesus' discussion about bread in a boat (8:13-21)

I will demonstrate this structural analysis more fully in chapter 3.

Intertextuality and Allusion

Though space in Mark's narrative may be examined in its social and geographical aspects, its historical and ideological dimensions can also be explored.[199] In these dimensions, space serves to recollect past events and connote symbolic meanings. In the present study, I will investigate how Mark's uses of the sea and the wilderness allude to the historical events of Israel's exodus, which had been interpreted and expressed in cosmological and eschatological dimensions in the OT and Second Temple Jewish literature. Jesus' sea miracles (4:35–41; 6:45-52) recall the victory over Israel's Egyptian pursuers at the Red Sea, and his feeding miracles (6:31-44; 8:1-10) echo the manna event in the wilderness. The spatial settings of the

---

199. This sentence uses the term "social" in a synchronic aspect and "historical" in a diachronic aspect.

sea and the wilderness thus play a role in connecting Jesus' miracles with the exodus events. The Markan spaces of the sea and the wilderness also carry cosmological and eschatological implications, in which Jesus' salvific ministries may be interpreted in the light of the new exodus anticipated in the OT and Second Temple Jewish literature.

I will search for the corresponding points between Jesus' sea and feeding miracles and the exodus events of the victory at the sea and the manna provision in the wilderness. This study will thereby also entail a typological approach in that it explores a correspondence between the exodus events (type) and Jesus' miracles (antitype).[200] However, I will not only examine the similarities between them in a historical dimension but also consider many and diverse cosmological and eschatological interpretations of the exodus events found in the later OT texts and Second Temple Jewish literature. Here the sea and the wilderness play a significant role in imbuing the exodus events with cosmological and eschatological implications. The sea and the wilderness do not simply serve as spatial settings that imply a connection between Jesus' miracles and exodus events; they also provide a theological impetus to understand Jesus' sea and feeding miracles in the light of the new

200. Goppelt, who argues strongly for the significance of typology in NT scholarship, presents a detailed and broad survey on the methods of using typology in late Judaism and the NT. He comments, "the typological use of the OT in the NT has always provided an example of a more profound interpretation of the OT and has motivated the search for a meaning that goes beyond the literal grammatical-historical explanation" (Goppelt, *Typos*, 7). According to Thiselton, many have explained typology as relying on a "correspondence between *events*" in comparison with allegory as relying on a "correspondence between *ideas*" (Thiselton, "Hermeneutics," *NDT* 294) While comparing typology with "direct prophecy"—that is, a direct prediction of a NT event—Osborne insists that "typology is indirect and analogously relates the Old Testament event to the New Testament event" (Osborne, *Hermeneutical Spiral*, 328). Within the frame of type and antitype, Ninow explains typology as follows: "a person, event, or institution ('type') in the OT corresponds to another one ('antitype') in the NT within the framework of salvation history. . . . The traditional understanding of biblical typology views the OT type as divinely ordained and a detailed predictive prefiguration of Jesus and the gospel realities brought about by him" (Ninow, "Typology," *EDB* 1341). For a detailed definition and explanation of typology, see Treier, "Typology," *DTIB* 823–27; Lampe and Woollcombe, *Essays on Typology*; Baker, *Two Testaments, One Bible*, 169–90. Evans regards typology as a hermeneutical premise rather than a methodological approach: "Typology is not so much a *method* of exegesis as it is a *presupposition* underlying the Jewish and Christian understanding of Scripture, particularly its historical portions. Typology is based upon the belief that the biblical story (of the past) has some bearing on the present, or, to turn it around, that the present is foreshadowed in the biblical story" (Evans, "Listening for Echoes," 48). However, typology is both presupposition and methodology. When we discuss the tendency of the NT writers who were willing to understand events in the light of OT stories, typology is presupposition. When we interpret the NT stories in the structure of type (the OT) and antitype (the NT), typology is methodology.

exodus and its cosmological and eschatological significance. In this sense, my methodological approach will incorporate attention to allusion (echo) as I compare Jesus' miracles with the exodus events on the basis of the spatial implications of the sea and the wilderness.

Before discussing allusion, we need to understand the concept of intertextuality, which refers to the relationship between texts. Since intertextuality provides the basic theory of how a text is related to and influenced by the earlier text or texts, a study of intertextuality is necessary for an understanding of the meaning and functions of allusion and echo. For this reason I will introduce intertextuality before explaining allusion and echo. These approaches will be applied to spatial analysis of the sea and the wilderness in chapter 4.

Intertextuality

The exploration of the use of the OT in the NT has concentrated on determining "which texts from the OT are cited in the NT, how they have influenced the text tradition, on which level of the text tradition this happened, and on the form of the text."[201] Only in reference to NT texts that are regarded as certainly quoting or alluding to OT texts had the use of the OT in the NT been significantly studied. When intertextuality was introduced and employed in biblical scholarship,[202] however, the study of the NT use of the OT entered a new phase. Brunson describes its impact as follows:

201. Brunson, *Psalm 118 in the Gospel of John*, 7. Porter enumerates the many terms used to describe the NT use of the OT: "citation, direct quotation, formal quotation, indirect quotation, allusive quotation, allusion (whether conscious or unconscious), paraphrase, exegesis (such as inner-biblical exegesis), midrash, typology, reminiscence, echo (whether conscious or unconscious), intertextuality, influence (either direct or indirect), and even tradition." In relation to the present study, I will introduce and employ the terms intertextuality and allusion (echo) to explain the NT use of the OT. See Porter, "Use of the Old Testament in the New Testament," 80.

202. Beal briefly introduces the history and meaning of "intertextuality" as follows: "This term [intertextuality] was first developed by Julia Kristeva. . . . Not to be confused with notions of literary borrowing or poetic influence, she understood it to describe every discourse, whether written or spoken. Every discourse is intertextual—'a field of transpositions of various signifying systems' (Kristeva, *Revolution in Poetic Language*, 60), 'an *intersection* of textual surfaces rather than a *point* (a fixed meaning)' (Kristeva, *Desire in Language*, 65). It is for this reason that every text is polyvalent. For Kristeva, and for others such as Jacques Derrida and Roland Barthes, the basic force of intertextuality is to problematize, even spoil, textual boundaries—those lines of demarcation which allow a reader to talk about *the* meaning, subject, or origin of a writing. Such borders, intertextuality asserts, are never solid or stable. Texts are always spilling over into other texts" (Beal, "Glossary," 22–23). Refer to Kristeva, *Desire in Language*; Kristeva, *Revolution in Poetic Language*; Derrida, "Living On," 75–176; Derrida,

Intertextuality, which was first used as a technical term in literary criticism, has only recently been applied to biblical studies, where it has significantly broadened the horizons of investigation. There is growing appreciation that the NT use of the OT goes far beyond the clear quotations and allusions, and that the meaning effects created by allusion are important for interpreting the passage in which they are embedded. Intertextuality raises questions rarely asked in the past, dealing with the relationship between texts created by alluding to or echoing a prior text, the changes of meaning and significance which the anterior text imports to the later text, and the continuity and discontinuity ("intertextual transformations") that takes place.[203]

Moore defines the meaning of intertextuality as used in modern literary criticism as follows: "Coined by Julia Kristeva, this term [intertextuality] denotes the multiple ways in which one text echoes, rewrites, or is otherwise intertwined with other texts, whether through overt citation and allusion, or—and this is much more Kristeva—through the sheer fact of its forming a node in a network that, for all intents and purposes, is boundless."[204] Intertextuality expands the boundaries of interpretation by pointing out that a given text is influenced not only directly by one or two immediately preceding texts but also indirectly by a diverse array of earlier texts, which may help establish the framework of the author's thought.

The concept of intertextuality should be explained more specifically, however, because the intertextual relationships could potentially be applied to all the other texts infinitely and indiscriminately.[205] It is essential to define

---

Dissemination; Barthes, "Theory of the Text," 31–47. Refer also to the following collection of articles that introduce the diverse meanings and functions of intertextuality: Clayton and Rothstein, *Influence and Intertextuality*. Intertextuality began to receive attention in biblical (especially NT) scholarship around 1989. According to Moyise, two books published in 1989 gave rise to a lively discussion of intertextuality in biblical writings (Moyise, "Intertextuality," 14–15): one is Draisma, *Intertextuality in Biblical Writings* and the other one is Hays, *Echoes of Scripture*.

203. Brunson, *Psalm 118 in the Gospel of John*, 7–8.

204. Moore, *Poststructuralism and the New Testament*, 130. One of the significant characteristics of intertextuality is "openness": "Intertextuality means that texts are open—open to all the effects of past texts and to the contexts of present readers." See Vanhoozer, *Is There a Meaning in This Text?*, 132.

205. Beal explains the reason of the difficulty to discuss intertextuality in biblical scholarship as follows: "Yet to anyone entering this new conversation it quickly becomes apparent that the application of this poststructuralist theoretical term is far from uniform; and the lines of influence by which it has been carried into biblical interpretation are nearly impossible to trace. One reason for this seemingly boundless dissemination of 'intertextuality' within our discipline is that it has been developed in

intertextuality when using this concept to interpret a text: "For the practice of intertextual reading . . . one must have such lines of delimitation, no matter how arbitrarily they may be set, and no matter how quickly they may be transgressed. That is, no intertextual reading can choose the 'general text'—everything, all at once, everywhere—as its object of interpretation."[206] Though intertextuality may simply be understood as the "relationship between texts,"[207] interpreters should provide their own account of the meaning and characteristics of intertextuality as applied to their study in order to place their use of the term on the broad spectrum of intertextuality.[208]

Intertextuality was first introduced as a technical term by poststructuralist literary critics.[209] In biblical scholarship, this term was also employed in reference to the exploration of relationships between biblical texts, but it is now dissociated from poststructuralists to some degree.[210] Though I use this term in the present study, I do not follow many poststructuralist tendencies, such as indeterminacy of textual meaning, infinite openness to all other

---

poststructuralism as a *theoretical* rather than a *methodological* term." See Beal, "Ideology and Intertextuality," 27.

206. Beal, "Ideology and Intertextuality," 28.

207. Vorster, "Intertextuality and Redaktionsgeschichte," 18. Vorster recommends reading Manfred Pfister's well-organized article to understand the concept of intertextuality. See Pfister, "Konzepte der Intertextualität," 1–30.

208. Culler explains the enormously diverse perspectives of intertextuality as follows: "Theories of intertextuality set before us perspective of unmasterable series, lost origins, endless horizons" (Culler, *Pursuit of Signs*, 109).

209. Poststructuralism is used as a broad term that includes deconstruction. Moore, *Poststructuralism and the New Testament*, 3. Vanhoozer says that "deconstruction is poststructuralist insofar as it denies the structuralist premises of an underlying system (e.g., of binary oppositions) that gives intelligibility to language and thought" (Vanhoozer, *Is There a Meaning in This Text?*, 52). I will here state my position against postmodern interpretation of language and knowledge. I put poststructuralism and postmodernism in the same category; the former focuses more on literary fields and the latter covers all ideologies and cultures in general.

210. According to Moyise, the idea of "intertextuality" is valuable in that it leads us to interpret a text in the aspect of "complexity and openness." He divides the use of this term into three categories: (1) "intertextual echo," focusing on the meanings of a text, which are resonated from prior texts; (2) "dialogical intertextuality," emphasizing on interactions between texts, which are performed in both directions; (3) "postmodern intertextuality," centering on the inability to determine the sole meaning of a text, which opens the possibility to create multiple meanings in a text. See Moyise, "Intertextuality," 17–18. While the first two approaches have the purpose of identifying meaning, the last approach presupposes an inherent unstableness of the meaning in texts. With the exception of those who use postmodern intertextuality, most biblical scholars employ intertextuality in relation to the first two approaches. In this sense, I state that the use of intertextuality of biblical scholarship is now separated from that of poststructuralism or postmodernism.

texts and contexts, reader-oriented interpretation, and skepticism toward the possibility of discovering the author's intention.[211] Kurz, who employs intertextuality to examine the use of Sir 48:1–6 in the plotline of Luke-Acts, rejects the concept of intertextuality as used by deconstructionists as follows: "This literary approach to intertextuality, however, differs from that of deconstruction, where intertextuality is a springboard for associate semiotic or cultural matters in general, or a way to dissociate concepts from their references so as to rewrite history according to contemporary ideologies and agendas."[212] In this study I will use an intertextual approach to help compensate for the weaknesses of traditional approaches to investigating relationships between texts.[213] Regarding the proper use of intertextuality in biblical studies, Osborne states that "intertextuality is best used as a study of

---

211. Sommer explains the concept of intertextuality used by poststructuralists as follows: "The intertextual approach relies heavily on structural linguistics and its postmodern heirs in seeing all signs, including those in a literary text, as meaningful only insofar as they stand in relation and opposition to other signs. As a result, any utterance signifies only in the context of other utterances, or as part of a sign system, such as a language. To understand any utterance is to put it in relationship with other utterances; and thus, any reader of a literary text necessarily connects it with other utterances.... It is the reader who interprets signs in the text by associating them with related signs in the reader's own mind. Of course, one reader's matrix of associations will differ from another's, so that the set of signs relevant for the intertextual approach can be quite broad.... Intertextuality, then, concerns itself with the relations among many texts; it is a synchronic, reader-oriented, semiotic method." See Sommer, *Prophet Reads Scripture*, 7.

212. Kurz, "Intertextual Use," 309.

213. In relation to the use of intertextuality, poststructuralists open the path to reading a text regardless of authorial intention, which consequently produces multiple meanings ("polyvalence" or "plurisignification") in the fixed text. "Since the perspective of the reader is crucial for the interpretation, polyvalence naturally results when various contemporary worldview are employed to examine the grid of the text" (Osborne, *Hermeneutical Spiral*, 475). In biblical scholarship, however, intertextuality is employed to examine the manner in which the NT uses the OT. Intertextuality focuses on how the NT writers used the OT texts, for example by understanding OT events typologically and applying the results to NT events. Midrashic exegesis and pesher patterns are also used by NT writers. Intertextuality covers these approaches, including traditional source criticism. On Midrashic exegesis, see Buchanan, *Introduction to Intertextuality*. This approach to interpreting the relationship between the OT and the NT is ultimately concerned with NT authors' multiple uses of OT texts to produce new NT texts. Moyise notes that scholars now tend to refer to "an author's intertextual use of traditions" rather than to "sources." This tendency suggests a recognition of the diversity and complexity of the process by which a text is created in interaction with prior texts; intertextuality is therefore also appropriately called "tapestry" or "mosaic." See Moyise, "Intertextuality," 15. I will use intertextuality understood in this way to explore relationships between texts in deeper and broader aspects beyond the examinations of traditional one-to-one correspondence between texts.

reuse of an Old Testament passage in a New Testament context, considering exactly how the dialogue between original meaning (Old Testament context) and new meaning (New Testament context) develops."[214]

Consideration of the intertexual use of the OT in the NT should not be limited to the examination of explicit correspondences between texts.[215] The traditional approach to exploring relationships between texts, "source-influence studies," is concerned mainly with determining what sources were employed in a text and showing how (or on what level) the antecedent texts influenced the text being considered.[216] In this old way of investigating the relationship between texts, however, studies of "the *function* of traces of anterior texts in later texts" and the "production and reception" of the texts are rare.[217] Intertextuality, however, offers a fresh interpretative tool for discovering the relationship between texts, showing "the ways a new text is created from the metaphor, images, and symbolic world of an earlier text or tradition"; in addition, "the interaction between a received text and a fresh social context brings a new textual and symbolic world into being."[218] In the present study I will employ the following understanding of intertextuality to

---

214. Osborne, *Hermeneutical Spiral*, 331.

215. Rosner argues that one should examine the NT use of the OT not only in "explicit" relationships between the texts, but also in their "implicit and instinctive" relationships. He explains a biblical quotation and its cumulative meanings as follows: "Obviously if a Biblical quotation is present (cf. [1 Cor] 5:13b; 6:16) it should be investigated as a possible doorway into a larger room of Scriptural teaching. Once this background material has been assembled it should be held up as a mirror against the relevant New Testament passage to see to what extent the influence of Scripture may be reflected. Having listened to the Bible's teaching on a subject one is ready to hear echoes (albeit with variations) in the New Testament." See Rosner, *Paul, Scripture, and Ethics*, 17–18.

216. Vorster explains the meaning and purpose of source-influence study as follows: "The theory of source-influence study is based on firm convictions and domain assumptions concerning texts and their origin and growth.... Source-influence studies are based on a particular view of what a text is. In New Testament scholarship texts are generally regarded as something which has developed into written documents and that it is possible to determine the presupposed texts on which these documents supposedly were based. The purpose of source-influence studies is to prove the use of sources and to demonstrate the debt of the authors of these texts to the precursor texts, be they actual or presupposed texts." See Vorster, "Intertextuality and Redaktionsgeschichte," 19–20.

217. Vorster, "Intertextuality and Redaktionsgeschichte," 15, 21. Vorster looks at three aspects of intertextual relationship: "First of all it is clear that the phenomenon text has been redefined. It has become a network of references to other texts (intertexts). Secondly, it appears that more attention is to be given to text as a process of production and not the sources and their influences. And thirdly it is apparent that the role of the reader is not to be neglected in this approach to the phenomenon of text."

218. O'Day, "Jeremiah 9:22–23 and 1 Corinthians 1:26–31," 259.

examine the sea and the wilderness in Jesus' sea and feeding miracles (Mark 4:35–41; 6:31–44; 6:45–52; and 8:1–10) in terms of the meanings suggested by interactions with the OT and Second Temple Jewish literature.[219]

First, intertextuality regards a text as a "network (or fabric) of traces."[220] When a text is created, it is connected with many earlier texts in complex relationships. It is important, however, to set limits on which earlier texts are related to the text being considered. One of the criteria used to select valid intertexts is evidence that the prior texts are related to the text in terms of "comparable contexts."[221] A text is created in the process of relating itself to anterior texts, and "comparable contexts" play a crucial role in placing a text in an intertextual relationship.[222] If Jesus' sea and feeding miracles are to be examined against the backgrounds of the sea and the wilderness, one should investigate prior texts in the OT and Jewish literature that include stories with the sea or wilderness as their background. These texts cannot all be examined, however, so it is necessary to narrow the number of possibilities. If Jesus' sea and feeding miracles reflect the exodus events, the imageries and traditions of the sea and the wilderness should be investigated in prior texts which contain the contexts of the exodus events.

Second, the intertextual relationship between texts is not so much "individual" as "cumulative."[223] When attempting to identify intertextuality between texts, one should begin by examining the prior text that shows explicit connections with the present text, but also, then, investigate other prior texts that present relatively implicit connections. Any author is affected by numerous other texts, so a given work, though most affected by another

---

219. In relation to intertextuality, I will here state my position on the NT use of the OT. NT writers did not use OT texts arbitrarily or subjectively, but employed the OT texts in something of a constant and unified way in view of the promise of the OT and its fulfillment in the NT. According to Osborne, "the early Christians (like the Jews) saw all salvation history (God working out his plan of salvation in human history) as a single continuous event." In this sense, "events in the past are linked to those in the present." See Osborne, *Hermeneutical Spiral*, 328. NT writers interpreted Jesus' actions in continuity with OT events. In other words, OT events were understood typologically by NT writers who saw and heard Jesus' life and ministry. Consequently, events experienced as promises in the OT were reenacted and fulfilled through Jesus' works in the NT. The use of the OT in the NT is based on the common theological understanding of "promise and fulfillment" in Jesus Christ. See also Beale and Carson, *Commentary*, xxiii–xxviii.

220. Vorster, "Intertextuality and Redaktionsgeschichte," 21.

221. Vorster, "Intertextuality and Redaktionsgeschichte," 21. According to Vorster, if a birth story is created, the intertextual relationships may be discovered in the prior texts that have similar contexts, namely birth stories.

222. Vorster, "Intertextuality and Redaktionsgeschichte," 21.

223. Rosner, *Paul, Scripture, and Ethics*, 19–20.

particular literary work, may also be influenced by many and diverse other texts. Images and meanings in the present text are accumulated through both explicit and implicit connections with prior texts.

Biblical writings in particular are closely related to each other in many complex ways. Biblical texts were not developed to correspond to prior texts in one-to-one relationships; rather, they were produced in collective and cumulative association with prior texts. Since the NT authors were significantly influenced by prior biblical writings, their writing might carry a particular meaning in relation to a particular OT text while also connoting other implications through its relation to other OT texts. In Mark, for example, the sea expresses diverse images and meanings derived from numerous earlier texts rather than a single image and meaning from a single prior text. If we study the image of the sea in Jesus' sea miracles with the supposition that these miracles reflect the victory at the sea in the exodus, we should examine this image not only in its original description in Exod 14 but also in later biblical writings that reinterpreted the exodus event in cosmological and eschatological terms. In Exod 14, the sea was physical water, but in the Psalms and the Prophets the image of the sea was reinterpreted as a representation of chaos with significant cosmological and eschatological resonances.[224] The sea in Mark's narrative therefore reflects not only the physical but also the cosmological and eschatological images of water.

Third, intertextuality looks at the ways in which images and meanings change when early texts are used in later texts.[225] Fishbane observes that we should pay particular attention to "how the texts that comprise it were revised and even reauthorized during the course of many centuries, and to how older traditions fostered new insights which, in turn, thickened the intertextual matrix of the culture and conditioned its imagination."[226] For example, if we assume that Mark used exodus themes in his narrative, we must not restrict our inquiry to exodus stories in the book of Exodus itself.[227] Mark might have used exodus themes as seen through the lens of Isaiah, who interpreted the exodus stories with his own view. For these reasons, we need to examine how exodus themes change between different OT texts. As Beale and Carson notes, "it is important to include reflection not

---

224. In chapter 4, I will discuss the images of the sea and the wilderness in relation to the exodus events in the OT and Second Temple Jewish literature, which had been reinterpreted with cosmological and eschatological implications.

225. Brunson, *Psalm 118 in the Gospel of John*, 8.

226. Fishbane, "Inner Biblical Exegesis," 20. In the field of biblical studies, Fishbane makes a great contribution to the study of intertextuality, which he calls "inner-biblical exegesis." See also Fishbane, *Biblical Interpretation*.

227. Beale and Carson, "Introduction," xxiv.

only on the use of the OT in the NT but also on the use of the OT within the OT. Sometimes a NT author may have in mind the earlier OT references but may be interpreting it though the later OT development of that earlier text."[228] Exploring the changes of images and meanings between OT texts may thus shed light on how NT authors interpreted OT events and how they presented events in their own narrative with these adopted viewpoints.

Fourth, intertextuality is concerned with how a text is produced in interaction with earlier texts. As Vorster asserts, "all texts can be regarded as the rewriting of previous texts, and also as reactions to texts."[229] The interpreter must consider how anterior texts are related, combined, and mixed in the process of producing the text. In the episode of Jesus' walking on the sea (6:45–51), for example, rescue and epiphany motifs and images appear together. To know how this NT text (6:45–51) used OT texts, we must first look for OT passages that include rescue and epiphany motifs and images. We then need to advance our investigation to learn how OT images and motifs have been transformed, united, fused, and molded in order to produce the new NT text. If we assume that Jesus' walking on the sea primarily alludes to the victory at the sea of the exodus story, then a rescue motif and image plays a main role in the episode and an epiphany motif and image serves as a supplement; in other words, the episode of Jesus' walking on the sea is primarily molded in the frame of the exodus story with a rescue motif and image, being complemented by an epiphany motif and image.[230]

Allusion

Hays states that "quotation, allusion, and echo may be seen as points along a spectrum of intertextual reference, moving from the explicit to the subliminal."[231] Thompson neatly defines these three elements of intertextuality in his study of Paul's epistles as follows:

> I will use 'quotation' to refer to instances in which the writer uses direct quotation with an explicit citation formula (e.g., γέγραπται γάρ). 'Allusion' will refer to statements which are *intended* to remind an audience of a tradition they are presumed to know as dominical; clear examples by this definition are 1 Cor. 7.10 and 9.14. 'Echo' or 'reminiscence' will refer to cases where the influence of a dominical tradition upon Paul seems

228. Beale and Carson, "Introduction," xxiv.
229. Vorster, "Intertextuality and Redaktionsgeschichte," 21.
230. I will discuss this conclusion at some length in chapter 4.
231. Hays, *Echoes of Scripture*, 23.

evident, but where it remains uncertain whether he was conscious of the influence at the time of dictating.[232]

According to Brunson, the theory of intertextuality has broadened and deepened our understanding of the NT use of the OT by recovering the "meaning effects created," and allusion and echo play a significant role in revealing intertextual relationships.[233] In relation to the present study, I will explain the function of allusion and echo and the ways in which they can be identified.[234]

Arguing that communication involves more than what is said directly, Brunson states the significance of allusion and echo in disclosing the relationship between texts as follows: "An allusion or echo in the form of a single phrase or word may appear atomistic, but when read against its original literary context, and in relation to its new setting, numerous unstated parallels and 'harmonics' may be overheard even though they have not been openly voiced."[235] Space connotes historical traces that may allude to or echo past events. In Mark, Jesus' miracles related to the sea and the wilderness may recollect and reenact the events from Israel's history that took place in similar settings.[236] In particular, these places serve as the settings of the "new exodus" accomplished by Jesus, alluding to and echoing both the original events in the book of Exodus and the images of the exodus in the later biblical writings such as the Psalms and Isaiah.[237] The present

232. Thompson, *Clothed with Christ*, 30.

233. Brunson, *Psalm 118 in the Gospel of John*, 10.

234. Though I will use allusion and echo to explore spatial meanings of the sea and the wilderness in the present study, the meaning of the term "quotation" needs to be introduced. Stanley defines quotation in a strict sense to explore Paul's citation of the OT in three aspects: "(1) those introduced by an explicit quotation formula ('as it is written,' etc.—the bulk of the texts); (2) those accompanied by a clear interpretive gloss (e.g., 1 Cor 15:27); and (3) those that stand in demonstrable syntactical tension with their present Pauline surroundings (e.g., Rom 9:7; 10:18; Gal 3:12)." See Stanley, *Paul and the Language of Scripture*, 37. Porter, however, pointed out a problem in defining quotation, raising the question of "how many words would qualify as a quotation" (Porter, "Use of the Old Testament in the New Testament," 95).

235. Brunson, *Psalm 118 in the Gospel of John*, 11.

236. Rhoads, Dewey, and Michie argues that spatial settings such as the Jordan River, the desert, the sea, and the mountains may both recall historical events and carry theological implications. For example, the desert implies a "place of testing," and the sea indicates a "place of chaos and destruction." See Rhoads et al., *Mark as Story*, 69–70.

237. Keesmaat describes the strength with which the exodus was recalled in the historical consciousness of Israelites. "Within Israelite historical consciousness the exodus held a central place. The exodus was recalled as the major formative event in Israelite history. It was seen as the event in which Israel was created; their history as a people was perceived to have begun at the exodus. As a result, the exodus was recalled as that

study will look at how the appearances of the sea and the wilderness in Jesus' sea and feeding miracles allude to or echo the exodus events even as they produce new exodus imagery. This will require the identification of criteria for identifying allusion and echo.

Allusion and echo may be distinguished in terms of an author's intentionality: the former is intentional and the latter is unintentional.[238] It can be difficult, however, to discern whether or not an author intended a particular intertextual connection.[239] An author's intentionality is therefore too subjective a criterion to effectively distinguish between allusion and echo. Osborne rightly identifies the characteristics of allusion and echo as follows: "Without any linguistic similarity the possibility of an allusion should not be pressed, but the possibility of an 'echo' may still be present if content points in that direction."[240] While allusion consists of linguistic correspondences between texts, echo includes similarities in content or context between texts that lack linguistic agreement. By this definition, my examination of the intertextual relationships surrounding the sea and the wilderness would seem to be concerned with echo, because it deals with similarities in the contexts of sea and wilderness narrative settings. However, my spatial study of the sea and the wilderness is designed to discover how historical and theological images and implications in the OT and Second Temple Jewish literature are related to Jesus' sea and wilderness miracles in Mark through both linguistic and thematic similarities. Echo may consequently be evaluated by the same criteria that are applied to allusion. In this study I will use "allusion" as methodological term related to the discovery of relationships between texts, while including the meaning of "echo." In conclusion, regarding echo as the atmosphere that is shared together between texts, I will employ "allusion" in evaluating intertextual relationships in terms of both linguistic and thematic correspondence between texts.

Though there are many methods for identifying allusion or echo,[241] this study will use four criteria for identifying allusions. I will not use a "purely"

---

which formed the identity of the Israelite people; they were a people who had once been slaves but had been saved from slavery by the Lord their God." See Keesmaat, "Exodus and the Intertextual Transformation," 35.

238. Keesmaat, "Exodus and the Intertextual Transformation," 32.

239. While Hays recognizes the difficulty of distinguishing between allusion and echo, he concludes that "*allusion* is used of obvious intertextual references, *echo* of subtler ones" (Hays, *Echoes of Scripture*, 29). Evans regards allusions as "verbal correspondence" and echoes as "thematic parallels" (Evans, "Listening for Echoes," 47). In the present study I will use the term "echo" to refer to the creation of a similar atmosphere between texts.

240. Osborne, *Hermeneutical Spiral*, 167.

241. E.g., Hays suggests seven criteria for evaluating allusions, though he uses the

audience-oriented or reader-response approach to identifying allusion, though I agree that allusion deals with images that must be shared between an author and a reader. A "purely" audience-oriented or reader-response approach, which neglects authorial intention by focusing on the reader's response, does not provide a solid foundation for identifying how NT authors used the OT texts—this approach may be arbitrary and vague.[242] My approach to allusion is therefore author-oriented or text-projected, making use of the following criteria.

First, an allusion must show basic "verbal agreement" between texts.[243] Without shared language, a similar atmosphere between texts is not by itself

term echo instead of allusion, understanding allusion and echo to belong to the same category. (1) *Availability*: "Was the proposed source of the echo available to the author and/or original reader?"; (2) *Volume*: "The volume of an echo is determined primarily by the degree of explicit repetition of words or syntactical patterns"; (3) *Recurrence*: "How often does Paul elsewhere cite or allude to the same scriptural passage?"; (4) *Thematic Coherence*: "How well does the alleged echo fit into the line of argument that Paul is developing?"; (5) *Historical Plausibility*: "Could Paul have intended the alleged meaning effect? Could his readers have understood it?"; (6) *History of Interpretation*: "Have other readers, both critical and pre-critical, heard the same echoes?"; and (7) *Satisfaction*: "With or without clear confirmation from the other criteria listed here, does the proposed reading make sense?" See Hays, *Echoes of Scripture*, 29–32. Thompson also suggests eleven criteria for evaluating allusions and echoes: verbal agreement, conceptual agreement, formal agreement, place of the gospel saying in the tradition, common motivation (rationale), dissimilarity to Graeco-Roman and Jewish traditions, presence of dominical indicators, presence of tradition indicators, presence of other dominical echoes or word/concept clusters in the immediate context, likelihood the author knew the saying, and exegetical value. See Thompson, *Clothed with Christ*, 30–36.

242. According to Porter, "if one is interested in establishing a given author's use of the Old Testament, it would appear imperative to orient one's discussion to the language of the author, rather than supposed, reconstructed 'knowledge' of the audience" (Porter, "Use of the Old Testament in the New Testament," 95). In the intertextual study of Ps 118 in John, Brunson states that his approach is "author oriented rather than reader centered": "This is, the focus of investigation is on what the author is attempting to do, rather than what the reader may or may not have perceived, with the understanding that the former may shed light on the latter" (Brunson, *Psalm 118 in the Gospel of John*, 13).

243. Osborne, *Hermeneutical Spiral*, 16/; Thompson, *Clothed with Christ*, 31–32; Brunson, *Psalm 118 in the Gospel of John*, 14. Leonard, who advances Fishbane's theory of inner-biblical allusion, suggests "eight principles as methodological guidelines" to discover the inner-biblical allusions in terms of verbal agreement. "(1) Shared language is the single most important factor in establishing a textual connection. (2) Shared language is more important than nonshared language. (3) Shared language that is rare or distinctive suggests a stronger connection than does language that is widely used. (4) Shared phrases suggest a stronger connection than do individual shared terms. (5) The accumulation of shared language suggests a stronger connection than does a single shared term or phrase. (6) Shared language in similar contexts suggests a stronger connection than does shared language alone. (7) Shared language need not be

enough evidence to establish a relationship; shared language in a similar context, however, suggests an association. If a particular word is used commonly between texts to describe a situation or action, it may provide a strong connection. For example, the Greek word ἐπιτιμάω (to rebuke), used in Mark 4:39 when Jesus calmed the roaring sea, is similarly employed in Ps 106(105 LXX):9 when God rebuked the Red Sea. In both texts the sea is personified and regarded as chaos in the light of the use of ἐπιτιμάω.[244]

Second, an allusion has "thematic coherence."[245] In other words, a text that alludes to prior texts shares the same or similar themes with the prior texts.[246] Jesus' two sea miracles (Mark 4:35–41; 6:45–52) allude to the exodus event of the victory at the Red Sea, which appears in Exod 14 and later biblical writings, and they share with the OT passages the theme of "deliverance at the sea." In addition, Thompson suggests "conceptual agreement" in regard to the use of vocabulary: "conceptual agreement is also a prerequisite, although it would be possible for an author deliberately to use the same language in a different sense (i.e., an antithetical or contrastive allusion)."[247] For example, as for the word "the sea," the ancient Israelites and their literature regarded it as chaos which threatened human beings and their voyages.[248] Here conceptual agreement on the sea may be found in Jesus' sea miracles, in that the sea in Jesus and his disciples' crossing is a chaotic force threatening their lives and journey.

Third, an allusion should be examined in consideration of "the individual writer's traits."[249] In Mark, the sea conveys the image of chaos in Jesus' sea miracles. While Luke tries to portray Jesus' life and ministry as a historical record (see Luke 1:1–4), Mark's description is more symbolic or theological. Mark employs the term "sea" (θάλασσα) rather than the more accurate geographical term, "lake" (λίμνη), likely to emphasize the char-

---

accompanied by shared ideology to establish a connection. (8) Shared language need not be accompanied by shared form to establish a connection." See Leonard, "Identifying Inner-Biblical Allusions," 246.

244. Chapter 4 contains detailed discussions of this.

245. Hays, *Echoes of Scripture*, 30; Thompson, *Clothed with Christ*, 32.

246. Leonard suggests six criteria for identifying the inner-biblical dependence of one text on another as follows: "(1) Does one text claim to draw on another? (2) Are there elements in the texts that help to fix their dates? (3) Is one text capable of producing the other? (4) Does one text assume the other? (5) Does one text show a general pattern of dependence on other texts? (6) Are there rhetorical patterns in the texts that suggest that one text has used the other in an exegetically significant way?" See Leonard, "Identifying Inner-Biblical Allusions," 258.

247. Thompson, *Clothed with Christ*, 32.

248. Propp, *Exodus 1–18*, 557.

249. Osborne, *Hermeneutical Spiral*, 167.

acteristics of "chaos," "threat," and/or "danger."[250] When Jesus rebukes the roaring sea, Mark's description of the sea is more personified than that of Matthew and Luke: Mark vividly portrays Jesus' action of rebuking the sea by using two imperative verbs: σιώπα, πεφίμωσο ("Quiet, Be still!" 4:39), while Matthew and Luke simply describe the fact that Jesus rebuked the sea without using imperative verbs.

Fourth, an allusion presents a "formal agreement"—that is, a "parallel in form (i.e., structure, number of elements)."[251] According to Brunson, "attention should be paid to structural correspondence such as similar contexts and circumstances."[252] Structural and contextual parallelism between texts serves to identify an allusion. In Exodus, the spatial movement of the Israelites in the exodus journey before entering Canaan roughly covers the sea, the wilderness, and the mountain; similarly, Mark shows Jesus' missional journey before entering Jerusalem taking him through the sea (4:35–41; 6:45–52), the wilderness (6:31–44; 8:1–10), and the mountain (9:2–8). We can thus identify a similar structural pattern of spatial movement connecting Exodus and Mark. In Mark 4:35—8:21, the spatial settings of the sea and the wilderness are repeated in a cyclic pattern.[253] In this section, Jesus twice begins a period of ministry by the sea and ends at the wilderness (4:35—6:44; 6:45—8:10); these places frame each cycle. The structural pattern of Mark's sea-desert spatial frame is also found in Ps 78:12–32, which describes the Israelites' journey from the Red Sea to the wilderness.[254] Allusion can be seen in the structural frame as well as its content.

Study Plan

This study will investigate Mark's presentation of the space where Jesus performed his ministry in Mark 4:35—8:21. I will examine Markan spatial presentation in three aspects. The first is "social space," which refers to the social environment of first-century Galilee, including social, economic, cultural, political, religious, and ethnic situations. I will explore how Mark

250. Malbon, "Jesus of Mark and the Sea of Galilee," 376.

251. Thompson, *Clothed with Christ*, 32.

252. Brunson, *Psalm 118 in the Gospel of John*, 32.

253. The structural analysis of a cyclic pattern in Mark 4:35—8:21 will be examined in chapter 3.

254. Kee notes that the twin motifs of God's rule over the sea and his provision in the wilderness appear in the Psalms (78:13-25; 106:9; 107:23-31) and Isaiah (40:12; 41:18; 51:10). See Kee, *Community of the New Age*, 112. The parallelism between Ps 78:12-32 and Mark 4:35—8:21 will be investigated in chapter 4.

represents these social circumstances in his narrative world. The second is "geographical space," which includes Mark's actual description of Jesus' geographical movement. I will examine how Mark uses literary techniques to arrange the route of Jesus' missional journey. The third is "allusive space," which evokes the memories of Israel's past; space here plays a role as the setting for recollection of events in Israel's history. I will consider how Mark's depiction of the sea and the wilderness alludes to the historical events of the exodus and their cosmological and eschatological significance.

This monograph consists of five chapters. Chapter 1 has introduced issues that have been raised about Markan spatial presentation. Attention should be paid to space, which has relatively been neglected in comparison with time, especially the eschatological aspects of time. In addition, methodological considerations for the examination of Markan spatial presentation were discussed. Three methodological approaches were suggested to explore three kinds of spaces. The first is a spatial theory (territoriality and representational space) for investigating how Mark presents the social circumstances of first-century Galilee in his narrative world (social space). The second is a narrative approach focusing on settings and Mark's rhetorical devices, used for a structural analysis of Mark 4:35—8:21 (geographical space). The third is an intertextual approach focusing on allusion, which sheds light on the spatial images and meanings of the sea and the wilderness in relation to the OT and Second Temple Jewish literature (allusive space).

Chapter 2 begins with a survey of Markan scholarship on the relationship between Galilee and Jerusalem. The exploration of the relationship between Galilee and Jerusalem helps facilitate an understanding of the characteristics of Galilean society, because Galilee was placed under the influence of Jerusalem. I will first introduce the discussions about how Mark understands the relationship between Jerusalem and Galilee, including debates on their relationship in historical, redactional, narratival, and social dimensions. Next, I will address the social environment of first-century Galilee in its social, economic, cultural, political, religious, and ethnic aspects, and then examine how Mark presents the social world of Galilee in his own narrative.[255] In this way I will demonstrate that Galilee provided fertile soil where Jesus' missional movement could originate and be successful.

Chapter 3 offers a structural analysis of Mark 4:35—8:21 based on Mark's geographical arrangement of Jesus' missional journey. I will begin with a review of previous structural analyses of Mark 4–8, which were based on the assumption of pre-Markan sources, compositional analysis, or the

255. With the exception of the comparisons between "historical" and "social," I use the term "social" in a comprehensive sense to include factors that could be described as "social," "economic," "cultural," "political," "religious," "ethnic," etc.

examination of Jesus' geographical movement. I will then use a narrative approach to detail the narrative structure of Mark 4:35—8:21, particularly focusing on the geographical settings of Jesus' missional movement and the rhetorical devices of parallelism. This structure consists of a cyclic pattern that includes two cycles, one focused on Jesus' ministry to the Jews and the other on his ministry to the Gentiles (4:35—6:44; 6:45—8:10), and a conclusion (8:11-21).

Chapter 4 addresses the spatial allusions associated with the sea and the wilderness, the two places that serve to frame each cycle (the sea appears at the beginning and the wilderness at the end). The use of the sea and the wilderness to form the structural framework of the two cycles plays a role in recollecting the exodus events of Israel's history. As the main function of setting in a narrative is to generate atmosphere, the spatial settings of the sea and the wilderness serve to evoke memories of events in Israel's history. Jesus' miraculous deliverances of his disciples at sea recall the victory at the sea in the exodus; his feeding miracles in the wilderness flash back to God's provision of manna in the wilderness in the exodus.

In this chapter, I will first examine the arrangement of the sea and wilderness events in Ps 78(77 LXX):12-32 and Mark 4:35—8:21, identifying the structural parallel between them. Second, I will look into the images and meanings of the sea and the wilderness in the original exodus events and then trace the changes in these images and their meanings presented by later OT texts and Second Temple Jewish literature. Third, I will demonstrate that Jesus' sea and feeding miracles allude to (echo) the exodus events as they appear not only in the historical description of Exodus but also in cosmological and eschatological representations in later OT texts and Second Temple Jewish literature. Jesus' sea and feeding miracles involve these accumulated images and meanings of the sea and the wilderness, as Mark describes Jesus' miracles as the new exodus. The sea and the wilderness in Jesus' miracles serve as spatial allusions to the past exodus while also signaling the new exodus carried out by Jesus. The spatial settings of the sea and the wilderness thus lead us to understand Jesus' missional movement in Mark 4:35—8:21 in the light of the new exodus.

Chapter 5 provides a conclusion to this study. Here I will summarize Markan spatial presentation in its "social," "geographical," and "allusive" aspects, which may provide a fresh hermeneutical frame for understanding Jesus' missional movement in Mark 4:35—8:21. I will also discuss what this study contributes to Markan scholarship and suggest some potentially fruitful directions for future biblical scholarship.

chapter 2

Social Space
The Social World of Galilee and Markan Spatial Presentation

Previous Studies on Markan Spatial Presentation

SINCE THE EARLY TWENTIETH century, the task of combining locality and theology has been performed in Markan scholarship.[1] The incipient investigations used historical and redactional methodologies to focus on the conflict between Galilee and Jerusalem, assuming the historical reality of a distinct Galilean community. With the development of literary approaches, the relationship between Galilee and Jerusalem has been explored in terms of Mark's presentation of narrative space. Scholars have also taken various approaches to understanding Mark's narrative space: spatial presentation based on a mythic structure, narrative space in social or cosmic settings, territorial space awaiting restoration for a greater Israel, and spatial presentation centered on the person of Jesus. In this chapter, I will first introduce the diverse discussions about "Mark and space."

---

1. See Malbon's and Stewart's summaries of the historical interpretations of the relation between regionality and theology in Galilee and Jerusalem: Malbon, "Galilee and Jerusalem"; Stewart, *Gathered around Jesus*, 1–29.

Galilee versus Jerusalem in Historical Studies

In the 1930s, Lohmeyer and Lightfoot began to explore Mark's spatial understanding of the relation between Galilee and Jerusalem.[2] They argue that there existed a confrontation between Galilee and Jerusalem, and that opposing doctrinal traditions originated from the local differences.[3] Galilee was the place of Jesus' acceptance and revelation, whereas Jerusalem was the sphere of his rejection. Jesus' ministry was positively active in Galilee in terms of his calling, teaching, healing, and miraculous works. In Jerusalem, however, he did not present sermons, miracles, or invitations to repentance.[4]

This contrast is demonstrated clearly in Jesus' proclamation that Galilee would be the place of his "eschatological return."[5] Jesus told his disciples that he would go before them to Galilee after being raised (14:28), and the young man at the tomb confirmed Jesus' words after his resurrection (16:7). However, the promise of his return does not simply indicate that he would be shown to the disciples in resurrection appearance. Rather, this proclamation has great significance: Galilee is uplifted as the location of the culmination of the ages.[6] Lightfoot describes Galilee as "the land where the divine fulfillment began and the land where it will receive its consummation."[7] Eschatological expectations, therefore, will be accomplished in Galilee rather than in the expected locale of Jerusalem.

On the basis of the relation between locale and theology, Lohmeyer and Lightfoot conclude that there were two geographical centers (Galilee and Jerusalem), each of which represented its own form of primitive Christianity. Mark's positive portrayal of Galilee as the place of Jesus' ministry and revelation implies that he uplifted Galilee rather than Jerusalem as the alternative locale of Jesus movement for the early Christians.

This theory, however, has some problems. First, no explicit proof that Galilee was a competing center against Jerusalem has been discovered.[8] Though Paul had some conflicts with the religious leaders from the Jerusa-

---

2. Lohmeyer, *Galiläa und Jerusalem*; Lightfoot, *Locality and Doctrine*. See also Stewart, *Gathered around Jesus*, 28.

3. Malbon summarizes historical interpretations of Mark's oppositional description between Galilee and Jerusalem from E. Lohmeyer (1936) through Robert Henry Lightfoot (1938) and Willi Marxsen (1956) to Werner Kelber (1974). See Malbon, "Galilee and Jerusalem," 242-55.

4. Lightfoot, *Locality and Doctrine*, 122-23.

5. Lohmeyer, *Galiläa und Jerusalem*, 73-77.

6. Lohmeyer, *Galiläa und Jerusalem*, 65.

7. Lightfoot, *Locality and Doctrine*, 124.

8. Davies, *Gospel and the Land*, 222.

lem church, conflict between Galilean Christians and Jerusalem Christians was not reported in early Christian literature.[9] It is therefore hard to demonstrate the existence of a Galilean Christianity which contrasted with Jerusalem Christianity. Second, Galilee is not always portrayed as accepting Jesus. Jesus was rejected by his hometown, which was in Galilee (6:1–6a).[10] Because of their refusal, he could not perform any mighty works there, with the exception of healing a few sick people (6:5). Third, ancient Jewish literature does not contain decisive and prevalent sources suggesting that messianic expectations were related to the region of Galilee.[11] For these reasons, it is difficult to assume that a primitive Galilean community and a primitive Jerusalem community each developed its own version of Christianity in competition with the other.[12]

Elliott-Binns's *Galilean Christianity* (1956) argues that while Christianity originated in Galilee, the center of the Jesus movement shifted from Galilee to Jerusalem at a very early stage, leading to the neglect of Galilean Christianity.[13] This tendency to ignore the Galilean roots of Christianity began with the later literature of the New Testament and continued to the most recent New Testament scholarship.[14] In opposition to this trend, Elliott-Binns emphasizes Galilean Christianity as a rival of Jerusalem Christianity:

> The Tübingen school of criticism tried to explain the history of the primitive Church on the basis of a conflict between St

---

9. Stewart argues that "though it is clear that some Jesus group members (notably Paul) did have difficulty with the leadership of the Jerusalem community over certain issues, there are no existing traditions that indicate that there was tension between Galilee and Jerusalem" (Stewart, *Gathered around Jesus*, 9).

10. In addition, local Pharisees and Herodians displayed serious opposition to Jesus at a Galilean synagogue (3:6). Freyne, "Geography of Restoration," 306.

11. In their exegesis of Γαλιλαία τῶν ἐθνῶν in Matt 4:15, Strack and Billerbeck insist that there was no source in the ancient literature expressing that the Messiah was explicitly connected to the region of Galilee (Strack and Billerbeck, *Kommentar zum Neuen Testament aus Talmud und Midrasch*, 160). Opposing Strack and Billerbeck, however, Wieder tries to find a relationship between the Messiah and Galilee in ancient literature, especially rabbinic materials (e.g., Karaite and Zoharitic sources). He argues that the Qumran sect geographically migrated to Damascus and expected that the messianic events might take place there. At that time, Damascus contained Lebanon and Anti-Lebanon, which included Upper Galilee. Therefore, Galilee belonged to the region of Damascus, where the messianic expectations were centered. See Wieder, *Judean Scrolls and Karaism*. In response to Wieder's insistence, Davies claims that the rabbinic materials suggested by Wieder are too late to be accepted as evidentiary sources (Davies, *Gospel and the Land*, 222–26).

12. Davies, *Gospel and the Land*, 222.

13. Elliott-Binns, *Galilean Christianity*, 11.

14. Elliott-Binns, *Galilean Christianity*, 11.

Paul, on the one hand, and the Twelve, especially St Peter, on the other hand. But a more convincing case, I would suggest, can be made out for a division between the early followers of Jesus in Galilee, probably including some at least of the Twelve, and the narrower Judaistic Christianity which was growing up at Jerusalem under the leadership of St James. . . .

Evidence for some kind of rivalry between Galilee and Jerusalem can clearly be seen in the N.T. itself, which contains what appear to be irreconcilable traditions as to the scene of the post-resurrection appearances of Jesus; and in the Gospel records there is a noteworthy difference of emphasis, with, on the one side, Mark, Q, and some of the matter peculiar to Matthew, and on the other, matter peculiar to Luke (and the early chapters of Acts) and John.[15]

Elliott-Binns suggests three distinct groups among the early churches: (1) the Jerusalem church led by James, which was conservative in keeping the Jewish traditions and maintaining contact with the Jews; (2) the Pauline churches, consisting of a larger proportion of the Gentiles, which showed a tendency toward a liberal interpretation of the gospel; and (3) the Galilean Christians, who were the first followers of Jesus (including some of the Twelve and perhaps Peter) and felt pride in their spiritual inheritance directly handed down by Jesus and jealousy toward the Jerusalem Church.[16] When the Roman army invaded Palestine, the two groups of Christians from Jerusalem and Galilee fled to Pella and assembled together. In doing so, they forgot their past rivalry and united.[17]

Elliott-Binns's theory has some distinct weaknesses, however. First and most notably, explicit evidence of the existence of a Galilean community has not been discovered in early Christian literature or other sources: "Outside the New Testament, information about a Galilean community is very scanty and late."[18] Second, the assumption that the leaders of a Galilean community were some of the Twelve, possibly including Peter, does not have convincing grounds. According to Elliot-Binns, because Mark's Gospel—which reflects the Galilean tradition as opposed to that of Jerusalem—speaks for Peter's standpoint, Peter might have been the leader of a Galilean community.[19] Yet Peter was one of the important leaders in the Jerusalem church, and there is no material indicating that he was in conflict with the Jerusalem

15. Elliott-Binns, *Galilean Christianity*, 11.
16. Elliott-Binns, *Galilean Christianity*, 62.
17. Elliott-Binns, *Galilean Christianity*, 68–69.
18. Stemberger, "Galilee—Land of Salvation?," 421–22.
19. Elliott-Binns, *Galilean Christianity*, 62.

church on behalf of a Galilean community. In addition, it is not clear that Galilean tradition was situated in conflict with that of Jerusalem. Third, it is too hypothetical to insist that the lost memory of a Galilean community is due to the migration of persecuted Galilean Christians into Pella, where they were united with Jerusalem Christians by discarding the rivalry between them. If a Galilean community with distinct spiritual pride could be so easily absorbed into a Jerusalem community at Pella and forgotten, it is difficult to imagine that these two communities were truly in competition. Finally, it is hard to find any evidence in the NT or other early literature to support the argument that a Galilean community had spiritual superiority to a Jerusalem community because they were taught directly from Jesus.

Galilee versus Jerusalem in Redactional Studies

In his 1956 book, *Der Evangelist Markus: Studien Zur Redaktionsgeschichte des Evangeliums*, Marxsen, who employs a redactional approach to study the Gospels, claims that the emphasis on Galilee in Mark originated from the redactor's intention.[20] Marxsen evaluates Mark's geographical description as follows:

> There are two possible explanations for Mark's geographical framework. One is that he constructs it for historical purposes but cannot achieve his goal, due to his ignorance of the territory or to incompleteness of his materials. In that case, the historical question is disposed of, since it led to the result that Mark was in error. The other explanation is that with his outline Mark has in mind a purpose other than the historical and uses the geographical data to express it. But then we must put the question in another way, since we can get an answer to our question only if the object of our inquiry at least implies it. The proper question is not the one which happens to interest us, but the one to which the person or thing interrogated aims to give the answer. Right here, this means that it is Mark who decides how the question ought to be put. But it is to be gleaned from the framework, from the redaction.[21]

According to Marxsen, Mark did not record the routes of Jesus' geographical movement with historical accuracy and chronological order due to his ignorance of Palestinian geography. Rather, he arranged (redacted) his collected materials with a theological purpose, bearing in mind Galilee's

20. Marxsen, *Mark the Evangelist*, 54–94.
21. Marxsen, *Mark the Evangelist*, 54–55.

"theological significance as the locale of the imminent Parousia."[22] "Mark's Galilean Gospel reflects no 'historical-geographical' interest. His concern might rather be termed 'eschatological-geographical.'"[23] Thus, Jesus' itinerary should be read through a theological lens.

Marxsen suggests three stages through which Mark was formed as a "Galilean Gospel."[24] The first stage is related to the "historical Jesus." At this stage, early Christian tradition arbitrarily linked certain locales with certain episodes. Marxsen thus asserts that the correlation between places and events of Jesus' ministry is weak. Concerning Galilee, though a large number of Galilean place-names are mentioned in Mark, "Galilee itself is not anchored in the tradition"—rather, the tradition reflects a "Palestinian Gospel" at this stage.[25] The second stage occurred during the period of "the primitive community" that was especially connected to Jerusalem. Marxsen argues against Lohmeyer that there is no information about the primitive community in Galilee. Instead, the shift from Jerusalem to Galilee took place because the Parousia was expected in Galilee. As the first coming happened in Galilee, the second coming was anticipated there as well. "Galilee thus becomes the new center."[26] The third stage includes Mark's redactional activity. Marxsen claims that Mark altered the tradition that had been handed down, intentionally filling Jesus' ministry in Galilee with positive images. Galilee does not simply mean the historical place where Jesus worked, but rather the locale where his eschatological ministry would unfold.[27]

Marxsen tries to uncover Mark's redactional activity by analyzing Mark's emphasis on Galilee.[28] For example, the addition of Galilee to place-names (Nazareth of Galilee [1:9]; the Sea of Galilee [1:16; 7:31]), and the statement that the large crowd from Galilee followed Jesus (3:7) is redactional.[29] Most notably, the expression and arrangement of 14:28 and 16:7,

22. Marxsen, *Mark the Evangelist*, 92.

23. Marxsen, *Mark the Evangelist*, 93.

24. Marxsen, *Mark the Evangelist*, 92–95.

25. Marxsen, *Mark the Evangelist*, 93. Marxsen, however, states the significance of Galilee in terms of the place-name "Nazareth": "On the other hand, it is quite clear that this area [Galilee] by implication has a slight advantage which—also by implication—is heightened by the traditional name 'Nazareth.'"

26. Marxsen, *Mark the Evangelist*, 93.

27. Marxsen, *Mark the Evangelist*, 94.

28. Marxsen, *Mark the Evangelist*, 57–95. Marxsen divides Mark into three sections ("Galilee Prior to the 'Journey Report'"; "Geographical Data of the 'Journey into Gentile Territory'"; "Galilee in the Passion Narrative") and analyzes his redaction in relation to the emphasis on Galilee.

29. Marxsen, *Mark the Evangelist*, 57–63. Stemberger refutes Marxsen's arguments by claiming that Galilee was frequently added to define Nazareth (e.g., Matt 2:22f.; Luke

which both originated from one saying, disclose Mark's redactional purpose of showing that the Parousia will be accomplished in Galilee.[30] In particular, Marxsen argues that 16:7, which was inserted in the abrupt ending of the Markan resurrection narrative (16:1–8), reflects Mark's view of the Parousia, not the emergence of the Risen Lord: "But then this redactional note cannot deal with an appearance of the Risen Lord awaited in Galilee: in Mark's context this passage can only refer to the expected Parousia."[31]

Stemberger, however, points out Marxsen's excessive interpretation to force the texts into his theory.[32] It is difficult to decide whether the names of Galilee in the texts came from traditions or redactions. Even if we admit that Galilee was redactionally inserted by Mark, it is hard to determine the purpose of Mark's redactional usages: we don't know whether he was intending to highlight Galilee as the place for the Parousia or not.[33] In addition, it is questionable whether 14:28 and 16:7 refer to the Parousia. Mark surely had knowledge of Jesus' resurrection appearance. As the sayings that Jesus will go ahead of the disciples and they will see him in Galilee in Matthew 26:32 and 28:7 refer to the appearance of the Risen Lord, the same sayings in Mark 14:28 and 16:7 indicate Jesus' resurrection appearance.[34] Parousia is not given as an experience for a few individuals, but proclaimed and accomplished as a cosmic event (cf. Mark 13).[35] Furthermore, while the apocalyptic passage of Mark 13 portrays the eschatological events as cosmic incidents that will happen in the future, it does not mention their occurrence in Galilee.[36] As every passion narrative in Matthew, Luke, and John ended with Jesus' post-resurrection appearances, Mark's ending may

---

1:26; 2:4, 39). See Stemberger, "Galilee—Land of Salvation?," 431–35. In addition, we cannot determine whether the expression in 3:7 ("the large crowd from Galilee followed Jesus") came from tradition or Mark's redaction.

30. Marxsen, *Mark the Evangelist*, 75–92. Lohmeyer also insists that the expression, ἐκεῖ αὐτὸν ὄψεσθε (there you will see him; 16:7), refers to the Parousia, not the Risen Lord. See Lohmeyer, *Das Evangelium des Markus*, 355–56.

31. Marxsen, *Mark the Evangelist*, 85.

32. Stemberger, "Galilee—Land of Salvation?," 434–35.

33. Stemberger, "Galilee—Land of Salvation?," 434.

34. Stemberger, "Galilee—Land of Salvation?," 427–28. Stemberger also argues that "by the time when Mark wrote, Peter, to whom this promise is especially addressed (16:7 *eipate tois mathētais autou kai tô Petrô*) had died, and Mark was probably in a position to know this (cf. Mark 10:39); Peter would no longer be there to expect the parousia."

35. Haenchen, *Der Weg Jesu*, 546.

36. Stemberger, "Galilee—Land of Salvation?," 428–29.

also refer to the Risen Lord's appearance in Galilee rather than alluding to the Parousia in Galilee.[37]

In his 1974 book, *The Kingdom in Mark: A New Place and a New Time*, Kelber emphasizes the collision of kingdoms and suggests Galilee as the new place of the arrival of the kingdom. He states that "eschatology is of ultimate concern to Mark, and the realized eschatology of the Galilean Kingdom serves as premise for, and holds the hermeneutical key to Markan theology."[38] Kelber, who believes that Mark's Gospel was written after AD 70,[39] claims that Mark's purpose was to proclaim "the presence of the Kingdom in Galilee" in response to the destruction of the temple. Thus, the focal point of Mark is not "the risen Christ," but "the presence of the Kingdom in Galilee."[40] Pointing out the weakness of Marxsen's exploration of 1:14–15, Kelber regards the essence of these verses not just as "the announcement of the Kingdom's imminent advent," but as "that of its establishment in the fullness of time and at a definite place."[41] Though he agrees that 14:28 and 16:7 are evidence of the existence of Galilean Christianity, Kelber considers 1:14–15 as "the gospel program," which serves as the key to understanding the kingdom theology of Mark.[42] He claims that because the verbs πεπλήρωται and ἤγγικεν (1:15) are in the perfect tense, they indicate the "continuation of a completed action,"[43] suggesting "the Galilean realization of the Kingdom," not "preparedness for the coming Kingdom."[44] Therefore, the kingdom of God had already come and been realized in Galilee.

Kelber also insists that the opposition between Galilee and Jerusalem came from Mark's rejection of the Davidic kingdom.[45] Kebler asserts that Jesus rejected the Davidic kingdom when he discussed the Davidic sonship of the Christ in the temple (12:35–37a). Kelber interprets Jesus' rhetorical

---

37. Stemberger, "Galilee—Land of Salvation?," 435–38. Stemberger notes two aspects of resurrection appearances: "Every resurrection appearance is two-sided: it connects with the past (normally the identification of the risen Lord with the earthly Jesus) and it points to the future (the command given by Christ)."

38. Kelber, *Kingdom in Mark*, 11.

39. Kelber, *Kingdom in Mark*, 1.

40. Kelber, *Kingdom in Mark*, 11.

41. Kelber, *Kingdom in Mark*, 6, 10.

42. Kelber, *Kingdom in Mark*, 3–15. Malbon explains Kelber's interpretation of 1:14–15 in relation to 14:28 and 16:7 as follows: "The initial (fulfilled, but concealed) appearance of the kingdom in Galilee (1:14–15) points to the final (revealed) appearance of the kingdom in Galilee (14:28; 16:7)." See Malbon, "Galilee and Jerusalem," 246.

43. Kelber here quotes Blass et al., *Greek Grammar*, 175.

44. Kelber, *Kingdom in Mark*, 11, 14.

45. Kelber, *Kingdom in Mark*, 95–97.

question, "David himself calls him Lord; so how can he be his son?" (12:37), as his rejection of Davidic sonship because the term κύριος represents the Son of God, not the Son of David.[46] Though Mark follows a "two-stage Christology" similar to that in Rom 1:3–4, he does not combine Davidic sonship with God's sonship like Matthew does.[47] Rather, Mark upholds an alternative understanding of Jesus as "the *Kyriotēs* of the Son of God" by denying "the scribes' Davidic sonship."[48] In accordance with this assertion, Kelber reads Jesus' entrance to Jerusalem (11:1–10) as having an "anti-Jerusalem" and "anti-Davidic" nuance: "11:1–10 does not depict Jesus' triumphal, messianic entry into Jerusalem, but the rejection of Davidic messianism outside of Jerusalem. The incident does not anticipate the realization of Jesus' messiahship in Jerusalem; rather, it casts doubt upon the messianic promise native to Jerusalem."[49] Galilee, therefore, is the new place of the kingdom of God, which is substituted for the kingdom of David in Jerusalem.

As discussed above, there is no evidence to suggest a conflict between the communities of Galilee and Jerusalem. Kelber's direct connection between geography and theology is therefore excessive. His exegesis of Mark is oversimplified and forcefully fit into the framework of the opposition between Galilee and Jerusalem. This faulty exegesis can be seen in Kelber's assertions regarding Mark 1:15. As France points out, Kelber's exegesis of 1:15 is a misguided attempt to label "ἡ βασιλεία τοῦ θεοῦ as some identifiable situation or event which 'arrives' at a particular time."[50] Mark does not explicitly mention that the kingdom of God has arrived at Galilee; he simply stated that when Jesus came to Galilee, he proclaimed the good news of God (1:14–15). Despite a longstanding debate about whether 1:15 implies a "realized" or a "futuristic" eschatology, no consensus has been reached.[51]

46. Kelber, *Kingdom in Mark*, 95.
47. Kelber, *Kingdom in Mark*, 96.
48. Kelber, *Kingdom in Mark*, 96.
49. Kelber, *Kingdom in Mark*, 96–97.

50. France, *Gospel of Mark*, 92. Kelber overstates the temporal significance of the perfect tense of the verbs πεπλήρωται and ἤγγικεν (1:15) by concluding that this implies realized eschatology. Verbs should be understood according to their nature, the context of the passages in which they appear, and their usages by an author.

51. Guelich introduces two different interpretations of ἤγγικεν as follows: "Lexical studies of ἐγγίζιεν have produced mixed results alternating between the meaning of 'nearness' and of 'arrival.' Dodd, claiming a common Semitic term (נגע, nāgaʻ—Hebrew; מטא, mĕṭaʼ—Aramaic) behind ἐγγίζιεν and φθάνειν (Matt 12:28; Luke 11:20) in the LXX, posited the meaning, 'has come,' from the Semitic terms (Dodd, *Parables*, 28–30). Kümmel, by contrast, concluded after examining the NT use of ἐγγύς and ἐγγίζιεν that the terms consistently denoted 'nearness' rather than 'arrival' (Kümmel, *Promise*, 19–25)." See Guelich, *Mark 1–8:26*, 44. Refer also to Dodd, *Parables of the Kingdom*;

Markan eschatology must be understood in terms of the classic expression, "already but not yet." France understands this tension and properly defines the nature of the kingdom of God in relation to its place and time:

> In the light of the widespread recognition that βασιλεία is essentially an abstract noun referring to the 'rule' or 'kingship' of God, the phrase ἡ βασιλεία τοῦ θεοῦ should not be read as a term with a single specific referent, whether a time, place, event, or situation. It is therefore not appropriate to ask whether 'the kingdom of God' is past, present, or future, as if it had a specific time-reference like 'the day of Yahweh.' God's kingship is both eternal and eschatological, both fulfilled and awaited, both present and imminent.[52]

Kelber's interpretation of 12:35–37a, where Jesus asks a question about the Davidic sonship of the Christ, is also problematic. According to Lane, the question in 12:35, 37 might be regarded as "a Haggada-question, a question of exegesis concerned with the reconciliation of two seemingly contradictory points of view expressed in Scripture."[53] These questions do not imply that the Christ is not the descendant of David, but that the Christ is superior to David.[54] Mark does not deny the Davidic sonship of Jesus, but rather positively portrays Jesus as the "Son of David" in blind Bartimaeus's confession (10:47–48) and in the crowd's acclamation of Jesus' entrance into Jerusalem (11:10, "Blessed is the coming kingdom of our ancestor David!").[55] In addition, there is no room to doubt that the first-century Christians ascribed the title "Son of David" to Jesus.[56] This passage (12:35–37a) is written not to reject the Davidic sonship of the Christ, but to express the importance of the identity of Jesus, who is indeed the Son of God, beyond the Son of David. Kelber's theory that Jesus established the kingdom of God in Galilee by rejecting the kingdom of David in Jerusalem is not valid; it is too difficult to find clear evidence of the conflict between the kingdom of God and the kingdom of David.[57]

Kümmel, *Promise and Fulfilment*.

52. France, *Gospel of Mark*, 93

53. Lane, *Gospel According to Mark*, 436. Lane follows David Daube's analysis on the types of question in Rabbinic Judaism. See Daube, *New Testament and Rabbinic Judaism*, 158–63.

54. Lane, *Gospel According to Mark*, 436–39. See also Hooker, *Gospel According to Saint Mark*, 292.

55. Stein, *Mark*, 596.

56. France, *Gospel of Mark*, 484.

57. Kee points out that Kelber's assumption of the rift between Galilee and Jerusalem is not convincing because it does not explicate "why the covenant community is

Galilee versus Jerusalem Based on a Mythic Structure

Malbon interprets Mark's geographical description "in the context of the text as a literary world," which is different from Kelber's view of the text as a historical world.[58] She explains the difference between a diachronic approach and a synchronic approach in narrative analysis as follows: "The diachronic dimension of a narrative is the chronological order in which events occur, the 'apparent content' of the narrative, while the synchronic dimension is the underlying, formal, theoretical organization of the narrative, its 'latent content.'"[59] In her 1986 monograph, *Narrative Space and Mythic Meaning in Mark*, Malbon explores the narrative structure of Mark by synchronically analyzing space.[60] On the basis of Lévi-Strauss's method of investigating myth,[61] she analyzes Mark's spatial references by examining three spatial suborders: "geopolitical space," "topographical space," and "architectural space." She conducts her study in three steps: "(1) isolating the *relations*, (2) examining the *sequence*, (3) analyzing the *schema*."[62] While investigating Markan space, she suggests utilizing the synchronic-schemata, which contain two opposing poles. In geopolitical space, the schemata are "Jewish homeland vs. foreign lands," "Galilee vs. Judea," and "environs of Jerusalem vs. Jerusalem proper." In topographical space, the schemata are "heaven vs. earth," "land vs. sea," and "isolated areas vs. inhabited areas." In architectural space, they are "house vs. synagogue—and temple," "room vs. courtyard," and "tomb vs. temple."

These schemata find their deepest level of meaning in a mythic structure and spatial framework that moves as the narrative goes on.[63] When a mythic structure operates in a text, irreconcilable opposites are exposed; myth mediates this opposition while new opposites, which successively replace the previous opposites, emerge progressively.[64] Malbon explains

---

redefined in Jerusalem at the temple (Kelber, *Kingdom in Mark*, 106), while the writer seems to know so little about the topography of Galilee that his accounts of itineraries of Jesus and the disciples are confusing and probably confused." See Kee, "Review," 123.

58. Malbon, "Galilee and Jerusalem," 247.
59. Malbon, "Galilee and Jerusalem," 248.
60. Malbon, *Narrative Space*. See also Malbon, "Galilee and Jerusalem," 247–55.
61. Though Malbon does not regard Mark as a myth, she believes that the structure of Mark can be investigated in a mythical dimension since a "mythic structure" may be "operative in a text" (Malbon, *Narrative Space*, 2).
62. Malbon, *Narrative Space*, 13.
63. Malbon, *Narrative Space*, xii.
64. Malbon, *Narrative Space*, 2–3.

the concept of myth and schemata as follows: "Myth is a way of thinking that involves the progressive mediation of a fundamental opposition," and "schemata suggest the fundamental opposition the myth seeks to mediate."[65] For example, the topographical schemata containing two opposing sides are "heaven vs. earth," "land vs. sea," and "isolated areas vs. inhabited areas." In these synchronic-schemata, heaven, land, and isolated areas represent "promise," while sea, earth, and inhabited areas represent "threat." These opposing sides are consequently arbitrated by a mediator such as "the way."[66]

Malbon also explains the relationship between Galilee and Jerusalem in terms of "'logical' or 'mythological' patterns of opposition and mediation."[67] Supposing that the geopolitical oppositions move toward mediation, she argues that the opposition between Jewish homeland and foreign lands is progressively replaced by the opposition between Galilee and Judea.[68] This later opposition (Galilee and Judea) is finally substituted by the opposition between environs of Jerusalem and Jerusalem proper. Among the schemata, the central axis in Mark is the opposition between Galilee and Judea.[69] At the mythical dimension, this opposition is mediated: "when Galilee, supposedly chaotic, connotes a new order, and Judea, supposedly orderly, represents chaos, the fundamental opposition is severely

---

65. Malbon, *Narrative Space*, 2–3.

66. Malbon, *Narrative Space*, 104. Malbon says that a way or a road serves as the final mediator in the topographical schema: "In a logical sense, a road is a transitional area between isolated areas and inhabited area. As outlined above in terms of the sequence, *hodos*, 'way' or 'road,' provides a unifying framework for the topographical suborder, a framework consisting of the first and final topographic references, scattered references throughout, and a significant cluster of references (8:27–11:9) at the narrative turning point." The topographical schemata are as follows (Malbon, *Narrative Space*, 97):

```
(promise)
           heaven
                    land
                            isolated areas
           mountain                          way
                    sea     inhabited areas
           earth
(threat)
```

67. Malbon, "Galilee and Jerusalem," 251.

68. Malbon, *Narrative Space*, 40–49.

69. Malbon says that both redaction criticism and structural analysis reveal the contrast between Galilee and Judea in Mark's narrative, the former focusing on a historical aspect and the latter on a literary aspect: "Structural analysis confirms the proposition of redaction criticism that the distinction between Galilee and Judea is pivotal for the Marcan Gospel. However, redaction critics, for example, Kelber, draw theological and historical conclusions from this observation, while structural critics draw literary and theological conclusions." See Malbon, "Galilee and Jerusalem," 252.

weakened."[70] In spite of mediation, Malbon states that Galilee and Jerusalem are still placed under strain.[71] In addition, after Jesus is resurrected, Mark points to a new location, neither Galilee nor Jerusalem, but somewhere in between these two poles: "Jesus is in movement; he is 'going before' (16:7); he is on the way."[72]

Malbon's structural analysis of space with a mythic dimension advances our understanding of space, especially in a synchronic dimension. It is doubtful, however, that she properly answers the questions that she herself poses and tries to prove: "(1) How is this opposition manifest in the narrative? (2) On what basis are these terms opposed? (3) Is any movement toward mediation of this opposition suggested in the narrative?"[73] She reduces diverse spatial referents into categories in order to make synchronic schemata consisting of opposing poles. For example, in a geopolitical schema, the Jewish homeland is opposed to foreign lands and they are characterized respectively as "the familiar" versus "the strange."[74] Though Malbon attributes "the familiar" to the Jewish homeland, Jesus was rejected by his hometown (6:1–6a). Furthermore, though Malbon asserts that "the strange" foreign lands are portrayed as "threatening,"[75] Jesus was also threatened in his Jewish homeland. In addition, as Stewart points out, "the idea that 'myth operates to mediate irreconcilable opposites by successively replacing them by opposites that do permit mediation' is not borne out in the geopolitical or architectural suborders since the original opposition pairs (strange vs. familiar and profane vs. sacred) are not ultimately mediated."[76] Stewart therefore asserts that only topographical schemata such as "heaven vs. earth," "land vs. sea," and "isolated areas vs. inhabited areas" are valid to explain mediation in a mythical structure.[77]

It is not mythic structure but diverse literary factors that serve to develop Mark's narrative. In addition, since Malbon's structural analysis is indifferent to "the surface structure of the text," narratival aspects such as characters, events, plot, and setting, are often overlooked.[78] As structuralists generally neglect discovery of the author's intention or purpose in a text,

---

70. Malbon, "Galilee and Jerusalem," 253.
71. Malbon, "Galilee and Jerusalem," 253.
72. Malbon, "Galilee and Jerusalem," 253.
73. Malbon, *Narrative Space*, 40.
74. Malbon, *Narrative Space*, 40–44.
75. Malbon, *Narrative Space*, 43.
76. Stewart, *Gathered around Jesus*, 24.
77. Stewart, *Gathered around Jesus*, 24.
78. Freyne, *Galilee, Jesus, and the Gospels*, 34.

Malbon also does not pay attention to the author Mark's intended meaning in the narrative.[79] Finally, Malbon's conclusion that Jesus' spatial location is somewhere between Galilee and Jerusalem is vague. It is difficult to envisage where Markan space stands toward the end of his book. Malbon's vague statement may be the result of an overemphasis on a literary (especially synchronic) approach, the focus of her methodology. Malbon writes that "in interpreting such a text, a historical approach is inadequate, a literary approach promising."[80] However, both historical and literary analyses are required for the proper interpretation of a text.[81]

Markan Narrative Space in Cosmic, Social, and Geographical Settings

Rhoads, Dewey, and Michie's *Mark as Story* (1999) present Markan narrative space in terms of cosmic and social settings.[82] Jesus' journey with his disciples serves as the "structural framework" of the whole Markan narrative, and the route of their itinerary is "around Galilee and up to Jerusalem."[83] These authors argue that "the settings in Mark are seldom neutral."[84] In a cosmic dimension, Mark's settings describe this world as inhabited by "God and angels, Satan and demons, unclean and clean animals, as well as humans."[85] The cosmic settings create social boundaries that separate people by dividing

---

79. Osborne points out the structuralists' indifference to discovering the "author's intended meaning" in a text as follows: "For structuralists, one cannot utilize a diachronic approach to the text in order to decipher what it means in the present. Therefore, this method (like phenomenological approaches) is unconcerned with the author's intended meaning and seeks only to uncover the structure behind the writer's expressed thought, the 'common world' of the underlying codes that address us directly." See Osborne, *Hermeneutical Spiral*, 473.

80. Malbon, "Galilee and Jerusalem," 255.

81. Malbon's interpretation of Mark is based on mythic structure and uses only a synchronic approach. A text should, however, be investigated in both dimensions, synchronic and diachronic. The synchronic and diachronic approaches may be compatible, co operative, and complimentary in interpreting a text. Kakkanattu mentions that "both synchronic and diachronic aspects are mutually complementary for the understanding of a Biblical text" (Kakkanattu, *God's Enduring Love*, 8). Moreover, the synchronic approach cannot be employed while excluding a historical aspect. Barr argues that "the synchronic should not be understood as an anti-historical aspect but as a deeply historical one" (Barr, "Synchronic, the Diachronic and the Historical," 5).

82. Rhoads et al., *Mark as Story*, 63–72.

83. Rhoads et al., *Mark as Story*, 63.

84. Rhoads et al., *Mark as Story*, 63.

85. Rhoads et al., *Mark as Story*, 64.

the holy from the unholy, the pure from the impure, and the clean from the unclean. The Israelites, who are holy before God, are distinguished from the impure Gentiles; religious leaders, who consider themselves clean, are distinguished from the defiled persons (e.g., demon-possessed persons, a woman with a hemorrhage, tax collectors, lepers, etc.).[86] The cosmic settings undergo changes, however, as this world is transformed through Jesus, the Son of God, and the coming of the kingdom of God:

> Into the midst of this bounded world gone awry, God opens the heavens and sends the spirit upon Jesus, who announces that "the rule of God has arrived." The arrival of God's rule changes cosmic space, because the power of God from above is now available on earth for healing and exorcism. The power of God's rule breaks out of local, national, and natural boundaries to make all space into God's space. After the execution and resurrection of Jesus, followers are to spread the holy power of the rule of God outward from Israel to the limits of the earth.[87]

In a political-cultural aspect, the social settings show that the Israelites are placed under the control of the Roman Empire, which evokes a suffering and threatening situation.[88] The society Mark describes is typical of ancient rural societies that feature a hierarchy ranging from small elite groups, including high-level political authorities and religious leaders, down to the common people who live below the level of subsistence and constitute the majority of the population of Israel. No middle class exists in this structure.[89] The Markan Jesus clamors for the radical reformation of this sociopolitical structure and proposes a new social order in which God reigns.[90]

Rhoads, Dewey, and Michie argue that Jesus' journey functions as the framework of the whole narrative in Mark and shows some distinct patterns.[91] For example, the settings of "beside the sea" or "crossing over the sea" to the east or west reveal the pattern of Jesus' movement in Galilee and its vicinity (Gentile territory). Here the narrative elements play a role of the indicator of whether Jesus took a journey in Jewish or Gentile territory. Similar patterns appear in the responses to Jesus' ministry: the responses

---

86. Rhoads et al., *Mark as Story*, 64.
87. Rhoads et al., *Mark as Story*, 65.
88. Rhoads et al., *Mark as Story*, 65–66.
89. Rhoads et al., *Mark as Story*, 65.
90. Rhoads et al., *Mark as Story*, 66.
91. Rhoads et al., *Mark as Story*, 66–69.

on the Jewish side are repeated on the Gentile side ("increasing popularity, intense opposition, withdrawal, and crowds in the desert").[92]

In addition, some settings allude to events that the Israelites experienced in their sacred history.[93] The Jordan River recalls the place where Israel entered into Canaan after the exodus; the "desert" recalls the Desert of Sinai, where the Israelites waited forty years to enter the promised land, as well as the place they had later crossed to return home after exile in Babylon; the "sea" recalls the Reed (Red) Sea, where God demonstrated his power to control the sea by separating the waters when the Israelites were chased by the Egyptian army; "mountains" recall Mount Sinai, where God revealed himself and gave the Law to Moses, and where the Israelites took refuge.[94]

Rhoads, Dewey, and Michie present a comprehensive understanding of Markan space as settings at a narrative level, discussing the nature and functions of Markan narrative space from various angles. Mark's narrative space both reveals the social environments of first-century Palestine and contains cosmic characteristics. Narrative scenes change according to Jesus' journeys, and his geographical (spatial) movement serves as the structural framework of Mark's narrative. In addition, some spatial settings evoke memories of Israel's history, functioning as the medium that connects events in Jesus' life with those of Israel's past. This comprehensive spatial understanding helps us discover the important characteristics of Markan space, which play a key role in the narrative analysis of Mark.

Galilee and Jerusalem as the Objects of Restoration

Freyne's 2001 article, "The Geography of Restoration: Galilee—Jerusalem Relations in Early Jewish and Christian Experience," argues that Mark does not place Galilee and Jerusalem in opposition, but rather presents both of them as objects to be restored.[95] Freyne analyzes the order of the geography listed in 3:7–8 and claims that Mark deliberately distinguishes Jewish regions from non-Jewish regions.[96] Galilee,[97] Judea, and Jerusalem

92. Rhoads et al., *Mark as Story*, 68.
93. Rhoads et al., *Mark as Story*, 69–70.
94. Rhoads et al., *Mark as Story*, 69–70.
95. Freyne, "Geography of Restoration," 304–7.
96. Freyne, "Geography of Restoration," 305.

97. Freyne suggests several elements to prove the Jewishness of Galilee in the Markan narrative. First, synagogues served as the community centers of Galilee, where people came together; second, the townspeople of Capernaum kept the Sabbath in that they brought all the sick and demon-possessed in the evening after sunset, namely the end of the Sabbath (1:32); third, Jesus ordered the healed leper to keep Moses's law by

belong to Jewish regions, while the regions across the Jordan (the region of the Decapolis), Tyre and Sidon, belong to non-Jewish regions. Mark takes Galilee as the departure point of Jesus' missional movement to non-Jewish regions, namely Gentile territory. Jesus traveled toward northern areas, Tyre and Sidon, and then moved to the east side of the Sea of Galilee through the regions of the Decapolis. This itinerary implies "Mark's concern with legitimisation of the gentile mission in the post-Easter situation (cf. Mark 13:10)."[98] Freyne states that the universal gathering of people around Jesus regardless of their ethnicity, which happened in Galilee, ultimately aims at the restoration of a "greater Israel":

> Both Jew and non-Jew gather around Jesus and his group as part of a multi-regional and multi-ethnic gathering of the nations and this pattern is continued in the two feeding miracles (Mark 6:35–44; 8:1–10). According to one version of restoration such a universal gathering was to take place in Zion (Isa 2:2–4), but in Mark it takes place in Galilee and Jesus travels from there to outlying regions, moving to the east (Decapolis), west (Tyre and Sidon) and north (Caesarea Philippi) before going south to Jerusalem, possibly therefore endorsing a greater Israel idea according to the lateral ethnicity model we have discussed.[99]

Freyne also argues that Mark does not describe Jerusalem in a negative way to place it in conflict with Galilee in the overall narrative plot.[100] When John the Baptist proclaimed a baptism of repentance for the forgiveness of sins in the wilderness, people from both Judea and Jerusalem came and were baptized by him, confessing their sins (1:1–6). They also came to Jesus when they heard his mighty works (3:8). The positive response of Judea and Jerusalem diminishes their negative portrayal.[101]

Freyne examines the relationship between Galilee and Jerusalem in historical and literary sources from the Hasmonean and Herodian periods,

---

showing himself to the priest and offering the sacrifices that Moses commanded for his cleansing, as the testimony to them (1:44). See Freyne, *Galilee, Jesus, and the Gospels*, 35.

98. Freyne, "Geography of Restoration," 305.

99. Freyne, "Geography of Restoration," 306.

100. Freyne, "Geography of Restoration," 306.

101. Freyne, "Geography of Restoration," 306. Freyne denies the dichotomous approach that claims that Markan geographical presentation of Galilee is positive while that of Jerusalem is negative. Opposition to Jesus took place not only in Jerusalem but also in Galilee: the local Pharisees conspired against Jesus with the local Herodians, plotting to kill him in a Galilean synagogue (3:6), and Jesus was rejected not only by his hometown but also by his mother and bothers (3:31; 6:1).

and explains it primarily in terms of socio-historical and anthropological factors, namely lateral and vertical ethnicity models. A lateral ethnicity model shows the expansion of territory for a greater Israel by attenuating kinship, social, or cultural ties; a vertical ethnicity model shows solid boundaries that separate the Jews from the Gentiles on the basis of the purity system reflected in the Jerusalem temple.[102] Freyne argues that both models of ethnicity in an anthropological aspect are "ideal types," which function "simultaneously, sometimes assisting and sometimes impeding the thrust of the other."[103] He applies these two models to Jesus' two different journeys in Mark's narrative. The journeys in and beyond Galilee correspond to the lateral ethnicity model, describing Jesus as the "charismatic itinerant engaged in messianic outreach," who broke through the demarcations between the Jews and the Gentiles.[104] The journey to Jerusalem, on the other hand, is in accord with the vertical ethnicity model, and can be regarded as a "ritual pilgrimage to the centre of Israel in order to renew it."[105] The Markan Jesus performed the "two modes of restoration"—namely, the lateral expansion of ethnic diversity and the vertical renewal of ethnic identity—and "both are transformed by a new synthesis in which ethnicity is affirmed both laterally and vertically."[106]

I agree with Freyne's understanding of Markan spatial presentation as the geography of restoration. Mark does not describe Galilee and Jerusalem in a conflict relationship, but portrays them as the spaces to be restored though Jesus' ministry. Though there exist conflicts between Jesus as a Galilean Jew and the religious leaders rooted in Jerusalem, Mark does not establish the mode of confrontation between Galilee and Jerusalem in his narrative. Rather, Mark shows that Jesus' ministry ultimately brings the restoration of the people of God by breaking down the ethnic boundary between the Jews and the Gentiles and renewing the identity of Israel. Here Galilee is the space where Jesus' missional movement gathers the people of God while destroying ethnic barriers, and Jerusalem is the space where Jesus' death and resurrection renew the identity of the people of God. This study regards Jesus' ministry in and beyond Galilee as his missional movement to the Jews and the Gentiles, dissolving barriers of class, gender, and

---

102. Freyne, "Geography of Restoration," 293, 310. Freyne explains "lateral and vertical ethnicity ideologies" in terms of anthropology as follows: "the one stressing the extensive dimension at the cost of an in-depth social bonding, and the other emphasising the intensive aspect by developing a tight-knit and circumscribed social culture."

103. Freyne, "Geography of Restoration," 293.

104. Freyne, "Geography of Restoration," 307.

105. Freyne, "Geography of Restoration," 307.

106. Freyne, "Geography of Restoration," 307.

race. Jesus' journeys beyond territorial boundaries consequently demonstrate that he is the Lord of all the people regardless their ethnicity and that his universal lordship extends beyond territorial limits.

Spatial Presentation Centered around Jesus

In his 2009 monograph, *Gathered around Jesus: An Alternative Spatial Practice in the Gospel of Mark*, Stewart explores how Mark understands and presents space. Stewart reports that there are two different groups of scholars evaluating Mark's geographical presentation. One group has argued that although Mark attempted to record the correct information, he did not have much knowledge of the geography of Palestine; the other group has claimed that Mark's geographical presentation was intended for mythological or theological purposes, and that he was not concerned with real and accurate geography.[107] Stewart states that his position is in the middle of these two groups: "While it seems unlikely that Mark was completely familiar with the geography of Palestine, his description of the territories through which Jesus travels is very much in line with Greek and Roman geographical tradition."[108] Further, "the central concept of ancient geography is the *oikoumenē*, or inhabited world."[109] This space, socially understood, is separated from non-inhabited areas of the world.[110] Greek and Roman geography is generally categorized into two types: "scientific" and "human."[111] Mark's geographical description is similar to the "human" type of geography.[112] Human geography is centered around the inhabited areas where people gather to live and socialize.[113]

Though Mark seems to follow human geography, he does not describe geography centered around ruling authorities or places of power. Instead, he provides a "new type of space centered around the person of Jesus in opposition to the civilized spaces of cities and the architectural spaces of

---

107. Stewart, *Gathered around Jesus*, 179.
108. Stewart, *Gathered around Jesus*, 179.
109. Stewart, *Gathered around Jesus*, 221.
110. Stewart, *Gathered around Jesus*, 221.
111. Stewart, *Gathered around Jesus*, 221. For the types of ancient Greek and Roman geography, refer to Stewart, *Gathered around Jesus*, 62–127.
112. Stewart, *Gathered around Jesus*, 179.
113. Stewart, *Gathered around Jesus*, 221. Human geography is mostly used "in forms of literature, ranging from historiography, novels, drama, comedy, epic, and even the geography itself."

synagogues and the temple."[114] In Mark, the "spatial practice of the temple/synagogue" is destined to come to an end and be replaced by the "new spatial practice" centered around Jesus, who exorcized demons, healed the people, and preached the gospel.[115] In this spatial practice performed by Jesus, "the kingdom of God exists spatially in the area around Jesus in which the new community 'gathers.'"[116] Stewart explicates the nature of the new space created by Jesus as follows:

> Jesus' new gathering, however, because of the power of the Holy Spirit, allows for the creation of pure spaces through exorcism. It is not Galilee and Jerusalem that are the primary points of opposition in the Gospel. Jesus' new gathering is not located specifically in the household. It is created in the spaces of the borderlands, areas that ancient geographers well knew were places for the formation of new movements. For the early Jews, these wilderness areas had always been the spaces for the formation of new spatial practices, especially in the Exodus and the return from exile. Jesus' new spatial practice, ultimately, will be fully consummated, according to Mark, when the Son of man returns, after the centers of civilization, that is, the temple and the city of Jerusalem have been destroyed.[117]

According to Brower, Stewart's exploration made an important contribution to Markan scholarship by pointing out that Markan spatial presentation demonstrates that the locus of purity is no longer the places of the synagogue and the temple, but the space centered around Jesus: "Geography is redrawn around Jesus."[118] Jesus destroyed the purity boundary of space built by the synagogue and the temple and created a new spatial configuration in which the kingdom of God would be realized through himself. I agree that Mark redefines space according to Jesus' ministry and his geographical movement. As Stewart says, Jesus refused the spatial practice of the vested rights (e.g., the cities, the synagogue, and the temple) and provided an "alternative spatial practice" centered around himself, in which the new community is established by breaking down the barriers of class, gender, and race.[119] In addition, while Jesus challenged the distorted authority of the synagogue and temple and was rejected by them, he performed

---

114. Stewart, *Gathered around Jesus*, 179–80.
115. Stewart, *Gathered around Jesus*, 224.
116. Stewart, *Gathered around Jesus*, 225.
117. Stewart, *Gathered around Jesus*, 225.
118. Brower, "Review," 56–57.
119. Stewart, *Gathered around Jesus*, 224.

his important ministry of teaching, caring, and revealing himself in the places such as the seaside (e.g., 4:1), the villages (e.g., 6:6b), the wilderness (e.g., 6:31–44; 8:1–10), the mountain (e.g., 9:2–8), the way (e.g., 8:27–38; 9:30–32; 10:32–34), and so forth. Jesus' movement did not originate from the center of power, but from the place where the new order and authority were ready to be accepted and the new gatherings were available. In relation to the present study, Jesus' spatial practice, which breaks down the ethnic boundary between the Jews and the Gentiles, is demonstrated by his geographical movement between Jewish and Gentile territory in his missional movement in 4:35—8:21.

Conclusion

The argument that Galilee and Jerusalem were situated in rivalry and conflict on the basis of the historical assumption of a distinct Galilean community lacks evidence. Not only have traditions and writings in support of this distinct community not been discovered, the competitive or strained relationship between the Galilean community and the Jerusalem community is also difficult to be found in Mark's narrative. Though it is evident that Mark presents Galilee and Jerusalem in different tones and colors, we may not say that they competed or clashed each other in terms of their leadership and theological positions. It is therefore hard to accept the theory that the Galilean community and the Jerusalem community had developed separate theologies and were in competition with each other in the early history of Christianity.

Galilee is also not an alternative to Jerusalem as a location for the expected Parousia or the eschatological realization of the kingdom of God. The suggestion that Mark 14:28 and 16:7 refer to the Parousia, rather than the emergence of the Risen Lord, is a forced interpretation. Like Matthew, Luke, and John, Mark tells his readers that the Risen Lord would appear in Galilee. The argument that Mark 1:15 refers to the Galilean realization of the kingdom of God is unpersuasive; we should instead interpret the presence of the kingdom of God in this verse according to "already but not yet" scheme. Additionally, Mark 12:35–37a does not refer to the rejection of the Davidic kingdom, giving Mark an anti-Jerusalem bent. In this passage, Mark demonstrates that Jesus is the Son of God beyond the Davidic sonship.

The analysis of space based on structuralism (e.g., a mythic structure) does not properly explain the relationship between Galilee and Jerusalem. This type of analysis assumes an opposing structure, and then posits a conflict relationship (between Galilee and Jerusalem) to fit into this structure.

The manner of developing a narrative does not always operate according to a fixed structure (a "deep structure"), and the diverse elements and multiple characteristics of a narrative should be considered to obtain an integral and comprehensive understanding of the text.

Like Freyne, I believe Mark describes Galilee and Jerusalem as objects to be restored. In Mark's narrative, Jesus' ministry focuses on the coming of the kingdom of God, and this implies the restoration of Israel in both Galilee and Jerusalem. Mark also portrays Galilee as the location of Jesus' missional movement by breaking down social barriers: people gather around Jesus as the people of God regardless of their ethnicity, gender, class, or economic standing. Jerusalem, due to its skewed temple-centered identity and transgression, is depicted as a place to be renewed through Jesus' death and resurrection.

Mark presents space centered around Jesus, with space unfolding in accordance with the route and place of Jesus' journey. As Stewart says, Jesus' geographical movement and his ministry provide a new spatial configuration focused not on the synagogue and the temple but on Jesus himself. Where Jesus goes, the people gather around him; where Jesus ministers to them, a new spatial configuration is established. It is not the places where power is concentrated (e.g., the synagogue and the temple), but the places ready to accept the new order and authority (e.g., the villages, the seaside, the wilderness, the mountain, and the way) where Jesus performs an alternative spatial practice by teaching, caring, healing, and revealing himself to the people of God. In relation to this study, Jesus' geographical movement between Jewish territory and Gentile territory in Mark 4:35—8:21 demonstrates his spatial practice of breaking down the barriers between the Jews and the Gentiles.

The present study deals with Jesus' ministry in and beyond Galilee in Mark 4:35—8:21, and this chapter seeks to explore the social space of Galilee and its Markan spatial presentation. In the following sections, I will investigate the social situations of first-century Galilee and explore how Mark depicts these circumstances. Mark portrays Galilee as the matrix for Jesus' missional movement, where the new spatial configuration, centered around Jesus, is created.

Social Circumstances of Galilee and Markan Presentation

The spatial investigation of Galilee must be performed in two aspects, historical and literary. First, our study needs to survey the historical situations of Galilee, especially its first-century social context. Ethnic, cultural, political, economic, and religious situations must be explored, since they serve as the primary setting of Mark's narrative. Second, our study calls for an investigation of Markan spatial presentation at a narrative level. We must examine how Mark understands Galilee and its vicinity and how he reflects this understanding in his own narrative.

In the present study, I will first survey the social environments of first-century Galilee and then examine how Mark presents them in his narrative world. This task will be performed in three areas: (1) the social situations of ethnicity, culture, and ethos; (2) the elements of social conflicts; and (3) the facility of geographical movement.

Ethnicity, Culture, and Ethos in Galilean Society and Markan Presentation

In terms of ethnicity and culture, Freyne introduces three views of Galilee.[120] The first is "Galileans as Israelites."[121] According to this view, Galilee, in contrast with Samaria, had remained ethnically exclusive despite the passing of many generations and even the invasion of Assyrian troops in 732 BC.[122] In Galilee, only a few members of the upper class were taken captive to Assyria, and the influx of non-Yahwists was minimal. Since Galilee had not undergone considerable ethnic changes, the Galileans readily participated in the independent movement of "the nation of the Jews" (ἔθνος τῶν Ἰουδαίων) in the second century BC, "accepting the Jerusalem temple as their natural cultic centre."[123] According to Freyne, however, this view is to be refuted because the Assyrian annals do not support the notion that only a few Galileans were captured by Tiglathpileser III. Rather, archeological excavation reveals that Galilee was devastated by the Assyrian conquest.[124]

The second view is "a pagan Galilee."[125] Isaiah's expression, "Galilee of the Gentiles" (9:1 [8:23 LXX], Γαλιλαία τῶν ἐθνῶν), which also appears in 1 Macc 5:15 (πᾶσαν Γαλιλαίαν ἀλλοφύλων: all Galilee of the Gentiles) and

---

120. Freyne, *Galilee, Jesus, and the Gospels*, 297–99.

121. Freyne introduces Alt's argument for the Galileans as Israelites. See Alt, "Galiläische Probleme," 363–435.

122. Freyne, "Geography of Restoration," 297–98.

123. Freyne, "Geography of Restoration," 298.

124. Freyne, "Geography of Restoration," 298. See also Younger, "Deportations of the Israelites," 201–27.

125. Freyne, "Geography of Restoration," 298–99. Freyne states that Bauer, Bertram, and Grundmann support "a pagan Galilee." See Bauer, "Jesus der Galiläer," 16–34; Bertram, "Der hellenismus in der Urheimat des Evangeliums," 265–81; Grundmann, *Jesus der Galiläer und das Judentum*.

Matt 4:15 (Γαλιλαία τῶν ἐθνῶν: Galilee of the Gentiles),[126] indicates that Galilee was regarded as a place fully influenced by pagan religion and culture. Because Galilee was encircled by Greek cities, Hellenism affected the Galileans heavily and directly. Galilee was thus under the "pagan ethos."[127] This view, however, exaggerates the influence of Greek cities and their culture in Galilee. Archeological remains do not provide decisive evidence as to whether Hellenism strongly influenced Galilee. In addition, Sepphoris and Tiberias do not show explicit pagan characteristics like "Scythopolis, Hippos, Gadara, or the Phoenician cities of the coast."[128] Fryene argues that "their impact on Galilean life was in the first instance social and economic rather than as centres of pagan culture that would be hostile to Jewish religious belief."[129]

The third view encompasses "a Jewish Galilee."[130] This option is to see "the ethnic situation of Galilee as thoroughly Jewish."[131] In connection to Galilee, the term Jewish/Ἰουδαῖος always indicates Judean in "a geographical rather than a religio-cultural sense."[132] The Galileans, who were composed of the old Israelites, had developed "their own distinctive ethos, customs, and belief."[133] In the period of Hasmonean expansion, the Galileans did not voluntarily accept the laws and duties that the Judeans made and imposed. Thus, the relations between them were increasingly strained. The Hasmonean dynasty colonized Galilee from the second century BC, and the Galileans became the object of reclamation.[134] In Galilee, therefore, the Galileans

126. Matthew's expression in the quotation of Isaiah, "Galilee of the Gentiles (Γαλιλαία τῶν ἐθνῶν)," does not refer to Jesus' direct ministry to the Gentiles in Galilee, but rather has the implication of foreshadowing Jesus' missional movement to the nations. As Keener says, "Matthew sees in Jesus' fulfillment of Isaiah's mention of a Gentile region an advance notice of further ministry to the Gentiles (cf. Isa 42:6; 49:6; 52:15)." In the first century, "Galilee was more Jewish than Gentile." See Keener, *Gospel of Matthew*, 146–47.

127. Freyne, "Geography of Restoration," 298.

128. Freyne, "Geography of Restoration," 298.

129. Freyne, "Geography of Restoration," 298. See also Freyne, *Galilee from Alexander the Great to Hadrian*, 101–54.

130. Freyne, "Geography of Restoration," 299.

131. Freyne, "Geography of Restoration," 299. Freyne asserts that the term "a Jewish Galilee" needs to be further clarified. Roughly speaking, "a Jewish Galilee" implies that Galilee was strongly influenced by the Judeans in social, cultural, and religious aspects, though the Galileans had their own identity that was different with that of the Judeans.

132. Freyne, "Geography of Restoration," 299. Freyne introduces Horsley's understanding of Galilean society. See Horsley, *Galilee*; Horsley, *Archaeology, History, and Society in Galilee*.

133. Freyne, "Geography of Restoration," 299.

134. Freyne, "Geography of Restoration," 299. In the Talmud, Yohanan be Zakkai, a

were ruled by the Judeans rooted in Jerusalem and Judea, naturally conflicting with Galilean society.[135] This view is also problematic, however, due to the lack of evidence for a "continued Israelite presence."[136] The position of "a Jewish Galilee" is similar to that of "Galileans as Israelites" in terms of the ethnic exclusivity of the population. However, these two positions differ in the way they interpret the situations of Galilean society. While the latter emphasizes the Galileans' voluntary submission to the power and cult of the Judeans and Jerusalem, the former highlights resistance to this power.

According to Freyne, almost all Jews were loyal to the Jerusalem temple. The temple serves as the center of their belief in the pre-70 period.[137] The Galileans were also faithful to the temple: they often made a voluntary pilgrimage to Jerusalem, gave the offering of half a shekel, and were even infuriated by attempts to defile the temple. They recognized themselves as "Yahweh-worshippers" through their emotional involvement and fidelity to the temple.[138]

Galilee, however, was placed under the control of the southern Jewish authorities: "the dominant strand were Ἰουδαῖοι, that is, people whose roots were southern and whose attachment to Jerusalem and its temple functioned as an important factor in defining and maintaining a separate identity in the north."[139] Freyne suggests two pieces of evidence to support this fact. First, in Josephus's *The Life*, Josephus claimed a prominent position of his priestly lineage that was connected to Jerusalem. The reason that he emphasized his priestly lineage was to establish a solid foothold in Galilee. His connection to Jerusalem served as the ground to reinforce his

---

great Pharisee who was trained in Galilee in the first century, deplored the situation of Galilee as follows: "O Galilee, O Galilee, in the end you shall be filled with wrongdoers!" (*y. Šabb.* 16:7 [15d]). The Judeans tended to disregard the Galileans.

135. Freyne, "Geography of Restoration," 299.

136. Freyne, "Geography of Restoration," 299.

137. Freyne, *Galilee, Jesus, and the Gospels*, 178. Freyne argues that loyalty to the temple played a role in overcoming the conflicts in Galilean society between rural peasants and ruling Jerusalem authorities. He explains conflict and harmony between Galilee and Jerusalem as follows: "An old and deep-seated attachment to Jerusalem and its temple, demonstrated particularly in fidelity to the pilgrimage, was capable of overcoming the social and economic tensions that existed between rural peasants from an outlying province and a ruling Jerusalem aristocracy who owned the better land and controlled the markets. In a word, a shared symbolic world-view, of which the Jerusalem temple was the central focal-point, compensated for the sense of alienation that was otherwise experienced by Galileans in a social world that was dominated by their religious leaders" (Freyne, "Galilee-Jerusalem Relations According to Josephus's Life," 607). See also Freyne, *Galilee from Alexander the Great to Hadrian*, 293–97.

138. Freyne, *Galilee, Jesus, and the Gospels*, 178.

139. Freyne, "Geography of Restoration," 300.

authority.[140] Second, in Mark 3:22 and 7:1, the scribes and the Pharisees came down from Jerusalem to Galilee in order to discredit Jesus' healing ministry and his disciples' behavior. This implies that the religious leaders in Jerusalem had the authority to inspect and control the social, cultural, or religious activities of the Galileans.[141]

Freyne argues that Galilean society showed two attitudes toward Jerusalem.[142] On the one hand, the Galileans were generally faithful to the Jerusalem temple and its religious authorities. On the other hand, they displayed a tendency to neglect the leadership of religious leaders rooted in Jerusalem. Despite their loyalty to the temple, the Galileans did not always follow Pharisaic halachic instructions. In addition, the Galileans had a different attitude toward the temple compared with that of the Judeans: "the temple itself may have had different symbolic value for differing strata of the Jewish society."[143] Freyne concludes that "Galilean attachment to the temple remained unimpaired, but that particular Pharisaic regulations had not been accepted in the province in the pre-70 period."[144]

Freyne's understanding of Galilean society fits well with Mark's description of Galilee. The Galileans were influenced and controlled by the Judeans in social, cultural, and religious aspects. Though it cannot be denied that the Gentiles such as Phoenicians, Itureans, Romans, and others also resided in Galilee and contributed to its population, Galilee was the land of the Jews under Jewish religious ethos. In addition, while Galilee was surrounded by Greek cities, and Sepphoris and Tiberias were built by Herod Antipas in Galilee, this does not prove that Galilee was completely Hellenized by them. Looking at its history and geographical location, Galilean society was much influenced by Gentile culture; nevertheless, it was still strongly placed under the Jewish ethos. Mark's portrayal of Galilee is full of Jewish colors, and Mark makes explicit divisions between the Jews and the Gentiles according to their territories: the Galilean crowds are separated from those of other regions (e.g., 3:7–8) and no Gentile character in Mark's narrative appears in Galilee. Despite the Jewish religious ethos in Galilee, however, the Galileans had their own identity, which was different from that of the Judeans who were rooted in Jerusalem.[145]

    140. Freyne, "Geography of Restoration," 300. See also Freyne, "Galilee-Jerusalem Relations."
    141. Freyne, "Geography of Restoration," 300.
    142. Freyne, "Galilean Religion," 105.
    143. Freyne, "Galilean Religion," 103.
    144. Freyne, "Galilean Religion," 105.
    145. When the social and cultural situations of first-century Galilee are explored, a distinction must be made between the "Galileans" and the "Judeans." They share their

Mark describes Galilee as a distinctive territory in terms of ethnicity and religious ethos. First, Mark distinguishes the crowds of the Galileans who were indigenous to the area from the crowds who came from the regions beyond Galilee. In Mark 3:7–8, the repetition of the phrase "the great multitude" (πολὺ πλῆθος, v. 7; πλῆθος πολύ, v. 8), indicates that the former usage refers to the Galilean crowd and the latter to the crowds from other regions.[146] According to France, "the use of two verbs, ἠκολούθησεν and ἦλθον πρὸς αὐτόν, has the effect of separating the Galilean crowd (who were already present to 'follow' him) from those from the more distant regions (who have first to 'come to him')."[147] Mark intentionally makes a distinction between the Galilean crowd and the crowds from other regions.

Second, Mark connects the ethnicity of Jesus' audience with their respective territories. Jesus' ministry to the Jews was performed in Galilee (Jewish territory), while his ministry to the Gentiles was done in Gentile territory.[148] In Mark, Jesus did not heal a single Gentile in Galilee, whereas in Matthew and Luke healings of the Gentiles took place in Galilee (e.g., the centurion in Capernaum in Matt 8:5–13 and Luke 7:1–10). This distinction in Mark is demonstrated well in Mark 4:35—8:21, where Jesus' missional activities to the Jews and the Gentiles are separated in terms of his geographical movement.

Third, Mark describes Galilee as the region that is placed under the influence of Jewish religious ethos, but has its own identity distinctive from that of Jerusalem and Judea. In Mark's narrative, the synagogues are frequently mentioned as religious centers in Galilee. As Freyne says, "mention of the synagogues of Galilee draws attention to the overall ethos that the author seeks to portray."[149] Jesus' early ministry in Galilee was performed

---

ethnicity, but they are separated in Mark's narrative in that the Galileans are controlled by the southern Judeans whose political power is based on the temple and Jerusalem. In the present study, however, when I use the term "Jews," it includes both the Galileans and the Judeans. The terms "Jews/Jewish" will be employed in contrast to "Gentiles/Gentile."

146. Lane, *Gospel According to Mark*, 129.

147. France, *Gospel of Mark*, 153. Freyne claims that the textual evidence shows that "an attempt has been made (either redactionally or in transmission) by the introduction of the verb ἠκολούθησεν to distinguish between the two groups," the Galileans who were native and the others who came from a distance. See Freyne, "Geography of Restoration," 305.

148. Wefald explores Jesus' separate Gentile mission in the first half of Mark by tracing the geographical and chronological movement of Jesus' journey. Wefald distinguishes Jesus' ministry to the Gentiles in Gentile territory from his ministry to the Jews in Galilee by employing narrative signals which reveal each Jewish and Gentile characteristic. See Wefald, "Separate Gentile Mission in Mark," 3–26.

149. Freyne, *Galilee, Jesus, and the Gospels*, 35.

in the synagogues.¹⁵⁰ The place of his first and public teaching was the synagogue in Capernaum (1:21), where he expelled an evil spirit; a man with a shriveled hand was healed in the synagogue (3:1); Jesus was rejected by his hometown when he taught in the synagogue of Nazareth (6:1–2); and Jesus met Jairus, one of the synagogue rulers, and healed his daughter's sickness (5:22). Most significantly, in a summary statement (1:39) Mark describes the synagogues as the central place of Jesus' preaching in his early Galilean ministry.¹⁵¹

The fact that a Jewish ethos prevailed in Galilee is also demonstrated by the concern in Galilee for the Sabbath and Mosaic Law.¹⁵² The crowd's decision to bring all the sick and demon-possessed to Jesus after sunset (1:32) implies that they intended to honor the Sabbath. Jesus' behavior also implies Galilean respect for Moses's laws: after healing a man with leprosy, Jesus commanded him to offer the sacrifices according to Moses's commandments (1:44).

Despite these implications in the text, the question remains as to how strongly the Galileans held to Jewish religious laws and traditions and how they understood them. According to Freyne, Mark's portrayal of the Galilean religious climate provides various options: "the depicted social world was Jewish, we saw, but that leaves many possibilities as regards the precise nature of the Galilean religious attitudes as envisaged by the author."¹⁵³ Though the religious climate of Galilean society clearly reflects Jewish influence, Mark presents that Galilean religious allegiance is not decided by "scribal influence" from Jerusalem.¹⁵⁴ The relationship between Galilee and Jerusalem was strained. Mark's narrative demonstrates this in the conflicts between Jesus and the religious leaders: Jesus of Galilee constantly comes into conflict with the religious leaders whose authority is rooted in Jerusalem, and the Galilean crowd, seeing the conflict between Jesus and religious leaders, show a favorable response to Jesus (e.g., 2:12). In Mark's narrative, Galilee was influenced by a Jewish religious ethos, but its religious attitude

---

150. The word "synagogue" (συναγωγή) and its cognates appear twelve times in Mark (1:21, 23, 29, 39; 3.1, 5.22, 35, 36, 38, 6.2; 12:39; 13:9). The first ten references to the synagogues are located in Jesus' Galilean ministry, but the last two references (12:39; 13:9) describe the scribes' status and thus relate not to the place of Jesus' ministry but to a place of persecution.

151. Donahue and Harrington states that "the stress on Jesus' synagogue preaching here may also reflect early missionary practice (see Acts 13:5; 14:1; 18:4)" (Donahue and Harrington, *Gospel of Mark*, 88).

152. Freyne, *Galilee, Jesus, and the Gospels*, 35.

153. Freyne, *Galilee, Jesus, and the Gospels*, 42.

154. Freyne, *Galilee, Jesus, and the Gospels*, 43.

was not fully in compliance with the religious authority based in Jerusalem. Galilee was ready to reject an old religious convention and to accept a new order of the kingdom of God; it therefore stood out as a potential place that would accept a new religious movement.

Conflicts in Galilean Society and Markan Presentation

Scholars have developed two opposing views of the Galilean social situation: "social conflict" and "social harmony."[155] In support of social conflict, Horsley suggests a social model of Galilee that incorporated political, economic, and cultural aspects.[156] Drawing from a socio-economic model, he insists on a power structure "between the village communities and their rulers."[157] In this model, he demonstrates a conflict in Galilee between peasants and landowners (or social elites) rather than between the Jews and Christians. Thus, Galilee was the place where common people, who constituted the majority of the population, suffered oppression from both Jewish authorities and Roman imperialism. As the leader of common people, Jesus protested against the ruling system with its vested interests and defended the traditional lifestyle of the village.

Freyne also attempts to analyze the cause of conflict in Galilee in the context of the political and economic climate of Herod Antipas's dominion.[158] In particular, the establishment of Sepphoris and Tiberias by Antipas brought changes to an economic structure in which urban centers controlled Galilean peasants' lives.[159] During the clashes between urban ruling

---

155. In his well-summarized articles dealing with the development of the interpretation of first-century Galilee, Moxnes introduces diverse opinions regarding Galilean society and categorizes them into two groups: conflict and harmony. See Moxnes, "Construction of Galilee—Part I," 26–37; Moxnes, "Construction of Galilee—Part II," 64–77.

156. Moxnes, "Construction of Galilee—Part II," 71. See Horsley, *Galilee*; Horsley, *Archaeology, History, and Society in Galilee*.

157. Horsley, *Archaeology, History, and Society in Galilee*, 10.

158. Freyne, *Galilee, Jesus, and the Gospels*, 135–75.

159. Freyne, "Jesus and the Urban Culture of Galilee," 75–121. Freyne, however, argues that despite the economic control exerted by Herodian cities, the Galileans showed strong allegiance to Jerusalem and its temple cult. "The fact that many of the villages were economically controlled by the Herodian cities of the Lower Galilee did not in any way destroy the much older and deeper loyalties to Jerusalem and its cult centre. Regardless of the amount of shared material culture that archaeology has uncovered, there is little evidence of any alternative myth emanating from the Greek cities that might have successfully competed for the loyalties of the villagers." See Freyne, "Urban-Rural Relations," 54.

power and rural resistance, a time characterized by oppression under the Herodian aristocracy and the religious leaders of Jerusalem, a "village and peasant ethos" emerged.[160] However, this conflict model, especially "the use of 'peasant' as *typos*," was disputed by Andrew Overman.[161] He refutes the socio-economic model and the supposed power struggle between peasants and rulers because these explanations rely on applying a peasants' insurrection model—which is based on the medieval and modern periods—to the common people of first-century Galilee.[162]

Instead of social conflict, Meyers argues for social harmony in Galilean society by highlighting the integrative dimensions of social activities.[163] From the investigation of archeological remains, he insists that urbanism and rural culture in Galilean cities and villages were situated in harmony. For example, pottery relics made it possible to trace the routes of the first-century trades in Palestine and its vicinity. The fact that these relics were discovered in widespread areas, not limited to cities, implies that there were economic relations between cities and villages. Such economic transactions made a society stable, which led to social harmony. This social harmony model is also problematic, however, because it interprets archeological remains to fit its purposes. The fact that relics were found in both cities and villages does not automatically imply social harmony. The economic interaction between cities and villages could also be interpreted as cities' exploitation of villages.[164] Archeological remains do not serve as positive evidence for social harmony.

Galilean society contained many conflict elements and Mark's narrative displays several conflict aspects disclosed by Jesus' ministry. With regard to Markan spatial presentation, I will explore the inherent conflicts in Galilean society that were uncovered through Jesus' ministry. The conflicts may be seen taking place between two opposing spaces: Galilee versus Jerusalem,[165] and villages versus cities.

160. Freyne, *Galilee, Jesus, and the Gospels*, 175. Moxnes explains a conflict model in Galilean society as follows: "Within the conflict pattern, the village population so to speak represents the ideal Jewish community, based on the 'old' values, whereas the cities represent a 'foreign' element of exploitation. Here Jesus becomes a leader for the village population, and his message and actions represent a religious expression of social protest. Thus, in a way the conflict pattern between Galilee and Jerusalem is replaced by an internal Galilean conflict between villages and cities." See Moxnes, "Construction of Galilee—Part II," 71.

161. Moxnes, "Construction of Galilee—Part II," 71–72.

162. Overman, "Jesus of Galilee and the Historical Peasant," 67–73.

163. Meyers, "Jesus and His Galilean Context," 57–66.

164. Moxnes, "Construction of Galilee—Part II," 72.

165. Though I agree that there was a conflict relationship between Galilee and

The conflict between Galilee and Jerusalem is apparent in the clashes between the Galilean Jesus and the religious leaders rooted in and influenced by Jerusalem. From a sociological perspective, Saldarini states that the Pharisees and scribes belong to the "retainer class" among upper classes in a first-century Palestinian society.[166] The retainer class worked for the benefits of the ruler and governing class and exerted their influence to the common people.[167] Located between the ruling class and the peasants, the Pharisees and scribes thrived in cities and towns, struggled to gain power and influence in Jewish society, and held influence with the public.[168] Though they did not have their own independent power, they exerted influence on society by enlisting the aid of the ruling powers or colluding with other upper classes.[169]

The Pharisees,[170] who formed not only a "religious group" but also a "political force which interacted with the governing class," served as "brokers" between the ruling power and the common people.[171] Though Mark

---

Jerusalem, this does not mean that there existed a Galilean Christian community in rivalry with a Jerusalem Christian community; that Galilee was seen as an alternative place for the coming of the kingdom of God or Parousia at the end of time; or that the mythic structure is operative in Mark's narrative, providing two opposing poles of Galilee and Jerusalem. Rather, their conflict relationship in Mark's narrative is related to the Galileans' openness to accepting the new authority of Jesus over that of Jerusalem, which was revealed through the conflicts between the Galilean Jesus and the religious leaders from Jerusalem.

166. Saldarini follows Gerhard Lenski's classification method to distinguish classes in agrarian empires, including the Roman Empire. Nine classes may be discerned: five upper classes (the ruler, the governing class, the retainer class, the merchant class, and the priestly class) and four lower classes (peasants, artisans, an unclean or degraded class, and the expendable class). Saldarini regards the Pharisees and scribes as a retainer class. See Saldarini, "Political and Social Roles," 200. Refer also to Lenski, *Power and Privilege*, 214–96.

167. Saldarini, "Political and Social Roles," 201.

168. Saldarini, "Political and Social Roles," 201.

169. Saldarini, "Political and Social Roles," 203–4.

170. We can obtain the information about the Pharisees from three source collections: the NT, Josephus's writings, and rabbinic literature. Though their descriptions of the Pharisees do not entirely agree with each other, the general conclusions may be suggested as follows: "They were a lay (not priestly) association who were thought to be expert in the laws; they were, in a sociological sense, "retainers" who brokered power between the aristocracy and the masses; they promoted a special living tradition in addition to the laws; they were very interested in issues of ritual purity and tithing; and they believed in afterlife, judgment, and a densely populated, organized spirit world." See Mason, "Pharisees," 1043.

171. Saldarini, "Political and Social Roles," 200.

does not describe the Pharisees as governmental or religious officials,[172] they are portrayed as a "potent political and religious force."[173] In contact with the ruling powers, the Pharisees as "unofficial ancillaries of the Jewish leadership" exercised their influence on the general populace.[174] In order to achieve their goal, they entered into political league with the Herodians (e.g., Mark 3:6) and were associated with the scribes rooted in Jerusalem (e.g., 7:1).[175] When Jesus began his ministry to the common people in Galilee, the strong opponents were none other than the Pharisees and scribes. As "unofficial patrons and brokers for the people," they might well regard Jesus, who challenged their authority and was popular among the people, as a threat to their force and influence.[176] "The Pharisees, one of many political and religious interest groups seeking power and influence over Jewish society, exercise influence on the people and compete with Jesus for social and political control."[177]

With the exception of two references (10:2; 12:13), Mark locates the Pharisees in a Galilean setting (2:16, 18, 24; 3:2, 6; 7:1, 3, 5; 8:11, 15).[178] However, they might be strongly connected to the temple and Jerusalem. For example, they were accompanied by the scribes who came from Jerusalem and criticized the disciples' behavior who were eating food with defiled hands, namely unwashed hands (7:1-5). Saldarini explains the association of the Pharisees in Galilee with the temple and the Jerusalem authorities as follows:

> The Pharisees must have worked for either the Temple leadership in so far as it was represented in Galilee, Herod Antipas's government, or landowners. The Pharisees' stress on tithing and priestly piety for the laity could have been attractive to the Jerusalem authorities who desired to collect tithes from all Jews in Palestine and who could have met resistance from Jews in Galilee, outside their political control. . . . If the Pharisees

---

172. Pickup, "Matthew's and Mark's Pharisees," 71.
173. Saldarini, "Political and Social Roles," 204.
174. Pickup, "Matthew's and Mark's Pharisees," 72.
175. Saldarini, "Political and Social Roles," 205.
176. Saldarini, "Political and Social Roles," 205.
177. Saldarini, "Pharisees," 5:295.

178. In Mark's narrative, the Pharisees are linked with Galilee whereas the scribes are strongly connected to Jerusalem. See Lührmann, "Die Pharisäer und die Schriftgelehrten im Markusevangelium," 169-85; Mowery, "Pharisees and Scribes, Galilee and Jerusalem," 266-68. While Josephus records that the Pharisees were closely associated with the leadership in Jerusalem, Mark displays their activity only in Galilee. See Saldarini, "Pharisees," 5:295.

in Galilee were representatives of the Jerusalem leadership, it would explain their small numbers in Galilee, their lack of mention in other sources, and their absence in accounts of indigenous Galilean society and leadership. It would also explain their hostility to Jesus and their willingness to form coalition with the Herodians to oppose him.[179]

Though the Pharisees had considerable influence on Galilean society and its populace,[180] they were closely related to the temple and Jerusalem authorities and they represented the Jerusalem leadership in Galilee. Jesus, who fought against the Pharisees and was welcomed by the Galilean crowd, was consequently situated in conflict with the Jerusalem leadership.

In Mark's narrative, the scribes are strongly linked with the temple and the authorities in Jerusalem.[181] Like the Pharisees, they may also be classified into the retainer class in Jewish society, serving as "bureaucrats, educators, and major and minor officials."[182] Basically, they were "Torah scholars who preserved and interpreted the Law in order to maintain its centrality in Judaism after the Exile and in the Diaspora."[183] In the first century, the scribes dwelt not only in Jerusalem but also in towns and villages in the provinces; Mark locates the scribes mostly in and coming from Jerusalem, while placing them merely two times in Galilee (2:6; 9:14).[184] Mark portrays the scribes as a political and religious force rooted in Jerusalem, representing its authority and influence in towns and villages of Galilee. Saldarini explains the status and roles of the scribes in the Gospels as follows:

> The presence of scribes in Jerusalem as officials and in Galilean villages as copyists and low-level officials is very probable. The gospels testify most reliably to scribes connected to the government in Jerusalem, and their role there seems to be as associates of the priests, both in judicial proceeding and enforcement of Jewish custom and law, and ongoing business in the Sanhedrin.[185]

---

179. Saldarini, "Political and Social Roles," 205.

180. Saldarini, "Political and Social Roles," 208. Saldarini states that "the Pharisees were recognized leaders in the Galilean community, according to Mark. This means that they had high standing in the community and influence, if not power, with the people and other leaders of the community."

181. "In Mark the scribes are associated with Jerusalem and the chief priests as part of the government of Judaism" (Saldarini, "Scribes," 5:1015).

182. Saldarini, "Political and Social Roles," 200, 205.

183. Paffenroth, "Scribes," 1773.

184. Saldarini, "Scribes," 5:1015.

185. Saldarini, "Scribes," 5:1015.

In Jesus' first public ministry in a Galilean synagogue (1:21–28), Mark describes Jesus as one who carried authority which differed from that of scribes. In contrast with the scribes' instruction, his teaching was new (διδαχὴ καινὴ κατ' ἐξουσίαν; "new teaching with authority," 1:27). According to France, "the general statement that his ἐξουσία differentiated his teaching from that of the γραμματεῖς suggests that he is already expressing some of the radical ideas, boldly contradicting accepted halakhic teaching, which will appear later in relation to, e.g., the Sabbath (2:23–3:6), the purity laws (7:1–23), or divorce (10:2–12). . . . They represent the old régime, challenged by the fresh new teaching of Jesus."[186]

In Mark, scribes are Jesus' strongest opponents, and "they are associated primarily (but not exclusively) with Jerusalem."[187] Meier claims that "to Mark's mind, which seems to move between the poles of Galilee and Jerusalem, scribes are especially associated with Jerusalem and hence with opposition to Jesus."[188] By connecting the scribes with Jerusalem,[189] Mark portrays Galilee as existing under the control of Jerusalem.[190] This is demonstrated clearly in the scribes' criticism of Jesus' sayings and deeds. The scribes who came down from Jerusalem accused Jesus of being possessed

---

186. France, *Gospel of Mark*, 102.

187. Donahue and Harrington state that the Jerusalem scribes played a crucial role in formulating a plot to kill Jesus (8:31; 10:33; 11:18; 14:1, 43, 53; 15:1, 31) (Donahue and Harrington, *Gospel of Mark*, 80). The scribes' major task was to interpret and preserve the law, and they were regarded as "guardians of tradition." The phrase "scribes of the Pharisees" (2:16) may imply that "scribes were associated with various sects and associations within first-century Judaism." See Twelftree, "Scribes," 1087. In relation to the law, their three major tasks were: "(a) to develop and interpret the Law pertinent to the times, (b) to teach students the Law, and (c) to act in judicial situations." See Guelich, *Mark 1–8:26*, 56. In Mark's narrative, the scribes always judge Jesus' words and deeds and criticize him.

188. According to Meier, scribes are rooted in Jerusalem, and Mark notes a few instances of those scribes' residence in Galilee: "possibly 1:22; 2:6, 16; the geographical setting in 9:11, 14 is unclear" (Meier, *Marginal Jew*, 554). For a discussion about the Pharisees' association with Jerusalem, see Vermès, *Jesus the Jew*, 56–57; Neusner, *First-Century Judaism in Crisis*, 38.

189. In Mark, the place-name "Jerusalem" appears 12 times (1:5; 3:8, 22; 7:1; 10:32, 33; 11:1, 11, 15, 27; 15:41). In two cases (3:22; 7:1), Jerusalem is connected to the scribes: οἱ γραμματεῖς οἱ ἀπὸ Ἱεροσολύμων καταβάντες (the scribes who came down from Jerusalem, 3:22); οἱ Φαρισαῖοι καί τινες τῶν γραμματέων ἐλθόντες ἀπὸ Ἱεροσολύμων (the Pharisees and some of the scribes who came from Jerusalem, 7:1).

190. Collins argues that if we assume that urban cities controlled the people of Galilee, Jerusalem might have had stronger influence on them than the Herodian cities did (Collins, *Mark*, 228). Freyne also says that "thus, insofar as any urban centre dominated the cultural life of Galilee, it would seem that it was Jerusalem, not the Herodian cities, that had the controlling influence over the majority of the population" (Freyne, "Urban-Rural Relations," 51).

by Beelzebub (3:22) and confronted Jesus about matters relating to ritual purity (7:1).[191] From the first scene of his public ministry (1:21–28), Jesus is portrayed challenging the authority and order (established by Jerusalem) with a "new teaching with authority" (1:27). The conflicts between Jesus and the scribes give us clues as to why the scribes came down from Jerusalem to disparage Jesus in the first place: the scribes thought that Jesus' ministry was already damaging "the absolute claim of their city and the basis for its control, the temple" (e.g., 2:1–12, 13–17; 3:20–30; 7:1–23).[192]

The response of the Galilean crowd to Jesus' ministry is different from that of the scribes. The first response of the crowd, gathered in a synagogue of Capernaum (1:21–28), is amazement (ἐξεπλήσσοντο, ἐθαμβήθησαν; 1:22, 27).[193] Their amazement carries the nuance of alarm, since Jesus' teaching and mighty works were unprecedented.[194] In the episode of the healing of a paralyzed man (2:1–12), Jesus came into conflict with scribes again. They questioned Jesus in their mind because he claimed authority to forgive sins. In response to their doubt, Jesus healed the paralyzed man in order to show his authority to forgive sins. Again, the crowds who witnessed this miracle were amazed (ἐξίστασθαι, 2:12). Though ἐξίστασθαι (2:12) is paralleled with ἐθαμβήθησαν (1:27), the nuance of amazement in this episode is different. This amazement is accompanied with the crowd's recognition that Jesus' authority came from God. The fact that the crowd glorified God (δοξάζειν τὸν θεόν, 2:12) after seeing Jesus' miracle has great implications. "Whereas the scribes took Jesus' words as a challenge to the prerogative of God, the crowd understood Jesus to be acting for God and with his approval."[195] In

---

191. Meier claims that "the references in 3:22 and 7:1, 5 create the impression of some sort of investigatory commission sent from Jerusalem to question or attack Jesus' activity in Galilee" (Meier, *Marginal Jew*, 554).

192. Freyne, *Galilee, Jesus, and the Gospels*, 47.

193. Mark uses various expressions to express the "amazement" of the crowd and the disciples at Jesus' teaching and mighty works: "ἐκπλήσειν (1:22; 6:2; 7:37; 10:26; 11:8); θαυμάζειν (5:20; 15:5, 44); ἐκθαυμάζειν (12:17); θαμβεῖσθαι(1:27; 10:24, 32); ἐκθαμβεῖσθαι (9:15); ἐξίστημι (2:12; 5:42; 6:51); cf. φοβεῖσθαι (4:41; 5:15, 33, 36; 6:50; 9:32; 10:32; 11:8) and ἔκφοβος (9:6)." See Lane, *Gospel According to Mark*, 72. Donahue and Harrington states that "the motif of surprise, wonder, awe, and fear" is one of the noticeable characteristics of Mark's narrative, and they classified these responses in five categories: "(1) in reaction to his teaching (1:22; 6:2; 10:24, 26; 11:18; 12:17); (2) as a conclusion to miracle stories (1:17; 2:12; 4:41; 5:15, 20, 33, 42; 6:50, 51; 7:37); (3) in narratives of divine epiphanies (4:41; 6:50–51; 9:6; 16:5, 8); (4) notices about the fright of the disciples at predictions of the Passion (9:32; 10:33; cf. 14:33, the fright of Jesus); and (5) reactions by opponents, both before and during the Passion of Jesus (11:18; 12:12; 15:5, 44)." See Donahue and Harrington, *Gospel of Mark*, 79.

194. France, *Gospel of Mark*, 102, 129.

195. France, *Gospel of Mark*, 129.

contrast to the scribes, the Galilean crowd accepted and acclaimed Jesus' words and deeds.[196] In Mark's narrative, therefore, the Galileans were not fully subordinated to the religious authority of Jerusalem but were in fact open to accept other authorities, not based on Jerusalem.

Though conflict between cities and villages does not appear explicitly in Mark, rural settings must play a significant role in understanding Jesus' ministry. In the general description of Jesus' itinerant ministry in Galilee, Mark 6:6b shows that Jesus' missional (teaching) activity centered around the villages ("Jesus went about the villages in a circuit, teaching": περιῆγεν τὰς κώμας κύκλῳ διδάσκων).[197]

In the Hellenistic world, a city (πόλις) and a village (κώμη) were clearly distinguished and their relationship was well-recognized.[198] According to Sherwin-White, Tiberias and probably Sepphoris were genuinely self-governing cities in Galilee, and they ruled just over their own urban areas. Caesarea Philippi, however, was a more powerful city with authority to rule not only its own urban area but also the adjacent territory.[199] Mark's expression of "the villages of Caesarea Philippi" (κώμας Καισαρείας τῆς Φιλίππου, 8:27) demonstrates "the relationship between the villages of a particular territory and the city to which they belonged."[200] France claims that "the plural together with the name of the city in the genitive clearly indicates small settlements associated with the city rather than the city itself."[201] In 8:27, Jesus and his disciples did not enter the city of Caesarea Philippi itself, but instead visited its surrounding territory, namely the nearby villages (κῶμαι).[202] France argues that Jesus' travel to Caesarea Philippi was not a

196. Freyne compares the Jerusalem crowd with the Galilean crowd in regard to receiving benefits from Jesus and freedom from religious authorities. "Yet despite the narrator's best effort to vindicate the Jerusalem populace, we cannot help noting that they were not the beneficiaries of any of Jesus' mighty deeds, only hearers of his teaching, rather like the experience in Nazareth, where he was not able to perform any of his works of power because of their lack of faith (6:5).... Thus a real contrast is set up between the freedom of the Galilean crowd, with its unbounded enthusiasm for Jesus to the end, and the people of Jerusalem, who though interested, are eventually brought under the control of their religious leaders, despite the reported fear of the crowd on the part of the authorities, should they move against Jesus, when first he arrived in the city (11:32; 12:12)." See Freyne, *Galilee, Jesus, and the Gospels*, 57.

197. In comparison with Mark, Matt 9:35 adds "cities" ("Jesus went about all the cities and villages, teaching": περιῆγεν ὁ Ἰησοῦς τὰς πόλεις πάσας καὶ τὰς κώμας διδάσκων).

198. Freyne, *Galilee, Jesus, and the Gospels*, 40.

199. Sherwin-White, *Roman Society and Roman Law*, 127.

200. Freyne, *Galilee, Jesus, and the Gospels*, 40.

201. France, *Gospel of Mark*, 328.

202. France, *Gospel of Mark*, 328. As the capital of a region, Caesarea Philippi

"mission" but a "retreat" to a rural area mostly populated by the Gentiles for the purpose of giving instructions to the disciples (8:27-38).[203] The same case may be discovered in Jesus' travel to the vicinity of Tyre (τὰ ὅρια Τύρου, 7:24). Jesus appeared not to enter Tyre itself but visited its vicinity (ὅρια), the administrative district controlled by Tyre. In Mark, Jesus is not generally a "frequenter of cities," but prefers to stay in the countryside.[204]

Matthew, Mark, and Luke do not always agree with each other on the distinction between a city and a village.[205] For example, while Matthew and Luke call Bethsaida a city (Matt 11:20-21; Luke 9:10),[206] Mark calls it a village (8:22-26). Scholars have debated whether Bethsaida was a city or a village.[207] Regarding Mark's reference to a village about Bethsaida in 8:22-26, as France assumes, "we envisage Jesus here (as later near Caesarea Philippi, v. 27) avoiding the city itself and visiting an outlaying settlement." Mark evidently calls Capernaum a city (1:33), which implies that he considered it to be the most important settlement.[208] When the people in the city sought Jesus during his incipient ministry in Capernaum, he said he would go to the neighboring villages (ἐχομένας κωμοπόλεις) to preach, which was his purpose for coming (1:38). Here the Greek κωμόπολις (a compound of κώμη and πόλις; literally, a "village-city"), used only here in the NT, refers to a settlement of middle size, something between a city and a village.[209] In

---

controlled a wide territory which would include many smaller settlements, namely villages.

203. France, *Gospel of Mark*, 328.

204. France, *Gospel of Mark*, 297.

205. Sherwin-White states that "Mark comes closer than any other Gospel to denoting the technical difference between a village and a true city" (Sherwin-White, *Roman Society and Roman Law*, 131).

206. John (1:44) and Josephus (*Ant.* 18:28) also call Bethsaida a city.

207. According to Josephus, under the tetrarch Philip Herod, the former village of Bethsaida gained new status as a city (Josephus, *Ant.* 18:28). It was renamed Bethsaida Julia after Caesar's daughter (Homan, "Bethsaida," 174). However, Lane argues that Mark's reference to Bethsaida as a village is correct because "despite its reorganization and new name it remained a mere toparchic capital (of Gaulanitis), and not a true city" (Lane, *Gospel According to Mark*, 283). See also Sherwin-White, *Roman Society and Roman Law*, 127-31.

208. France, *Gospel of Mark*, 112. Capernaum, which is mentioned three times in Mark (1:21; 2:1; 9:33), serves as the base camp for Jesus' ministry. Jesus went out for mission from there and came back again to there. Jesus' missional works, however, took place mostly in villages and rural terrain.

209. France, *Gospel of Mark*, 112. France states that κωμόπολις technically means "a settlement which is more than a village but cannot claim the status of πόλις." It also refers to "a city that has only the position of a κώμη as far as its constitution is concerned" ("κωμόπολις," BDAG 580).

his usage of κωμοπόλεις, which are placed in a lower level than Capernaum, Mark portrays Jesus as "moving from the centre of local influence into a rather more 'grassroots' ministry."[210]

In Mark, πόλις is used eight times (1:33, 45; 5:14; 6:33; 6:56; 11:19; 14:13, 16). Three of these uses refer to Jerusalem (11:19; 14:13, 16). In 1:45, Jesus could not go into πόλις openly, because the people spread the news about him. In 5:14, when Jesus expelled demons at the seashore in the region of the Gerasenes, the people went to πόλις to report his miracle. In 6:33, the people came out from πόλις to follow Jesus, who went away in a boat to the wilderness. In 6:56, πόλις is used to describe Jesus' universal mission ("wherever he went, into villages or cities or fields": ὅπου ἂν εἰσεπορεύετο εἰς κώμας ἢ εἰς πόλεις ἢ εἰς ἀγρούς). With the exception of the use of πόλις in reference to Capernaum in 1:33, the term πόλις is not directly used as the background of Jesus' ministry in Galilee and its vicinity. Though cities are mentioned in Mark, the perspective in the narrative is "outdoor and rural for the most part,"[211] and Jesus' ministry is mainly portrayed in the settings of villages and rural landscapes. Jesus also taught the crowd with parables, which have the context of a rural lifestyle (e.g., 4:1-34); even during his stay in Jerusalem, Jesus employed rural imagery in his teaching (e.g., 12:1-9; 13:28-30).[212]

Further, Mark refuses to mention the names of cities built by Herod (e.g., Sepphoris, Tiberias, and Machaerus) even in the episode of Herod's birthday celebration.[213] In regard to Mark's reason for not mentioning these cities, Freyne assumes that Jesus intentionally stayed away from these cities in order to avoid conflict with Herodian power, which had led to the execution of John the Baptist (6:14-29).[214] On the other hand, Moxnes suggests that this refusal might be Mark's "strategy to recreate the landscape in accord with the traditional village landscape with its kinship solidarity."[215] Rural settings in Mark's narrative lead us to envisage "the kingdom of God as

210. France, *Gospel of Mark*, 113.

211. Freyne, *Galilee, Jesus, and the Gospels*, 41. Cf. Mark 6:56, where Mark's narrative presents "a threefold division of settlement": village (κώμη), city (πόλις), and field (ἀγρός).

212. Freyne, *Galilee, Jesus, and the Gospels*, 39.

213. Freyne, *Galilee, Jesus, and the Gospels*, 40.

214. Freyne, *Galilee, Jesus, and the Gospels*, 139-40.

215. Moxnes, "Construction of Galilee—Part II," 75. Moxnes states that "the conflict pattern between Galilee and Jerusalem is replaced by an internal Galilean conflict between villages and cities." Whereas cities present the image of "exploitation," villages appear as the place of "the ideal Jewish community." "Jesus becomes a leader for the village population, and his message and actions represent a 'religious' expression of a social protest" (Moxnes, "Construction of Galilee—Part II," 73).

a landscape with an alternative spatial management of power."[216] According to Stewart, "Mark rejects the current social configuration of space and establishes a new one in which proximity to Jesus is the key element."[217] For example, though Jesus' ministry was first carried out in synagogues, the synagogue was replaced by the house as the place of meetings. The synagogue became a hostile place for Jesus (3:1–6) where he was rejected even by his hometown (6:1–6); in contrast, the house became the site of intimate meetings where "table-fellowship is established (2:15; 6:10; 14:3, 14)."[218] Mark focuses on rural settings to show that Jesus' missional movement did not originate from the place where political, economic, and religious powers were concentrated. The villages, and not the cities, were the better place for Jesus to begin with his missional movement in Galilee. In Mark's narrative, Jesus created a new configuration of space by his missional movement.

Jesus was rejected by religious leaders in the synagogues and the temple, where the existing authorities were active. In contrast, Jesus was usually accepted in rural settings. He called the disciples at the seaside of Galilee (1:16–20), taught the crowd beside the sea (2:13; 4:1), and miraculously delivered the disciples on the sea, disclosing his identity as the Savior (4:35–41; 6:45–52). He went out to the desert for prayer (1:35), led his disciples to the wilderness for rest (6:31), and fed a large crowd there (6:31–44; 8:1–10). He predicted his death and resurrection on the way (8:31; 9:31; 10:33–34), and he revealed himself before the disciples in the glory of the transfiguration on the mountain (9:2–8). According to Stewart, the wilderness and mountains especially serve as locations for the "identity formation" of God's people:

> In the desert, people come to John the Baptist, forsaking centers of civilization in order to be baptized. Crowds are fed miraculously in the desert, recalling the miraculous feeding of the Israelites during their wilderness wanderings and instituting a new spatial practice in contrast to that of the temple and synagogue. Jesus chooses his disciples on a mountain, and revelation of his identity in the Transfiguration occurs on the mountain. . . . [Wilderness] is mostly a positive place in the Gospel and establishes a space for the formation of the new community of the kingdom of God.[219]

---

216. Moxnes, "Construction of Galilee—Part II," 75. As regards the study of spatial management, Sawicki suggests its three fields: ethnicity, gender, and the presence of the Roman Empire in Galilee. See Sawicki, "Spatial Management of Gender and Labor in Greco-Roman Galilee," 7–28.

217. Stewart, *Gathered around Jesus*, 224.

218. Freyne, *Galilee, Jesus, and the Gospels*, 62.

219. Stewart, *Gathered around Jesus*, 210.

I do not agree with the argument that Mark describes Galilee as the physical place where the kingdom of God is realized. In addition, there is no textual evidence that Mark's description of Jesus' ministry, which focuses on the rural terrain, was intended to elevate Jesus as a rural protester against the power of the city. Instead, Mark's portrayal of villages and the rural landscape in Jesus' Galilean ministry represents his own spatial configuration. Jesus gathered his people for the new community not in the closed place, where the powers were already established and concentrated, but in the open place, where a new spatial configuration could be created for the kingdom of God. In this respect, villages and rural areas serve as the space where Jesus' missional movement could successfully unfold.

Markan Presentation of Galilee as the Geographical Center of Jesus' Missional Movement

Mark portrays Galilee as the first place where Jesus proclaimed the kingdom of God (Mark 1:14–15).[220] After John the Baptist was put into prison, Jesus came to Galilee and preached the good news of God. In John's ministry, however, there was no reference to Galilee (1:5); apart from Jesus himself, only people from the Judean countryside and Jerusalem came to John to be baptized in the Jordan River.[221] France suggests that the absence of "Galilee" in 1:5 may imply that John's baptizing ministry was towards the southern region of the Jordan River.[222] However, the fact that Jesus came from Nazareth of Galilee to be baptized by John (1:9) also indicates that people from Galilee could come to John regardless of the geographical location of his ministry.[223] In addition, if we consider Mark's exaggerated expression, "all (πᾶσα, πάντες)" the people in 1:5, there is no reason not to mention crowds from other regions receiving

---

220. In his work *Jewish War*, Josephus suggests the detailed delineation of the boundaries of Galilee, dividing Galilee into two areas, the Upper and Lower Galilee: "Now Phoenicia and Syria encompass about the Galilee, which are two, and called the Upper Galilee and the Lower . . . they are bounded on the south with Samaria and Scythopolis, as far as the river Jordan; on the east with Hippene and Gadaris, and also with Gaulanitis, and the borders of the kingdom of Agrippa; its northern parts are bounded by Tyre, and the country of the Tyrians" (Josephus, *War* 3:35–40). Though Mark's geographical description of Galilee is not detailed in comparison with that of Josephus, their thoughts on general outline of geography of Palestine and its surrounding regions are not different to each other.

221. Boring, *Mark*, 50.

222. France, *Gospel of Mark*, 67.

223. France, *Gospel of Mark*, 67. France notes that "it has the effect of making the appearance of Jesus ἀπὸ Ναζαρὲτ τῆς Γαλιλαίας in v. 9 the more striking; he is not part of the Judean crowd, but a stranger from the far north."

John's baptism. It can be concluded, therefore, that Mark deliberately limits John's ministry to Judea and Jerusalem in order to present a geographical and ethnic contrast between John's ministry and that of Jesus.

The range of Jesus' ministry is vast and boundless in terms of geography and ethnicity, and Galilee serves as the central place for his missional movement. Though the starting point of his ministry was Galilee (1:14) and his incipient ministry focused on Galilee (1:39), his fame spread widely beyond Galilee in every direction—to Judea, Jerusalem, Idumea, and the regions across the Jordan and around Tyre and Sidon—and those who heard about him came to Galilee (3:7–8).[224] In his later Galilean ministry, Jesus himself attempted to take a journey into Gentile territories (4:35—9:50) and carried out mighty works. As Malbon says, Galilee was "the gathering place for the various multitudes (3:7–8) as well as the home base for Jesus' foreign travel."[225] Galilee, then, was not only the starting point of Jesus' ministry but also the outpost of his mission to the Gentiles.

Mark lists regions and cities in 3:7–8, and their order reflects a division between Jewish and Gentile territories:[226] "Jesus departed with his disciples to the sea and a great multitude from Galilee followed him; hearing all the things that he was doing, a great multitude came to him from Judea, Jerusalem, Idumea, beyond Jordan, and the region around Tyre and Sidon." The first three regions (Galilee, Judea, and Jerusalem) are part of Jewish territory, while the latter four regions (Idumea, beyond Jordan, and the region around Tyre and Sidon) are a part of Gentile territory. In these verses, Mark depicts Galilee as the center of these surrounding regions: Judea and Jerusalem locate to the south, Idumea even father to the south, the land beyond Jordan to the east, and the regions around Tyre and Sidon to north—to the west of Galilee is the Mediterranean Sea.[227]

---

224. Though Mark begins to portray Jesus' ministry in Galilee after the arrest of John the Baptist (1:14), John's Gospel records Jesus' ministry in Judea before the arrest of John the Baptist (3:24). In John's account, John the Baptist introduced Jesus as the Lamb of God at Bethany on the other side of the Jordan (1:28–29) and two of John's disciples followed Jesus (vv. 35–39). In the Passover, Jesus cleared the temple and performed miracles in Jerusalem, in which Jesus was known to many people (2:13–23). Jesus went into the Judean countryside and baptized at Aenon near Salem, where John the Baptist also was baptizing (3:22–23). Jesus' fame might therefore spread not only to the Judeans, but also to those who came from outside of Judea to keep the Passover.

225. Malbon, *Narrative Space*, 43.

226. Freyne, "Geography of Restoration," 305.

227. Boring, *Mark*, 97–98. Malbon describes the regions of Judea and Jerusalem as west of Galilee in order to emphasize the centrality of Galilee or to highlight the contrast between the west as Jewish territory and the east as Gentile territory: "After referring to a multitude following Jesus from Galilee, the narrator refers to a multitude coming from Judea and Jerusalem (west), and from Idumea (south), beyond the Jordan

Galilee functions as a central base from which Jesus could easily access regions in all directions, especially Gentile regions. Three distinct times, Jesus started a journey from Galilee to Gentile territory and then came back to Galilee again. The first journey to a Gentile region led across the sea toward the east side of the Sea of Galilee, the region of the Garasenes near Decapolis (5:1–20). The second was an overland route—the second attempt at travelling eastward across the sea was aborted (6:45–52)—that took Jesus northwest from Galilee to the vicinity of Tyre and then on a roundabout path through Sidon toward the Sea of Galilee in the midst of the region of the Decapolis (7:24—8:9). The third was a sea-crossing and overland tour to the area northeast of Galilee, covering first Bethsaida, then the villages around Caesarea Philippi, and up to a high mountain (8:22—9:29).

Jesus encountered no obstacles to prevent him from going into Gentile territory: "movement into gentile regions seems relaxed and informal."[228] His repeated crossings of the Sea of Galilee, moving both west and east, and his free journeys into the Gentile regions of the north imply that easy contact was possible between the Jews and the Gentiles in spite of their ethnic and religious divisions.[229] Freyne claims that "the most striking feature of Mark's presentation is the fact that, though Jewish in its overall ethos, it allowed for easy contact with the surrounding regions."[230] Jesus' easy crossing of the physical boundaries between Jewish and Gentile territories indicates that Galilee was an open area with porous boundaries.[231] In addition, his free intercourse with the Gentiles in his travels implies that he worked by going beyond the social, cultural, and religious boundaries between the Jews and the Gentiles.[232] For all these reasons, Galilee was the place where

---

(east), and Tyre and Sidon (north). Galilee and Judea constitute the Jewish homeland, and the other regions and cities establish the boundaries of the foreign regions surrounding the Jewish homeland." See Malbon, *Narrative Space*, 42.

228. Freyne, *Galilee, Jesus, and the Gospels*, 35.
229. Freyne, *Galilee, Jesus, and the Gospels*, 40–41.
230. Freyne, *Galilee, Jesus, and the Gospels*, 50.
231. Freyne, *Galilee, Jesus, and the Gospels*, 54–59.
232. Rhoads explains social boundaries in terms of Jesus' network for mission: "In the narrative, the boundary definition of the Jesus network effectively cuts across all other boundaries for identifying God's people, especially those set by the authorities of Israelite society. The authorities as portrayed in Mark's story have set different boundaries, according to their interpretation of God's will, as the means to determine who is with God and who is against God: clean/unclean; Jew/Gentile; those who follow the traditions of the elders/those who do not; God's land/Gentile land; the 'righteous' according to the Law/the 'sinners.' The Jesus network cuts across all these traditional boundary lines: village of origin, ties of ancestry, family, class, nationality, religious belief and practice, and ascribed power roles." See Rhoads, *Reading Mark*, 110–11.

Jesus began his missional movement and it continued to serve as the home base from which he traveled into Gentile territory, tearing down obstacles between the Jews and the Gentiles.[233]

Conclusion

In this study, Markan spatial presentation of Galilee was explored in three aspects. First, Mark describes Galilee as having a Jewish religous ethos. The Galileans were influenced and ruled by the Judeans whose authority came from the temple and Jerusalem. This effect is seen in ethnic, cultural, and religious aspects. Despite the strong influence of the southern power, however, the Galileans were ready to accept the order and values of the new world, which would be different from that of the temple and Jerusalem.

Second, social conflict centers on opposing spaces: Galilee versus Jerusalem, villages versus cities. In Mark's narrative, the Galileans welcomed Jesus' teaching and mighty works as new authority that weakened the power of Jerusalem. Mark also portrays Jesus' ministry against the background of rural terrain, not in the setting of cities. Jesus did not perform significant ministries in the cities, which stood for vested interests and the power of the elites. Rather, he went about among the villages, teaching people and sending out his disciples to do ministry. Jesus' ministry is positively portrayed in Galilee and the villages, not in Jerusalem and the cities. In Galilee and its vicinity, Jesus' missional movement focusing on villages and rural areas provides a new spatial configuration for the kingdom of God, which is different from the existing spatial configuration established by Jerusalem and cities.

Third, Galilee is depicted as both the center toward which people from every direction gathered to see Jesus and the outpost from which he journeyed to meet them. In addition, Jesus' travels and ministry between Galilee and Gentile territory demonstrate the breaking down of barriers between the Jews and Gentiles. Galilee therefore serves as the matrix where Jesus' missional movement could successfully develop.

---

233. Looking at Jesus' travels beyond Galilee and exploring the Gentile countries and cities in the surrounding area will expand and enrich our knowledge of Jesus' ministry. Moxnes points out the lack of studies on the neighboring regions of Galilee and emphasizes the significance of these areas as follows: "To put it another way, scholars have focused on the road between Galilee and Jerusalem but have overlooked the much closer areas to the North, East, and South, that are all within easy walking distance from the hills overlooking the Sea of Galilee. . . . It is at least possible that closer studies of these areas and the interrelations between them and Galilee, will provide a broader picture of the context of the Galileans and also of Jesus." See Moxnes, "Construction of Galilee—Part II," 74.

chapter 3

Geographical Space
Structural Analysis of Mark 4:35—8:21

IN THE PREVIOUS CHAPTER, I discussed Markan scholarship on locality and the relationship between Galilee and Jerusalem, exploring how Mark understood and presented social space in his Gospel. In this chapter, I will perform a structural analysis of Mark 4:35—8:21 with an eye toward the narrative presentation of geographical space. I will first introduce various structural analyses of Mark 4–8 and then suggest my narrative structure based on Mark's geographical arrangement, literary techniques, and boat and bread motifs. In doing so, I will show how Mark's spatial presentation achieves his theological purposes.

Survey of Previous Structural Analyses of Mark 4–8

Scholars have held diverse opinions on the literary structure and theological themes of Mark 4–8.[1] In his 1901 book, *The Messianic Secret*, Wrede argues that Mark does not display a well-organized structure because he does not systematically arrange his historical traditions but rather connects them to display his own "dogmatic or semi-dogmatic ideas": "In actual fact he [Mark] did not think through from one point in his presentation to the next."[2] In addition, since it is hard to find any pattern of arrangement that is able to show segments containing several minimal units, Wrede denies the presence of segmentation in Mark's literary structure. Elsewhere in

---

1. For a summary of structural analyses of Mark 4–8, see Fowler, *Loaves and Fishes*, 5–42.

2. Wrede, *Messianic Secret*, 129–32.

Markan scholarship, however, there have been many attempts to analyze the structure by finding the pattern of arrangement, source distinction, or segmentation.[3]

Structure Based on Pre-Markan Sources

On the basis of the assumption of pre-Markan sources, scholars have attempted to discover cyclic patterns, especially of two parallel cycles or catenae. Two feeding stories, which show an explicit doublet, provides a ground for proposing various cyclic patterns. By including one or both of the feeding miracles in the structure, some have tried to find the cyclic patterns in Mark 6–8, others in Mark 4–6, and still others in Mark 4–8.[4]

Many scholars have theorized a cyclic pattern in Mark 6–8: Mark 6:31—7:37 was repeated in 8:1–26(30).[5] In his 1942 article, "A Marcan

---

3. See Petersen, "Composition of Mark 4:1–8:26," 192–93. Petersen enumerates various proposals on the pattern of arrangement: "Proposals range from the modest arguments of H.-W. Kuhn to the immoderate assertions of R. Pesch, although breaks in chaps. three and six, as noted earlier, still result. Variety is also a hallmark of yet other approaches, such as the focus on intrinsic formal (triadic) patterns by Alfaric, Lohmeyer, Albertz, and Schweizer, on the extrinsically oriented ring composition suggested in an early work by Pesch and in a new one by F. G. Lang, on the compositional influence of liturgical calendars (Bowman; Carrington), and on OT typology (Farrer). And geography, whether simple (Marxsen) or complex (Kümel), still has its advocates."

4. Fowler, *Loaves and Fishes*, 5–6.

5. The parallelism between Mark 6:30—7:37 and 8:1–26(30), on the accounts of the two feeding miracles, has long been recognized. Van Oyen presents a well-summarized survey of the history of interpretation of the doublet structure in these two pericopae in terms of pre-Markan miracle cycles (Van Oyen, *Interpretation of the Feeding Miracles*, 1–19). I will shortly introduce Van Oyen's survey.

In the nineteenth century, Weizsäcker (*Untersuchungen über die evangelische Geschichte*, 69–70) believed that the feeding miracle was preserved twice in the oral tradition and the two feeding miracles in Mark were located at the beginning of two paricopae, which show a cyclic pattern in a shared thematic parallel (Weizsäcker, *Untersuchungen über die evangelische Geschichte*, 69–70).

6:33–44	Jesus' benefactions	8:1–10
7:1–23	opposition of the Pharisees	8:11–13
7:24–30	orientation towards the Gentiles	8:14–21
7:31–37	miracles as the breakthrough of Jesus' power	8:22–26

Soden followed Weizsäcker, suggesting three parallels in the two cycles: miracles of the loaves (6:31–44; 8:1–10); conflict stories (7:1–23; 8:11–13); and healing (7:31–37; 8:22–26) (Soden, "Das Interesse des apostolischen Zeitalters an der evangelischen Geschichte," 147–51).

Arguing for a doublet cycle, Volkmar provided a different structure in terms of the

Doublet: Mark vi.31–vii.37, and viii.1–26," Jenkins suggests a doublet of Mark 6:31–8:26, appealing to verbal agreement.[6] He provides a table that shows distinctive and common features of each parallel unit as follows:

---

scope of pericopae (6:1—7:23; 7:24—8:26) and the method of distinction. According to Volkmar, the main theme of 6:1–8:26, the "universality of Jesus' mission," is approached as a dialectic between thesis (Israel: 6:1—7:23) and antithesis (opposition to Israel: 7:24—8:26). See Volkmar, *Marcus und die Synopse der Evangelien*, 341–42.

6:1–13	Jesus repudiated; mission disc.	7:24–37	Jesus with the Gentiles
6:14–29	Interruption	8:1–3	interruption: three days
6:30–52	loaves, lake, incomprehension	8:1–13	loaves, crossings, sings
6:53—7:23	Helping everywhere; (un)clean	8:14–26	Blindness of the disciples

In the twentieth century, scholars continued to discuss the parallelism between 6:30—7:37 and 8:1–26(30), suggesting a threefold to sixfold parallel. See Weiss, *Das älteste Evangelium*, 204–26; Wellhausen, *Das Evangelium Marci*, 52–65; Meyer, *Ursprung und Anfänge des Christentums*, 125; Jenkins, "Marcan Doublet," 87–111; Schmid, *Das Evangelium Nach Markus*, 147–48; Best, *Temptation and the Passion*, 120; Haenchen, *Der Weg Jesu*, 283–84; Pesch, *Naherwartungen*, 60–62; Perrin, *New Testament*, 239; Barnwell, *Our Story According to St. Mark*, 146.

According to Taylor, the general agreement on the parallel structure is as follows (Taylor, *Gospel According to St. Mark*, 628):

1. The Feeding of the Five Thousand.	1. The Feeding of the Four Thousand.
2. The Crossing and Landing.	2. The Crossing and Landing.
3. The Controversy with the Pharisees about Defilement.	3. The Controversy with the Pharisees about Signs.
4. The Syro-Phoenician Woman (The Children's Bread).	4. The Mystery of the Loaves (The Leaven of the Pharisees).
5. The Healing of the Deaf and Mute.	5. The Healing of the Blind Man.

With regard to "the motif of understanding," Lane proposed two cycles, both of which begin with a feeding and end with a confession of faith (6:31—7:37 and 8:1–30) (Lane, *Gospel According to Mark*, 269).

Ch. 6:31–44	Feeding of the Multitude	Ch. 8:1–9
Ch. 6:45–56	Crossing of the Sea and Landing	Ch. 8:10
Ch. 7:1–23	Conflict with the Pharisees	Ch. 8:11–13
Ch. 7:24–30	Conversation about Bread	Ch. 8:14–21
Ch. 7:31–36	Healing	Ch. 8:22–26
Ch. 7:37	Confession of Faith	Ch. 8:27–30

6. Jenkins, "Marcan Doublet," 87–111. Though many have suggested the parallelism between 6:31—7:37 and 8:1–26(30), detailed explanations are relatively scanty. Jenkins presents an exhaustive explanation for this doublet structure. See Fowler, *Loaves and Fishes*, 7. In this study, I will argue against a doublet structure between these two pericopae, discussing Jenkins's hypothesis.

Word	Mark A Distinctive Features	Mark A/B Common Features	Mark B Distinctive Features	Word
220	I. 6:31–44 Jews Shepherdless disciples to Jesus 5 loaves 2 fishes glance to heaven 12 *kophinoi* 5,000	I. DESERT FEEDING *Jesus, disciples* and *crowd* in *desert place*; *crowd excites Jesus' pity*; *Jesus and disciples* discuss *how to feed crowd*; *bread and fish* produced, *blessed, broken, distributed*; *baskets filled with* surplus pieces; thousands of people	I. 8:1–9a Gentiles? Decapolis? 3 days, no food Jesus to disciples 7 loaves few 'fishlets' 7 *spurides* about 4,000	125
138	II. 6:45–52 Jesus walks on the water	II. VOYAGE ACROSS LAKE	II. 8:9b–10a	13
72	III. 6:53–56 Gennesaret Summary	III. ARRIVAL	III. 8:10b "Dalmanoutha"	5
395	IV. 7:1–23 Scribes from Jerusalem Hand-washing Korban What defiles	IV. CONFLICT WITH AUTHORITIES *Pharisees*	IV. 8:11–12 Sign from Heaven	38
130	V. 7:23–30 Tyre Syro-Phoenician (misplaced)	V. AVOIDING REALM OF ANTIPAS *Rebuke*	V. 8:13–21 Other side warning: remember loaves	108

113	VI. 7:31–37 deaf-stutterer "ephphatha"	VI. HEALING EAST OF LAKE *Healing privately by spitting* *Command to tell no one*	VI. 8:22–26 blind man, men as trees	
1032	Total		Total	369[A]

A. Jenkins, "Marcan Doublet," 91.

Jenkins identifies six similar stories that are arranged in the same order.[7] He claims that the two sections (6:31—7:37 and 8:1–26) form a doublet in their similarities and differences.[8] Similarities, including verbal agreements, contents, and the same order of events, suggest the presence of a doublet;[9] dissimilarities also evince a doublet. Jenkins asserts that the stories had been changed as the tradition developed, and he proposes five criteria to identify how they were changed during transmission.

> But it may be said with some repeated from time to time, or passed on to be repeated by others (a) it tends to get shorter the more it is repeated, or handed on; (b) displacements and omissions occur as well as additions which may be inferred from the original story or which make it more satisfactory to the mentality of the story-teller; (c) the story remains recognizably the same story; (d) the most stable elements of the story are those which arouse specific interests; (e) the least stable are details such as names (especially foreign names) and numbers.[10]

On the basis of these criteria, Jenkins suggests that 8:1–26 was treated and altered more than 6:31—7:37 in the process of oral transmission.[11] The length of the second sequence is one third of the first sequence. The first sequence is more preserved and less influenced by the community than the second sequence. In addition, the differences in details such as "names,

---

7. Jenkins, "Marcan Doublet," 90.
8. Jenkins, "Marcan Doublet," 92–93.
9. Jenkins, "Marcan Doublet," 92–93. Jenkins argues that the feeding miracle did not repeat historically since the disciples, who had experienced the miracles of the five thousand feeding, could not have questioned Jesus about the problem of the lack of food at the event of feeding the four thousand in 8:4 ("His disciples replied, 'How can one feed these people with bread here in the desert?'"). Therefore, one of two feeding miracles was made by following the other, forming a doublet.
10. Jenkins, "Marcan Doublet," 89.
11. Jenkins, "Marcan Doublet," 92–93.

numbers, motives, times" support the presence of a doublet rather than counter it.[12]

With the exception of the two feeding stories, however, I do not believe that these parallels evince a doublet. Though Jenkins claims that the parallel stories are matched as a doublet form, they simply correspond to each other in terms of the similarities of general contents, locales, characters, or motifs.[13] The common features of stories II (Mark A [6:45–52] vs. Mark B [8:9b–10a]; Voyage Across the Lake) and III (Mark A [6:53–56] vs. Mark B [8:10b]; Arrival) are related solely to Jesus' itinerary pattern (sea-crossing), not to shared events. The reason for the shortened stories in Mark B II and III is not the many repetitions in the process of transmission, but Mark's effort to describe Jesus' voyage simply. There is no apparent evidence that these corresponding stories show the characteristics of a doublet. In addition, Jenkins does not explain the absence of a second boat trip in Mark A, which must correspond to the second boat trip in 8:13 of Mark B.[14]

Jenkins argues that the descriptions of locales in Mark A are more historically accurate than those in Mark B and so Dalmanutha in Mark B III (8:10b) is a "memory-corruption of Gennesaret" in Mark A III (6:53).[15] In addition, if the names in a narrative are not familiar, they might be omitted or changed into "unrecognizable, especially foreign names."[16] However, the argument that Dalmanutha was an unexpectedly changed name due to its unfamiliarity is not acceptable because there was no reason for Mark to record a cryptic name instead of another, more familiar name.[17] It is more probable to assume that mysterious names are original, because they might have been changed into more familiar names in the process of tradition.[18]

12. Jenkins, "Marcan Doublet," 92.
13. Fowler, *Loaves and Fishes*, 9.
14. Jenkins, "Marcan Doublet," 105.
15. Jenkins, "Marcan Doublet," 103.
16. Jenkins, "Marcan Doublet," 102

17. The place-name Dalmanutha is completely unknown outside of this reference. It is conjectured to be the same as Magadan in the parallel passage Matt 15:39. This assumption is not reliable, however, because Magadan is located on the eastern side of the Sea of Galilee and Mark describes Dalmanutha as situated on the western side of the sea. See Lane, *Gospel According to Mark*, 271. Another option is Magdala, which is found as a textual variant in Matthew and is located at the western side of the sea. As Dalmanutha is derived from an Aramaic term for "wall," and Magdala from an Aramaic term for "tower," possibly meaning "walled city," Dalmanutha may be identified with Magdala. See Donahue and Harrington, *Gospel of Mark*, 245–46; Lane, *Gospel According to Mark*, 271. As we have no idea of where it was located, however, "there is no value in mere speculation" (France, *Gospel of Mark*, 309).

18. Guelich argues that Dalmanuth was not a Markan corruption in transmission,

As Gundry points out, the geographical designation of Dalmanutha not only supports tradition, but also historicity: "For who would insert a regional name of opaque reference?"[19] In addition, the contents and lengths of Mark B II and III are too short to be compared with Mark A II and III in the light of a doublet.

In the stories IV (Mark A [7:1–23] vs. Mark B [8:11–12]; Conflicts with Authorities), there are similarities in characters (Pharisees) and situations (conflicts). These two stories are, however, difficult to pair as a doublet because Mark A IV has the form of Jesus' long saying containing the instruction of clean and unclean, but Mark B IV is Jesus' simple response to Pharisees' asking for a sign from heaven. In terms of both content and length, they cannot be regarded as a doublet.

As regards the stories V (Mark A [7:24–30] vs. Mark B [8:13–21]; Avoiding Realm of Antipas), Jenkins claims that a passage was misplaced because 6:51–52 (Mark A II; the motif of "the hardened heart") must have been placed in Mark A V in order to correspond to Mark B V's hardened heart motif (8:17–18).[20] He also insists that the route in 7:31 showing Jesus' avoidance of Antipas's territory might be contained in both stories of Mark A V and Mark B V, but was misplaced in Mark A V and lost in Mark B V.[21] However, Jenkins tries too hard to fit these stories into a doublet. The motif of the hardened heart in 6:51–52 fits better with Jesus' walking on the sea (Mark A II) than with the Syrophoenician woman's daughter (Mark A V), and the location of 7:31 in the text is right to show Jesus' overland journey.

In relation to topographical referents of the stories VI, Jenkins suggests that Bethsaida in 8:22, despite its location in Mark B's section, may not be the corrupted-name but rather the historically accurate name due to the

---

but was preserved in pre-Markan tradition: "Since Mark does not create specific place names elsewhere in his redaction and since one is more likely to use a well-known rather than a rare place name when creating a scene, this geographical reference most likely belongs to a pre-Markan tradition" (Guelich, *Mark 1–8:26*, 413). See also Schmid, *Das Evangelium nach Markus*, 210; Pesch, *Das Markusevangelium 1:1–8:26*, 405–6; Fowler, *Loaves and Fishes*, 51–53.

19. Gundry, *Mark*, 403. Gundry postulates the reason for the obscurity of the place name Dalmanutha as follows: "Presumably Dalmanutha was somewhat recognizable at one time, but not so much as to have made its way into extant literature, and therefore probably not so much as to have come to mind for the fabrication of an inauthentic itinerary." For the reason nothing is known about Dalmanutha, France assumes that "there were small fishing villages along the lake which are not otherwise recorded and which have left no trace in later place names" (France, *Gospel of Mark*, 309).

20. Jenkins, "Marcan Doublet," 105.

21. Jenkins, "Marcan Doublet," 105.

familiarity of tradition.[22] Though he admits the possibility that Bethsaida in 8:22 was located "through misplacement" of the destination of Jesus' voyage in 6:45 of Mark A II (Jesus' walking on the sea; 6:45–52), he argues that it is more probable to suppose that the place-name Bethsaida was well preserved in the process of tradition, because Bethsaida was familiar to those who lived outside of Palestine. For instance, a feeding miracle occurs at Bethsaida in Luke, and Bethsaida is described as Philip's hometown in John, which originated from Asia Minor. Names such as Bethsaida, therefore, could be suitable due to familiarity to the Markan community.[23] However, this suggestion also shows lack of evidence because we cannot be sure whether or not Bethsaida was a familiar name to those who read or heard Mark.[24]

Jenkins's attempt to show a doublet between 6:31—7:37 and 8:1–26 is riddled with holes and inconsistencies. He employs form- and redaction-critical methods to prove a doublet, but in so doing he modifies or relocates many parts of the text with uncertain assumptions and criteria. In addition, as Fowler points out, Jenkins postulates a doublet based not on sameness between the paralleled stories in all aspects of vocabulary, plot, and characters, but on "the point of contact between matched elements," such as "a repeated motif, overlapping sets of characters, a common geographical locale, and the recurrence of a particular healing technique."[25] Jenkins's arguments for the presence of a doublet are therefore unpersuasive: he only shows Mark's literary use of a cyclic pattern by noticing the repeated motifs and characters, and especially by tracing the circle of Jesus' geographical movement (Mark II, III, V, and VI). Though Jenkins doubts the accuracy of Mark's geographical description due to memory-corruption of place-names, he tries to discover a cyclic pattern in Jesus' geographical movement running though Mark 6–8.

In his 1976 commentary, *Das Markusevangelium 1. Teil: Einleitung und Kommentar zu Kap. 1:1–8:26*, Rudolf Pesch proposes a cyclic pattern of miracle stories in pre-Markan materials.[26] He insists that Mark received

22. Jenkins, "Marcan Doublet," 108–9.

23. Jenkins, "Marcan Doublet," 109.

24. It is widely agreed that Mark's audience was composed mainly of Gentile Christians, likely in Rome. Mark is assumed to have been written to a Roman audience because of its "Latinisms," "translation of Aramaic expressions," and "explanation of Jewish customs." See Carson and Moo, *Introduction to the New Testament*, 182–83. Therefore, the argument that Mark's audience was familiar to the place-name, Bethsaida, is not persuasive, because they were presumably unfamiliar with Jewish geography and customs.

25. Fowler, *Loaves and Fishes*, 8–9.

26. Pesch, *Das Markusevangelium 1–8:26*, 277–81. Keck argues that 3:7ab, 9, 10 came from "Urtext," which may be discovered similarly in 4:35–41; 5:1–20, 21–43;

a series of miracles (3:7—6:56) that described Jesus as the eschatological prophet who delivered the people of God from distress. This miracle collection shows a chiastic structure with an intercalation (*Schachtelung*) as follows:

> A: Summary (3:7-12)—a tremendous gathering to the healer and exorcist, Jesus.
>> B: Stilling of the storm (4:35-41)—greater than Jonah; exorcistic power over wind and sea like Yahweh.
>>> C: Healing of the Gerasene demoniac (5:1-20)—Son of the Most High God; the exorcistic conqueror of heathen disorder.
>>>> D: Healing of a woman with a hemorrhage and resurrection of Jairus's daughter (5:21-43)—greater than Elijah/Elisha; power over sickness and death.
>>> C^1: Feeding of the five thousand (6:32-44)—the endtime shepherd of Israel: giver of eschatological fullness.
>> B^1: Walking on the sea (6:45-51)—In Jesus Yahweh has appeared.
> A^1: Summary (6:53-56)—a tremendous gathering to the healer who brings salvation in all directions.[27]

Pesch regards Mark as a conservertive redactor and thinks that the literary technique of intercalation does not come from Mark himself, but from a pre-Markan redactor. In the pre-Markan stage, the miracle stories already existed as a collection in connection to the seafaring imagery.[28] The boat motif plays the role of connecting these stories and making the boundary of the miracle collection. Pesch, however, ignores the fact that the boat journey does not end at 6:56, but continues to 8:21.[29] He excludes 8:1-21

6:31-52, and 6:53-56 with regard to "the boat and the idea of touching Jesus" (Keck, "Mark 3:7-12 and Mark's Christology," 341-48). Guelich states that Keck's view may serve as a ground for Pesch's argument of the cyclic structure of miracle stories in that the summary of Jesus' healing ministry in 3:7-12 is in parallel with the healing summary in 6:53-56 (Guelich, *Mark 1–8:26*, 143). Kuhn also proposes a similar structure of a pre-Markan collection in 3:7—6:56, suggesting 3:7-12 and 6:53-56 as the parallel summaries in this pericope (Kuhn, *Ältere Sammlungen im Markusevangelium*, 191–213).

27. Pesch, *Das Markusevangelium 1:1–8:26*, 279. English translation mine.
28. Pesch, *Das Markusevangelium 1:1–8:26*, 278.
29. Gundry, *Mark*, 160–61. Gundry also argues that 3:7-12 is unlikely to serve as "the introduction to a pre-Markan collection of miracle stories." Rather, "from the start Jesus' withdrawal to the sea was related to the conspiracy against his life (3:6)" and "the following statements summarize according to tradition what occurs at the present time and place on account of what he has been doing earlier and elsewhere."

on the basis that it belongs to the material of Markan redaction rather than pre-Markan redaction, but Fowler questions Pesch's distinction between Markan redaction and pre-Markan redaction by considering the boat motif: "how is one to distinguish between the admittedly *Markan* redactional use of the boat motif and the *pre-Markan redactional* use of the motif?"[30] Pesch does not provide reasonable grounds for limiting the boat motif to 6:56. In addition, we cannot neglect the fact that the parallels in 3:7—6:56 extend to Mark 8 (e.g., the explicit parallel between the feedings of five and four thousand in 6:45–52 and 8:1–10).[31]

Those who argue for a cyclic pattern in Mark 3(4)–6 and 6–8 under the assumption of a pre-Markan collection of miracle stories face a problem in that the parallels which compose a cyclic pattern cannot be found only on each side, 3(4)–6 and 6–8. Rather, they should be discovered in the integrative section, 3(4)–8. Fowler properly points out the weakness of the hypotheses of pre-Markan cycles on each side as follows:

> There is an intersection in the data examined in the attempts to find pre-Markan cycles behind Mark 4–6 and 6–8. The cycles found in Mark 4–6 overlap with those of Mark 6–8, so one cannot legitimately pursue either enterprise in isolation from the other.[32]

Another attempt to theorize a cyclic pattern of miracle stories has focused on Mark 4–8. In his 1970 article, "Toward the Isolation of Pre-Markan

---

30. Fowler, *Loaves and Fishes*, 18. Neirynck also points out the difficulty of distinguishing between Markan and pre-Markan redaction, simply investigating the vocabulary as regards a boat itinerary (Neirynck, "L'Évangile de Marc," 167). I argue the boat motif in relation to Jesus' travel to other regions begins with 4:35 and ends at 8:21. In 1:19–20, a boat simply serves as a background for the workplace of James and John; in 3:9, a boat is used to keep the people from crowding Jesus; in 4:1, a boat is employed for Jesus to teach toward the crowd along the seashore. The sea-crossings by a boat appear in 4:35—8:21.

31. Though Keck, Pesch, and Kuhn recognize the parallelism between the two feeding miracles, they do not give consequence to this parallelism, excluding it in their cycles. One of the reasons to neglect the two feeding miracles and their significance is to regard "one a copy of the other" in a different genre. As Fowler says, "it will not suffice to deny, as Keck, Pesch, and Kuhn have done, a complete correspondence between 6:30—7:37 and 8:1–26, acknowledge nevertheless the parallel feeding stories, and proceed to look elsewhere (e.g., Mark 4–6) for a pre-Markan cycle" (Fowler, *Loaves and Fishes*, 22–23). Marcus states that those who argue for the pre-Markan collection in 3:7–6:56 (e.g., Keck and Pesch) neglect "the parallels between some of the Markan passages and John 6, since these parallels extend into the doublet in Mark 8, suggesting that if there was a pre-Markan source, it did not end at 6:56." He demonstrates that Mark 6:34—8:33 is in parallel with John 6:1–71. See Marcus, *Mark 1-8*, 256.

32. Fowler, *Loaves and Fishes*, 23.

Miracle Catenae," Achtemeier studies the structure of Mark 4:35—8:26 with the assumption of "a pre-Markan cycle of miracles."[33] He argues for "a two-fold source" displayed in doublets such as two sea miracles, two feeding episodes, two healings accompanied by spitting, and so on. Such repetition, then, forms the basis of Mark's characteristic literary style and produces a structural framework. Achtemeier suggests two groups of miracle stories in the form of two catenae in 4:35—6:44 and 6:45—8:26. Though they do not show exact parallelism,[34] these two groups share a similar pattern in terms of the arrangement of episodes.

Achtemeier performs his study in two stages, first examining the materials not related to miracle stories and then exploring the miracles stories themselves.[35] These investigations are done by identifying evidence of Markan editorial activity. Among the non-miraculous materials, only the material about the death of John the Baptist (6:17–29), in which few editorial activities appear, circulated independently in its present form in the pre-Markan tradition.[36] Other materials were subject to Markan editorial activity, collected and modified to form the present arrangement.

Achtemeier pays attention to ten miracle stories in Mark 4:35—8:26 and argues that they were circulated "in the form of two catenae, identical in arrangement (sea miracle, three healing miracles, and a feeding miracle) but not in content."[37] He proposes the following structure:

---

33. Achtemeier, "Toward the Isolation," 265–91. Schmidt introduces the tradition of two cycles in Mark 4–8 as follows: "There may also have been early collections of miracle stories, such as a source for the three miracles in Mark 5. It is also noteworthy that they are preceded by a sea-crossing story (4:35–41) and followed eventually by a feeding story (6:35–44). Mark is unique in presenting a repetition of this cycle (6:47–52; 7:24—8:10). Scholarly opinion differs on whether there were one or more such cycles circulating earlier than Mark, or if the author of Mark is responsible for developing them. The shape of these collections seems influenced by the exodus tradition, featuring sea-crossing and feeding stories, and by the collection of Elijah and Elisha stories (1 Kings 17–19; 2 Kings 1–9)." See Schmidt, *Gospel of Mark*, 9.

34. Achtemeier enumerates the discordant parts that do not show parallelism between the two cycles: "In the first cycle, the healings (5:1–43) precede the account of Jesus' preaching (6:1–6), whereas in the second block, the preaching and disputes (7:1–23) occur in the midst of the healings (6:53–56, 7:24–37). The material on John the Baptist in the first cycle has no counterpart in the second, whereas the material at the end of the second grouping (8:11–21) has no counterpart in the first. And the healing at Bethsaida (8:22–26) ends the second section in a way quite unlike the ending of the first block (with a feeding, 6:34–44)." See Achtemeier, "Toward the Isolation," 265.

35. Achtemeier, "Toward the Isolation," 266.

36. Achtemeier, "Toward the Isolation," 270, 274.

37. Achtemeier, "Toward the Isolation," 290.

Catena I	Catena II
4:35–5:43; 6:34–44 (with 4:35; 5:21c; 5:43a; and 6:34bc as probably editorial, and 5:24 and 6:35b as clearly editorial)	6:45–51; 8:22–26; 7:24b–30, 32–37; 8:1–10 (with 6:45c, 50c, 51b; 7:36; and 8:1a as editorial)
Stilling of the Storm (4:33–41)	Jesus Walks on the Sea (6:45–51)
The Gerasene Demoniac (5:1–20)	The Blind Man of Bethsaida (8:22–26)
The Woman with a Hemorrhage (5:25–34)	The Syrophoenician Woman (7:24b–30)
Jairus's Daughter (5:21–23, 35–43)	The Deaf-Mute (7:32–37)
Feeding of the 5,000 (6:34–44, 53)	Feeding of the 4,000 (8:1–10)[A]

A. Achtemeier, "Toward the Isolation," 291.

In terms of the order in these two catenae, two stories were rearranged by Mark. First, the woman with a hemorrhage (5:25–34) was placed before Jairus's daughter (5:21–23, 35–43) in the pre-Markan cycle. These two stories, which are presently combined as an intercalation structure, were separated in the original form. They differ in their literary and linguistic aspects: while the former story uses the historical present tense and short sentences with comparatively few participles, the latter employs the aorist and imperfect tense and longer sentences with repeated participles.[38] Mark combined these two stories into one by inserting the woman with a hemorrhage into the middle of the story about Jairus's daughter.[39] Achtemeier argues that the woman with a hemorrhage preceded Jairus's daughter in the original order of the pre-Markan cycle. Mark 5:21ab is the introductory part of the story of the woman with a hemorrhage, and the same phrase, "a large crowd" (ὄχλος πολύς), is repeated in v. 24 as the backdrop of reintroduction of this story. On the other hand, v. 21c serves as the introduction of Jairus's daughter.[40] The Markan editorial activity of v. 21ab and v. 21c therefore reflects the original order of these two stories: in the light of the order of v. 21ab and v. 21c, the woman with a hemorrhage connected to 21ab precedes Jairus's daughter connected to 21c.

Second, Achtemeier claims that the blind man at Bethsaida (8:22–26) was placed right after Jesus' walking on the sea (6:45–51) in the second

---

38. Achtemeier, "Toward the Isolation," 277.

39. Achtemeier, "Toward the Isolation," 277–78. Achtemeier claims that there is no theological intention in this intercalation structure: "Nor is there any need for this kind of framework for the story of the woman with the flow of blood. The account is complete in itself and gains little from its present position, either in terms of necessary information or theological point, which could not be gotten were the story set in another framework. There is no compelling reason, then, why the stories had to be combined by the tradition in order for either of them to be understood or valued."

40. Achtemeier, "Toward the Isolation," 278.

catena, corresponding to the Gerasene demoniac (5:1–20) in the first. According to Achtemeier, the geographical description in 8:22, "and they came to Bethsaida" (καὶ ἔρχονται εἰς Βηθσαϊδάν), provides the key to unlock the original order of pre-Markan cycle.[41] The place-name Bethsaida appears two times in Mark (6:45; 8:22). The first is Jesus' voyage toward Bethsaida (6:45), which strangely ends with the arrival at Gennesaret (6:53);[42] the second is Jesus' arrival at Bethsaida (8:22), which serves as the introduction to the blind man at Bethsaida. The destination of Jesus' voyage in the first story is in accord with his arrival in the second story, and so the two are connected to each other in sequence. The blind man at Bethsaida (8:22–26) therefore followed Jesus' walking on the sea (6:45–51) in the pre-Markan cycle.

In his analysis of the seams between stories, Achtemeier focuses primarily on discovering Markan editorial activity, attempting to restore pre-Markan forms from the present stories by identifying two miracle catenae in which miracle stories correspond to each other. Though it is worth investigating a cyclic pattern in Mark 4:35—8:26, Achtemeier's attempt to establish the original order of the stories within miracle collections is unpersuasive. Indeed, the possibility of separating the pre-Markan sources from the final composed text of Mark is itself questionable. As Neirynck comments, the fact that repetition or duality is an innate literary characteristic of Mark makes it doubtful that one can distinguish between pre-Markan sources and Markan redactional elements or between tradition and redaction.[43]

It is possible to identify at least four difficulties with Achtemeier's proposal. First, Achtemeier argues that 5:21ab originally functions as the introduction of the woman with a hemorrhage (5:25–34) while v. 24 is Mark's

---

41. Achtemeier, "Toward the Isolation," 285.

42. Achtemeier, "Toward the Isolation," 284. With the aid of Snoy's study, Achtemeier suggests that the arrival at Gennesaret (6:53) is the conclusion of the feeding of the five thousand (6:34–44), thus paralleling the ending of the feeding of the four thousand (8:1–10), namely the arrival at Dalmanutha (8:10): "Snoy, in a thorough and fruitful study, has suggested that vs. 53 (the departure by sea, in this instance to Gennesaret) may in fact represent the original conclusion to the story of the feeding of the 5,000, since the account of the feeding of the 4,000 ends in a similar way (the departure by sea, in this instance to the regions of Dalmanutha, 8:10). It is, of course, quite like Mark to insert one story into another. If that is the case, it would explain how the geographical problem arose; in his desire to connect both stories to the disciples' lack of understanding (vs. 52), Mark is willing to tolerate the geographical difficulties which result from that connection (i.e., the order to go to Bethsaida now precedes the arrival at Gennesaret, due to the insertion of vss. 45–51 between vss. 44 and 53), just as, in his desire to connect the two incidents, he is willing to tolerate the ambiguity with regard to the dismissal of disciples and crowds (vss. 45 f.)." Refer to Snoy, "La rédaction marcienne," 234.

43. Neirynck, *Duality in Mark*, 77.

redactional attempt to reintroduce this story by inserting the repeated phrase "a large crowd" (ὄχλος πολύς). In addition, v. 21 is closely connected with the previous story. Therefore, the woman with a hemorrhage follows the Gerasene demoniac (5:1–20) and precedes Jairus's daughter (5:21–23, 25–43). However, there is no ground to argue that v. 21ab serves only to introduce the woman with a hemorrhage. Verse 21ab may also function as the introduction of Jairus's daughter. A crowd gathering around Jesus when he got out of a boat is not a special case but a recurring event in the Markan narrative (e.g., 6:53–56). It is therefore difficult to determine the original order of these two stories.

Second, while Achtemeier argues for a doublet between the two healing miracles that involve spitting (7:32–37; 8:22–26),[44] he does not identify them as counterparts in two catenae. If these two healings correspond to each other in terms of the use of spittle, Achtemeier should have placed them in different catenae in order to preserve the parallelism.[45] Instead, he put them both in the second catena.

Third, with the exception of two sea miracles and two feeding miracles, Achtemeier does not present a full description of parallelism in the six healing miracles. Fowler states that "it is clear that Achtemeier somehow regards the catenae as parallel to each other—but just exactly how they are parallel, how this came about, or what significance the parallelism has is never explained."[46]

Finally, Achtemeier insists that Mark was not interested in geography, so geographical descriptions which seem to be inconsistent were generated by Mark's careless redactional process—for example, the landing of the boat at Gennesaret (6:53) instead of Bethsaida (6:45) is due to Mark's editorial confusion of Bethsaida in 8:22.[47] Though abrupt changes of spatial locations occasionally occur in Mark, we cannot say that they came from Mark's inattention to geography or careless redaction.[48] Gundry argues that "the

44. Achtemeier, "Toward the Isolation," 265.

45. Fowler, *Loaves and Fishes*, 29.

46. Fowler, *Loaves and Fishes*, 28.

47. Achtemeier, "Toward the Isolation," 282–84. For similar arguments for careless redaction regarding the geographical referent in 6:56—in other words a conflict in traditions—see Marcus, *Mark*, 436; Hooker, *Gospel According to Saint Mark*, 171; Guelich, *Mark 1–8:26*, 356–57.

48. There are several possible ways to resolve the discrepancy between the voyage toward Bethsaida (6:35) and the arrival at Gennesaret (6:53), which Achtemeier ascribes to Mark's editorial activity of ignoring geographical accuracy. Some scholars have argued that the reason for aborting the voyage toward Bethsaida was to delay their arrival there until the disciples recognized Jesus' Gentile mission. See Malbon, *Narrative Space*, 27–29; Smith, "Bethsaida via Gennesaret," 349–74. Others argue that

discrepancy between setting out for Bethsaida (v 45) and arriving at Gennesaret (v 53) is so glaring that to regard either location as a redactional intrusion is to make the redactor almost unbelievably inept."[49] It seems likely that the change of destination in this voyage was due to the adverse wind, which may be a natural corollary that complies with the text itself.[50] In addition, the landing at Gennesaret serves as the geographical setting of Jesus' proclamation that "all foods are clean" (7:19) in Jewish territory,[51] which implies the breaking down of barriers between Jews and Gentiles. After this declaration in Jewish territory, Jesus ventured to take an overland tour toward Gentile territory to the northeast.

Mark's geographical description is not inaccurate, but carefully designed so that the narrative as a whole develops with Jesus' geographical movement. The overall and explicit framework of Mark may be constructed in Jesus' journeys from Galilee to Jerusalem: Galilean Ministry (1:1—8:21), Journey to Jerusalem (8:22—10:52), and Jerusalem Ministry (11:1—16:8). In Mark 4:35—8:21, it is possible to discern a cyclic pattern based on Jesus' geographical movement; by presenting two cycles, one focused on the Jews (4:35—6:44) and the other on the Gentiles (6:45—8:21), this organizational structure serves to demonstrate the universality of Jesus' mission to both the Jews and the Gentiles.[52] Mark's literary techniques and theological intentions can be discovered by tracing Jesus' geographical movement and the spatial changes between episodes. Achtemeier, however, fails to notice the literary and theological significance of Mark's geographical description.

---

the landing at Gennesaret, not Bethsaida, is due to the disciples' disobedience. See Schreiber, *Theologie des Vertrauens*, 96–97. Still others insist that the failure of the disciples to arrive at Bethsaida was due to the wind against them, and so they might have altered their destination and landed the boat at Gennesaret. See Edwards, *Gospel According to Mark*, 202; Gundry, *Mark*, 346; Stein, *Mark*, 331.

49. Gundry, *Mark*, 346.

50. Some commentators have argued that because the strong wind calmed down, a boat could reach the original destination, Bethsaida. See Guelich, *Mark 1–8:26*, 356; Hooker, *Gospel According to Saint Mark*, 171. Edwards, however, argues against this assumption, saying, "I doubt that the situation seemed so simple to the disciples in the boat. After straining at the oars for the better part of the night, I suspect, they were happy to put in at Gennesaret rather than row another eight miles to Bethsaida" (Edwards, *Gospel According to Mark*, 203).

51. This declaration should be performed in Jewish territory (Gennesaret), not in Gentile territory (Bethsaida: Mark's narrative regards Bethsaida as Gentile territory in the light of narrative signal "crossing over"), because the purity system that separated the Jews from the Gentiles was carried out in Jewish territory.

52. This will be discussed in greater detail in my structural analysis below.

Structure Based on Compositional Analysis

In his 1980 article, "The Composition of Mark 4:1–8:26," Petersen proposes a compositional structure of Mark 4:1—8:26 and discusses its hermeneutical significance.[53] Petersen argues that this section of Mark's Gospel is organized into triadic clusters consisting of three minimal units (three cycles), with two intervals between the clusters.

	A/a	B/b	C/c
Cycle One: 4:1—5:20			
	4:1–30	4:35–41	5:1–20
Interval One: 5:21—6:29			
	5:21–43	6:1–6a	6:6b–29
			6:6b–13;
			14–16;
			17–29
Cycle Two: 6:30–56			
	6:30–44	6:45–52	6:53–56
Interval Two: 7:1–37			
	7:1–23	7:24–30	7:31–37
	7:1–13;		
	14–15;		
	17–23		
Cycle Three: 8:1–26			
	8:1–12	8:13–21	8:22–26[A]

A. Petersen, "Composition of Mark 4:1–8:26," 205. This diagram represents the synchronic relations among each A, B, and C unit in the three cycles.

In this structure, the sea-crossings serve as the central axes of the triadic cycles, and the overland journey marks an interval.[54] Petersen stresses the significance of geography and motifs for an understanding of this section's compositional structure: "a combination of topographical content and repeated content is an unambiguous key to the formal structure of Mark 4:1–8:26."[55]

---

53. Petersen, "Composition of Mark 4:1–8:26."
54. Petersen, "Composition of Mark 4:1–8:26," 196.
55. Petersen, "Composition of Mark 4:1–8:26," 193.

Each cycle (4:1—5:20; 6:30-56; 8:1-26) shows a similar pattern of topographical locations. Each A unit (4:1-34; 6:30-44; 8:1-12) portrays Jesus' sayings and deeds to the crowds "on one side of the sea"; each B unit (4:35-41; 6:45-52; 8:13-21) describes Jesus' interaction with the disciples "in the boat while in transit across the sea"; and each C unit (5:1-20; 6:53-56; 8:22-26) depicts Jesus' healing miracles at his "debarkation on the other side of the sea."[56] The A, B, and C units in each cycle are thus connected by a boat motif and the sea-crossings (B units) are centrally located between A units and C units:[57] the pattern of topographical location is "seaside/sea/seaside."[58] The two interval sections (5:1—6:29; 7:1-37) exhibit a similar pattern, as Jesus undertakes an overland journey "away from and back to the sea."[59]

This triadic structure is hermeneutically significant in that the A, B, and C units in each cycle—though the C units are only partially involved—represent the compositional theme, namely, "the failure of the disciples to understand."[60] The B units in particular repeatedly show the disciples' incomprehension of who Jesus is.

In the two interval sections, "seeing, hearing, and understanding" are the important elements that comprise the theme of the episodes.[61] For example, in the first interval Herod misunderstood Jesus' identity as John the Baptist *redivivus* (6:6b-29), and in the second interval Pharisees misinterpreted ritual purity (7:1-23). Petersen claims that the combination of the "Pharisees" and "Herod" in 8:15 ("Watch out for the yeast of the Pharisees and the yeast of Herod") represents an "allusion" to these two units, and that the warning about their yeast is therefore related to the ignorance that is the key prevailing issue in 4:1—8:26.[62] The compositional structure that Pe-

---

56. Petersen, "Composition of Mark 4:1-8:26," 196.

57. Petersen, "Composition of Mark 4:1-8:26," 196. Petersen suggests that sea-crossing is the core element forming the compositional framework in 4:1-8:26: "Our first clue to compositional arrangement is therefore the topography of sea transit. It leads us to the second clue, namely, the repetitive quality of the three boat episodes. The repetition produces the first compositional break in the mere sequence of minimal units in 4:1-8:26."

58. Petersen, "Composition of Mark 4:1-8:26," 197.

59. Petersen, "Composition of Mark 4:1-8:26," 197.

60. Petersen, "Composition of Mark 4:1-8:26," 207, 212. According to Petersen, though the themes of the episodes of the C units are not directly related to the disciples, who are described only as bystanders, these episodes are associated with the "understanding" of the disciples.

61. Petersen, "Composition of Mark 4:1-8:26," 209-11.

62. Petersen, "Composition of Mark 4:1-8:26," 211. Petersen explains the reason for combining the "Pharisees" and "Herod" in 8:15 as follows: "It is curious that in B^3

tersen proposed provides a hermeneutical framework for Mark 4:1—8:26, a section focused on revealing the disciples' incomprehension of who Jesus is despite Jesus' instructions in his acts and sayings.[63]

Petersen summarizes how the three cycles in 4:1—8:26 are composed from the perspective of topographical arrangement as follows:

> This review of the topographical sequence of episodic (minimal) units demonstrates three compositional points. First, peculiar to 4:1–8:26 is a distinction made between minimal units on the basis of sea transit on the one hand and of land travel on the other hand. Second, three minimal units associated with sea transit appear in three separate segments or cycles. In each cycle the topographical location is respectively on one side of the sea (A), on the sea in a boat (B), and on the other side of the sea (C). Third, those minimal units associated with land travel appear in two places, namely, as intervals between the first and second cycles (5:21–6:29) and between the second and third cycles (7:1–37).[64]

There is, however, a critical defect in Petersen's compositional analysis, which he himself acknowledged:[65] it is difficult to discover a seaside/sea/seaside pattern in the third cycle. To make his proposal work, Petersen combined two different episodes—the feeding of the four thousand (8:1–10) and the Pharisees' demand for a sign (8:11–12)—into one unit (A^3, 8:1–12).[66] He

---

Jesus warns the disciples about 'the leaven of the Pharisees and the leaven of the Herod' (8:15). The reference to the Pharisees in 8:15 is in all probability related to 8:11–12, but I suggest that, in view of the extensive allusions in B^3 to earlier units, the *conjunction* of the 'Pharisees' and 'Herod' in 8:15 is an allusion to the two composite units in the intervals, and that the compositional content of these units identifies the 'leaven' as a metaphor for understanding things in human terms—surely it is not a metaphor for seeking signs from heaven (8:11–12), which is only a symptom of the wider problem of understanding that Mark is concerned with. If this interpretation of the 'leaven of the Pharisees and the leaven of Herod' is correct, it also provides *a* motive for the composition of the two composite units—to spread the wealth of ignorance."

63. Petersen, "Composition of Mark 4:1–8:26," 217.

64. Petersen, "Composition of Mark 4:1–8:26," 199–202. As for the two intervals, Petersen also suggests three compositional characteristics: "First, there is no internal topographical change that would justify positing independent episodes or minimal units. Second, the distinction between their component parts is signaled by the focus on actors other than Jesus: the twelve, Herod, and the baptist; the Pharisees and scribes, the people, and the disciples. And third, the second and third parts each follow from the immediately preceding parts in such a way that the third part is never connected in the same way with the first one."

65. Petersen, "Composition of Mark 4:1–8:26," 199.

66. Petersen, "Composition of Mark 4:1–8:26," 199.

regards the boat trip to the district of Dalmanutha in 8:10 as a side trip rather than a sea-crossing because there is no sea-crossing signal such as εἰς τὸ πέραν or διαπεράω.⁶⁷ The A³ unit (8:1-12) thus has a seaside setting. The formulaic signal for a sea crossing appears in 8:13 (εἰς τὸ πέραν), so the B³ unit (8:13-21) becomes a sea-crossing episode.⁶⁸ Finally, the setting of the C³ unit (8:22-26) is the seashore because Jesus' healing miracle happens after his debarkation. Petersen argues along these lines that the third cycle (8:1-26) shows the pattern of seaside (A³)/sea (B³)/seaside (C³).

There are, however, significance problems with Petersen's attempt to identify this pattern in the third cycle. First, 8:1-10 and vv. 11-12 cannot be legitimately combined into one (A³) unit—the two stories are simply too different. While 8:1-10 is a feeding miracle, 8:11-12 is the Pharisees' demand, with the impure intention of testing Jesus, for "a sign from heaven."⁶⁹ Second, the boat trip toward the region of Dalmanutha (8:10) should not be regarded as a side trip because, given the route of Jesus' overland journey in 7:31, the feeding of the four thousand (8:1-10) likely occurred on the eastern shore of the Sea of Galilee.⁷⁰ Jesus' movement to the region of Dal-

---

67. Petersen, "Composition of Mark 4:1–8:26," 199. Petersen argues that the boat trip in 8:10 corresponds to a side trip oversea in 6:31-32.

68. Kelber also does not consider the boat trip (8:10) as a sea-crossing to the west because there is no crossing signal (εἰς τὸ πέραν, διαπεράω). Jesus still stayed on the eastern shore in 8:1-12, and the final voyage toward the west (εἰς τὸ πέραν, v. 13) was performed in vv. 14-21. See Kelber, *Kingdom in Mark*, 61.

69. The Pharisees' request for "a sign from heaven" (8:11) does not directly refer to a miracle such as Jesus' previous feeding miracle. Here the Pharisees' demand is not a miracle (δύναμις), but a sign (σημεῖον), and these terms should be distinguished. In the Synoptic Gospels, σημεῖον is never employed for Jesus' δύναμις. See Rengstorf, "σημεῖον," 7:235. As Edwards says, "Jesus had done miracles all along, with which the Pharisees cannot have been unfamiliar" (Edwards, *Gospel According to Mark*, 235). Therefore, if the Pharisees wanted to see Jesus' miracles like a previous feeding miracle, they should have used δύναμις instead of σημεῖον. The request for a sign focuses on "the question of authentication," addressing whether Jesus' ministry came from God himself and was manifested and authorized by him. See France, *Gospel of Mark*, 311. Rengstorf states that "the demand for a sign has to do with the reciprocal relation between Jesus and God on the one hand and on the other hand the relation of those who are interested in a sign to Jesus in the sense of a religious relation (πίστις)" (Rengstorf, "σημεῖον," 7:235). The Pharisees' demand for a sign is the request for "an act by which God would reveal his approval of Jesus in an irrefutable way." The expression, "from heaven" (ἀπὸ τοῦ οὐρανοῦ) as a "circumlocution for 'from God,'" enhances this argument. In addition, the request by the Pharisees for a sign was intended to test Jesus, as Satan tempted Jesus. See Stein, *Mark*, 375. According to Lane, "in this context 'a sign from heaven' signifies a public, definitive proof that God is with him" (Lane, *Gospel According to Mark*, 276-77). Therefore, there is no connection between 8:1-10 and 11-12.

70. I will explain the route of Jesus' overland journey in 7:31 in my structural analysis based on geographical analysis.

manutha, which was located on the western side of the Sea of Galilee, after performing the feeding miracle on the eastern side should be seen as a sea-crossing from east to west. Sea-crossings can be recognized when the narrative signals of a sea-crossing (e.g., εἰς τὸ πέραν, διαπεράω) are employed, or when the definite place-name of a voyage's destination appears in the text. Mark 6:32, for example, depicts a side trip by boat: Jesus just took a boat to go a deserted place, and there is no crossing signal or destination place-name. On the other hand, while 8:10 lacks a narrative signal, the announced destination of the voyage (the region of Dalmanutha) establishes the event as an east-to-west sea-crossing. Petersen's attempt to discover the pattern of Jesus' geographical movement is commendable, but the triadic structure he proposes is faulty in that it does not show the actual route indicated by the text in the third cycle.

Structure Based on Jesus' Geographical Movement

According to Hedrick, there is an obvious difference between Mark 1–13 and Mark 14–16 in terms of "formal narrative literary features."[71] While the literary style of Mark 1–13 is too "episodic" to be integrated, Mark 14–16 is well organized in a "chronological framework."[72] Hedrick argues, however, that the episodic events in Mark 1–13 can be bundled into distinct groups on the basis of geographical and spatial distinctions: "the geographical references and spatial locations, regardless of the occasional problem they pose, constitute the only immediately recognizable over-all narrative structure to an otherwise highly episodic narrative."[73] The "evident overall framework," according to which the individual and independent episodes of Mark 1–13 are organized into sub-groupings, is thus shown to be "geographical."[74]

Mark did not simply record the route of Jesus' geographical movement. Instead, he attempted to use geographical and spatial description to demonstrate the purpose and theological significance of Jesus' journey. These can be discovered through the use of structural analysis based on geography.[75] In 1956, for example, Marxsen underlined the importance of

71. Hedrick, "What Is a Gospel," 256.
72. Hedrick, "What Is a Gospel," 260.
73. Hedrick, "What Is a Gospel," 259.
74. Hedrick, "What Is a Gospel," 257.
75. Hedrick, "What Is a Gospel," 255. Hedrick notes the relationship between form and content as follows: "Because form and content are closely related, content should be considered in determining an author's narrative 'plan;' yet it seems more reasonable to consider content *in the light of* a prior analysis of narrative structure."

Mark's geographical description in the account of Jesus' journey into Gentile territory,[76] and in 1973, Kümmel noted the geographical significance of Galilee as "the point of departure of the Gentile mission."[77]

In the present study, an examination of the narrative structure of Mark 4:35—8:21 based on a geographical analysis of Jesus' itinerary may show how Mark delivers his theological themes. Most importantly, this structural analysis explicates Jesus' missional works to the Jews and the Gentiles. In his 1974 book, *The Kingdom in Mark: A New Place and a New Time*, Kelber rejects Achtemeier's idea that Mark's arrangement was based on his collection of pre-Markan materials.[78] Instead, Kelber argues that Mark reordered his source materials according to his own theological purposes. Kelber insists that Mark portrayed Jesus' journey of Mark 4:35—8:21 in the context of boat trips in order to bring "logic and unity" to this pericope.[79] He suggests that "the Jewish designations" and "the Gentile designations" are employed to distinguish between Jewish and Gentile territories. The Sea of Galilee becomes the dividing point between west and east; the western side is presented as Jewish territory and the eastern side as Gentile territory.[80] Through Jesus' missional works in both sides of the sea, including in the northern Gentile cities, the barriers between the Jews (west) and the Gentiles (east) were broken down, making possible the unity and expansion of the kingdom of God. In this process, Jesus constantly tried to explain who he was and what he was doing, but the disciples remained ignorant of his identity and the meaning of his works.

In his 1981 monograph, Fowler rejects Kelber's argument because it is difficult to find evidence that the west and east represent Jewish and Gentile territories, especially in the stories of two feedings.[81] Fowler is skeptical of attempts to connect geographical locations to ethnic groups. He also rejects the idea that the geographical description of Jesus' itinerary in Mark 4–8 reveals Mark's theological purpose on the grounds that Mark was not only indifferent to the accurate portrayal of geographical locales, but even confused regarding the names of some cities and villages around the Sea of Galilee. Using the method of redaction criticism, Fowler argues that Mark created the story of the feeding of the five thousand (6:30 44) from the story of the feeding of the four thousand (8:1–10), which was fundamentally "a

---

76. Marxsen, *Mark the Evangelist*, 66–75.
77. Kümmel, *Introduction to the New Testament*, 86–89.
78. Kelber, *Kingdom in Mark*, 45–65.
79. Kelber, *Mark's Story of Jesus*, 30.
80. Kelber, *Kingdom in Mark*, 48–62.
81. Fowler, *Loaves and Fishes*, 54–68.

traditional story taken by Mark from his *Vorlage*," with slight modifications made to show the disciples' ignorance, clearly revealed in 8:19–21.[82] Fowler thus refutes the claim that the two feeding stories were arranged geographically so that one was for the Jews and the other for the Gentiles.

In his 1985 dissertation, "Rhetoric and Meaning in Mark 6:30–8:10," Phelan points out that Fowler neglects the significance of 7:1–23 in relation to 8:1–10.[83] Phelan argues that the main purpose of this passage (7:1–23) is not to criticize the traditions of the elders, but to declare that "all foods are clean" (καθαρίζων πάντα τὰ βρώματα; 7:19), which implies that all people are clean.[84] The feeding of the four thousand (8:1–10) is therefore connected to the Gentiles who were declared to be clean in the previous passage (7:1–23). Phelan notes that this central section (6:30–8:10) focuses on the identity of Jesus and his mission to those who were accepted as the people of God regardless of their ethnicity.

In her 1984 article, "The Jesus of Mark and the Sea of Galilee," Malbon presents a structural analysis of Mark 4–8 that stresses the significance of the Sea of Galilee as "the geographical focal point for the first half of the Gospel of Mark, the center of the Marcan Jesus' movement in space (7:31)."[85] Three sea-crossing episodes—"stilling the storm" (4:37ff.), "walking on the sea" (6:47ff.), and "conversation about bread" (8:14ff.)—are elaborately composed to "dramatize both teaching and healing."[86] The Sea of Galilee plays the role not only of a "boundary" between west (the Jewish side) and east (the Gentile side) but also of a "bridge" between them.[87] Malbon charts Jesus' voyage, centered around the Sea of Galilee, as follows:

---

82. Fowler, *Loaves and Fishes*, 37–38. Fowler argues that "the presence of a striking number of *hapax legomena* and the conspicuous absence of Markan vocabulary and literary characteristics leads one to conclude that the bulk of Mark 8:1–10 was obtained by Mark from his *Vorlage*, although the pericope does bear the signs of some Markan redaction, especially at the beginning (8:1–2), and at the end (8:10)."

83. Phelan, "Rhetoric and Meaning," 181.

84. Phelan, "Rhetoric and Meaning," 224.

85. Malbon, "Jesus of Mark and the Sea of Galilee," 363.

86. Malbon, "Jesus of Mark and the Sea of Galilee," 364.

87. Malbon, *Narrative Space*, 43.

MARCAN SEA VOYAGES

West (Jewish)	Sea of Galilee	East (Gentile)
(teaching in parables beside the sea)		
4:35–36, start of W-E crossing ⟶	4:37–41, calming of sea ⟶	5:1, arrival at country of Gerasenes
	⟵	5:21, E-W crossing
(healing Jairus's daughter and hemorrhaging woman)		
6:1, return to patris		
(rejection in patris; mission of disciples; account of death of John; return of disciples)		
6:32, W-W side trip by boat ⟶		
(feeding 5,000) ⟵		
6:45, Jesus' command to disciples for W-E crossing to Bethsaida; departure of disciples by boat ⟶	6:47–52, disciples in boat; Jesus walking on sea, saying "ego eimi"	
6:53, arrival at Gennesaret ⟵		
of disciples and Jesus		
(healing sick; arguing against Pharisees concerning ritual purity)		
7:24, 31, W-E movement by northerly, overland route ⟶		*(healing Syrophoenician woman's daughter in region of Tyre and Sidon)*
		7:31, movement through the Decapolis *(healing deaf man in the Decapolis; feeding 4,000)*

8:10, arrival at Dalmanutha ←─────────────────	8:10, E-W crossing
(conversation with Pharisees concerning "sign from heaven")	
8:13, W-E crossing ──→ 8:14–21, conversation with disciples about 'bread' ──→	8:22, arrival at Bethsaida *(healing blind man—in two stages)*ᴬ

A. Malbon, "Jesus of Mark and the Sea of Galilee," 369.

With the help of Kelber and Malbon's studies, Wefald wrote the 1995 article "The Separate Gentile Mission in Mark: A Narrative Explanation of Markan Geography, the Two Feeding Accounts and Exorcisms," which explores the separate Gentile mission in the first half of Mark by tracing the geographical and chronological movement of Jesus' journey.[88] Using the method of narrative analysis, he argues that Jesus took four journeys into Gentile territory marked by four "narrative signals": "(1) Jesus encountering Jewish religious leaders, (2) the presence of Jewish worship centers, (3) obvious Gentile markers such as 'swine,' and (4) a non-exclusive understanding of Kelber's signals of 'to cross over' and 'the other side' (as modified by Malbon's interpretation of the boat trip of 6:45)."[89] He identifies the four journeys as follows: "Journey 1 is from 4:35 to 5:21, Journey 2 is from 6:45 to 6:53 (aborted), Journey 3 is from 7:24 to 8:10, and Journey 4 is from 8:13 to 9:30."[90] Wefald uses these narrative signals to compare Jesus' mission to the Jews and his mission to the Gentiles, especially in the cases of the two exorcisms (1:21–28 and 5:1–20) and two feeding miracles (6:30–44 and 8:1–10). He argues that "meaningful geographical references reveal a geographically and chronologically separate mission by Jesus in his exorcistic activity, the two feeding accounts, and the bread conversation, which flesh out a clear narrative of parallel yet different missions to the Jews and the non-Jews."[91]

---

88. Wefald, "Separate Gentile Mission in Mark," 3–26.

89. Wefald, "Separate Gentile Mission in Mark," 12–13.

90. Wefald, "Separate Gentile Mission in Mark," 13. Iverson's 2007 monograph offers a similar structural analysis of Jesus' journeys into Gentile territory. The first journey into Gentile territory is 5:1–20, the second (failed) is 6:45–53, the third is 7:24—8:9, and the fourth is 8:22—9:29. See Iverson, *Gentiles in the Gospel of Mark*.

91. Wefald, "Separate Gentile Mission in Mark," 26.

The Narrative Structure of a Cyclic Pattern in Mark 4:35—8:21 Based on Geographical Arrangement, Literary Parallelism, and Boat and Bread Motifs

Mark wrote his Gospel with a special focus on time and space. His narrative of Jesus' ministry in Galilee and its vicinity (1:1—10:52) generally follows the route of Jesus' geographical movement, and his account of Jesus' ministry in Jerusalem (11:1—16:8) is arranged according to a day-by-day timeline. Mark's narrative has both synchronic and diachronic characteristics in its plot: the episodes of Mark 4:35—8:21 are synchronically repeated with parallelism (e.g., two sea miracles and two feeding miracles) and diachronically progress with Jesus' geographical movement. "Repetitive parallelism" moves a narrative ahead in "synonymous, antithetical, or synthetic, i.e., climactic" ways.[92] Petersen explains the diachronic and synchronic characteristics of narrative and their interactions in Mark 4:1—8:26 as follows:

> The synchronic dimension of verse represents a playful poetic and semantic interference of the more normal diachronic communication of content. Parallelism interrupts the merely sequential flow of content through a systematic repetition that requires readers and hearers to move forth and back through the text rather than simply straight through it. Once a parallel is discerned it becomes necessary to pause, however momentarily, and synthesize the relations between the parallels before moving forward through the text. Now Mark's narrative is clearly written in prose form. I submit, however, that the parallelism between the cycles in 4:1–8:26 plays a closely comparable role to that of parallelism in verse, that it is comparable to climactic parallelism in particular, and that the parallels represent a hermeneutically significant interplay between the synchronic and diachronic display of content.[93]

I will explore the structure of Mark 4:35—8:21 using both diachronic and synchronic approaches. Diachronically, a narrative develops as Jesus' ministry expands with his geographical movement; synchronically, similar episodes are repeated and appear as parallels. Here, in the interaction

---

92. Comparing the proposed three cycles with "the parallel lines of Hebrew poetry (*parallelismus membrorum*)" in his compositional analysis of 4:1—8:26, Petersen says that "the display of content, the communication, moves forward through a formal system of 'recurrent returns' or 'repetitive parallelism'" (Petersen, "Composition of Mark 4:1–8:26," 203).

93. Petersen, "Composition of Mark 4:1–8:26," 203–4.

between the diachronic and synchronic aspects of the narrative, a cyclic pattern can be discerned.

According to Malbon, "geographical distinctions and recurring events" divide Mark 4:35–8:26 into two sub-sections: the first journey (4:35—6:44) and the second journey (6:45–8:26).[94] Kelber divides Mark into four sections (1:1—4:34; 4:35—8:21; 8:22—10:52; 11:1—16:8) and gave 4:35—8:21, in which Jesus went on distinct missions to the Jews and to the Gentiles, spreading the kingdom of God and unifying the people of God regardless of their ethnicity, the title "Expansion and Unity of the Kingdom."[95] My analysis will incorporate elements of both these approaches: I will divide Mark 4:35—8:21 into two cycles (4:35—6:44; 6:45—8:10) and one conclusion (8:11–21), in which Jesus' missional movement is expanded to the Jews and the Gentiles by breaking down the barriers between them. Two sea miracles (the departure of a boat toward the east: 4:35-41 and 6:45-52) and two feeding miracles (6:31-44 and 8:1-10) mark the beginning and end of each cycle, and the final boat trip serves as a conclusion (8:11-21). The following table identifies the two cycles as parallels based especially on spatial (geographical) analysis.

---

94. Malbon, *Hearing Mark*, 35. Malbon divides Mark into four sections (1:1—4:34; 4:35—8:22[26]; 8:22[26]—10:52; 11:1—16:8) and placed the episode of the blind man at Bethsaida (8:22-26) as an overlapping part between the second and third section. The topic of the second section is "community." See Malbon, *Hearing Mark*, 35-53, 55-56.

95. Kelber, *Kingdom in Mark*, 45-65. See also Kelber, *Mark's Story of Jesus*.

Cycle I	Cycle II
Jesus' Ministry in Galilee and Its Vicinity (4:35—6:44)	Jesus' Expanded Ministry Beyond Galilee (6:45—8:10)
a. **The Sea Miracle** of Jesus' Calming the Storm (4:35–41)	a. **The Sea Miracle** of Jesus' Walking on the Water (6:45–52; Summary of Healing Ministry, 53–56)
b. Healing of a Demon-Possessed Man (5:1–20) in <u>Gentile Territory</u>	b. The Episode Including *Jesus' Saying* in Relation to the Implication of Mission: Instructions on Clean and Unclean (7:1–23) in <u>Jewish Territory</u>
c. Healing of Jairus's Daughter and a Woman with a Hemorrhage (5:21–43) in <u>Jewish Territory</u>	c. Healing of a Syrophoenician Woman's Daughter (7:24–30) in <u>Gentile Territory</u>
d. The Episodes Including *Jesus' Saying* about Mission (6:1–30): A Prophet without Honor (6:1–6a); Jesus' Sending out the Twelve (6:6b–13, 30); The Execution of John the Baptist (6:14–29) in <u>Jewish Territory</u>	d. Healing of a Deaf and Mute Man in <u>Gentile Territory</u> (7:31–37)
e. **The Feeding Miracle** to the Jews (6:31–44)	e. **The Feeding Miracle** to the Gentiles (8:1–10)
Conclusion	
i. Pharisees' Seeking a Sign (8:11–12) ii. The Discussion about Bread on the Sea (8:13–21)	

My structural analysis will address the weaknesses of the previously suggested structures and present an integrative investigation of the narrative structure of 4:35—8:21 on the basis of geography, while also considering Mark's literary techniques and motifs.

The structures proposed by scholars who assume an important role played by pre-Markan materials (e.g., Jenkins, Pesch, Achtemeier et al.) are commendable for their investigations of a cyclic pattern in Mark 4–8, but there are several critical problems with these studies. First, attempts to use historical-critical approaches to distill pre-Markan sources from the present text and reconstruct the original form of the tradition, which is assumed to include pre-Markan miracle collections, are simply too hypothetical. It is also difficult to distinguish between pre-Markan and Markan redactional activity.[96] Second, conflicts have developed between those who argued for a cyclic pattern in 6–8 (e.g., Jenkins) and those who claimed to find a similar pattern in 4–6 (e.g., Pesch). As Fowler points out, the overlap between the cycles in 4–6 and 6–8 can be discovered in terms of parallels, so the cycles must be investigated in 4–8.[97] Third, it is inconsistent to change the sequence of miracle episodes in the text in order to show parallelism (e.g., Achtemeier). If we can arbitrarily manipulate the arrangement of episodes in the present text in order to present parallelism, numerous kinds of parallels may be constructed in Mark 4–8. Finally, as Neirynck argues, duality and repetition are among Mark's stylistic characteristics,[98] so a cyclic pattern in the narrative must be examined in terms of Mark's literary techniques, not the assumption of pre-Markan sources.

My study of the structure of this passage may overcome these problems. First, I will examine a cyclic pattern in 4:35—8:21 of the present text without presupposing the uncertain hypothesis of pre-Markan miracle collections. Second, on the basis of the explicitly exposed parallelism—e.g., two sea miracles (4:35–41; 6:45–52) and two feeding miracles (6:31–44; 8:1–10)—I will investigate a cyclic pattern in Mark 4–8 rather than 4–6 or 6–8. Third, I will explore a cyclic pattern by tracing Jesus' geographical movement without changing the order of episodes in the text. Fourth, I will give due consideration to Markan literary techniques—especially repetition, which grounds the other literary devices—in my structural analysis because these techniques play a significant role in the establishment of a cyclic pattern. Finally, I will consider the motifs of boat and bread, which serve not only to construct the frame of a cyclic structure but also to disclose Mark's theological themes in this pericope.

My analysis has been assisted by scholars who have developed structures with relation to geographical description. Petersen provides a compositional structure, focusing on the arrangement of episodes centered on the Sea of Galilee in a "seaside/sea/seaside" pattern. He does not, however, trace Jesus' geographical movement, and so fails to investigate the significance of the route of Jesus' itinerary. Tracing Jesus' distinctive missional journey to Jewish and Gentile territories is important if one is to grasp Mark's geographical arrangement, which may reveal the purpose of Jesus' journey. Studying a compositional pattern in a synchronic aspect alone may neglect the process of narrative development (e.g., we must consider that Jesus'

---

96. Neirynck, "Evangile de Marc," 167; Fowler, *Loaves and Fishes*, 18.
97. Fowler, *Loaves and Fishes*, 23.
98. See Neirynck's exhaustive study on Markan duality. Neirynck, *Duality in Mark*; Neirynck, "Duality in Mark"; Neirynck, "Duplicate Expressions in the Gospel of Mark."

geographical movement in Mark 4–8 shows the expansion of his ministry from Jewish land to Gentile land).[99] Wefald, on the other hand, proposes a structure by tracing Jesus' geographical movement and distinguished between Jesus' missions to Jewish and Gentile territories, but he fails to consider Mark's literary techniques. Kelber and Malbon pays attention to Jesus' geographical movement in Mark 4:35—8:21(26), presenting Jesus' mission to the Jews and the Gentiles, but they do not provide detailed structural analyses of this pericope.

My structural analysis is significant in its integrative approach to Mark 4:35—8:21. Diachronically, the geographical movement of Jesus' itinerary will be traced in the process of the narrative development; synchronically, the episodes of his ministry will be investigated in the light of Mark's literary technique of parallelism; thematically, boat and bread motifs will be explored in terms Mark's theological intention. All of these approaches will serve to construct a structure with a cyclic pattern.

This study will be performed in three steps. The first step is to set up the boundary of the pericope 4:35—8:21. The second step is to trace how Jesus' geographical movement is configured and examine how the episodes are arranged in a repetitive form. In doing this, I will explain the cyclic pattern in the two sections (4:35—6:44; 6:45—8:10). The third step is to explore how the concluding episodes (8:11–21), especially their use of the boat and bread motifs, are connected to the two cycles and deliver the theme of Mark 4:35—8:21.

Setting up the Boundary

The "geographical and thematic indicators" are the most useful means to divide Mark into several parts and to analyze its structure.[100] According to Witherington, both macro- and microstructures can be examined in Mark,[101] and the analysis of macrostructure should precede that of microstructure in a consideration of how the narrative of Mark progresses in the overall frame. Collins suggests some criteria to determine the structure of Mark or divide it into parts: "explicit changes in spatial location or temporal

---

99. Though Petersen notes the significance of both synchronic and diachronic approaches, his structural analysis was performed primarily with a synchronic approach.

100. Collins, *Mark*, 89.

101. Witherington, *Gospel of Mark*, 36. Baarlink surveys twenty-seven structures of Mark. See Baarlink, *Anfängliches Evangelium*, 75–78.

setting, the introduction of one or more characters, or a shift in topic."[102] These criteria will be employed in my structural analysis of Mark 4:35—8:21.

To begin, it is evident that Mark is largely divided into three parts based on the areas of Jesus' ministry and his geographical movement from Galilee to Jerusalem: Galilee (1:1—8:21), the way to Jerusalem (8:22—10:52), and Jerusalem (11:1—16:8). According to Kümmel, the use of loose words or phrases, such as "καὶ, πάλιν, ἐκεῖθεν, ἐν ἐκείναις ταῖς ἡμέραις, ἐξελθών," to connect individual episodes or sayings reveals a lack of "biographical-chronological interest."[103] Mark instead composed his sources "in a broad stroke" with "a geographical arrangement (Galilee—Galilee and surrounding regions—journey to Jerusalem—Jerusalem)."[104] Kümmel asserts that Mark's geographical locales have theological significance: Galilee is the "place of Jesus' eschatological activity and the point of departure of the Gentile mission," while Jerusalem is the "place of origin of the Jewish obduracy toward Jesus."[105] As Kümmel says, Mark shows a "geographical-theological"[106] or "geographical-thematic" structure.

In the present study, I divide Mark into four parts in relation to Jesus' geographical movement: Jesus' early ministry in Galilee (1:1—4:34); his expanded ministry in and beyond Galilee (4:35—8:21); his ministry on the way to Jerusalem (8:22—10:52); and his final ministry in Jerusalem (11:1—16:8). The boundary of the second part (4:35—8:21), on which the present study is focused, is determined by three elements: the geographical expansion of Jesus' ministry, a boat motif, and a shift of theme.

First, the first voyage of Jesus and his disciples across the Sea of Galilee serves as the turning point of Jesus' ministry beyond Galilee and to the Gentiles; the second part of Mark's Gospel therefore begins with 4:35. Jesus' ministry is performed only in Galilean areas in 1:1—4:34, but after 4:35

---

102. Collins, *Mark*, 87.

103. Kümmel, *Introduction to the New Testament*, 85.

104. Kümmel, *Introduction to the New Testament*, 82–86. Kümmel divides Mark into five parts based on geographical criteria: "Part One: Jesus in Galilee 1:14–5:43; Part Two: Jesus as Itinerant Within and Outside Galilee 5:44–9:50; Part Three: Jesus on the Way to Jerusalem 10:1–52; Part Four: Jesus in Jerusalem 11:1–13:37; Part Five: Passion and Resurrection Narrative 14:1–16:8." He explains the purpose of Mark's geographical arrangement as follows: "It is evident that Mk himself has essentially created the itinerary of Jesus, so it may also be inferred that the pervasive concentration in Galilee of the activity of Jesus arises from a theological motive. The idea that Mk could not have Jesus journey to Jerusalem more than once because the way to Jerusalem is for Jesus the anabasis into the heavenly sanctuary, or that 'Galilee of the Gentiles' for Mk includes the pagan places such as Tyre, Sidon, and Caesarea Philippi, is completely contrived."

105. Kümmel, *Introduction to the New Testament*, 88–89.

106. Kümmel, *Introduction to the New Testament*, 89.

Jesus expands his ministry by journeying into Gentile territory. Geographical references, such as "to the other side" (εἰς τὸ πέραν, 4:35) and "to the country of the Gerasenes" (εἰς τὴν χώραν τῶν Γερασηνῶν, 5:1), indicate that Jesus attempted to travel out of Galilee.[107] Jesus made trips in and beyond Galilee by means of five crossings of the Sea of Galilee between Jewish and Gentile territories (4:35; 5:21; 6:45; 8:10; and 8:13) and two overland journeys, one in Jewish territory (6:6b) and the other in Gentile territory (7:24). In addition, an examination of Jesus' geographical movement between Jewish and Gentile territories reveals Jesus' distinctive mission to the Jews and the Gentiles. His itinerary consists of: the first boat trip to Gentile territory (4:35–5:20); the return to Jewish territory (5:21–43); the overland journey in Jewish territory (6:1–44); the second attempted but aborted boat trip to Gentile territory (6:45–52); the return to Jewish territory (6:53—7:23); the overland journey to Gentile territory (7:24—8:9); the return to Jewish territory (8:10–12); and the final boat trip (8:13–21).

Second, in this pericope (4:35—8:21) Jesus frequently crosses the Sea of Galilee for his missional journeys by boat, and a boat motif plays a significant role in contouring the structure of this section.[108] Woodroof explains the significance of the boat motif in shaping Jesus' itinerary and ministry as follows:

107. Hedrick proposes an outline of Mark 1:2—13:37 according to "geographical and spatial shifts": "I. At the Jordan in the Wilderness, 1:2–14a"; "II. In Galilee, 1:14b–4:34"; "III. A Trip out of Galilee, 4:35–5:20"; "IV. Return to Galilee, 5:21–7:23"; "V. A Trip to Tyre and Sidon and the Decapolis, 7:24–31"; "VI. Return to Galilee, 7:31–8:12"; "VII. A Trip to the Tetrarchy of Philip, 8:13–9:29"; "VIII. Return to Galilee, 9:30–50"; "IX. Journey to Jerusalem, 10:1–11:10"; "X. Two Preliminary Entries into Jerusalem, 11:11–26"; "XI. Events in and around the Temple, 11:27–13:37." Hedrick insists that while Mark 14–16 has a "chronological framework," Mark 1–13 is composed of individual episodes clustered by a "geographical framework." See Hedrick, "What Is a Gospel," 257–60.

108. In Mark 4:35—8:21, there is a boat motif in contouring the itinerary of Jesus' missional movement and disclosing its significance. Three major functions of a boat motif can be found in this section. First, a boat serves as a means for "crossing" between west (Jewish territory) and east (Gentile territory). Jesus' missional journeys toward Gentile territory and back to Jewish territory begin and end with crossings of the Sea of Galilee. Second, a boat serves as a "place of revelation." In the two sea miracles (4:35–41; 6:45–52), Jesus revealed himself as the Savior, delivering the disciples while calming the storm and walking on the sea. The disciples were in a boat not only as they witnessed these miracles, but also as they grew astonished and questioned Jesus' identity (e.g., 4:41). It was also in a boat that Jesus reminded them of the miraculous feedings through which he disclosed his identity (8:13–21). Third, as Kelber notes, a boat serves as a "vehicle of unification" (Kelber, *Mark's Story of Jesus*, 41–42). The Sea of Galilee was a barrier between west and east, separating the Jews and the Gentiles. A boat, however, functions as a vehicle to cross over this barrier, in which Jesus' mission of unifying the Jews and the Gentiles was successfully performed.

The 'boat' becomes important to Mark's story in one narrow portion of his narrative—4:1–8:21. Only in this section do Jesus and his disciples appear 'in the boat' and 'on the sea.' Prior to this, Galilee defined the scope of Jesus' activity, while "the way" and "Jerusalem" dominate the sections which follow. But over these four and one half chapters, it is the boat which provides the primary organizing motif for Jesus' travels and work.[109]

The word "boat" (πλοῖον) appears 17 times in Mark (1:19, 20; 4:1b, 36a, 36b, 37a, 37b; 5:2, 18b, 21b; 6:32, 45b, 47a, 51, 54; 8:10b, 14), and "small boat" (πλοιάριον) appears once (3:9).[110] Though images of a boat as a setting in Mark's narrative occur before 4:35, the actual use of a boat to cross the Sea of Galilee as part of a voyage begins in 4:35. The boat trips end at 8:21 with a discussion between Jesus and the disciples about bread in a boat (8:13–21). This serves as the conclusion to the second part of Mark (4:35—8:21), and no further references to a boat appear after this episode.[111] Instead of a boat motif, "the way motif" prevails in the following part of Mark (8:22—10:52).

It may be questioned, however, whether the episode of Jesus' healing of a blind man at Bethsaida (8:22–26) should be included in the second (4:35—8:21) or third (8:27—10:52) part of Mark.[112] Some commentators have argued that this healing episode belongs to the second part, and therefore ends the second part at 8:26.[113] Because the pattern of Jesus healing on the seaside after a sea-episode appears consistently throughout the second

---

109. Woodroof regards boats in Mark as a metaphor for the church, but his claim seems to be allegorical to some degree. Woodroof, however, highlights the significant functions of boats in each episode of Mark 4:1—8:21. For example, the boat in the parable of the sower (4:1–34) functions as a *"gathering place* (where the disciples enjoy the immediate presence of their master)," a *"boundary marker* (to indicate between those 'on the outside' and the inner circle of disciples)," and a *"teaching platform* (from which both the crowds and the disciples are informed of spiritual matters)"; the boat in the episode of Jesus' calming the storm (4:35–41) serves as a *"place of testing* (where disciples feel threatened)," a *"place of safety* in the storm (where disciples are protected by Jesus)," an *"environment for building faith* (where disciples are challenged to trust in Jesus)," a *"spiritual battleground* (where God meets and defeats Satan)," and a *"place to experience the saving power of Jesus".* See Woodroof, "Church as Boat in Mark," 231–49.

110. Malbon, *Narrative Space*, 53.

111. Lührmann, *Das Markusevangelium*, 139.

112. Opinions differ as to the division of this section and whether this miracle story serves as the ending of the second part, the beginning of the third part, or a bridge between the two parts. See Stein, *Mark*, 386–87; Brooks, *Mark*, 132–33.

113. See Guelich, *Mark 1–8:26*, 316–18; Evans, *Mark 8:27–16:20*, 3–4; Healy, *Gospel of Mark*, 159–60; Petersen, "Composition of Mark 4:1–8:26," 193–94; Hooker, *Gospel According to Saint Mark*, 200–1.

part,¹¹⁴ the blind man at Bethsaida is included in this part. Geographically, the directional change of Jesus' journey toward Jerusalem, where he would die and be resurrected, begins with Peter's confession (8:27–33).¹¹⁵ This confession is the "watershed" of Mark's narrative and Jesus' three passion predictions (8:31; 9:31; 10:33–34) serve as a framework for the third part.¹¹⁶ It follows, therefore, that the third part starts from 8:27.

Nevertheless, it is difficult to decide which part of Mark's narrative the blind man at Bethsaida (8:22–26) belongs to, because it functions as a bridge between the second and third parts.¹¹⁷ According to Williams, the blind man at Bethsaida functions as a "transitional episode" that both echoes the healing of a deaf and mute man in the previous narrative (7:31–37) and foreshadows the healing of blind Bartimaeus in the following narrative (10:46–52).

> The healing story has significant connections with the preceding material because of its similarity to the healing of the deaf man and its contrast with the continuing blindness of the disciples. However, the healing of the blind man also encourages anticipations of the following narrative. The healing of the blind man creates the expectation that others will come to see and to understand.¹¹⁸

Donahue and Harrington also argue that the story of the blind man at Bethsaida (8:22–26) is related to the previous healing of a deaf and mute man (7:31–37), with which it shares verbal and ritualistic similarities, and also to the following healing of blind Bartimaeus (10:46–52), which also depicts gaining sight as a symbol for understanding who Jesus is.¹¹⁹ Despite

---

114. For example, the healing of a Gerasene demoniac (5:1–20) is located after Jesus' calming the storm (4:35–41); the summary of healing many people at Gennesaret (6:53–56) is placed after Jesus' walking on the water (6:45–52); the healing of a blind man at Bethsaida (8:22–26) is situated after the discussion about bread on the sea (8:13–21).

115. Healy, *Gospel of Mark*, 159.

116. Hooker, *Gospel According to Saint Mark*, 200; Petersen, "Composition of Mark 4:1—8:26," 193–94.

117. Malbon suggests an overlapping structure about a blind man at Bethsaida between the second and third part, because this episode functions as both the conclusion of the second part and the introduction of the third part. See Malbon, *Hearing Mark*, 55.

118. Williams, *Other Followers of Jesus*, 127–37.

119. Ritualistic similarities indicate Jesus' healing actions of spitting and touching. See Donahue and Harrington, *Gospel of Mark*, 257–58; Collins, *Mark*, 397–98.

the difficulty of determining which part of Mark the blind man at Bethsaida belongs to, a thematic change helps resolve the problem.

Third, a shift in theme determines the boundary between the second and third parts. Though the blind man at Bethsaida serves as a "transitional" episode between the preceding and following parts, it plays the role of introducing a new theme for the third part of Mark, namely "the 'way' of Christian discipleship" "from blindness to sight."[120] The second part of Mark ends with Jesus' discussion of bread with his disciples in a boat (8:13–21) and the third part begins with the healing of a blind man at Bethsaida (8:22–26).

The second, third, and fourth parts of Mark can be distinguished by their emphases on different traits of Jesus' ministry, which help disclose the themes of each part. The second part is dominated by a number of Jesus' miraculous works; the third parts focuses on his passion prediction while narrating only three miracles—two healing miracles (8:22–26 and 10:46–52), which serve as the brackets of this part, and one exorcism (9:14–29) in the context of a controversy discussion; the fourth part features Jesus' suffering in Jerusalem, where he performed no miraculous works except for a negative miracle of cursing of a fig tree.[121] The second part shows how great, glorious, and praiseworthy Jesus was by focusing on his miracles; the third part presents Jesus' ultimate purpose in coming to earth, revealed in his sayings; and the fourth part demonstrates how he accomplished the will of God through his suffering.

The third part of Mark, then, functions as a transitional section between the second and fourth parts.[122] As the narrative focus shifts from glory to suffering, Jesus is seen predicting his passion to the disciples and teaching them about discipleship (e.g., "denying oneself, taking up one's cross, and following Jesus," 8:34). Throughout the third part, the disciples fail to grasp what Jesus means in his sayings, despite his passion predictions. The disciples here may be regarded as "blind" to Jesus' teaching.[123] In the introductory episode of the third part, the blind man at Bethsaida, who was healed in two steps, symbolically refers to the disciples' blindness. Johnson states that "as long as they [the disciples] cannot understand the significance of Jesus' passion and the direction it gives Christian discipleship, they, like the blind man in 8:22–26, will only have partial vision."[124]

---

120. Healy, *Gospel of Mark*, 159; Boring, *Mark*, 231–307.
121. Boring, *Mark*, 231.
122. Boring, *Mark*, 231. See also Williamson, *Mark*, 149.
123. Marcus, *Mark 8–16*, 589. See also Johnson, "Mark 10:46–52," 191–204.
124. Johnson, "Mark 10:46–52," 203.

According to Boring, "the major thematic transition that occurs in this section [the third part] is the transition from veiled, parabolic speech and actions to clear and explicit revelation from God/Jesus regarding the identity of Jesus and his function in the divine plan of salvation."[125] The story of the blind man at Bethsaida (8:22–26), which serves as an introduction to the third part (8:22—10:52) parallels the story of blind Bartimaeus (10:46–52) that acts as its conclusion.[126] These two miraculous gifts of sight form literary brackets or inclusio,[127] which symbolically imply "the 'blindness' of the disciples."[128]

Best argues that the two-stage healing of the blind man at Bethsaida in 8:22–26 refers to the two steps involved in the realization of who Jesus is, while the gaining of sight is a "metaphor for the gift of spiritual understanding."[129] The two stages in healing represent the progression "from partial understanding to complete understanding."[130] The following episode of Peter's confession (8:27–33) indicates his incomplete comprehension of Jesus' identity or "half-sight," which fails to recognize Jesus as the suffering

---

125. Boring, *Mark*, 232, 257–58.

126. Since the episodes in Mark are arranged geographically, the final episode of the third part (8:22—10:52) should occur just outside of Jerusalem. Jericho where Jesus healed blind Bartimaeus, is "the last city in the Jordan River Valley before Jerusalem," and so the third part ends at the episode of blind Bartimaeous. See Stein, *Mark*, 491. In Mark's narrative, Bethsaida belongs to Gentile territory because it is located at the eastern side of the Sea of Galilee in the light of the narrative signals of a sea-crossing (e.g., εἰς τὸ πέραν, διαπεράω). After the final boat trip to Bethsaida, Jesus no longer journeyed oversea, but only traveled on foot. From here, he went to a northern Gentile area, the villages of Caesarea Philippi (8:27), came back to Galilee (9:30), and then went into the region of Judea and beyond the Jordan (10:1). In each territory—a Gentile region (8:31), Galilee (9:31), and Judea and beyond the Jordan (10:33–34)—Jesus predicted his death and resurrection. Therefore, the new journey (to Jerusalem), which mainly focuses on predicting Jesus' passion, begins with Gentile territory, the eastern village of Bethsaida, and so the third part geographically starts at 8:22.

127. Donahue and Harrington, *Gospel of Mark*, 257–58. Hooker explains the connection between these two healing miracles and the themes of discipleship and suffering as follows: "There is yet another parallel to this narrative in the story of the healing of another blind man, Bartimaeus, in 10:46–52. In this story, too, the theme of faith (Bartimaeus appeals to Jesus as 'Son of David') and discipleship (he follows Jesus 'in the way') are close to the surface. Some commentators therefore divide the gospel at 8:22, arguing that these two healings of blind men form an 'inclusio' and mark the beginning and end of the section about the way of the Cross and the meaning of discipleship." See Hooker, *Gospel According to Saint Mark*, 197. Refer also to Collins, *Mark*, 91.

128. France, *Gospel of Mark*, 320.

129. Best, "Discipleship in Mark," 325.

130. Williams, *Other Followers of Jesus*, 132.

Messiah.¹³¹ At the end of the third part, blind Bartimaeus, who represents an "exemplary figure" of faith, is completely healed in one step, sees Jesus immediately, and follows him on the way.¹³² Mark uses these two minor characters to illustrate the process of becoming a true disciple, even as the disciples themselves remain in a state of incomprehension. "At the outset Mark reminds the reader how difficult it can be to see these things clearly, while at the end Mark 10:46–52 illustrates a clear-sighted faith in Jesus the Son of David as the agent of God's healing power and the enthusiastic and wholehearted response that he evokes from people of faith."¹³³ In conclusion, the two miraculous healings of the blind function as the brackets of the third part of Mark. The second part ends at 8:21.

Two Cycles Based on Geographical Arrangement and Literary Parallelism

My structural analysis seeks primarily to explore how the individual episodes and sayings of 4:35—8:21 are arranged, presenting a cyclic pattern in a narrative dimension. For this study, I will employ a narrative approach,¹³⁴ focusing particularly on Mark's geographical arrangement by tracing Jesus' missional journeys and examining Markan literary parallelism.¹³⁵ This

---

131. Best, "Discipleship in Mark," 325.

132. Though Bartimaeus belongs to the crowd and is not a disciple of Jesus, he shows true discipleship. He is an "exemplary" figure in both his faith and following: "He possessed insight into the messianic identity of Jesus, since he addresses Jesus as the Son of David. Moreover, he addresses Jesus as his teacher, so that he expresses the commitment of a disciple. Like the twelve disciples, he is also sacrificial, leaving behind what he has in order to follow Jesus on the way. Thus, Bartimaeus is exemplary not only because of his faith, but also because he is a follower of Jesus." See Williams, *Other Followers of Jesus*, 152–66. According to Best, the sayings and actions of Bartimaeus produce a "'discipleship' atmosphere" (Best, *Following Jesus*, 141) In addition, as Williams says, since the words such as ἀκολουθέω ("to follow") and ὁδός ("way"), which are applied to Bartimaeus, are related to discipleship in a metaphorical significance, Bartimaeus can be regarded as an exemplary figure for discipleship. See Williams, *Other Followers of Jesus*, 160–63.

133. Donahue and Harrington, *Gospel of Mark*, 319.

134. See chapter 1 on methodological considerations for a discussion of narrative settings, and rhetorical devices.

135. In fact, this structural analysis is related to a composition approach, which focuses primarily on the arrangement of sources in the narrative. A composition approach as a means of analyzing a structure explores how sources were arranged and how they were combined and integrated in a "holistic" way. It can be more precisely understood if we compare it with a redaction approach. Smalley explains the difference between redaction criticism and composition criticism as follows: "In fact, however,

structural analysis will be performed largely in the light of narrative settings (i.e., time, space, and social circumstances)—particularly spatial (geographical) settings—and Markan rhetorical devices.

I will perform this structural analysis of 4:35—8:21 in two steps. The first step is to trace the route of Jesus' geographical movement in order to discover a cyclic pattern. The second is to examine the parallelism between the two cycles in a geographical framework. In doing so, I will show how the episodes and sayings are arranged to form a cyclic pattern in the light of Mark's geographical description. This analysis will also take into account Mark's literary techniques.

Tracing Jesus' Geographical Movement

The geographical setting of Jesus' ministry in the first half of Mark (1:1—8:21) is Galilee, and the Sea of Galilee forms the geographical central point of his expanded ministry in and beyond Galilee in the second half of his Galilean ministry (4:35—8:21). Three voyages across the Sea of Galilee serve as the framework of this section: Jesus' calming the storm (4:35-41), walking on the water (6:45-52), and discussing bread on the sea (8:13-21).[136]

'redaction' and 'composition' criticism, although close together, are strictly speaking different disciplines. One (redaction criticism) is the study of the observable changes introduced by the Gospel writers into the traditional material they received and used. The other (composition criticism) examines the *arrangement* of this material, an arrangement which is motivated by the theological understanding and intention of the evangelists." See Smalley, "Redaction Criticism," 181. Osborne regards composition criticism as the developed stage of earlier redaction criticism and explains the relationship between redaction criticism and composition criticism in this way: "There are two foci for the discipline: (1) the editorial alterations of the traditions (this is the primary concern of earlier redaction critics) and (2) the process by which the authors combined the traditions into a holistic work (this is called composition criticism)." See Osborne, "Redaction Criticism," 199-200. According to Petersen, compositional analysis requires two tasks; the first task is to explore "the segmentation of the narrative" which is made up of "minimal compositional units" and the second is to examine how the 'compositional building blocks' are arranged." See Petersen, "Composition of Mark 4:1-8:26," 186. Composition and narrative approaches also differ in some aspects. In relation to the present study, the main difference is that a composition approach is concerned with the arrangement of the sources (the traditions) in a given text and a narrative approach is involved with the arrangement of the passages in a narrative plot. For the structural study, however, they do not conflict with each other, but instead are complimentary for the integral understanding of a text's arrangement. A composition approach is more useful for the synchronic study of structure and a narrative approach for diachronic study.

136. Malbon, "Jesus of Mark and the Sea of Galilee," 363.

In this framework, this part of Mark (4:35—8:21) consists of two literary building blocks (4:35—6:44; 6:45—8:10) and one concluding section (8:11–21). The two sea miracles (4:35–41; 6:45–52) are placed at the beginning of each block, and the two feeding miracles (6:31-44; 8:1-10) are located at the end of each block. These two blocks establish two cycles, exhibiting a cyclic pattern that can be discovered by tracing Jesus' geographical movement. The pattern of geographical movement is similar in the two cycles, though the routes of the two journeys are different.

In the first cycle, Jesus traveled from the western seaside across the Sea of Galilee to the region of the Gerasenes (4:35-5:20). After healing a Gerasene demoniac, Jesus returned to the western shore in a boat and cured Jairus's daughter and a woman with hemorrhage (5:21-43). Jesus then left the west coast of the Sea of Galilee, took an inland journey to Nazareth, where he was rejected by his own hometown (6:1-6a), and then traveled among villages teaching (6:6b). The execution of John the Baptist is inserted in the episode of Jesus' sending out the disciples (6:7-30). After finishing their mission to Galilee the disciples returned to Jesus (v. 30), who then performed the miracle of feeding the five thousand in the wilderness along the west coast of the Sea of Galilee (6:31-44).[137]

In the second cycle, Jesus set out to sail to the eastern port city of Bethsaida, but this attempt was aborted, and he landed on the western shore at Gennesaret, where he healed many people (6:45-56).[138] Jesus engaged in a

---

137. We can infer that the wilderness was located on the west coast of the Sea of Galilee because, after the feeding miracle, Jesus ordered the disciples to sail to the other side (εἰς τὸ πέραν, v. 45), namely to Gentile territory (the east side of the sea).

138. As discussed above, though many assumptions have been suggested to explain the change of destination from Bethsaida to Gennesaret, the voyage toward Bethsaida was aborted due to the adverse storm. In particular, the description of the disciples straining at the oars against the wind in Mark 6:48 implies that they exerted themselves to make headway but had difficulty reaching their destination. In the previous sea episode of 4:35-41, however, there is no reference to the disciples struggling against the windswept sea; they were just flustered with fear. In comparison with the sailing of 4:35-41, the voyage of 6:45-52 explicitly shows that the disciples tried to reach their destination but were in trouble. Edwards suggests a concrete possible route and process for this voyage, including the alteration of destination, in 6:45-52 as follows: "We do not know the exact location of the feeding of the five thousand, but the general vicinity appears to have been in the hill country north of Capernaum and west of Bethsaida. A boat crossing from there to Bethsaida leads due east (or perhaps slightly northeast) along the north coast of the lake. Gennesaret, however, lay some eight miles southwest of Bethsaida and some four miles south of Capernaum on the west side of the lake. Mark does not account for this triangular voyage. One way to make sense of it is to assume that the battering wind from the northeast (v. 48) blew the boat southeast in the direction of Gennesaret, where Jesus and the disciples then put ashore." See Edwards, *Gospel According to Mark*, 202.

controversy with religious leaders from Jerusalem about clean and unclean, and in Galilee he declared that all foods are clean (7:1–23). After this proclamation, Jesus took an overland journey toward the northwest, entered a house in the region of Tyre, and healed a Syrophoenician woman's daughter (7:24–30). Tyre, located around 40 kilometers south of Sidon and around 45 kilometers from Acco, was a significant city with a long history on the Phoenician coast.[139] The region of Tyre (τὰ ὅρια Τύρου, v. 24) generally refers to the "area under the jurisdiction of the coastal city of Tyre bordering on the north of Galilee."[140] The straight-line distance between the western shore of the Sea Galilee—the starting point of Jesus' journey toward southern Syria might be Gennesaret (6:53)—and Tyre is around 55 kilometers.[141] Lane states that the territorial district of Phoenicia, adjacent Galilee, was around 32 kilometers from Capernaum.[142] Jesus crossed over the frontier of northern Galilee and went into the region of Tyre in southern Syria.

The important, though confused, summary of the route of Jesus' round trip from northwest to southeast is described in 7:31: Καὶ πάλιν ἐξελθὼν ἐκ τῶν ὁρίων Τύρου ἦλθεν διὰ Σιδῶνος εἰς τὴν θάλασσαν τῆς Γαλιλαίας ἀνὰ μέσον τῶν ὁρίων Δεκαπόλεως ("And again departing from the region of Tyre, he went through Sidon toward the Sea of Galilee, through the midst of the region of the Decapolis").[143] The following two episodes—the healing of a deaf and mute man (7:31–37) and the feeding of the four thousand (8:1–10)—share the geographical information from 7:31.

Scholars have suggested diverse interpretations of 7:31. According to France, the phrase διὰ Σιδῶνος ("through Sidon") indicates that Jesus' journey was a roundabout one because he took a detour to reach the southeast area.[144] Jesus set out northward to Sidon from the region of Tyre, then reached south to the Sea of Galilee "in the midst of" (ἀνὰ μέσον) the region of the Decapolis.[145] Mark's description of Jesus' geographical movement is

139. Katzenstein, "Tyre," 6:686.

140. Guelich, *Mark 1–8:26*, 384. See also Dalman, *Sacred Sites and Ways*, 195–208.

141. I calculated the straight-line distance between Tyre and Gennesaret. Gennesaret is located between Capernaum and Magadan.

142. Lane, *Gospel According to Mark*, 259.

143. The above translation is mine.

144. France, *Gospel of Mark*, 301–2. Brooks claims that the phrase "through Sidon" demonstrates Jesus' missional journey to Gentile territory: "The expression 'through Sidon' is shorthand for 'through the region of Sidon' and does not necessarily indicate that Jesus entered the city itself. Sidon's territory probably extended at least twenty miles to the east of the city itself. It was important for Mark to show that Jesus spent some time in Gentile territory—also the Decapolis—in order to provide some justification for the Gentile mission in his own day." See Brooks, *Mark*, 122.

145. Guelich suggests two options for interpreting ἀνὰ μέσον τῶν ὁρίων Δεκαπόλεως,

intended to show that Jesus journeyed beyond Jewish territory. Lane explains the route of Jesus' roundabout trip described in 7:31 as follows: "Jesus apparently journeyed northward to the district of Sidon and then turned southeastward through Philip's territory toward a point on the eastern shore of the Lake of Galilee within the region of the Decapolis."[146] Though I generally agree with Lane's description of Jesus' itinerary, the best interpretation of ἀνὰ μέσον τῶν ὁρίων Δεκαπόλεως is "going through the midst of the region of the Decapolis," rather than his rendering, "within the region of the Decapolis." My translation of the phrase keeps with the meaning of "the midst of" (ἀνὰ μέσον),[147] which demonstrates that Jesus' missional ministry was performed in more extensive areas of Gentile territory as he visited the region of the Decapolis.

Lane argues that the route of 7:31 might be delineated in order to show that Jesus remained in Gentile territory, presenting "strong Gentile

---

especially focusing on ἀνὰ μέσον. The first is simply to interpret the phrase as *"within the territory of the Decapolis,"* which implies that the Sea of Galilee is *within* the territory of the Decapolis (e.g., Cranfield, *Gospel According to Saint Mark*, 250; Lane, *Gospel According to Mark*, 265). However, "this reading conflicts with the geographical data, since the sea borders only a part of the Decapolis and certainly is not in the middle of it." It is also weak on lexical grounds because ἀνὰ μέσον does not simply mean "within" (Lang, "'Über Sidon mitten ins Gebiet Der Dekapolis," 153). Guelich's second option is to insert *"through"* in front of "the midst of" to form *"through the midst of* the territory of the Decapolis" (e.g., Lang, "'Über Sidon mitten ins Gebiet Der Dekapolis," 152-54). Though this rendering also has a lexical problem, it keeps the meaning of "the midst of" and provides an understandable route to the Sea of Galilee: Jesus reached the Sea of Galilee by going through the midst of the territory of Decapolis. See Guelich, *Mark 1–8:26*, 392. The latter option is better in that it may properly explain the route of Jesus' roundabout journey without damaging the meaning of "the midst of."

146. Lane, *Gospel According to Mark*, 256. Though we do not know the exact route of Jesus' journey in 7:31, Edwards assumes the following: "From the region of Tyre Jesus travels over twenty miles north to Sidon, then southeast across the River Leontes, and from there further south through Caesarea Philippi to the Decapolis on the east side of the Sea of Galilee" (Edwards, *Gospel According to Mark*, 223). Guelich introduces two further suggestions. The first is "a route from Tyre via Sidon across to Caesarea Philippi and down through Philip's territory to the sea at Hippos" (e.g., Dalman, *Sacred Sites and Ways*, 200–1; Cranfield, *Gospel According to Saint Mark*, 250; Lane, *Gospel According to Mark*, 265). "It is difficult, however, to include the route going though 'the middle of the Decapolis.'" The second suggestion is a travel "from the territory of Tyre north to Sidon then across Lebanon to the territory of Damascus which bordered the eastern territory of Sidon and then southeast through perhaps the Decapolis cities of Dium, Abila, Gadara and eventually through Hippos to the sea" (e.g., Lang, "Über Sidon mitten ins Gebiet Der Dekapolis," 152–54). See Guelich, *Mark 1–8:26*, 392–93. The second route presents a better description than the first because it may satisfy the expression of "the midst of the Decapolis."

147. Guelich, *Mark 1–8:26*, 393.

association."[148] Donahue and Harrington also claim that the purpose of Mark's description in 7:31 is that "Mark wants to have Jesus move north, then east, and finally south to compass the whole of the southern Phoenician (Gentile) territory prior to his journey to Jerusalem in 8:22–10:52."[149] Mark also describes Jesus as staying "near the east side of the lake" in the light of 8:10. Stein, however, rejects the idea that Jesus' destination in 7:31 is the east side of the Sea of Galilee.[150] Because there is no reference to "crossing over" the Sea of Galilee using a phrase such as εἰς τὸ πέραν ("to the other side"; 4:35; 5:1, 21; 6:45; 8:13), the two events (7:32–37; 8:1–10) took place on the same—western—side of the Sea of Galilee as 8:11–13. The voyage toward Dalmanutha in 8:10 is therefore a side trip.

The purpose of the geographical description in 7:31 is to show that Jesus took a mission to the whole of Gentile territory on the way to his final destination on the east coast of the Sea of Galilee. In the description of Jesus' movement ("Then he left the region of Tyre and went through Sidon") Mark carefully presents Jesus' itinerary in Syria. While Matthew simply describes Jesus as entering the region of Tyre and Sidon (Matt 15:21), Mark divides Jesus' visit to Syria into two steps: entering the region of Tyre (Mark 7:24), and departing from Tyre to go through Sidon (v. 31). In addition, while Matthew does not mention the return route to reach the Sea of Galilee (Matt 15:29), Mark describes the journey to the sea in detail (departing from Tyre and going through Sidon toward the Sea of Galilee, through the midst of the region of the Decapolis, Mark 7:31). Moreover, Mark could have combined Tyre and Sidon into one expression while portraying Jesus' entrance to a house in Syria in 7:24 (compare his earlier use of the expression "Tyre and Sidon" in 3:8),[151] but instead he carefully separated Jesus' visitations between Tyre and Sidon in 7:24, 31 for the purpose of presenting his wide circuit journey from northwest to southeast in Gentile territory. The expression "in the midst of" (ἀνὰ μέσον) the region of the Decapolis implies that Jesus' ministry covered Gentile territory and that he sojourned there. The Markan expression "he came to" (ἦλθεν εἰς; 1:14, 29, 39; 5:1; 6:53; 8:10; 9:33; 14:16) indicates that "the following incident/event takes place in the location described by the 'to' (εἰς)."[152] After his round trip, then, Jesus reached the eastern side of the Sea of Galilee.

148. Lane, *Gospel According to Mark*, 256–57.
149. Donahue and Harrington, *Gospel of Mark*, 239.
150. Stein, *Mark*, 357–58.
151. See Gundry, *Mark*, 378.
152. Stein, *Mark*. 358. Though Stein argues that Jesus reached the west coast of the Sea of Galilee (Jewish territory), I argue its location was the east coast (Gentile territory).

If we connect Jesus' itinerary around the region of the Decapolis in 7:31 with the expression "during those days" (ἐν ἐκείναις ταῖς ἡμέραις) in 8:1, the miracle of the feeding of the four thousand (8:1–10) happened on "the east side of the Sea of Galilee" in Gentile territory.[153] In the light of Jesus' extensive journey in 7:31, some of the crowd who came from a great distance (ἀπὸ μακρόθεν ἥκασιν) in 8:3 might be Gentiles who followed Jesus from the regions he visited earlier.[154] In addition, the fact that the two episodes (7:31–37; 8:1–10) have Gentile characteristics[155] indicates that these events took place in Gentile territory. The two episodes thus share the geographical information from 7:31, taking place on the east side of the Sea of Galilee in Gentile territory. After feeding the four thousand, Jesus returned west to the region of Dalmanutha by boat (8:10).

Tracing Jesus' geographical movement in each cycle establishes four aspects of the cyclic pattern. First, each cycle includes two sea-crossings from west to east and back from east to west. The four references to crossing over the sea appear in 4:35, 5:21, 6:45, and 8:10. In the first cycle, Jesus traveled over the sea by a boat from west to east (4:35) and then returned from east to west (5:21). In the second cycle, Jesus attempted to cross over from the west to Bethsaida in the east, but this voyage was aborted and he landed on the west side at Gennesaret (6:45, 53). Jesus then journeyed by land in the areas of Tyre, Sidon, the coast of the Sea of Galilee, and the region of the Decapolis (7:31) and finally reached the east side of the Sea of Galilee, from where he returned west to Dalmanutha (8:10).

Second, Jesus took an overland journey in each cycle. In the first cycle, after being rejected by his hometown (6:1–6a) Jesus went around teaching from village to village in Galilee (6:6b) and sent his disciples out into Galilee with mission commandments (6:7–13, 30). In the second cycle, after a controversy with Jewish religious leaders about the law of purity and his proclamation that all foods are clean (7:1–23), Jesus ventured into Gentile territory, traveling toward the northwestern cities of Tyre and Sidon before coming down to the east side of the Sea of Galilee in the region of the Decapolis (7:24–37).

---

153. Edwards, *Gospel According to Mark*, 229.

154. According to Guelich (*Mark 1–8:26*, 404), the phrase ἀπὸ μακρόθεν ἥκασιν could "allude to Gentiles as constituents of the crowd" (Guelich, *Mark 1–8:26*, 404). Danker also argues that this expression indicates "Gentiles," which may reflect Josh 9:6 LXX and Isa 60:4 LXX (Danker, "Mark 8:3," 215–16).

155. For a detailed discussion of the Gentile characteristics in these two episodes, see Iverson, *Gentiles in the Gospel of Mark*, 57–77.

In addition, the pattern of Jesus' overland journey is similar in the two cycles: seaside (seashore)/land/seaside (wilderness).[156] In the first cycle, after sea-crossings back and forth (4:35—5:20), Jesus healed Jairus's daughter and a woman with a hemorrhage at the seashore (5:21–43). He then traveled inland to Nazareth (6:1–6a). After being rejected by his hometown people, he took an overland tour, giving his disciples a mission commandment and sending them to the villages of Galilee (6:6b–30). Finally, Jesus and his disciples withdrew to the wilderness, and Jesus fed five thousand people along the western seaside (6:31–44). In the second cycle, after aborted sea-crossings back and forth (6:45–52), Jesus healed many people at the seashore (6:53–56) and discussed distinctions between clean and unclean, proclaiming that all foods are clean (7:1–23). He then traveled overland into Gentile territory, progressing toward the region of Tyre, through Sidon, and through the middle of the Decapolis before reaching the Sea of Galilee (7:24–36). Finally, Jesus fed four thousand people in the wilderness along the eastern seaside (8:1–10). The following table presents the cyclic pattern of seaside/land/seaside centered on an overland journey in each cycle.

	Cycle I	Cycle II
Seaside	Sea-crossings (4:35—5:20) and healing at the seashore (5:21–43)	Sea-crossings (6:45–52) and healing at the seashore (6:53–56; teaching about clean and unclean [7:1–23])
Land	Overland Journey (6:1–30)	Overland Journey (7:24–37)
Seaside	Feeding the five thousand in the wilderness beside the sea (6:31–44)	Feeding the four thousand in the wilderness beside the sea (8:1–10)[157]

156. In his compositional analysis of Mark 4:1—8:26, Petersen suggests the pattern of seaside/sea/seaside in three cycles and inland tours in two intervals located among three cycles (Petersen, "Composition of Mark 4:1–8:26," 188; especially see the diagram of three cycles and two intervals). This pattern is inversely used to demonstrate my proposed pattern, seaside/land/seaside, though my detailed divisions of passages differ from Petersen's.

157. My overall structure, which presents two cycles with juxtaposition, is based on the sea (4:35–41; 6:45–52), the land (5:1—6:30; 6:53—7:37), and the wilderness (6:31–44; 8:1–10). The above table seems to be in conflict with my overall structure in terms of the detailed divisions of passages; however, since this table focuses solely on the pattern of an overland journey in each cycle by paying attention to the beginning and ending points of travel, namely the seaside, it does not disagree with my overall structure. In addition, the sea miracles in the sea are included in the beginning parts, and the feeding miracles in the wilderness are contained in the ending parts.

Third, in each cycle Jesus began his ministry at the sea and ended it in the wilderness. In each cycle, Jesus began his journey by sailing to the east; the miracles of calming the sea (4:35–41) and walking on the sea (6:45–52) took place in the process. His final destination in each cycle is the wilderness (ἔρημός [6:32]; ἐρημία [8:4]), where he fed the five thousand on the west side of the Sea of Galilee (Jewish territory) and the four thousand at the east side of the Sea of Galilee (Gentile territory).

Finally, the Decapolis,[158] which is the focal point of Jesus' Gentile mission, plays the role of connecting the two cycles. In the beginning of the first cycle, Jesus visited the region of the Gerasenes and met a demon-possessed man (5:1–20). Jesus expelled the demons from the man and healed him; the man then proclaimed in the Decapolis how much Jesus had done for him. In the end of the second cycle, Jesus reached the region of the Decapolis (7:31) and healed a deaf and mute man (7:31–37). According to Donahue and Harrington, Mark establishes a pattern where a report about Jesus spreads in Gentile areas and then Jesus performs miracles there.[159] Those who lived in the region of the Decapolis and heard about Jesus in the first cycle were able to see his mighty works in the second cycle. Therefore, the Decapolis serves as the first and last stop for the Gentile mission.

In conclusion, Jesus' journey in each cycle shows a similar pattern of geographical movement: (1) a journey from west to east by sea and a return from east to west; (2) an overland journey through either Jewish or Gentile territory; (3) a movement from the sea in the first event to the desert in the final event; and (4) Gentile mission around the focal point of the Decapolis.

The two cycles differ, however, according to their varying territorial emphases. In the first cycle, Jesus' ministry was performed mainly in Jewish territory, with the exception of the healing of a Gerasene demoniac in the Decapolis (5:1–20). On the contrary, in the second cycle his ministry occurred mostly in Gentile territory, with the exception of the controversy

---

158. "The Decapolis" (Δεκάπολις) literally means the "ten cities" in Greek, but the number of cities has not been exactly determined. All the cities are located to the east of the Jordan River except for Scythopolis (Beth-shan), which is located on the plain of lower Galilee. The Decapolis is known as a "league of independent cities organized by Pompey," but their political union is not found in documents. The reason that they seemed to be united as one is "their Hellenistic character, which distinguished them sharply from neighboring populations, Jews to the W, Nabataeans to the S, highland tribes or semi-nomads to the N." The Hellenistic nature of the Decapolis is shown in their "origin," "institutions," and "culture." See Rey-Coquais, "Decapolis," 2:116–21.

159. A similar pattern appears in John, in that "people proclaim Jesus but faith comes from direct contact" (John 4:28–30, 39–42). In addition, the healed Gerasene demoniac plays the role of "a prototype of the Christian missionary" in the region of the Decapolis. Donahue and Harrington, *Gospel of Mark*, 168, 239.

with religious leaders in Jewish territory (7:1–23). Jesus' geographical movement in each cycle can be outlined as follows:

Cycle I	Cycle II
1. W to E (sea-crossing: 4:35—5:20)	1. W to E (aborted) but returned to W (sea-crossing: 6:45—7:23)
2. E to W (sea-crossing: 5:21-43)	2. W to E (outland journey beyond Galilee [overland: 7:24-37])
3. W (inland journey of Galilee [overland: 6:1-30])	3. E (the wilderness near the Sea of Galilee [8:1-9])
4. W (the wilderness near the Sea of Galilee [6:31-44])	4. E to W (sea-crossing: 8:10)

Parallels between the Two Cycles

I will examine the parallels between the two cycles in a geographical framework, which may further explicate the cyclic pattern in Mark 4:35—8:21. According to Williams, Mark displays a "series of repeating scenes,"[160] and Mark's literary technique of repetition plays a significant role of forming a pattern in a narrative. In repetition, similarities and dissimilarities appear together. Williams suggests four functions of repetition.[161] The first function is "emphasis" which facilitates clear understanding of the narrative by underscoring the idea that Mark considers as significant.[162] The second is the establishment of "variations," in which the narrative resonates as different events or characters are found in similar situations.[163] The third is the promotion of "new developments in character and plot" through variations in repeated episodes.[164] The fourth function is setting "expectations"

---

160. Williams, *Other Followers of Jesus*, 52.

161. Williams, *Other Followers of Jesus*, 52–54.

162. Williams, *Other Followers of Jesus*, 52–53. For example, after Jesus' proclamation of the coming of the kingdom of God with the request to repent and believe in the gospel in Mark 1:14–15, the people in the following miracles consistently and repeatedly respond to Jesus by showing faith. This repetition demonstrates Mark's emphasis on faith.

163. Williams, *Other Followers of Jesus*, 53. According to Williams, "placing different characters in similar situations allows the narrator to explore possible responses. Through his repeated depiction of minor characters and their reactions to Jesus, Mark is able to define in a greater way his understanding of the proper response to Jesus."

164. Williams, *Other Followers of Jesus*, 53. For example, Mark shows a series of characters in similar situations, but then develops his narrative by presenting variations in these situations. In relation to the present study, a Jewish woman with a hemorrhage

by which readers may anticipate subsequent situations in a framed pattern, assuming that "the pattern will continue."[165]

Rhoads, Dewey, and Michie claim that Mark's compositional structure is not so much clearly linear as repetitive: "The Markan episodes are intertwined with each other by the repetition of words and phrases, the occurrence of foreshadowings and retrospections, similarities of scenes and situations, and the clustering of episodes in concentric or parallel patterns."[166] Repetition occurs among characters, settings, themes, or verbal agreements, and involves many similarities. Repetition does not mean exact sameness, however; rather it refers to a consistent pattern in the midst of variations.[167] In order to find a pattern, one needs to discover similar situations and to explore how variations take place in these situations. Variations occur when characters or other elements are changed in the midst of similar situations.[168] Therefore, the focal point of discovering a pattern is to find similar situations in the episodes. Though repetition should be studied from every literary aspect such as characters, themes, settings, and verbal agreements, it is necessary to examine similar situations in order to discover a pattern.[169] Here, I will discover similar situations especially from the "settings" of the episodes.

---

shows great faith to Jesus (5:21–43) in the first cycle (4:35—6:44) and a Gentile Syrophoenician woman with a demon-possessed daughter demonstrates great faith to Jesus (7:24–30) in the second cycle (6:45—8:21). Both characters are women, but their ethnicity is different. Here, Mark's narrative develops in terms of the expansion of Jesus' missional journey, from the Jews to the Gentiles. There is repetition in relation to the characters' gender and faith, but variation in repetition in terms of their ethnicity, which develops the narrative by demonstrating that Jesus' ministry expands from the Jews to the Gentiles.

165. Williams, *Other Followers of Jesus*, 54. For example, Jesus repeatedly commands the people who are healed by him not to tell the healing miracles, but they do not keep his word, spreading the news about his miraculous works. This pattern is discovered in the leper (1:44–45), the Gerasene demoniac (5:19–20), the people who see the healing of a deaf and mute man (7:36), and the people's restraint of blind Bartimaeus from crying out for Jesus' mercy (10:48). "Through repetition, Mark creates the expectation that minor characters will speak freely when they are confronted by the miraculous power of Jesus."

166. Rhoads et al., *Mark as Story*, 47. According to Dewey, "Mark does not have a clear linear structure, rather it consists of forecasts and echoes, variation within repetition, for a listening audience" (Dewey, "Mark as Interwoven Tapestry," 234).

167. Williams states that "the narration of similar situations with variations adds resonance to the story" (Williams, *Other Followers of Jesus*, 53).

168. Williams, *Other Followers of Jesus*, 53.

169. Rhoads, Dewey, and Michie suggest eight types of repetitive patterns in Mark's narrative: "verbal thread," "foreshadowing and retrospection," "two-step progressions," "type-scenes," "sandwich episodes," "framing episodes," "episodes in a concentric

According to Rhoads, Dewey, and Michie, "settings serve many functions: generating atmosphere, providing the occasion for a conflict, revealing traits of the characters as they interact with settings, and evoking associations present in the culture of the audience."[170] In general, settings give us information about "where," "when," and "how" actions take place.[171] Therefore, settings are investigated in three aspects, namely "locale," "time," and "circumstances."[172] In the present study, I will discover a cyclic pattern in Mark 4:35—8:21, which is constructed on the basis of repetition, in other words parallelism. In a narrative dimension, I will discover parallelism between the two cycles in the frame of the narrative settings, namely space, time, and circumstances. "Where" is related to space, in which I will examine the similar pattern of Jesus' geographical movement in the two cycles. "When" is concerned with "time," in which I will investigate the similar situation that narrative time creates in the two cycles. "How" is involved with circumstances, in which I will explore the similar context, namely social, political, cultural, religious, economic, etc., in the two cycle. Though I mainly focus on the similar settings to demonstrate my proposed cyclic pattern, I will also examine parallels between the two cycles in regard to characters, themes, and verbal expressions, which are necessarily significant to discover a cyclic pattern.

As we previously examined, a cyclic pattern of Jesus' journey can be discovered by tracing the route of his geographical movement. From now on, this pattern will be explored by investigating parallelism between the two cycles in similar situations, namely settings and other repetitive elements. Here, it is necessary to define the terms of geography and space that I employ. I use the term "geography" to emphasize the route in which Jesus took a journey, so geography is connected to a movement between places. However, I employ the term "space" to highlight the significant settings in which the events happened: space, therefore, connotes peculiar or allusive significance. Nevertheless, the usages of these terms overlap sometimes.

The spatial settings in each cycle largely consist of three parts: the sea (4:35–41; 6:45–52), the land (5:1—6:30; 6:53—7:37),[173] and the wilder-

---

pattern," and "progressive episodes in series of three." See Rhoads et al., *Mark as Story*, 47–55.

170. Rhoads et al., *Mark as Story*, 63.

171. Powell, *What Is Narrative Criticism?*, 69.

172. Abrams and Harpham, *Glossary of Literary Terms*, 330. More detailed studies of settings require "the cosmic depiction of space and time, the culture and society of the story world, geographical locations, humanly constructed spaces, and so on" (Rhoads et al., *Mark as Story*, 63).

173. Though sea trips by boat appear in the overland journey of the first cycle (5:21;

ness (6:31–44; 8:1–10). In each spatial setting, Jesus performed the nature miracles of calming the sea and walking on it, the healing miracles—both exorcism and curing sickness—on the land, and the feeding miracles of the five thousand and the four thousand in the wilderness.

In the first miracles (sea miracles: 4:35–41; 6:45–52) of each cycle, similar situations are discovered. In both episodes, the spatial setting is the sea. Geographically, the voyages are sea-crossings (εἰς τὸ πέραν [to the other side: 4:35; 6:45]) from west to east. The time is the evening (ὀψίας γενομένης [when evening came: 4:35; 6:47]), which alludes to a terrifying situation at night.[174] The circumstance is the disciples' desperate struggle against a furious wind (λαῖλαψ μεγάλη ἀνέμου [a great windstorm: 4:37]; ὁ ἄνεμος ἐναντίος αὐτοῖς [a wind against them: 6:48]).

We can also find similar situations in the last miracle of each cycle (the feeding miracles: 6:31–44; 8:1–10). In both episodes, the spatial setting is the wilderness near the Sea of Galilee, on the west side of the sea (Jewish territory) in the first cycle and on the east side (Gentile territory) in the second. Reference to time indicates the critical need for food or the state of starvation.[175] The phrase ἤδη ὥρας πολλῆς ("the hour is already late"),[176] repeated twice in 6:35, creates a sense of crisis regarding the need to feed the people,[177] while the length of the journey with Jesus (ἤδη ἡμέραι τρεῖς, "already three days") in 8:2 highlights that the crowd might be hungry.[178] The circumstance is the predicament of the crowd, which arouses Jesus' compassion. In the account of the feeding of the five thousand Jesus was moved with compassion because the people were like sheep without a shepherd (6:34), while in the feeding of the four thousand Jesus had compassion because the people had nothing to eat (8:2).

6:32), I place them in the overland journey in the large frame. When we study settings in detail, we will explore their functions as settings.

174. Donahue and Harrington, *Gospel of Mark*, 157.

175. Donahue and Harrington, *Gospel of Mark*, 205, 244.

176. In Greek literature, the phrase ὥρας πολλῆς sometimes means a "late hour," and in this verse it indicates the late afternoon, when the normal dinner time was approaching. France, *Gospel of Mark*, 256.

177. Donahue and Harrington, *Gospel of Mark*, 205.

178. Donahue and Harrington, *Gospel of Mark*, 244. There is another nuance of time for three days. The term "three days" evokes anticipation that a significant event may occur. In the OT, important events happened after a three-day journey ("Gen 30:36; Exod 3:18; 5:3; 8:27; Num 10:33; Josh 1:11") or a three-day hunger or fasting ("1 Sam 30:12; Esth 4:16"). According to Boring, the time setting in 8:2 ("in those days": ἐν ἐκείναις ταῖς ἡμέραις) provides "little chronological information, but is a biblical formula with eschatological overtones" (Boring, *Mark*, 219).

The first and last miracles of each cycle are clearly parallel to one another, presenting variations on similar events in similar settings.[179] It is more complicated to discover parallelism between the remaining episodes of the two cycles and arrange them with a repetitive form.[180] Nonetheless, a cyclic pattern with parallelism can be consistently tracked through these episodes. Though there is little reference to time settings in these episodes, spatial and circumstantial settings and other elements such as characters, themes, and verbal expressions can be examined for parallelism. Within the frame of the sea and feeding miracles that serve as brackets, the remaining episodes in each cycle show a chiastic structure at a narrative level as follows:

179. I have refrained from examining the parallel elements of characters, themes, and verbal expressions between the two sea miracles and between the two feeding miracles because the similar situations between them can be clearly seen in the similar locales, time, and circumstances.

180. Malbon suggests parallelism of the episodes between the two sea-feeding blocks with respect to Jesus' "mighty deeds" (δυνάμεις, 6:2) as follows:

Calming the sea	Walking on the sea
Healing the Gerasene demoniac (a Gentile)	Healing many at Gennesaret (Jews)
Healing the hemorrhaging woman and Jairus's daughter (two Jews)	Healing the daughter of the Syrophoenician woman and the deaf man in the Decapolis (two Gentiles)
Feeding the five thousand (Jews)	Feeding the four thousand (Gentiles)

She demonstrates a parallelism between the two building blocks, presenting the contrast between Jewish and Gentile characters. See Malbon, "Echoes and Foreshadowings in Mark 4–8," 219–22. There are, however, several weaknesses in her parallel structure. First, "healing many at Gennesaret (Jews)" in the second block does not parallel with "healing the Gerasene demoniac (a Gentile)" in the first block, because the former is simply a summary of Jesus' healing of the crowd. In addition, the summary does not include any individual or particular character who plays a significant role in an episode comparable to that of the Gerasene demoniac. Second, Malbon claims that the healing of the hemorrhaging woman and Jairus's daughter (two Jews) corresponds to the healing of the daughter of the Syrophoenician woman and the deaf man in the Decapolis (two Gentiles). The two episodes in the former healing correspond only to the daughter of the Syrophoenician woman, excluding the deaf man in the Decapolis, because the former two episodes are combined in a sandwich structure. In addition, the central and common theme—a woman's faith and the healing of a daughter—in the former two episodes only appears in the episode of the daughter of the Syrophoenician woman. Third, as Malbon herself says, the three episodes in the second block are not connected sequentially in one cluster like the three in the first block.

[The sea miracle of Jesus' calming the storm (4:35-41)]
A — A demon-possessed man (5:1-20)
   B — Jairus's daughter and a woman with a hemorrhage (5:21-43)
      C — Jesus' saying about mission to the Jews, including some episodes (6:1-30)
[The feeding miracle of the five thousand (6:31-44)]

[The sea miracle of Jesus' walking on the water (6:45-52); healing summary (6:53-56)]
      C' — Jesus' saying in relation to the implication of mission to the Gentiles (7:1-23)
   B' — A Syrophoenician woman's daughter (7:24-30)
A' — A deaf and mute man (7:31-37)
[The feeding miracle of the four thousand (8:1-10)]

First, the narrative settings of a demon-possessed man (5:1-20) and a deaf and mute man (7:31-37) are similar.[181] In the first cycle, Jesus met a demon-possessed man who lived among the tombs in the region of the Gerasenes after the first crossing the Sea of Galilee to Gentile territory (5:1-3). Jesus healed the demon-possessed man, who proclaimed how much Jesus had done for him in the Decapolis (5:20).[182] In the second cycle, Jesus arrived at the Sea of Galilee in the midst of the region of the Decapolis by way of Tyre and Sidon (7:31) and met a deaf and mute man who had a speech impediment (7:32). This miracle took place before the last sea-crossing back to Jewish territory. We can thus observe the similar settings of the two episodes: they took place near the Sea of Galilee (θάλασσα, 5:1; 7:31) and are related to the region of the Decapolis (Δεκάπολις, 5:20; 7:31).[183] In addition, the Decapolis serves as the connecting point between the two episodes: the formerly demon-possessed man proclaimed Jesus' mighty work to the people of the Decapolis at the beginning of the first cycle (5:20), and those who lived in the region of the Decapolis brought a deaf and mute man to Jesus at the end of the second cycle (7:31-32).

A similar response to Jesus' healing miracles appears in both episodes. At the end of each episode, people were astonished by Jesus' mighty work

---

181. Williams, *Other Followers of Jesus*, 45.

182. The demon-possessed man plays the role of a forerunner for the preparation of Jesus' ministry in Gentile territory as John the Baptist does in Jewish territory (Wefald, "Separate Gentile Mission in Mark," 13-14). In addition, "the prototype of the Christian missionary" can be discovered in a demon-possessed man who proclaimed what Jesus had done (Donahue and Harrington, *Gospel of Mark*, 168).

183. Williams, *Other Followers of Jesus*, 45-46. In Mark, the Decapolis appears only in 5:20 and 7:31.

(5:20; 7:36–37). In the first cycle, the healed man began to proclaim (ἤρξατο κηρύσσειν, 5:20) how much Jesus had done for him, and all were amazed (ἐθαύμαζον, 5:20). In the second cycle, the intensity of the proclamation and amazement increases with the healing of the deaf and mute man: the more Jesus commanded people to tell no one, the more zealously they proclaimed it (μᾶλλον περισσότερον ἐκήρυσσον, 7:36), and those who heard it were astonished beyond measure (ὑπερπερισσῶς ἐξεπλήσσοντο, 7:37).

Second, the interwoven story of Jairus's daughter and the woman with a hemorrhage in the first cycle (5:21–43) can be compared with the account of the Syrophoenician woman's daughter in the second cycle (7:24–30).[184] The geographical settings of the two stories are different, however. The episodes of Jairus's daughter and the woman with a hemorrhage took place on the west shore of the Sea of Galilee (5:21) right after a sea-crossing from the east; the episode of the Syrophoenician woman's daughter occurred in the region of Tyre (7:24)—northern Gentile territory—during an overland journey. Though the geographical settings differ between the episodes, the spatial setting of the miracles is the same: both take place in a house. In the first cycle Jesus entered Jairus's house (οἶκος, 5:38) and healed his daughter; in the second, Jesus entered a certain house (οἰκία, 7:24) and conversed with a Syrophoenician woman who found her daughter healed when she returned to her own house (οἶκος, 7:30).

The more significant aspect of the settings of these two episodes is their social circumstances. Two characters, a woman and a daughter, play an important role in both.[185] In particular, the woman with a hemorrhage (5:25–34) and the Syrophoenician woman (7:24–30) serve as exemplary figures who show true faith,[186] despite the fact that both held low social positions in the ancient world.[187] In the first cycle, the woman with a hem-

---

184. The healings of Jairus's daughter (5:21–24; 35–43) and the woman with a hemorrhage (5:25–43) are regarded as one unit since they are intertwined in a sandwich structure.

185. In both episodes, women show true faith and daughters are healed.

186. An episode about a woman with a hemorrhage (5:25–34) is intercalated in the middle of a healing story of Jairus's daughter (5:21–24; 35–43), and the two stories consist of a sandwich structure (A-B-A'): the B-section (a woman with hemorrhage) serves as the "theological key" to interpret the A and A'-sections (a healing story of Jairus's daughter). In the light of the B-section, the central theme in this sandwich structure is faith. Edwards, *Gospel According to Mark*, 11–12.

187. Women in Jewish society generally belonged to the lower class and their social status appears in the saying that "man gives thanks that he is not an unbeliever or uncivilized, that he is not a woman and that he is not a slave"—"Among the Rabb. it is traced back to R. Jehuda b. Elaj (c. 150 AD)" (Oepke, "γυνή," 1:777). According to Scholer, women were portrayed negatively, especially as sexual tempters, by male writers, and their roles were limited to household chores as wife and mother. The

orrhage suffered not only from physical illness, but also from social and religious discrimination.[188] Menstruation was regarded as a source of ritual impurity (Lev 15:19–27; Josephus *J.W.* 5.227), and the woman who discharged blood for twelve years was isolated from her community.[189] In the second cycle, Mark describes the woman with a demon-possessed daughter with the double expression Ἑλληνίς, Συροφοινίκισσα to describe her ethnicity—she is introduced as a Gentile woman of Syrian Phoenicia (7:26). Edwards argues that we can read v. 26 as a "crescendo of demerit": "she is a woman, a Greek Gentile, from infamous pagans of Syrian Phoenicia."[190] Jesus compared the Gentiles to dogs (κυναρίοις, v. 27), which was insult to the Gentile woman.[191] In the Jewish world, the Gentile woman was placed far from God's blessings ("Let the children first be fed, for it is not fair to take children's bread and throw it to the dogs," v. 27). It is clear, then, that the women in the two cycles both experienced exclusion from the Jewish

---

first-century historian Josephus insists that "women should be submissive" because the Law prescribes women to be "inferior in all matters" (Josephus, *Ag. Ap.* 2.201). Sirach even narrates the state of women's nature as follows: "better is the wickedness of a man than a woman who does good; it is woman who brings shame and disgrace" (Sir 42:14). On the other hand, positive pictures of women have also been discovered in Second Temple sources: some women occupied a leading position in synagogues, and Jewish women sometimes took "initiative for their lives and activities" independent from male domination. In general, however, Jewish society and culture showed "androcentric and patriarchal" characteristics and Jewish women became passive and submissive, though we cannot say that they were severely oppressed and rejected from society. See Scholer, "Women I: Gospels," 1095–96. In Greek culture, most women were set apart from society and only lower-class women were compelled to leave home to draw water and handle business in the marketplace. Greek women were depreciated by men and were thought to lack moral conscience. They were forced to stay at home, conducting household affairs. "Conversation with males outside the family was forbidden to citizen-class women, and even communication between spouses was limited." It was therefore unusual for Jesus to converse with a Syrophoenician woman in Mark 7:24–30. See Kroeger, "Women in Greco-Roman World and Judaism," 1276–77. Despite their low-level status, "the Greek ideal of woman is a lofty one. Greek poetry offers a wealth of impressive and imperishable types of womanhood both in the physical and the spiritual sense" (Oepke, "γυνή," 1:777–78). Roman women could have relatively more freedom than Greek women, engaging in many and diverse social activities. See Kroeger, "Women in Greco-Roman World and Judaism," 1277.

188. France, *Gospel of Mark*, 236.

189. Edwards, *Gospel According to Mark*, 163.

190. Edwards, *Gospel According to Mark*, 218.

191. Though κυνάριον (little dogs or puppies) is the diminutive form, the nuance of its severity does not decrease: "The diminutive form (used in biblical literature only in this pericope), perhaps indicates the status of the dogs in Jesus' image as dogs of the house rather than of the yard, but it does not remove the harshness of picturing Gentiles en masse as 'dogs' as opposed to 'children'" (France, *Gospel of Mark*, 298).

community because of their social status, yet both overcame adversities and obtained what they sought by faith.

Finally, though it is difficult to discover similarities in the settings of Jesus' saying about a mission to Jews (6:1–30) and his saying about clean and unclean with its implications for a mission to the Gentiles (7:1–23), the similarity between these two pericopae can be found in their common theme of "mission." In the first cycle, after Jesus was rejected by his hometown (6:1–6a) he went around teaching from village to village in Galilee and sent out his disciples with a mission commandment (6:6b–13, 30). In this section, the episode of Herod's execution of John the Baptist is inserted by stealth, seeming irrelevant to the mission theme. As Edward points out, however, the two episodes of Jesus' mission commandment and sending of the Twelve (6:6b–13, 30) and the execution of John the Baptist (6:14–29) are connected in a sandwich structure.[192] The death of John the Baptist points to martyrdom, which serves as prefiguration of the death of Jesus and his followers. By inserting the episode of John the Baptist's execution (6:14–29) into their mission activities (6:6b–13, 30), Mark intended to show that the disciples' mission should involve sacrificial commitment to the point of death. "The sandwich structure draws mission and martyrdom, discipleship and death into an inseparable relationship."[193] The section as a whole, therefore, deals with mission to the Jews.

In the second cycle, after Jesus engaged in a controversy about Jewish tradition with the Pharisees and some of the scribes (7:1–13), he explained what is clean or unclean (vv. 14–23), teaching that people are not made unclean by what goes into them, but by what comes out of them. In his instruction about purity and impurity, Jesus declared that all foods are clean (v. 19). This means that all people, regardless of their ethnicity, are clean[194] and can be the people of God. With this proclamation, Jesus took an overland journey toward Gentile territory to the north (v. 24), where he met the Syrophoenician woman (vv. 24–30). Jesus' instruction about clean and unclean is thus related to the Gentile mission, and indeed the following episodes (7:24–30, 31–37; 8:1–10) show Jesus' mission to the Gentiles.

The Final Section as Concluding the Two Cycles

The concluding section (8:11–21) contains two episodes: the Pharisees' request for a sign (8:11–12) and the discussion of bread on the sea (8:13–21).

192. Edwards, *Gospel According to Mark*, 189.
193. Edwards, *Gospel According to Mark*, 189.
194. Phelan, "Rhetoric and Meaning," 224.

In the first episode, Jesus returned to the west, the region of Dalmanutha (8:10), where he met the Pharisees. The fact that Jesus met Jewish religious leaders implies that he came to Jewish territory.[195] Like the first and second cycles, this concluding section begins in Jewish territory.

In this episode, the Pharisees ask Jesus for "a sign (σημεῖον) from heaven." Here a "sign" does not simply mean a miracle, but "a public, definite proof that God is with him."[196] The Pharisees could undoubtedly know about Jesus' miraculous works, because his reputation as a miracle worker had been spread not only to the Jews but also to the Gentiles (1:32–34, 45; 3:7–12; 5:19–20; 6:53–56; 7:25, 32).[197] Their request for a sign is seeking not the reproduction of a miracle but some kind of "authentication" that Jesus' activity comes from God.[198] Though their seeking a sign is intended to test Jesus (8:11), this is related to his identity as God's agent.

Jesus' refusal of the Pharisees' request for a sign implies that the miracles he had already performed truly came from God. The divine approval of his miraculous works was denied by Jewish religious leaders such as the scribes who witnessed Jesus' exorcism and reproached him because they thought that he was possessed by Beelzebub and cast out demons by the ruler of the demons (3:22). In 8:12, Jesus refused to give a sign to the Pharisees due to their unbelief and dishonest motive. The unfaithful and rebellious generation seeks a sign, "since they have rejected the 'signs' that God has already given them through Jesus' ministry."[199] Jesus' refusal to provide a sign indicates that only those who have faith can recognize that what he said and did came from God. This episode (8:11–12) therefore serves as the conclusion of the two cycles (4:35—6:44; 6:45—8:10) because Jesus' refusal

---

195. "Jesus' encountering Jewish religious leaders" serves as the narrative signal to show that Jesus is in Jewish territory. Wefald, "Separate Gentile Mission in Mark," 12–13.

196. In the OT and Second Temple Jewish literature, the concept of a sign implies a "token which guarantees the truthfulness of an utterance or the legitimacy of an action" (Lane, *Gospel According to Mark*, 276–77). The term σημεῖον is not used to signify a miracle in the Synoptic Gospels. See Guelich, *Mark 1–8:26*, 413.

197. Guelich, *Mark 1–8:26*, 413.

198. According to France, the sign that the Pharisees request is to have a supernatural character, as it comes "from heaven" (ἀπὸ τοῦ οὐρανοῦ) (France, *Gospel of Mark*, 311). Gibson states that this expression contains an apocalyptic tone (Gibson, "Jesus' Refusal," 37–66). On the contrary, Marcus asserts that the phrase ἀπὸ τοῦ οὐρανοῦ may be a "circumlocution for 'from God'" (Marcus, *Mark 1–8*, 499). There are two ways of interpreting ἀπὸ τοῦ οὐρανοῦ: an apocalyptic implication and a "periphrase for 'from God.'" Of the two options, Guelich believes that the latter understanding better fits the context of this episode. See Guelich, *Mark 1–8:26*, 413–14.

199. Guelich, *Mark 1–8:26*, 414.

of the Pharisees' request demonstrates that his previous miraculous works and sayings (4:35—8:10) were, in fact, authenticated by God.

In the second episode (8:13–21), the discussion between Jesus and his disciples about bread on the sea is connected to both the sea miracles (4:35–41; 6:45–52) and the feeding miracles (6:31–44; 8:1–10) and delivers the theme that Jesus is the Savior who feeds both the Jews and the Gentiles.[200] This episode (8:13–21) includes the boat and bread motifs which play the role of connecting the previous sea and feeding miracles. There are four connecting points between the discussion on the sea and the previous sea and feeding miracles.

First, this episode (8:13–21), like the two sea miracles (4:35–41; 6:45–52), is set on the sea. Just as three passion predictions function as the central axes of 8:22—10:52 with its "way motif," three sea events (4:35–41; 6:45–52; 8:13–21) serve as a framework of 4:35—8:21 with its "boat motif."[201] The two sea miracles and the discussion on the sea have a boat motif and a sea setting in common.

Second, over the course of the three sea episodes, the disciples' incomprehension becomes worse in a sort of "downward spiral," and this too connects the episodes.[202] In the first sea episode (4:35–41), Jesus rebuked the disciples' lack of faith (4:40), and they asked each other with fear, "Who then is this?" (4:41). In the second episode (6:45–52), they mistook Jesus for a ghost as he walked on the sea, "for they did not understand about the loaves and their heart was hardened" (6:52).[203] In the third episode (8:13–21), the disciples' lack of understanding is intensified by Jesus' twofold reproaches: "Do you still not perceive or understand? Are your hearts hardened?" (8:17). The first charge about the disciples' lack of understanding ("Do you still not perceive or understand?" 8:17) is related to the first sea episode ("Who then is this?" 4:41). The second charge about the disciples' hardened heart ("Are your hearts hardened?" 8:17) is connected to the second sea episode ("for their hearts were hardened," 6:52).

Third, the disciples' fearful rhetorical question about Jesus' identity in the first sea episode (4:35–41) was answered by Jesus' rebuke-laden

---

200. Malbon claims that "the sea conversation echoes not only the preceding two sea incidents but especially the preceding two miraculous feeding stories" (Malbon, "Echoes and Foreshadowings in Mark 4–8," 214–15).

201. Malbon, "Echoes and Foreshadowings in Mark 4–8," 214.

202. Boring, *Mark*, 225.

203. The second sea miracle (6:45–52) is connected to the preceding feeding miracle (6:31–44). The reason that the disciples mistook Jesus for a ghost is their incomprehension of the preceding feeding miracle (6:52); the disciples' misunderstanding of Jesus' walking on the sea is thus connected to their failure to understand his feeding miracle.

rhetorical question in the discussion on the sea (8:13–21).²⁰⁴ In the first sea episode, the disciples who saw Jesus calm the sea asked each other, "Who then is this?" (τίς ἄρα οὗτός ἐστιν;, 4:41). In the conclusion, Jesus asked his disciples—who still failed to realize Jesus' identity despite having experienced the two feeding miracles—"Do you still not understand?" (οὔπω συνίετε;, 8:21). Though Jesus' saying to the disciples takes a form of question, it is a rhetorical question designed to make the disciples recognize who Jesus is. Jesus' question in 8:21 thus serves as the answer to the disciples' question about his identity in the first sea miracle in 4:41. The first question in this section (4:35—8:21) is answered by the last question in the same section. Furthermore, Jesus' rhetorical question (8:21) not only exposes the disciples' lack of understanding but also discloses his identity as the Savior.

Finally, this episode explicitly mentions the two earlier feeding miracles. Aware of the disciples' discussion about having no bread among them, Jesus reminded them of the miraculous feedings. He first asked them how many baskets full of broken pieces they picked up when he broke the five loaves for the five thousand; they replied that twelve baskets were collected (8:19). He then asked again how many basketfuls they gathered when he broke the seven loaves for the four thousand; they answered that seven baskets were collected (8:20). By referring to each of the two feedings, this episode is connected to both these miracles with a bread motif. Though the disciples' lack of understanding is highlighted in this episode, the narrative also reveals who Jesus is: the Savior who feeds both the Jews and the Gentiles. This episode thereby concludes the two cycles not only by alluding to the two sea miracles and mentioning the two feeding miracles but also by contrasting the disciples' incomprehension with Jesus' greatness as the Savior who fed all the people, regardless of their ethnicity.

Scholars differ in their interpretation of the main theme of Mark 4–8. Petersen argues that Mark 4:1—8:26 is primarily concerned with the "disciples' incomprehension despite Jesus' expectation of them and despite his attempts to explain things to them."²⁰⁵ Petersen's interpretation of Mark 4–8

---

204. According to Malbon, Jesus and the disciples are the main characters of the three sea events (4:35–41; 6:45–52; 8:13–21), and "the theme of the disciples' response to Jesus and their understanding of his person and his actions is central in each case and is twice highlighted in a concluding rhetorical question (4:41; 8:21)" (Malbon, "Echoes and Foreshadowings in Mark 4–8," 214).

205. Petersen, "Composition of Mark 4:1–8:26," 217. For an emphasis on discipleship in Mark 4–8, see Fowler, *Let the Reader Understand*. Arguing for the disciples' incomprehension of Jesus as the central theme of Mark's narrative, Tyson emphasizes their blindness as follows: "Their recognition of Jesus is only partial, due to their blindness and their hardness of heart. Moreover, their incomplete understanding is actually a misunderstanding of the nature of Jesus. . . . There are many instances of the disciples'

focuses on discipleship. Malbon, on the other hand, claims that the central theme of 4:1—8:21 is "the search for understanding—understanding of who Jesus is and thus of what following him entails."[206] She thus identifies a Christological perspective as key to understanding Mark 4-8.

Christology and discipleship are combined and interact with each other in Mark 4-8,[207] but I will give more weight to Christology than to discipleship. The emphasis on the disciples' incomprehension of Jesus' iden-

blindness—they do not understand the stilling of the sea (4:41), the feeding of the five thousand (6:32)." If so, what is Mark's purpose in saying this? According to Tyson, "the most obvious answer is that Mark is aware of a significant difference between his own point of view and that of the disciples. To Mark the disciples' understanding of Jesus' Messiahship is a misunderstanding." See Tyson, "Blindness of the Disciples in Mark," 261-63. While highlighting the negative images of the disciples in Mark, Weeden explains the progression of a serious deterioration in the relationship between Jesus and the disciples, "from imperceptivity (1:16-8:26) to misconception (8:27-14:9) to rejection (14:10-72)" (Weeden, "Heresy That Necessitated Mark's Gospel," 66). See also Weeden, *Mark-Traditions in Conflict*. Tromcé believes that Mark negatively portrayed the disciples in order to challenge the hierarchic leadership in the Jerusalem community (Tromcé, *Formation of the Gospel According to Mark*, 1975). Kelber claims that "Mark's story is essentially that of the conflict and break between Jesus and the Twelve" (Kelber, *Mark's Story of Jesus*, 88). See also Kelber, *Kingdom in Mark*; Kelber, *Oral and the Written Gospel*. For arguments that Mark portrayed the disciples' incomprehension with a "pastoral" purpose of presenting the difficulty of discipleship, see Best, *Following Jesus*; Tannehill, "Disciples in Mark."

206. Malbon, "Echoes and Foreshadowings in Mark 4-8," 227-28. For the emphasis on Christology in Mark 6-8, Matera asserts that "the theme of the disciple's incomprehension in 6:14-8:30 serves the Christological function of heightening the mystery of Jesus' identity." The disciples' incomprehension is not so much a "failure" to understand Jesus' identity as "the hardening of their heart," in which Mark tells us that "the mystery of Jesus' person is too great for human beings to perceive without divine assistance." See Matera, "Incomprehension of the Disciples," 172. Catchpole also argues that the disciples' incomprehension is "inevitable and christologically conditioned," and that humans can know who Jesus is only "through revelation" (Catchpole, "'Triumphal' Entry," 327). For a Christological interpretation of 8:13-21, see Hooker, *Gospel According to Saint Mark*, 192-96. Gundry consistently writes his commentary on Mark from a Christological perspective, especially focusing on "an apology for the cross" (Gundry, *Mark*).

207. Handerson who studies Christology and discipleship in Mark in the context of Jewish apocalyptic, summarizes a general agreement in Markan scholarship on Christology, discipleship, and the interactions between them. "Put simply, a broad consensus of scholarship maintains that only in light of the cross do the disciples (and thus the readers) gain full disclosure of Jesus' identity, which is that of a crucified and raised messiah. Taken a step further, scholars generally agree that it is only when Jesus' followers have endorsed this proper Christological understanding that they are fully enabled to serve as Jesus' disciples. In this view, not only does Mark's gospel itself primarily intend to advocate 'Christological correctness,' but it also assesses the disciples' faithfulness according to their grasp of who this Jesus really is." See Handerson, *Christology and Discipleship in the Gospel of Mark*, 9.

tity inversely exposes his mercy and greatness as he consistently performed mighty works despite his followers' ignorance. In addition, Jesus' rebuke of the disciples' lack of understanding serves as a way to press them to recognize who he is. In the final sea episode (8:13–21), Gundry emphasizes a Christological understanding by exploring the meaning of the basketfuls of leftovers.[208] To add the adjective πλήρεις ("full") after the phrase πόσους κοφίνους κλασμάτων ("how many baskets of broken pieces") in 8:19 implies "superadequacy."[209] The point of Jesus' question about leftovers is to emphasize the surpluses beyond what was needed for the feedings themselves, so that "the superadequacy of Jesus' miraculous power" appears prominently.[210] Taking a Christological perspective, Hooker explains the implications of the discussion between Jesus and the disciples (8:13–21), focusing on Jesus' identity and divine power.

> This passage raises great problems for the modern reader. Is Mark implying that the disciples are foolish to worry about bread because, whenever they are short of food, Jesus can always multiply it? The fact that Jesus talks here about the leaven of the Pharisees and the leaven of Herod, however, and that this leaven cannot be interpreted literally suggest that Mark is hinting that the real significance of the feeding miracles is to be found at a deeper level than the physical. He does not suppose that Jesus will always satisfy hunger or that his follower will never go short again. Rather, in multiplying the loaves, Jesus has demonstrated his divine power and revealed who he is. Because they have failed to see the point and do not realize who Jesus is, the disciples show that they are indeed in great danger from the leaven of the Pharisees and of Herod.[211]

In conclusion, Mark 4:35—8:21 focuses on Jesus' identity and his power as revealed in his mighty works. As Malbon says, "twice the disciples have witnessed the power of Jesus over the sea and over the bread, power like that of Yahweh over the Read (or Reed) Sea and over the manna."[212]

---

208. Gundry, *Mark*, 407–10.

209. Gundry, *Mark*, 410. As in Mark 8:19, superadequacy appears in 8:20. It is more surprising, however, in that the adjective πλήρεις is changed into the noun πληρώματα, which implies "its advancement ahead of the reference to fragments."

210. Gundry, *Mark*, 410.

211. Hooker, *Gospel According to Saint Mark*, 196.

212. Malbon, "Jesus of Mark and the Sea of Galilee," 367.

Conclusion

Many have attempted to analyze the structure of Mark 4–8, and many diverse structural analyses have been suggested. Some scholars have studied this passage under the assumption of pre-Markan sources, others have taken a compositional approach, and still others have traced Jesus' geographical movement. Despite the diverse approaches, however, most of these structural analyses were performed in the light of repetitive patterns of Mark's narrative.

Mark's overall structure is based on distinct geographical areas of Jesus' ministry: Galilee (1:1—8:21); journey to Jerusalem (8:22—10:52); and Jerusalem (11:1—16:8). Though Jesus' ministry in Jerusalem is described chronologically, his ministry in and beyond Galilee is arranged to follow his geographical movement. Mark 4:35—8:21 in particular shows a cyclic pattern in the geographical route of Jesus' missional journey; this reflects Mark's use of repetition as a literary technique. Not only do similar contents and contexts of the episodes appear repeatedly, their spatial arrangement is also repetitive. The beginning and ending of the two cycles (4:35—6:44; 6:45—8:10) take place in the same space: the sea (4:35-41; 6:45-52) and the wilderness (6:31-44; 8:1-10). In each cycle, Jesus' journey begins with a voyage from west to east across the Sea of Galilee, during which he delivered the disciples from the roaring sea. He returned again from east to west by sea-crossing. Jesus also took an overland journey in each cycle. The final episodes of both cycles end at the wilderness, where Jesus fed the five thousand (Jews) and the four thousand (Gentiles). In each cycle, the focal locale of his Gentile mission is the Decapolis. The repetitive pattern of the route of Jesus' geographical movement and its spatial arrangement creates a structure of two cycles in Mark 4:35—8:10, and 8:11-21 serves as the conclusion of the two cycles. In this spatial framework, the similarity and variation of episodes between the two cycles are discovered.

Jesus' missional (geographical) movement between west (Jewish territory) and east (Gentile territory) implies the breaking down of the boundaries of ethnicity, gender, and class. First, the pattern of Jesus' missional journey by sea-crossings between west and east demonstrates that he worked to destroy the ethnic barrier between the Jews and the Gentiles. In addition, after proclaiming that "all foods are clean" (7:19) in Jewish territory, Jesus took a journey to Gentile territory and met a Syrophoenician woman (7:24-30). His behavior here indicates that belonging to the people of God is not limited to the Jews, but expands to the Gentiles; regardless of ethnicity, those who believe the gospel of Jesus can be part of the people of God. Second, Jesus demolished the gender barrier between males and females. Not only did Jesus satisfy Jairus's request for his daughter's healing, he also cured the suffering of a woman with a hemorrhage (5:21–43). Here faith serves as the main requirement to be healed by Jesus; Jesus praised the woman's faith, saying, "Daughter, your faith has healed you" (5:34). Regardless of gender, faith is the ground for membership in the people of God.[213] Third, Jesus dismantled the class barrier between high and low positions in society. Regardless of their social position—Jairus was a revered synagogue ruler, while the woman with a hemorrhage was an unclean outcast—Jesus welcomed all people and healed them. In this way, Jesus revealed his missional movement as the unification and expansion of the kingdom of God. As Kelber says, "The Two are the One. The dimensions of the Kingdom of God are universal."[214]

In Mark 4:35—8:21, Christology and discipleship appear together. Jesus consistently tried to show his identity by performing miraculous works, but the disciples still failed to recognize who he is. Though Christology and discipleship are intertwined in the episodes, this section ultimately presents Jesus' identity as the Savior who delivers, heals, and feeds all people, both the Jews and the Gentiles. This Christological implication is evident especially in Jesus' sea and feeding miracles, which reflect imagery from the exodus. As God redeemed the Israelites at the Red Sea and fed them with manna in the wilderness, Jesus delivers his disciples at the Sea of Galilee and feeds the crowds with bread in the wilderness. In the next chapter, I will examine the exodus imagery in Mark 4:35—8:21 in the light of spatial understanding and explore its significance for Christology.

---

213. Kelber demonstrates the equality of males and females by connecting gender and territory: "Mark's concern for unity and equality extends to this treatment of males and females. It is difficult to overlook his effort to place males and females on either side of lake so as to assure their equal standing in the new community. On the Jewish side the evangelist tells of a father and the raising of his daughter (5:21–24, 35–42), as well as of the healing of a woman (5:25–34). On the Gentile side he gives an account of a mother and her daughter (7:24–30), and two additional accounts each dealing with a male sufferer (5:1–20; 7:32–37). Males and females on the Jewish and Gentile side are incorporated in the Kingdom of God." See Kelber, *Mark's Story of Jesus*, 42.

214. Kelber, *Mark's Story of Jesus*, 42.

chapter 4

Allusive Space

Spatial Allusions of Exodus Imagery in the Sea and the Wilderness

SOME OF THE SPATIAL settings in Mark's narrative—the Jordan River, the sea, the wilderness, the mountain, and so on—lead us to look back to past events in the history of Israel.[1] These biblical landscapes allude particularly to the event of the exodus, in which God delivered his people from bondage in Egypt. According to Piper, "there was nothing in that series of historical events that left such an everlasting imprint on the mind of the Israelites as the exodus story did, with the miraculous deliverance from servitude in Egypt, the forty years migration in the wilderness, and the legislation on Mount Sinai."[2] The exodus story had been told and retold as it was handed down across the generations: the Israelites not only established their identity on the historical experience of their forefathers in the exodus from Egypt, they also anticipated their own deliverance in the light of this event.[3]

---

1. Rhoads, Dewey, and Michie note that these settings make readers reminisce about old memories of Israel's past and relate Jesus' salvific ministry with God's deliverance of the Israelites (Rhoads et al., *Mark as Story*, 69–70). Smith explores the theological meanings of Mark's spatial description in relation to the OT background, especially the exodus, and described places such as the Sea of Galilee, the Jordan River, mountains, and wilderness. See Smith, *Lion with Wings*, 152–56.

2. Piper, "Unchanging Promises," 3.

3. Anderson states the significance of the exodus as the starting point of Israel's history: "Israel's life-story did not really begin with the time of Abraham or even the Creation, although the Old Testament in its present form starts there. Rather, Israel's history had its true beginning in a crucial historical experience that made her a self-conscious historical community—an event so decisive that earlier happenings and subsequent experiences were seen in its light. This decisive event—the great watershed of

Clifford observes the significance of the exodus and its three critical epochs as follows:

> Many Christians find the Christian Bible, comprised of the Old and New Testament, diffuse, lacking unity, and therefore difficult to use in systematic theology. Yet the Bible itself uses a powerful organizing principle that spans both testaments and unites them, namely the Exodus in its dual aspects of liberation and formation. There are three Exodus moments. Exodus I is the thirteenth-century BCE foundational event. Exodus II is its sixth-century renewal. Exodus III is the first-century CE climactic renewal of Israel by Jesus.[4]

Among all the events of the exodus from Egypt, the most decisive and deeply imprinted on Israel's memory may have been the crossing of the Red Sea, the provision of manna in the wilderness, and the giving of the Law at Mount Sinai.[5] The sea, the wilderness, and the mountain were thus remembered as the places where God's mighty works were performed and his revelation disclosed. Exodus imagery associated with these spatial settings appeared repeatedly in the Old Testament, Second Temple Jewish literature, and the New Testament; the Psalms, the Prophets, and Second Temple Jewish writings in particular told and retold the story of the exodus and applied exodus imagery to contemporary situations by employing these key settings. The sea, the wilderness, and the mountain thus played a significant role in recalling the events of the exodus to the Israelites.

Mark portrays Jesus as the one who delivers the people of God from evil powers. According to Fisher, Jesus' redemptive works may be understood as "a greater and new exodus" in comparison with the original.[6]

Israel's history—was the Exodus from Egypt. Even today the Jewish people understand their vocation and destiny in the light of this revealing event which made them a people and became their undying memory." See Anderson, *Understanding the Old Testament*, 8.

4. Clifford, "Exodus in the Christian Bible," 345.

5. Though events like the ten plagues, the Passover, water from the rock, and the Israelites' rebellion against Moses are also important in the exodus story, memories about the places where events took place are related to the sea, the wilderness, and the mountain.

6. Fisher argues that "one way of describing the redemption through Jesus Christ is as a new and greater Exodus, the telling of it patterned after the Exodus story" (Fisher, "New and Greater Exodus," 69). The Jordan River is also a reminder of the exodus story, alluding to the entering of the Promised Land. It functions as the barrier between the wilderness and the Promised Land, and Joshua parted the water for the Israelites to cross the river in the same way the previous generation had crossed the Red Sea. See also Piper, "Unchanging Promises," 17; Rhoads et al., *Mark as Story*, 69; Smith, *Lion with Wings*, 154.

The main spatial settings that recall the exodus events in Mark's narrative are: the sea, where Jesus calmed the roaring sea and walked on the water (4:35–41; 6:45–52); the wilderness, where Jesus fed the five thousand and the four thousand (6:31–44; 8:1–10); and the mountain, where Jesus was transfigured (9:2–8). Jesus' later Galilean ministry (4:35—8:21) and his journey to Jerusalem (8:22—10:52) unfold among the sea, the wilderness, and the mountain, and these places form the framework of Mark's narrative while echoing the exodus events. In the present study, I will explore how the spatial settings of the sea and the wilderness serve as the structural framework of Mark 4:35—8:21 and how they reflect the exodus events of the victory at the Red Sea and the provision of manna in the wilderness.

Intertextual Relationship between Ps 78(77):12-32 and Mark 4:35—8:21

Sea-Desert Twin Motifs in the Exodus Story

Kee argues that the two consecutive episodes of Jesus' feeding of the crowd and walking on the water in Mark 6:31–52 and John 6:5–21 had been handed down together in the tradition.[7] Emphasizing the new exodus in Mark, Kee claims that "the twin motifs of God's command over the waters and his feeding his own in the desert" frequently appear together in Psalms (Ps 78:13–25; 106:9; 107:23–31) and the later prophetic traditions (Isa 40:12; 41:18; 51:10).[8] Jesus' sea and feeding miracles may be understood in terms of the twin motifs that reflect the exodus events.

Though the presence of the twin motifs in the paired episodes of the sea and feeding miracles (Mark 6:31–52; John 6:5–21) is significant, the order of the two episodes does not correspond to that of the original exodus: while the feeding of the crowd in the wilderness precedes Jesus' walking on the sea in the paired episodes of Mark and John, the feeding of the Israelites with manna in the desert follows the crossing of the Red Sea in the original exodus. If Mark used exodus imagery in his narrative, the sea miracle should precede the feeding miracle, following the original order of events.

The twin motifs of the sea and feeding miracles can be discovered in a separate form in Mark's narrative, repeated twice and forming a framework for the cyclic pattern in 4:35—8:10. In the two cycles (4:35—6:44; 6:45—8:10), the first pair of sea and feeding miracles is 4:35-41 and 6:31-44; the second is 6:45-52 and 8:1-10. This manner of pairing episodes according

---

7. Kee, *Community of the New Age*, 112.
8. Kee, *Community of the New Age*, 112.

to a cyclic structure differs significantly from Kee's pairing of the consecutive episodes in 6:31–52 (Jesus' feeding of the five thousand [6:31–44] and his walking on the sea [6:45–52]). Paired as I propose, the sea and feeding miracles in each cycle take place in the same order as the events of the original exodus. In the first pair, Jesus calmed down the sea by rebuking the roaring sea and then fed the five thousand in the wilderness; in the second pair, Jesus walked on the sea and then fed the four thousand in the wilderness. In each cycle, then, the twin motifs recall the events of the exodus from Egypt, namely God's mighty work of parting the Red Sea to allow the Israelites' crossing (Exod 14:15–31) and his feeding of the Israelites in the wilderness (16:1–12).

Kee insists that the twin motifs are found "in Psalms in celebration of God's past acts on behalf of Israel" and "in the later prophetic tradition, where the events of the Exodus serve as the model for the awaited eschatological redemption of the chastened, renewed nation."[9] In the history of the Israelites, the exodus events had been diversely interpreted by different authors, traditions, and generations. To properly understand Mark's use of exodus imagery and its theological significance in his account of Jesus' sea and feeding miracles, it is therefore necessary to explore how the exodus events, especially those containing the twin motifs, were presented in the OT and Second Temple Jewish literature.

Structural Parallels between Ps 78(77):12–32 and Mark 4:35—8:21

The Psalms contain many mentions of the exodus (e.g., Ps 66, 77, 78, 80, 81, 95, 105, 106, 114, 134, 135, 136).[10] Piper sorts these psalms into three

---

9. Kee, *Community of the New Age*, 112.

10. Nixon introduces ten psalms related to the exodus story and explained their characteristics as follows: "There is also fairly frequent reference to the Exodus in the Psalter. Apart from isolated allusions, we find most of the material in ten psalms. Psalm 66 celebrates God's deliverance of his people starting with the Exodus. Psalm 77 is a personal psalm in which the writer is led from personal trouble to the greatness of the Redeemer God. Psalm 78 is a recital of the Exodus event with lessons drawn from it. To these last two psalms in particular we owe the emphasis on Israel as a flock led by God. Psalm 80 is a plea for God to act again as He has acted before and Israel is described as a vine as well as a flock. Psalm 81 calls for the obedience of the people to the God who had delivered them. Psalms 105 and 106 go together—the emphasis in the former being on the greatness of Yahweh and in the latter on the rebelliousness of the people. Psalm 114 is a celebration in vivid poetic language of God's victory at the Exodus. Psalms 135 and 136 are psalms of praise to Yahweh in which His work of creation is associated with His work of redemption." See Nixon, *Exodus in the New Testament*, 8–9. See also Piper, "Unchanging Promises," 5; Kee, *Community of the New Age*, 112.

categories based on thematic divisions.[11] First, Ps 78, 81, and 95 remind the Israelites of "the kindness of God" which led them "to repent and give up their unbelief"; second, Ps 105, 106, 114, 134, and 136 focus on "the praise of God" for "the great things God has accomplished"; third, Ps 77 gives "comfort derived from history" to people in agony.[12] The references to and imagery of the exodus in these psalms thus show (1) God's goodness in leading people to repentance from unbelief; (2) the greatness of God's mighty works; and (3) God's comfort of distressed people. In relation to the twin motifs of the sea and the wilderness, I will especially examine the structural pattern and theological theme of Ps 78:12-32 (77:12-32 LXX) and compare it with Mark 4:35—8:21.[13]

According to Clifford, Ps 78(77 LXX), the longest psalm that reviews the history of Israel,[14] consists of five parts: an introduction (vv. 1-11), two recitals (vv. 12-32; 40-64) and two sequels (vv. 33-39; 65-72).[15] As seen in the outline below, the two recitals and two sequels exhibit strong parallelism.

---

11. Piper, "Unchanging Promises," 5. "Exhortation and praise" most frequently appear in these psalms.

12. Piper, "Unchanging Promises," 5.

13. Brunson argues that the Gospel of John presents "structural parallels" of "works and signs" between the exodus led by Moses and Jesus' ministry: "In evoking the works/signs parallels to Moses it was no doubt John's intention to take the reader back to the exodus and portray Jesus as the leader of a new or second exodus. However, the Johannine Jesus associates his ministry principally with the Father not with Moses.... In many of the exodus parallels to Jesus' ministry it is the works of Yahweh that Jesus reproduces: It is Yahweh who opened the Red Sea, guided Israel with the pillar of fire, gave the Law, instituted the first covenant, healed those who looked at the serpent, and provided bread and water in the wilderness. If the people grumbled against Moses, they did so even more against God." See Brunson, *Psalm 118 in the Gospel of John*, 162. Mark also follows an exodus pattern and compares Jesus' ministry with that of Moses. Jesus may be portrayed as the one greater than Moses, but Jesus' ministry is eventually associated with God's mighty works rather than Moses.' In Mark's narrative, Jesus is the one who worked miracles that only God can do.

14. Cf. According to Mays, Ps 105, 106, and 136 are frequently categorized as "historical psalms" due to the "common dominant feature," though these Psalms cannot be said as "historical" since they are related to "the past and its bearing on present and future" (Mays, *Psalms*, 254). See also Hossfeld and Zenger, *Psalms 2*, 286. There has been a discussion about the genre of Ps 78. Kraus regards it as a historical psalm (Kraus, *Psalms 60-150*, 535-48). On the contrary, Eissfeldt classifies it as a wisdom poem (Eissfeldt, *Old Testament*, 124-27). Gunkel considers it as a mixture of genres, namely "Sagenerzählung" (legend), "Hymnen" (hymn), "prophetische Mahnrede" (prophetic warning), and "Weisheitsdichtung" (wisdom poetry) (Gunkel, *Die Psalmen*, 342). For a discussion of genre, see Hossfeld and Zenger, *Psalms 2*, 286-87.

15. Clifford, "In Zion and David," 129.

Introduction: vv. 1-11 (30 cola)
Liturgical officer addresses all Israel to reveal the true meaning of the covenantal traditions, to instill fidelity to those traditions, and to provide a negative example of infidelity.

First Recital:	*Second Recital:*
Wilderness Events	From Egypt to Canaan
vv. 12-32 (47 cola)	vv. 40-64 (55 cola)
Gracious act (vv. 12-16)	Gracious act (vv. 44-55)
Rebellion (vv. 17-20)	Rebellion (vv. 56-58)
Divine anger & punishment	Divine anger & punishment
(manna and quail) vv. 21-32	(destruction of Shilo) vv. 59-64
Sequel vv. 33-39 (16 cola)	*Sequel* vv. 65-72 (17 cola)
Total cola: 63	Total cola: 72[16]

---

16. Clifford, "In Zion and David," 129. Clifford focuses on the structure and arrangement of the source in Ps 78(77) and discovers its outline with "the aid of formal devices such as repetition of key words and phrases, chiasm, paronomasia or word play, and especially in the parallel structure of the two historical recitals" (127). For those who follow the structural analysis laid out by Clifford, see Mays, *Psalms*, 255; Tate, *Psalms 51-100*, 287-88. Coats, who emphasizes traditions, proposes a structure composed of "a twofold introduction" (vv. 1-8 [1-4 and 5-8]) and "three different units of traditions" (vv. 9-72): "the positive tradition of Yahweh's aid to Israel in the wilderness" (vv. 9-16); "the negative element of Israel's idolatry in the land" (vv. 44-66); and "the murmuring tradition as it appears in the Pentateuch (vv. 17-41 and 67-72). See Coats, *Rebellion in the Wilderness*, 223-24. Campbell, who stresses the theme of rejection and election, suggests the following structure (Campbell, "Psalm 78," 59-60):

I. Introduction	vv. 1-8
II. Recital of history (theologically interpreted)	vv. 9-72
1. Recital of rejection	vv. 9-64
a. Rejection of Yahweh by Israel	vv. 9-58
b. Rejection of Israel by Yahweh	vv. 59-64
2. Recital of election	vv. 65-72
a. Introduction	vv. 65-66
b. Statement of election	vv. 67-72
i. Negatively: rejection of Joseph/Ephraim	v. 67
ii. Positively: election of Judah, Zion, and David	vv. 68-72

Goldingay proposes a concentric structure, arguing that the main theme of Ps 78(77), located at the center, is "Israel's failure and God' grace" (vv. 32-43) (Goldingay, *Psalms 42-89*, 480-81):

Each of the recitals shows the same pattern: "recitation of the LORD's marvelous deeds for Israel, an instance of failure, the responding divine wrath, a concluding account of how the LORD maintained the relation with his sinful people."[17] The order of the exodus events in the first recital (78[77]:12–32),[18]

> Statement of purpose: to get people to listen and submit to God (vv. 1–8)
> Ephraim's failure (vv. 9–11)
> God and Israel in the wilderness (vv. 12–31)
> The characteristic dynamics of that relationship (vv. 32–43)
> God and Israel from Egypt to Shiloh (vv. 44–64)
> Ephraim's rejection and God's choice of David (vv. 65–72)

In a similar way, VanGemeren suggests a symmetrical structure, claiming that "the psalmist alternates between Israel's rebellion and God's faithfulness." He first presents a large fame—"Call to Wisdom (vv. 1–4)"; "Lesson from Israel's History (vv. 5–64)"; and "Good News: God Has Chosen David (vv. 65–72)"—and then provided the symmetrical structure of the central didactic section as follows (VanGemeren, *Psalms*, 591):

> Past and future generation (vv. 5–8)
> Israel in Egypt and in the wilderness (vv. 9–16)
> Israel in the wilderness (vv. 17–31)
> God's mercy on a rebellious people (vv. 32–39)
> Israel in Egypt and in the wilderness (vv. 40–55)
> Judgment on a rebellious generation (vv. 56–64)

Though it is difficult to determine the structure of Ps 78(77), Clifford's proposed structure is persuasive because it takes into consideration many diverse literary and thematic elements that contribute to poetic structure: e.g., repetition, paronomasia, literary and thematic parallelism. Despite scholarly disagreement on the structure of Ps 78(77), there is the general consensus that this Psalm shows the contrasts between Israel's disbelief and God's grace and between the rejection of Ephraim and the election of David.

17. In agreement with the Clifford's proposed structure, May suggests the following simple structure for Ps 78(77): "introduction" (vv. 1–11); "the failure of the ancestors of the wilderness generation" (vv. 12–39); "the failure of the ancestors that happened in Ephraimite territory" (vv. 40–72). Psalm 78 shows the characteristics of a "parable (*mashal*)" and "riddles (*hidot*) from the past" (v. 2). It is *mashal*, in that it deals with instruction: those who hear it will be taught not to follow their ancestors' unfaithfulness and disobedience. It is also *hidot*, in that it contains inference: from the events in the past, those who hear it will infer meanings in the present. See May, *Psalms*, 255.

18. Clifford argues that Ps 78(77) does not follow the order of the exodus described in the Pentateuch: "The stories, however, are not in the order in which they are found in the Pentateuch, nor do they function in the same way. The desert wanderings come *before* the exodus from Egypt. The miracle of water in the desert is bound in with the crossing of the Red Sea, unlike the Pentateuchal tradition. The story of the manna, which in the Pentateuch is a story of grace, is joined to the narrative about the quail, becoming the instrument of God's punishment upon disbelief." See Clifford, "In Zion and David," 124–25.

in which the psalmist recasts the records of the Exodus in the Pentateuch, is as follows: the crossing of the Red Sea, the guiding by cloud and fire, and the provision of drink by splitting rocks in the wilderness (vv. 12–16); Israel's failure in faith by grumbling about God's supply of bread and meat (vv. 17–20); Israel's unbelief in spite of God's provision of manna and quail and his wrath against them (vv. 21–32). The core passages in three parts of the first recital are as follows.[19]

> 13 He broke asunder a sea (θάλασσαν) and brought them through;
> made the water stand like a wineskin.
> 14 And he led them with a cloud by day,
> and all the night long with an illumination of fire
> 15 He broke asunder a rock in a wilderness
> and gave them drink as form a voluminous deep.
> 16 And he brought out water from a rock
> and brought down waters like rivers. (Psalm 77:13–16 LXX)
>
> 19 And they spoke against God and said,
> "Surely, God will not be able to spread a table in the wilderness (ἐρήμῳ)?"
> 20 Even though he struck a rock so that waters gushed out,
> and wadis deluged,
> surely, he cannot also give bread or spread a table for his people?" (vv. 19–20)
>
> 23 And he commanded the clouds above,
> and opened heaven's doors,
> 24 and he rained down manna (μαννα) for them to eat,
> and heaven's bread (ἄρτον) he gave them.
> 25 Bread of angels man ate;
> provisions he sent them in abundance. (vv. 23–25)
>
> 32 Amidst all these things they still sinned,
> and they did not believe in his marvels. (v. 32)

The first recital begins with the crossing of the sea (θάλασσαν) and ends with God's provision of bread (μαννα, ἄρτον) and meat in the wilderness (ἐρήμῳ). In the middle of this frame, God's miraculous works in the wilderness—such as the leading with cloud and fire and the supply of water—are described, along with the Israelites' complaint about the lack

---

19. Because Mark is believed to refer to the LXX version of the Hebrew Bible, I include relevant LXX passages. The English translation is taken from Albert and Wright, *New English Translation of the Septuagint*.

of God's provision. In the conclusion of the first recital, the psalmist laments that the Israelites showed unbelief despite their experience of God's mighty works.

In the sequence of the exodus of Pentateuch,[20] the feeding miracle in the wilderness follows the crossing of the Red Sea and precedes the provision of water by the splitting of rocks.[21] Psalm 78(77), however, does not follow this order of events; the sequence in Ps 78(77):12–32 is the crossing of the Red Sea, the provision of water by the splitting of rocks, and the feeding miracle in the desert.[22] Clifford argues that the reason for uniting the two episodes of the sea-crossing miracle and the provision of water into one great miracle is to make the Israelites' rebellion appear still more vicious.[23] In addition, God's mighty power in these two episodes is expressed in the same verb, "to split" (בקע, διαρρήγνυμι; used of God's splitting the sea and the rocks in 78[77]:13, 15).[24] These miraculous works related to water

---

20. Patterson divides the major stages of the Israelites' journey from Egypt to Sinai, which are differentiated by the repeated phrase "and they departed from," as follows: "The narrative of the Re(e)d Sea crossing forms a pivotal part of a larger narrative detailing the Hebrews' journey from Egypt to Sinai (Exod 12:37–19:2). The major stages of the itinerary are marked structurally by the recurring phrase 'and they departed from.' The narrative traces the Israelites' movement from Egypt to Succoth (12:37—13:19), from Succoth to the sea (13:20—15:21), from the sea to the oasis at Elim (15:22–27), from Elim to the Desert of Sin (16:1–36), from Sin to Rephidim (17:1–18:27), and from Rephidim to Sinai (19:1–2)." See Patterson, "Victory at Sea," 44. Harvey suggests the five significant events of the exodus story as follows: "(1) Israelites' departure from Egypt; (2) the miraculous crossing of the Red Sea; (3) wandering and grumbling in the wilderness; (4) God's revelation at Sinai; (5) the Israelites' entry into the Promised Land." See Harvey, "La typologie," 383–86.

21. Hossfeld and Zenger, Psalms 2, 286.

22. Hossfeld and Zenger, Psalms 2, 286. Hossfeld and Zenger argue that the portrayal of the exodus events in Ps 78(77) takes a "local progression" rather than "temporal progression": "Beginning in Egypt, v. 12; wilderness, vv. 15, 17, 19, (40); (Egypt, vv. 43, 51); wilderness, v. 52; land/mountain, v. 54; Shiloh, v. 60; Mount Zion, v. 68."

23. Clifford, "In Zion and David," 132. In contrast with Clifford, Kraus claims that the psalmist simply combined the manna story with the rock story by way of "original transitions," not paying attention to the "chronological order": "The singer of Psalm 78 waives all given dispositions of tradition; he does not strive for chronological succession but combines the individual transmissions by means of original transitions. Thus a reflection about the people that leads to the story of the manna is immediately joined to the miracle of the rock." See Kraus, Psalms 60–150, 127. However, Kraus does not give a proper explanation for why the psalmist arranged the rock story in front of the manna story. Clifford's argument is more convincing than that of Kraus, in that the psalmist probably separated the crossing of the Red Sea and the provision of manna in the wilderness, while combining the crossing of the Red Sea and the provision of water by the splitting of rocks in order to describe Israelites' rebellion as more evil one.

24. Clifford, "In Zion and David," 132. In Hebrew poetry, the sea (v. 13) is paralleled with the river (v. 16) in the similar setting of "the waters" (מים, ὕδωρ; vv. 13, 15, 16).

function as signs for the Israelites to test God by questioning whether he who supplied water could provide bread and meat in the desert (vv. 19–20). In response to their rebellious attitude, God, full of rage, opened the doors of heaven and rained down manna and meat upon them (vv. 21–24). While manna was God's gracious gift to Israelites in the Pentateuch, it is here given under "the sign of divine wrath."[25] Psalm 78(77):32 serves as the conclusion of the first recital and tells us of the "sad result" of the Israelites' repeated and unceasing sins and disbelief in spite of God's mighty works for them.[26]

Mays states that biblical instructions are passed down to future generations in two ways:

> The way of God and the way of the ancestors (Hebrew "fathers") are woven together. The people of God are instructed, not only by what God has done and said, but also by what the fathers and mothers in the faith have done and said. The biblical *torah* of the first five books and the four Gospels is composed in that way. The speaker uses examples of failure by the ancestors. There is irony here; those who passed on the tradition also failed it. Every generation will have to reckon with the fact that the story tells of failure as well as faithfulness.[27]

Despite God's mighty works, the Israelites failed to stand in the faith (Ps 78[77]:32). Likewise, though Jesus performed miraculous works, especially the two feeding miracles, the disciples failed to understand who Jesus is and forgot what Jesus had done for them (Mark 8:13–21).

According to Hossfeld and Zenger, Ps 78(77) is directly cited twice in the NT.[28] First, Ps 78(77):2 (ἀνοίξω ἐν παραβολαῖς τὸ στόμα μου φθέγξομαι προβλήματα ἀπ' ἀρχῆς, "I will open my mouth in parables; I will utter hidden things from of old") is employed as the introduction to the explanation of a parable in Matt 13:35 (ἀνοίξω ἐν παραβολαῖς τὸ στόμα μου, ἐρεύξομαι κεκρυμμένα ἀπὸ καταβολῆς [κόσμου], "I will open my mouth in parables; I will utter things hidden from the foundation of the world"). Second, using the quotation formula "as it is written" (καθώς ἐστιν γεγραμμένον), John 6:31 (ἄρτον ἐκ τοῦ οὐρανοῦ ἔδωκεν αὐτοῖς φαγεῖν, "He gave them bread

---

25. Clifford, "In Zion and David," 133. In response to the Israelites' hideous testing of God, he not only supplied them with food, but also smote them at the same time. This implies the close relationship between "God's grace and his judgment." See Weiser, *Psalms*, 541.

26. Tate, *Psalms 51–100*, 291.

27. Mays, *Psalms*, 257.

28. Hossfeld and Zenger, *Psalms 2*, 301.

from heaven to eat") cites Ps 78(77):24 (ἄρτον οὐρανοῦ ἔδωκεν αὐτοῖς, "He gave them the bread of heaven"). In addition to the explicit and direct quotations of Ps 78(77) in Matthew and John, many allusions to Ps 78(77) can be found in other NT writings that reflect the events of the exodus. Hossfeld and Zenger explain the allusions of Ps 78(77) in the NT as follows:

> There is another focus of reception of Psalm 78 in the historical reflection in 1 Corinthians 10. In v. 3 Paul alludes to the miracles of the manna and the quails from Ps 78:24ff. In v. 4 he recalls the water miracle in Ps 78:15–16, and in v. 5 he recalls the death of the Israelites in the wilderness according to Ps 78:31. In 1 Cor 10:9 he may also be alluding to the theologoumenon of Israel's sinful testing of God in Ps 78:18, 56. Acts 8:21 uses the reproach of Ps 78:37a (their heart did not cling to God) as a reason for the judgment on Simon Magus.[29]
>
> Like John's Gospel, Rev 2:17 takes up the manna verse in Ps 78:24. In Rev 16:4 and 13 the plague narrative is brought in; there may be a reference to the first plague as it is described in Ps 78:44 (water into blood) and to the second frog plague as developed in Ps 78:45.

Psalm 78(77) may have been well-known to the NT writers and regarded as the historical record and explanation of the exodus events. As Hossfeld and Zenger state, "evidently early Christian scriptural interpretation was aware of Psalm 78 as an independent account of history."[30]

Mark's Gospel also contains quotations of and allusions to the Psalms,[31] and I argue the sea and feeding miracles in Mark may allude to the exodus events described in Ps 78(77). Because "the crossing of the sea and the gift of manna are the central miracles in the Exodus story,"[32] Ps 78(77):12–32 may use these two miracles to give an instruction. In a similar way, Mark may follow Ps 78(77) by providing a lesson from the sea and feeding miracles. In its account of sea and feeding miracles, Ps 78(77) contrasts the Israelites' ceaseless disbelief and rebellion with God's merciful deliverance and provision. Similarly, Mark 4:35—8:21 contrasts the disciples' persistent incomprehension and hardened hearts with Jesus' merciful redemption and care.

---

29. Hossfeld and Zenger, *Psalms 2*, 301.

30. Hossfeld and Zenger, *Psalms 2*, 301.

31. Arguing for the significance of Mark's use of the Psalms, Geddert lists Mark's direct quotations from the Psalms as follows: "God's voice from heaven at Jesus' baptism quotes Psalm 2; the pilgrims who celebrate the king on the colt quote Psalm 118; Jesus then also quotes Psalm 118 and later Psalm 110 in the temple, and he quotes Psalm 22 from the cross" (Geddert, "Use of Psalms in Mark," 111).

32. Hooker, *Gospel According to Saint Mark*, 169.

Despite seeing God's mighty works, the Israelites constantly grumbled and even rebelled against God (Ps 78[77]:17). Likewise, despite witnessing Jesus' miracles, the disciples constantly displayed their incomprehension of Jesus' identity and even developed hardened hearts (Mark 8:17). Nevertheless, God guided the Israelites and provided for them in his mercy, and Jesus cared for and fed the disciples and the crowd in his grace. Donahue and Harrington note the thematic pattern of Israel's failure and God's merciful guidance in the wilderness wanderings of the exodus, seen in both Ps 78(77) and Mark:

> [A] motif that may influence the failure of disciples and of the crowds in Mark is the pervasive rhythm of the Old Testament in which God's love is met by infidelity and failure, but only to be renewed by God. This theme appears in the early narratives of Israel's rebellions in the wilderness, where the people reject Moses's leadership and their own deliverance from Egypt. . . . This cycle pervades the retelling of the Exodus narratives in Psalm 78 and characterizes the calls to repentance or return in the prophetic writings (Isa 1:17–19; 40:2; 44:21–23; 59:13; Lam 4:12–14, 21–23).[33]

We can also discover verbal parallels between Ps 78(77) and Mark 4:35—8:21. Collins asserts that Ps 78(77) has an intertextual relationship with the account of the feeding of the five thousand in Mark 6:31–44.[34] Mark 6:42 (καὶ ἔφαγον πάντες καὶ ἐχορτάσθησαν, "and they all ate and were satisfied") is similar to Ps 78(77):29 (καὶ ἐφάγοσαν καὶ ἐνεπλήσθησαν σφόδρα, "and they ate and were filled exceedingly").[35] In addition, the image of a crowd "like sheep without shepherd" (ὡς πρόβατα μὴ ἔχοντα ποιμένα) in Mark 6: 34 refers to images of the exodus guided by God in Ps 78(77):52–55, 70–72 (ἀπῆρεν ὡς πρόβατα τὸν λαὸν αὐτοῦ, "he led out his people like sheep," v. 52; ἔλαβεν αὐτὸν ποιμαίνειν Ιακωβ τὸν λαὸν αὐτοῦ, "he brought him to be the shepherd of his people Jacob," v. 71).[36]

---

33. Donahue and Harrington, *Gospel of Mark*, 33.

34. Collins, *Mark*, 326. See also Guelich, *Mark 1–8:26*, 336; Stein, *Mark*, 313; Garland, *Mark*, 257; Hooker, *Gospel According to Saint Mark*, 169.

35. While Ps 78(77):29 employs the similar word ἐμπίμπλημι ("to satisfy" or "to fill quite full") which "prepares for the criticism of the people's attitude in the following verse of the psalm," Mark used the word χορτάζω ("to satisfy," v. 42) which implies "the modest nature of the banquet hosted by Jesus." The word πάντες ("all") in Mark 6:42 indicates "the greatness of the miracle" by Jesus: πάντες serves as the preparation to disclose the number of the crowd who ate in v. 44. Collins, *Mark*, 326.

36. Watts, "Mark," 159.

Marcus also suggests parallels between Ps 78(77) and Mark 8:1–12 (the feeding of the four thousand and looking for a sign to test God):

Mark 8:4 "Where will anyone be able (δυνήσεται) to get the loaves (ἄρτων) to satisfy these people here in the wilderness (ἐπ' ἐρημίας)?"	Ps 78(77):19–20 "Will God be able (δυνήσεται) to prepare a table in the wilderness (ἐν ἐρήμῳ)? . . . Is he able to give bread (ἄρτον)?"
Mark 8:11 "Seeking from him a sign from heaven, testing (πειράζοντες) him."	78(77):18 "They tested (ἐξεπείρασαν) God in their heart."[A]

A. Marcus, *Mark 1–8*, 483–84.

Marcus claims that Mark's use of "the exodus typology" of Ps 78(77) can be seen not only in striking verbal parallels but also in his use of the thematic pattern of wilderness wanderings.[37] Mark's narrative follows the pattern of the exodus in Ps 78(77):19–20: just as the Israelites grumbled about their situations and tested God even after experiencing his mighty works, Jesus' disciples doubted his ability to provide food in the wilderness and his opponents tested him even after seeing and hearing his miracles.[38]

Parallels in pattern (order), setting, wording, and theme between Ps 78(77):12–32 and Mark 4:35—8:21 demonstrate the intertextual relationship between the two passages. According to Swartley, "in Psalm 78 (see vv. 13–31) Israel's deliverance from bondage, its rebellion in the wilderness, and God's guidance and provision of bread from heaven are all intertwined."[39] In Ps 78(77):12–32, we see a pattern of deliverance at the sea, Israel's rebellion, provision of food in the wilderness, and lamentation for Israel's unbelief. A similar pattern appears in Mark 4:35—8:21: the disciples' deliverance at the sea, Jesus' rejection by his hometown, the feeding of the disciples and the crowd in the wilderness, and lamentation over the disciples' incomprehension and hardened hearts. Here, the sea and the wilderness function as the main settings that reveal a similar pattern in the two texts.

The sea-crossing and the feeding of the people serve as the framework for the beginning and ending of episodes in both Ps 78(77):12–32 and Mark 4:35—8:21. The crossing of the Red Sea corresponds to the crossing of the Sea of Galilee; the feeding with manna and meat in the wilderness corresponds to the feeding with bread and fish in the wilderness. The conclusions of both texts are similar, in that the Israelites and the disciples continued in a state of unbelief despite experiencing miracles. Both concluding statements

37. Watts, "Mark," 481, 495.
38. Watts, "Mark," 495.
39. Swartley, *Israel's Scripture Traditions and the Synoptic Gospels*, 46.

are laments for failure in faith and understanding: in spite of the feeding miracles, the Israelites still sinned and did not believe (Ps 78[77]:32), and the disciples did not yet understand (Mark 8:21). In their use of the deliverance at the sea and the provision in the wilderness as a bracketing framework (Ps 78[77]:12–31 and Mark 4:35—6:44; 6:45—8:10), and in their concluding notes of unbelief (Ps 78[77]:32 and Mark 8:11–21), Ps 78(77):12–32 and Mark 4:35—8:21 exhibit structural parallelism. Therefore, as Psalm 78(77):12–32 uses the miracle episodes to draw a contrast between the Israelites' unbelief and God's merciful works in the exodus story, Mark follows this structural pattern by contrasting the disciples' incomprehension with Jesus' gracious ministry in the miracle stories.

Within this framework, doubt and rejection of God and Jesus appear in both texts alongside miraculous works. In the first recital in Ps 78(77):12–32, God showed the mighty works of leading the Israelites by cloud and fire and of giving the provision of water by splitting rocks (vv. 14–16), but the Israelites rebelled against him and tested him by demanding food (vv. 17–22). In the first cycle in Mark 4:35—6:44, Jesus performed miraculous works such as exorcism (5:1-20) and healing (vv. 21-43), but his hometown took offense at him (6:1-6a).[40] Both the Israelites and the disciples forgot the miraculous works they had seen (Ps 78[77]:11; Mark 8:14) and rejected God and Jesus.[41]

Both texts also show a cyclic pattern: in Ps 78(77):12–32, 40–64, two recitals are concluded with two sequels (vv. 33–39, 65–72), and in Mark 4:35—6:44; 6:45—8:10, two cycles are followed by a conclusion (8:11–21). According to Greenstein, "the two-dimensional mapping of Psalm 78's structure produces a cyclic pattern of ideological significance": God's mighty and gracious acts and the Israelites' disobedience appear at the same time.[42]

---

40. The execution of John the Baptist (Mark 6:14–29) also implies the rejection of Jesus, since John's death alludes to Jesus' death: "Mark's account of John's death prepares for his story of Jesus' death." See Donahue and Harrington, *Gospel of Mark*, 202.

41. The fact that the disciples forgot to bring bread is connected to their imperceptiveness of the meaning of Jesus' miraculous feedings of the five thousand and the four thousand.

42. Greenstein, "Mixing Memory and Design," 199. Watts also points out a similar pattern between Ps 78(77) and Mark 4-8 in terms of the sea and feeding episodes, focusing particularly on shepherd imagery: "Interestingly, just as Ps 78 links God's care for Israel in his power over the sea and provision of food in the exodus (78:12-20) with his appointment of David to shepherd them (78:70-72), so too Mark presents Jesus as Israel's shepherd in the context of a feeding followed by a demonstration of his power over the sea on behalf of the Twelve, the Israel that he has reconstituted around himself (see 6:51-52, where Mark links the significance of both events)." Mark may have intentionally presented Jesus' miracle as the awaited new exodus, with the sea and the wilderness serving for its setting. Watts emphasizes that "Mark's motif of the fulfillment

Mark 4:35—8:21 also shows the mixture of two motifs, presenting a cyclic pattern: Jesus' miraculous and gracious works and the disciples' ignorance. In conclusion, the parallelism between the first recital of Ps 78(77):12–32 and the first cycle and conclusion of Mark (4:35—6:44; 8:11–21) may be summarized in terms of their verbal and thematic agreement and similarity of order and setting as follows:[43]

Psalm		Mark
78(77 LXX):13	the crossing of the sea (θάλασσα)	4:35–41
78(77 LXX):14–16	the miraculous works	5:1–43
78(77 LXX):17–20	the rebellion and rejection	6:1–6a (cf. 6:14–29)
78(77 LXX):23–29	the provision of bread (ἄρτος) in the wilderness (ἔρημος)	6:31–44
78(77 LXX):18	the testing (πειράζω) of providing a sign	8:11
78(77 LXX):11[44]	the forgetting (ἐπιλανθάνομαι) of the mighty works	8:14
78(77 LXX):32	the failure of belief and understanding	8:21[45]

The Sea and the Wilderness as the Spatial Settings of the New Exodus

The sea and the wilderness have special meanings in the exodus story, and they were interpreted symbolically, cosmologically, and eschatologically in the OT and Second Temple Jewish literature. I will now explore the images of the sea and the wilderness in the OT, especially Psalms and Isaiah, and in some Second Temple Jewish literature, and examine how these spatial

---

of return from exile and his high Christology are in view." See Watts, "Mark," 161.

43. As we have seen, the second cycle of Mark 6:45—8:10 also shows parallelism with Ps 78(77):12–32. The bracket frames of the sea and wilderness miracles are parallel between Mark and the psalm. The doubt of the Israelites and the disciples that God and Jesus are able (δύναμαι) to give loaves (ἄρτος) in the wilderness (ἔρημος) also appears in both texts (Ps 78[77]:19–20; Mark 8:4). In addition, the Israelites tested (ἐκπειράζω, Ps 78[77]:18) God and the Pharisees tested (πειράζω, Mark 8:11) Jesus.

44. Though Ps 78(77):11 belongs to the introductory part, this verse serves as the ground of the interpretation of the exodus events in the following recitals. Since the Israelites forgot God's miraculous works, they constantly failed to have faith and kept on sinning.

45. Mark 4:35—8:21 follows the pattern of the description of the exodus events in Ps 78(77):12–32, in which both conclusions are the failure of faith and understanding of the Israelites and the disciples.

settings using exodus imagery serve to deliver the theological themes of Jesus' Galilean ministry in Mark 4:35—8:21.

The Sea and the Exodus Imagery

David Mathewson described the symbolic usages of the sea in the OT and Second Temple Jewish literature as follows:

> The sea functions metaphorically as a symbol of chaos and evil and stands in antipathy toward God and his people. . . . The sea is often depicted as the place of primordial chaos which stands in opposition to creation (Ps 104:6–7; cf. Gen 1:2–10) and the source of hostility and of the bestial adversaries of God and his people (cf. Isa 27:1; 51:9–10; Dan 7:2–3; *1 En.* 60:7–8; *4 Ezra* 6:49–52; *2 Bar.* 29:4; *Apoc. Ab.* 21:4). God's overt opposition to the hostile sea is a fairly widespread motif in the OT (Job 7:12; 26:12; Ps 18:15; 29:3; 74:13–14; 77:16; 89:9–10; Jer 5:22; 51:36; Nah 1:4; Hab 3:8; cf. *1 En.* 101:7). Thus Yahweh is angry with and rebukes the hostile sea; Yahweh even on occasion dries up its waters.[46]

In the creation story of Genesis, the waters (1:2) are separated into two kinds, the waters below the expanse and the waters above the expanse (v. 7), and the waters under the sky are gathered into one place and called the sea (v. 9). In v. 2, the waters in creation are described in parallel phrases: "over the surface of the deep (תְהוֹם, ἄβυσσος)" and "over the waters (מַיִם, ὕδωρ)."[47] The waters here can be associated with the image of the deep.[48] Though the תְהוֹם ("the watery deep") is a chaotic image, it is never personified like Tiamat, the Babylonian goddess of the primeval ocean of *Enuma Elish*.[49] Some scholars have attempted to connect תְהוֹם with Tiamat,[50] claiming that the creation in Genesis may allude to the account of creation from a cosmic

---

46. Mathewson, "New Exodus," 245–46. For an intensive study of the sea (the waters), see Reymond, *L'eau, sa vie, et sa signification*. See also Baker's short but well-summarized article about the meaning and functions of the wind and the waves in the OT and the NT (Baker, "Wind and the Waves").

47. Mathews, *Genesis 1–11:26*, 134.

48. The "deep" is actually synonymous with the "waters." Wenham, *Genesis 1–15*, 17.

49. Walton, *Genesis*, 73.

50. E.g., Gunkel argues that the deep (תְהוֹם) in Gen 1:2 has the background of Babylonian myth (Gunkel, *Schöpfung und Chaos in Urzeit und Endzeit*, 16–30). See also Otzen et al, *Myths in the Old Testament*, 33–34.

battle with Tiamat in Babylonian myth.[51] This argument, however, has failed to gain adherence.[52] As Walton maintains, "[the] lack of personification in Genesis removes from the element of chaos any sense of evil."[53] In addition, the etymological similarity between *těhôm* ("the deep") in Gen 1:2 and *Ti'âmat* ("Tiamat") in Babylonian and Ras Shamra mythology cannot be used as evidence that Genesis borrowed mythological conceptions from neighboring religions.[54] Though the waters that are expressed as "the deep" seem to express the image of chaos in Gen 1:2, they do not carry implications of threat or evilness.[55] According to Mathews, "Genesis identifies the waters only for what they are, creations subject to the superintendence of God."[56] Genesis 1 tells us that the "waters," which are described as the "deep" in v. 2 and become the "sea" in v. 9, are placed under the control of God in his creation.

In the exodus story, the waters (the sea) bear implications of threat, chaos, or evil force. Ringgren states that "the sea plays a crucial role in the narratives describing the deliverance of Israel from Egypt."[57] In the historical description of the crossing of the Red Sea (Exod 14:13–31) and the songs of Moses and Miriam praising God's mighty work of parting the waters (15:1–21), the sea was not only an obstacle and threat that the Israelites had to overcome in order to escape from the Egyptian army but also an object

---

51. Anderson, *Creation versus Chaos*, 42–45.

52. Rad says that Gen 1:2 does not seem to borrow the conceptions of Babylonian and Ras Shamra mythology. Rather, this verse presents the "peculiar intermediate state between nothingness and creation, i.e., the chaos, the subject of a theological declaration." Here, chaos simply indicates "the threat to everything created," because "all creation is always ready to sink into the abyss of the formlessness." He also maintains that there is no idea of *creatio ex nihilo* in this verse. See Rad, *Genesis*, 50–51. However, I do not believe this verse carries any implication of a threat that may lead creation into destruction. Rather, it implies that everything was under God's control at creation, and so Gen 1 depicts *creatio ex nihilo*.

53. Walton, *Genesis*, 73. See also Hamilton, *Book of Genesis*, 110–11.

54. Wenham, quoting Heidel, maintains that "both Hebrew and Babylonian *Ti'amat* are independently derived from a common Semitic root" (Wenham, *Genesis 1–15*, 16). See also Heidel, *Babylonian Genesis*, 98–101. Matthews also says that "the Babylonian and Hebrew terms for "deep/ocean" are related to a common Semitic word, and therefore the Hebrew is not a derivative of Tiamat linguistically" (Matthews, *Genesis 1–11*, 134). For a detailed discussion of the etymology of תְּהוֹם, see Tsumura, *Earth and the Waters*, 45–52.

55. Walton asserts that "there is nothing sinister or menacing about this chaos in Genesis; it is simply the indication that God has not yet done his work" (Walton, *Genesis*, 74).

56. Mathews, *Genesis 1–11*, 134.

57. Ringgren, "יָם, *yām*," 6:94.

that God could control and manipulate in order to redeem his people. When the Israelites camped before Pi-hahiroth, between Migdol and the sea, the chasing Egyptians nearly reached the Israelites' camp (vv. 1–9). In great fear, the Israelites cried out to God and reproached Moses because of the serious threat of the death at the hands of the Egyptian army (vv. 10–12). God commanded Moses to raise his staff and stretch out his hand over the sea. The waters were divided, the sea became dry land, and the Israelites safely crossed over the sea while the Egyptians drowned as the waters flowed back over them (vv. 13–31). In this episode, God is portrayed as the one who has the mighty power to rule over the waters. God's power, magnificence, and greatness were disclosed as he first made the waters unthreatening to the Israelites and then used the waters as an instrument to defeat the Egyptian army.

According to Stegner, "the story of Israel's deliverance at the sea, as recorded in Exod 14, was not static, but continued to grow and change with the addition of new exegetical traditions."[58] The historical event at the Red Sea was reinterpreted and represented in different tones and dimensions, namely cosmological and eschatological. In the song of Moses and Miriam that praises God's victory at the Red Sea (Exod 15:1–21), the image is subtly changed from neutral waters (מַיִם) to chaotic waters (תְּהֹמֹת).[59] In his exegesis of Exod 15:8, Durham describes this shift as follows:

> There is here a subtle but important shift from "waters" (מים) and "currents" (נזלים), neither of which refers to the primordial waters of chaos . . . to "ancient deep," תהמת. The implication, at the very least, is that the visible waters in their everyday flow were thrust aside to make way for the temporary release of the devastating rebellion-waters from their subterranean prison. Then these same waters, the very symbol of disorder in motion, are "made solid," "stilled" in the middle of the sea.[60]

---

58. Stegner, "Jesus' Walking on the Water," 215–16.

59. Tromp argues that the Hebrew תְּהֹמֹת, has a primordial force: "Hebrew $t^ehôm$ is a vigorous and often grim word, which never entirely renounced its mythical past. A primordial strength pervades $t^ehôm$ throughout. It stands for: a) the primeval ocean; b) the waters round the earth after creation, which continually threaten the cosmos; c) these waters as a source of blessing for the earth. The word denotes chaotic water, both at the time of creation and after it" (Tromp, *Primitive Conceptions*, 59–61). For further discussion of the primordial waters, see Reymond, *L'eau, sa vie, et sa signification*, 167–76, 182–94. Though it is not necessary to connect "the deep" (תְּהֹמֹת) of Exod 15:5, 8 with that of Gen 1:2, this word here implies chaos as a threatening force to human beings.

60. Durham, *Exodus*, 207. He argues that Exod 15:4–8 portrays "the victory with allusions to Yahweh's prior victory over the cosmic chaos-waters."

In order to show God's sovereignty over the cosmos and his incomparable power and holiness—"Who is like you, O LORD, among the gods? Who is like you, majestic in holiness, awesome in glory, doing wonders?" (15:11)—the victory at the Red Sea is retold using cosmological expressions in the song of Moses and Miriam. According to Watts, "Yahweh's victory over his enemies, expressed in creational 'chaos-defeating' language, is characteristic of the ancient Divine-Warrior Hymns of early Israel, of which Exod 15 is perhaps the finest early example."[61]

The sea (the waters), symbolizing chaos,[62] here plays a significant role in the development of a cosmological understanding of this victory.[63] Not only the Egyptian army but also the sea as chaos threatened the Israelites.[64] God, however, delivered the Israelites by using the chaos-waters to drown the Egyptian army: both threats were subjugated by his power.[65] God's defeat of the Egyptian army consequently reveals his power to rule over chaos in the universe. God's victory over historic enemies by controlling chaos demonstrates his universal sovereignty over both earthly nations and cosmic forces.[66]

The Psalms frequently use the image of the sea in the exodus story to glorify God's power and sovereignty. The psalmists praise God's mighty works of dividing the sea and leading the Israelites to pass through it: "You divided the sea by your might" (Ps 74:13); "He turned the sea into dry land; they passed through the river on foot (66:6)";[67] "He divided the sea and let them pass through it and made the waters stand like a heap" (78:13).[68]

---

61. Watts, *Isaiah's New Exodus and Mark*, 160.

62. Here, "the sea is personified to some degree": the sea (the waters) is portrayed as אַדִּירִים (mighty) in v. 10 and is conveyed by three different terms that are the subject of a series of actions, "the waters (מַיִם) piled up," "the deep waters (תְּהֹמֹת) congealed" (v. 8), and "the sea (יָם) covered them" (v. 10). Dozeman, *Commentary on Exodus*, 338.

63. In the expression of v. 12, "the earth swallowed them," the earth has a cosmic image like the sea, indicating "nether world," or "underworld." See Durham, *Exodus*, 207; Dozeman, *Commentary on Exodus*, 338.

64. According to Propp, the Israelites saw the sea as "a disquieting reminder of Chaos threatening the habitable realm" (Propp, *Exodus 1–18*, 557).

65. Bruckner, *Exodus*, 142.

66. Bruckner, *Exodus*, 143. Bruckner communicates the significance of the songs of victory over chaos and historic enemies (e.g., Ps 77:19–20; 89:9–10; 114:1–7) as follows: "These songs of victory over the chaos of nature and history make the point that the fear of the ancient Near East does not hold sway. The Lord's victory over the pharaoh was also a victory over the symbols of chaos in the ancient Near East."

67. In this verse, the passing through the Red Sea (יָם) in the exodus story corresponds to the crossing of the Jordan River (נָהָר). See Ringgren, "יָם, yām," 6:95.

68. Goldingay maintains that Ps 78:13 intends to emphasize God's mighty work over the sea and his power to control it rather than to describe God's destruction of the

God's control of the sea is repeatedly mentioned in the Psalms as evidence of God's redemptive power to deliver Israel. As Curtis notes, "the depiction of Yahweh in the praises of Israel includes a number of statements which imply that he has the waters in complete subjection."[69]

The sea (the waters) is often personified in the Psalms. Psalm 77:17 describes the sea (the waters)[70] as one who saw God and trembled before his presence: "When the waters saw you, O God, when they were afraid, the deep [תְּהֹמוֹת] trembled." This verse is related to the exodus story because v. 20 presents the image of passing through the sea (the waters):[71] "Your way was through the sea, your path, through the mighty waters." Verses 17 to 21 thus portray "the demonstration of God's power in theophanic intervention."[72] The waters are described anthropomorphically as afraid and troubled in order to intensify the depiction of God's mighty works. The waters, which correspond to the deep (תְּהֹמוֹת, v. 17), are regarded as chaos,[73] and the chaotic waters should be tamed and conquered by God.[74] The sea is also personified in Ps 114:3, 5: "the sea looked and fled." As Allen says, the personified description of the sea is related to theophany: the appearance of God's overwhelming power made the chaotic waters so afraid that they fled without fighting.[75]

In Ps 106(105 LXX), a historical poem that recounts the exodus from Egypt, the sea is again personified and rebuked by God: "He rebuked (וַיִּגְעַר) the Red Sea, and it dried up; he led them through the deep (תְּהֹמוֹת), as

---

Egyptian army. See Goldingay, *Psalms 42–89*, 490.

69. Curtis, "'Subjugation of the Waters,'" 245. In this article, Curtis deals with the motif of "the subjugation of the waters," and discusses whether this motif contains "mere poetic imagery" or reflects "the tension between the cults of Yahweh and Baal."

70. Hossfeld and Zenger state the conflict between the superior power of God and the chaotic force of the waters in a cosmic dimension as follows: "It is true that the emphasis on the element of water has an obvious association with the passage through the sea, but here it is a matter of the mythical-cosmic confrontation between the superior God-king and the waters of chaos" (Hossfeld and Zenger, *Psalms 2*, 279).

71. Ringgren, "יָם, yām," 6:93.

72. Tate, *Psalms 51–100*, 275.

73. Curtis argues that the "Reed Sea" is paralleled with "deeps" (Curtis, "'Subjugation of the Waters,'" 249).

74. I previously explained the meaning of the word "the deep" (תְּהֹמוֹת), as the chaotic waters in the song of Moses and Miriam in Exod 15:1–21.

75. Allen argues that "the imagery used of creation in Ps 104:7–8 is here used of Israel's history. Behind the present use of the metaphor stands the holy-war tradition expressed in Exod 15:14–16; Deut 11:25; Josh 2:9–11; Hab 3:7" (Allen, *Psalms 101–150*, 142).

through the wilderness (מִדְבָּר)"; "καὶ ἐπετίμησεν⁷⁶ τῇ ἐρυθρᾷ θαλάσσῃ καὶ ἐξηράνθη καὶ ὡδήγησεν αὐτοὺς ἐν ἀβύσσῳ ὡς ἐν ἐρήμῳ" (v. 9 LXX). The Hebrew word תְּהֹמוֹת (the deep)—also used in Exod 15:5, 8—is employed here to present the chaotic character of the sea. This psalm recalls the Israelites' rebellion against God at the Red Sea (Ps 106[105]:7) and reveals God's power to subjugate the waters by rebuking the Red Sea (v. 9).⁷⁷ According to Goldingay, though the expressions of rebuking and withering the sea do not correspond to the "Exodus formulations," it was natural to connect this imagery to the victory at the Red Sea.⁷⁸ The historical event of the exodus at the Red Sea is expressed in the cosmic imagery of God's rule over chaos.⁷⁹

Imagery of the sea and the waters is also associated with the exodus story in Isaiah. Isaiah envisages the new exodus from Babylon by recalling the exodus from Egypt. He anticipates the impending redemption of Israel because God's past deliverance serves as the evidence of his power to deliver Israel again.⁸⁰ Among the many allusions to and mentions of the new exodus in Isaiah,⁸¹ sea/waters imagery associated with the exodus story appears in Isa 43:16–17; 50:2; and 51:9–10.

Isaiah 43:16–17 portrays God's deliverance of the Israelites in the sea and his victory over the Egyptian army.

> This is what the LORD says—
> he who made (הַנּוֹתֵן) a way in the sea,
> a path through the mighty waters,
> who brought out (הַמּוֹצִיא) chariots and horses,

76. The Greek verb ἐπιτιμάω is similarly used in Mark 4:39 when Jesus rebuked the wind to be still. As Jesus calmed down the sea by his word, "to rebuke the wind," God's "word" also has the power to subjugate the sea by rebuking it: "His [God's] power extends also to his word, because by his 'rebuke' (cf. v. 9; cf. 104:7; Isa 50:2; Na 1:4) he brought the sea to submission (cf. 65:7; 104:7)" (VanGemeren, *Psalms*, 783).

77. Curtis, "'Subjugation of the Waters,'" 249.

78. Goldingay claims that these expressions are related to the imagery of "a deity's victory over cosmic tumultuous waters" in creation. In Ps 18:15(16), 104:7, God's rebuke (גְּעָרָה) of the waters (מַיִם) or the deep (תְּהוֹם) is connected to the imagery of the creation. See Goldingay, *Psalms 90–150*, 228.

79. Goldingay, *Psalms 90–150*, 228.

80. Ringgren, "יָם, *yām*," 6:95.

81. The new exodus motifs appear especially in Isa 40–55. Anderson suggests ten passages presenting the new exodus imagery among these chapters: "(1) 40:3–5 The highway in the wilderness; (2) 41:17–20 The transformation of the wilderness; (3) 42:14–16 Yahweh leads his people in a way they know not; (4) 43:1–3 Passing through the waters and the fire; (5) 43:14–21 A way in the wilderness; (6) 48:20–21 The exodus from Babylon; (7) 49:8–12 The new entry into the Promised Land; (8) 51:9–10 The new victory at the sea; (9) 52:11–12 The new exodus; (10) 55:12–13 Israel shall go out in joy and peace" (Anderson, "Exodus Typology in Second Isaiah," 181–82).

the army and the power,
and they lay there, never to rise again,
they are extinguished, quenched like a wick.

The following verses (vv. 18–21) also describe his future activity in the new exodus and Smith says its significance as follows: "If God has the power to overcome the power of the sea and the horses and chariots of their past enemies, surely he can transform the future by reversing the curses of the past and bringing water and blessing to his land and his people."[82] Isaiah's eschatological vision of future deliverance is firmly based on God's past action of rescuing the Israelites from Egypt.[83] The climax of his deliverance took place in the sea where his mighty power to defeat the Egyptian army was revealed. By employing participles (הַנּוֹתֵן, "the one who makes" in v. 16; הַמּוֹצִיא, "the one who causes to bring out" in v. 17), Isaiah emphasizes "who God is and what he has done."[84] The sea and the waters that were controlled by God serve as the instruments to reveal God's power and greatness.

In Isa 50:2, the sea is rebuked by God: "By my rebuke (בְּגַעֲרָתִי), I dry up the sea."[85] The sea is here personified and regarded as the force of chaos; God's action of rebuking the sea shows his supreme authority and rule over the universe. According to Smith, however, it is questionable to which tradition Isa 50:2 belongs: "(1) about God's past power to dry up the Red Sea so that the Israelites could be delivered from a past enemy; (b) from hymnic literature that praises God's sovereignty over nature; or (c) from traditions

82. Smith, *Isaiah 40–66*, 208.

83. Pao explains the significance of Isaiah's combination of the past and the present as follows: "This blending of the past and the present is typical of the act of re-enacting the Exodus event in Isaiah 40–55; and to understand this simply as a 'typology' does not fully explicate the complex nature of the relationship between the two. Moreover, the 'former' act apparently becomes the basis without which the 'latter' would not be possible" (Pao, *Acts and the Isaianic New Exodus*, 54). Smith also notes that God's "eschatological plan" is trustworthy since he performed successfully his "past plan." In Isa 43:18, the listeners are urged to forget God's past deeds because God is still alive and is doing a new thing which is greater than anything witnessed in the past. The waters that serve as an instrument to kill the Egyptians in the past are provided to God's people as the fountain of life: "I provide water in the wilderness, rivers in the desert, to give drink to my chosen people" (v. 20). See Smith, *Isaiah 40–66*, 208–10.

84. Smith, *Isaiah 40–66*, 209.

85. Kee says that the imagery of the waters is used as "the fulfilment of the eschatological hope." He suggested two instances of the eschatological significance of the water imagery in terms of the rebuke of the waters in Isaiah. First, Isa 17:13 describes "the rebuke of the new situation in which God brings the nations under his control as the 'rebuke' of the waters." Second, in Isa 50:2, the image of God's drying up the sea indicates "an eschatological picture of the ultimate victory of God over the evil powers." See Kee, "Terminology of Mark's Exorcism Stories," 236.

about God's ecological transformation (either renewal or degradation) of nature."[86] Isaiah 50:2 employs exodus imagery with both historical and cosmological implications in order to demonstrate God's power to deliver his people and his sovereignty over the universe. The words of Isa 50:2—"Was my *hand* [יָד] too short to redeem you? . . . By my *rebuke* [גְּעָרָה] I dry up the sea"—contain imagery that closely parallels two expressions associated with the exodus imagery in Isa 51:9 ("the *arm* (זְרוֹעַ) of the LORD") and Ps 106:9 ("*rebuking* (גָּעַר) the sea"). Given this similarity, we can infer that Isa 50:2 also refers to the exodus story. Goldingay agrees that the verb "rescue" (נָצִיר) in Isa 50:2 describes the end of "an experience of servitude or danger or attack," so this sentence fits well with the exodus.[87] Though he acknowledges the exodus implication in this verse, Goldingay argues that the imagery of rebuking the sea is "more associated with the tumultuous powers that Yhwh brought under control at creation."[88] Since historical and cosmogonic types are mixed in the exodus motifs, the imagery that evokes God's redemptive works in the exodus can also be understood in the light of his creative acts. In Isaiah's vision (especially Isa 40–55), creation is not so much "a once-for-all past event" as "an ongoing or present reality."[89] God, who demonstrated his power to control the sea by separating the waters in the first exodus, also presents his power to subjugate chaos by rebuking the sea as a creative act in the new exodus.[90] The image of drying up the sea also has eschatological significance in that God eventually wins the victory over evil forces.[91]

In Isa 51:9–10, the imagery of the sea and the waters is associated with the exodus story and expressed in the cosmogonic dimension.

> Awake, awake, put on strength,

---

86. Smith, *Isaiah 40–66*, 376.

87. Goldingay, *Message of Isaiah 40–55*, 398.

88. Goldingay, *Message of Isaiah 40–55*, 398–99. Goldingay states that "the prophet affirms that Yhwh still possesses the power to control the tumultuous forces of disorder, the power that was utilized at the exodus but goes back to creation."

89. Goldingay, *Message of Isaiah 40–55*, 432.

90. Pao mentions that "the Exodus event is understood against the creation myth of the cosmic defeat of Rahab and the sea (50:2; 51:9–11); and the creative act of God is repeatedly evoked (40:12–31; 42:5; 44:24; 45:9–18; 48:12–13; 51:12–16)" (Pao, *Acts and the Isaianic New Exodus*, 56). Watts explains God's creative power to redeem Israel as follows: "It is affirmed that Yahweh has created the world and its history (e.g., עשׂה: 44:24; 45:7, 12; ברא: 40:26, 28; 45:12; יצר: 45:7, 18; יסד: 48:13) and in particular Jacob-Israel (עשׂה: 43:7; 44:2; ברא: 43:1, 7; 44:2, 21; יצר: 45:9, 11). On the strength of this evidence Yahweh announces his intention to use his creative power and wisdom to deliver Jacob-Israel and to restore the land in a New Exodus (51:9–10; 44:27 and 50:2)" (Watts, *Isaiah's New Exodus and Mark*, 40).

91. Kee, "Terminology of Mark's Exorcism Stories," 236.

> O arm of the LORD;
> Awake, as in days of old,
> > in the generations of long ago.
> Was it not you who cut Rahab (רַהַב) to pieces,
> > who pierced the dragon (תַּנִּין)?
> Was it not you who dried up the sea (יָם),
> > The waters of the great deep (תְּהוֹם);
> who made the depths of the sea
> a way for the redeemed to cross over?

Isaiah yearns for the strength of the arm of the LORD to deliver his people, "making possible the New Exodus and Return to Zion."[92] According to Pao, the prophet reworked the exodus traditions by transforming them into the paradigm of the eschatological new exodus.[93] This task was performed in two ways: first, through the presentation of the exodus as "a future event promised on the basis of God's action in the past"; second, through "the reformulation of the original Exodus story with the cosmogonic one, thus emphasizing the (new) Exodus as a creative event."[94] Verses 9–10 can be understood in these two aspects of Isaianic transformation of the exodus pattern. On the one hand, the prophet emphasized that it was the LORD who dried up the sea (the waters) and made a path to cross them. The ground for anticipating the future event that God promised comes from the past event that he performed at the Red Sea. On the other hand, the prophet associates the sea and the waters with the imagery of Rahab (רַהַב) and the dragon (תַּנִּין),[95] which were destroyed by God. The historical event of the exodus from Egypt was reinterpreted in terms of a cosmic event associated with God's creative act.[96]

Since 51:9–10 reflects the exodus story, the destruction of Rahab and the dragon is connected to the parting of the Red Sea. In a historical aspect, "Rahab" refers to Egypt (e.g., Isa 30:7, where Egypt is called Rahab who sits still; Ps 87:4, where Rahab and Babylon appear together) and the dragon

---

92. Martin, "Exegesis of Isaiah 51:9–11," 151. The imagery of the arm of Yahweh plays an important part in the exodus traditions (e.g., Exod 15:6; Isa 51:9), and the usage of the term "arm" is related to the "language of cosmic and holy warfare" (Martin, "Exegesis of Isaiah 51:9–11," 153–54). For the image of the arm of the Lord, see Seely, "Image of the Hand of God in the Exodus Traditions."

93. Pao, *Acts and the Isaianic New Exodus*, 56.

94. Pao, *Acts and the Isaianic New Exodus*, 56.

95. Baltzer argues that Rahab (רַהַב), the dragon (תַּנִּין), the sea (יָם), and the primordial waters (תְּהוֹם רַבָּה) are the names or descriptions of myth (Baltzer, *Deutero-Isaiah*, 356).

96. According to Achtemeier, in Isa 51:9–10, "the author identifies the act of dividing the waters at the time of creation with the act of dividing the waters to redeem his people from bondage in Egypt" (Achtemeier, "Person and Deed," 175).

stands for Pharaoh (e.g., Ezek 29:3).[97] Rahab and the dragon are also images of the cosmic world. Isaiah employs this imagery to demonstrate that God alone is the Creator and Lord of the universe who subjugated the evil force of chaos in creation. According to Oswalt, Rahab and the dragon were drawn from the mythic images of the ancient Near East, but Isaiah does not follow established mythic ideas but employs this imagery to present God's supremacy in the universe.

> [I]t is also clear that those terms [Rahab and dragon] are not limited to those historical referents. As is known from Ugaritic studies, *the twisting monster* is a figure in the struggles of Baal with the god of the sea, Yam, as is 'Leviathan,' which is equated with the monster in Isa. 27:1. Given these facts, and the evidence that the myth of the struggle of the gods with the sea monster was known in one form or another all over the ancient Near East, one has reason to believe that Isaiah is here, as in 27:1, utilizing this acquaintance among the people for his own purposes. It is important to note that the allusions to Near Eastern myths in the Bible all occur after 750 B.C., long after the basic antimythic character of biblical faith had been established. Thus there is an appeal here neither to some current Hebrew myth nor to some original one, now dead. Rather, just as a contemporary poet might allude to the *Iliad* or the *Odyssey*, utilizing imagery familiar to his hearers but that is hardly part of their belief system, so Isaiah uses the imagery of the well-known stories of creation to make his point. It was not Baal or Marduk or Ashur who had any claim to being the Creator—it was the Lord alone.[98]

I do not believe that the use of the imagery of Rahab and the dragon implies that the Israelites' faith was based on mythic concepts or theologies; rather, this language and imagery was employed in opposition to other ancient Near Eastern myths to describe God's sovereignty over the universe and his supremacy over other gods.[99]

---

97. In the OT, the imagery of Rahab (רַהַב) and the dragon (תַּנִּין) is connected to Egypt, and in particular Rahab serves as a symbol of Egypt in other passages of the OT (implicitly Ps 87:4; explicitly Isa 30:7). Goldingay, *Message of Isaiah 40–55*, 432. See also Oswalt, *Book of Isaiah*, 341.

98. Oswalt, *Book of Isaiah*, 341–42.

99. In his exegetical comments on Isa 51:9–11, Martin correctly explained the use of myths in the OT as follows: "As will be seen in the exegesis, a prominent feature of the passage is its adaptation of the language and imagery of Near Eastern mythology. A myth can be defined as a story of gods or other superhuman beings told to account for the presence and order of the world, for some custom or institution, or for a natural

God's mighty work in parting the waters implies his creative act of destroying the chaos represented by Rahab and the dragon. Isaiah thus associates the historical event of the victory at the sea with a creative event; in this way, the exodus event expands to a universal event.[100] In Isaiah's vision, God's victory at the sea is elevated to a triumph over chaos in which universal salvation is accomplished. The sea here plays an important role as the medium that connects the historical event of the exodus with a creative event. Therefore, the deliverance of the Israelites at the sea ultimately indicates the God's victory over the chaos-waters. The sea, which in cosmological and eschatological terms stands for chaos, is the object to be subjugated and defeated by God in the new exodus.

The Sea as the Setting of the New Exodus in Jesus' Sea Miracles (Mark 4:35–41 and 6:45–52)

As previously discussed, in Exodus and the later OT literature the sea and the waters represent an obstacle or the power of chaos that threatens the people of God. However, the negative images of the sea inversely serve as instruments to disclose God's power over the chaotic forces and his sovereignty over the universe. The sea in the exodus was an obstacle to Israel's escape from the Egyptian army, but the Israelites crossed over it by God's miraculous power. The victory at the Red Sea has also been reinterpreted in terms of a cosmological dimension. God's destruction of the Egyptian army at the sea is identified with his defeat of the chaotic force of the sea. God is

---

phenomenon such as a storm or the appearance of vegetation in the spring. Israel's neighbors preserved many such myths, and the Israelites were undoubtedly familiar with them. In several Old Testament passages, including Isa 51:9–11, the writers have apparently—it is safe to say almost surely—worked the language and imagery of these myths into passages about Yahweh and his creative and redemptive activity in history. This is not to say that these writers were in any way suggesting that the Israelite beliefs concerning God and his activity were myths. Rather, they were using this familiar language and imagery of Near Eastern mythology as a poetic device for affirming Israel's faith in Yahweh's concrete activity. At the same time, they were making the point that it was Yahweh, not the fantastic figures of Semitic mythology, who was really responsible for the natural and historical order of the world" (Martin, "Exegesis of Isaiah 51:9–11," 152).

100. According to Pao, in the ancient traditions of Israel, the exodus story is not and should not be interpreted separately from the creation story. Pao agrees with Clifford's idea of "two ideal types": in a modern sense, while the "historic type" is regarded as "redemption," the "cosmogonic type" is considered as "creation." At the advent of Israel as the people of God, both types become the same event; redemption and creation are understood together, not being separated from each other. Pao, *Acts and the Isaianic New Exodus*, 57. Refer to Clifford, *Fair Spoken and Persuading*, 18, 23.

therefore revealed as the supreme ruler over both the earthly nations and the cosmic world.

Jesus' sea miracles in Mark 4:35–41 and 6:45–52 reflect this exodus imagery, with the setting of the sea recollecting the victory at the Red Sea.[101] In these stories the sea is not simply an obstacle to Jesus and his disciples' voyage, but rather has the significance of a chaotic force that echoes the exodus event with all its cosmological and eschatological implications. In the present study, I will examine the implications and functions of the sea and examine the exodus imagery in each sea miracle in Mark.

Jesus Calming the Storm (4:35–41)

In the first sea miracle, Jesus' calming the storm (4:35–41), the sea serves as an obstacle preventing the disciples from reaching their destination. When Jesus and his disciples were sailing on the Sea of Galilee, a great windstorm and furious waves came upon them and the ship was about to be wrecked (4:37). As the Red Sea was a barrier to the Israelites escaping from Egypt, the Sea of Galilee was an impediment to the disciples reaching the opposite shore. Both the Israelites and the disciples were in danger even of death in the sea.

In Mark's narrative, the sea is not only physical water but also has an image of chaos. Mark portrays the sea as a chaotic force threatening the disciples who wished to cross over it. According to Elizabeth Struthers Malbon, Mark prefers the term "sea" (θάλασσα) to "lake" (λίμνη) that is the more geographical accurate term,[102] because "sea" has overtones of hazard or chaos:

> [I]t is clear that the Marcan application of the term *thalassa* rather than *limnē* to the lake of Galilee serves well its narrative and theological purposes. Though *limnē* is more geographically precise, the more ambiguous *thalassa* is rich in connotations from the Hebrew scriptures. Mark presupposes the connotation of the sea as chaos, threat, danger, in opposition to the land as order, promise, security.[103]

---

101. Chapman suggests three prominent scenes to evoke Mosaic imagery: the separating of the water in the sea, the giving of manna in the wilderness, and the grant of the Law in the mountain (Chapman, *Orphan Gospel*, 51–61).

102. Malbon, "Jesus of Mark and the Sea of Galilee," 376.

103. Malbon, "Jesus of Mark and the Sea of Galilee," 376.

When the furious sea threatened them, Jesus rebuked the wind and commanded the sea to be muzzled (v. 39).[104] The verbs "to rebuke" (ἐπετίμησεν, indicative) and "to be muzzled" (φιμώθητι, imperative), which are used to describe Jesus' expulsion of the unclean spirit in Mark 1:25, are employed in the same moods in 4:39 to describe his calming of the sea.[105] On the basis of the usage of the two verbs in an exorcism, Jesus' calming the stormy sea may be regarded as another type of exorcism.[106] France, however, rejects this idea: "that is a lot to build on two verbs, each of which has a much wider use than in specifically exorcistic contexts."[107] In his view Mark's wording is a mere "anthropomorphism," but not a portrayal of the storm as demonic.[108]

Though the sea is not directly called Satan or a demon, Mark's portrayal of the sea is not simply an anthropomorphism of nature,[109] but rather presents the sea as a chaotic force. In comparison with the parallel passages of Matthew (8:23–27) and Luke (8:22–25), Mark portrays the chaotic and threatening nature of the sea most strongly. All three synoptic Gospels use the indicative verb of "to rebuke" (ἐπιτιμάω) toward the winds and the sea, but while Matthew and Luke use no imperative verbs, Mark includes two imperative verbs—σιώπα, πεφίμωσο ("Quiet, be still!" 4:39)—directed toward the roaring sea, one of which (πεφίμωσο) is used to expel the evil spirit in 1:25 (φιμώθητι). The use of two verbs (ἐπιτιμάω and φιμόω) in the same combination found in the exorcism narrative (an indicative form of "to rebuke" followed by the imperative "be still" in 1:25) demonstrates that the sea is seen as an evil (chaotic) force in Mark's account (4:39).[110] In the expression "even the wind and the sea obey him" (καὶ ὁ ἄνεμος καὶ ἡ θάλασσα ὑπακούει αὐτῷ; 4:41), the wind and the sea together take a singular form

---

104. Though Jesus rebuked the wind and told the sea to be muzzled, the objects of Jesus' rebuke are both the wind and the roaring sea.

105. Stein, *Mark*, 243.

106. Twelftree also argues that the act that Jesus' rebuking the furious wind in Mark 4:39 reflects his rebuking demons in 1:25, so the wind and the sea may be regarded as demons: "This perspective on the story is further endorsed when we note the way Jesus is said to speak to or 'rebuke' (*pephimōso*, Mk 4:39) the wind and the sea as if they are demons, reminiscent of the language of the exorcisms (cf. *phimōthēti*, 1:25)" (Twelftree, *Jesus the Miracle Worker*, 70).

107. France, *Gospel of Mark*, 224.

108. France, *Gospel of Mark*, 224. France suggests the examples of anthropomorphism of the rebuking of the sea in Ps 18:15; 104:7; 106:9; Isa 50:2; Nah 1:4.

109. Edwards argues that "Mark's description of the stilling of the storm exceeds the Hebrew penchant for personalizing nature" (Edwards, *Gospel According to Mark*, 149).

110. When Jesus rebukes (ἐπετίμησεν) Peter as Satan in 8:33, the following verb of ἐπετίμησεν is imperative: "Get behind me" (ὕπαγε ὀπίσω μου).

of the verb ὑπακούω ("to obey"), indicating that they are regarded as "one force."[111] In addition, the sea is personified by the use of the verb ὑπακούω, which is an intensification of the verb ἀκούω ("to hear"): "Jesus, here the teacher mighty in word and work, receives the response of submission from the forces of nature."[112] According to Collins, "the reason why the wind and sea are treated like demons is that demons or evil spirits were thought to be responsible for inclement weather. There is evidence in both Greek and Jewish literature, early and late, for the personification or demonization of wind and sea."[113] Even more significantly, the Greek verb ἐπιτιμάω ("to rebuke") is related to the censure of demonic forces elsewhere in Mark's narrative. This verb is used by Jesus to warn and expel demons in 1:25, 3:12, and 9:25; it is also employed three times in the context of Jesus' prediction of his suffering, death, and resurrection (8:27–38),[114] most importantly when Jesus rebuked Peter as Satan because Peter set his mind on the things of men rather than the things of God (v. 33).

According to Kee, the Synoptic Gospels' use of ἐπιτιμάω to describe exorcism has no parallel in non-Jewish sources.[115] The verb is not used as a term of control over demonic forces in the Hellenistic miracle stories;[116] it is used in association with exorcisms only in the Jewish world.[117] The background of exorcism in Mark's narrative is connected to "the cosmic plan of

111. Donahue and Harrington, *Gospel of Mark*, 159.

112. Donahue and Harrington, *Gospel of Mark*, 159–60.

113. Collins, *Mark*, 261. See also Loos, *Miracles of Jesus*, 642.

114. The Greek ἐπιτιμάω is used three times in the pericope of Jesus' passion prediction (8:27–38). First, Jesus warned (ἐπετίμησεν) the disciples not to tell anyone about him (8:30). Second, Peter rebuked (ἐπιτιμᾶν) Jesus for his prediction of suffering (v. 32). Third, Jesus rebuked (ἐπετίμησεν) Peter as Satan, for he did not have in mind the things of God, but the things of men (v. 33). The verb ἐπιτιμάω is also used by the disciples and the people in 10:13, 48, but in this case it is not connected to demons: the disciples rebuked those who were bringing little children (v. 13), and the people rebuked blind Bartimaeous for his shout to Jesus (v. 48). Jesus' use of ἐπιτιμάω, however, is strongly related to his rebuke of evil forces.

115. Kee, "Terminology of Mark's Exorcism Stories," 240. For an examination of the language used in 4:35–41, refer to Kittel, "'Wer ist der?' Markus 4:35–41," 517–42.

116. Kee argues that "at the outset the understanding of Jesus' exorcism and healings was radically different from the significance which formally comparable acts had among the hellenistic wonder-workers. In the pagan sources, the actions either have meaning as events in themselves (reports of cures, evidences of magical power), or they are told to create a supernatural aura around an esteemed figure of the past." See Kee, "Terminology of Mark's Exorcism Stories," 240–42, 246.

117. Kee, "Terminology of Mark's Exorcism Stories," 232. Kee examines the relationship between the Hebrew גער and the Greek ἐπιτιμάω and argues that the usages of גער beyond the lexical considerations serve as the background to interpret Mark's exorcism stories.

God by which he was regaining control over an estranged and hostile creation, which was under subjection to the powers of Satan."[118] In his rebuke of the sea, Jesus is depicted as the eschatological conqueror who defeats an evil force.[119] Therefore, Jesus' stilling of the storm not only presents a Christological declaration of Jesus' lordship over "nature," but also manifests his sovereignty over "the cosmic world" by using the word, "to rebuke" (ἐπιτιμάω), to express power over the evil forces.[120]

As we have seen, the imagery of rebuking the sea is connected to the victory at the sea in the exodus story. In Ps 106:9 and Isa 50:2, passages that are explicitly connected to the exodus imagery, God rebuked the sea and dried it up in order to rescue his people. The personified sea is understood as chaos to be destroyed. The historical imagery of the exodus event is here combined with the cosmic imagery of a creative event: the sea, representing chaos, plays a role in combining these two imageries[121] as God's rescue of his people at the sea is identified with his rebuke and conquest of the chaotic forces in a creative event.[122] God's redemptive work is interpreted in the light of his creative work in order to show his sovereignty over the universe. Likewise, Jesus' deliverance of the disciples at the sea is depicted in the light of a cosmic (creative) event as he rebukes the chaos-sea. "Just as God defeated chaos in his act of creation, an act paralleled by his redemption of Israel, so here Jesus also defeats that symbol of chaos, the stormy sea, in the course of redemptive life."[123] The description of the sea in terms of chaos rebuked by Jesus demonstrates that Jesus is the universal ruler over the cosmic world, as well as nature, in his redemptive work.

118. Kee, "Terminology of Mark's Exorcism Stories," 246.

119. Marcus, *Mark 1–8*, 337. Jesus' exorcistic activity to rebuke the sea fulfills the eschatological aim of defeating the evil power. See also Kee, "Terminology of Mark's Exorcism Stories," 246.

120. Kee, "Terminology of Mark's Exorcism Stories," 244. Edwards, placing an emphasis on Christology, argues that the goal of calming the storm is to show that "Jesus does what only God can do" (Edwards, *Gospel According to Mark*, 150).

121. In Isa 51:9–10, Yahweh as "Creator-Warrior" defeats "the watery-chaos-monster at the Exodus." Likewise, Jesus is demonstrated as the same "Creator-Warrior," when he rebukes the chaos-sea. Watts, *Isaiah's New Exodus and Mark*, 161.

122. Achtemeier says that "Israel understood its redemption in terms of a creative act which was paralleled only by God's original act of creation, when he overcame the primeval chaos" (Achtemeier, "Person and Deed," 175). In Psalms, Isaiah, and the later OT passages, God's defeat of chaos in his creative act just has the purpose of demonstrating that he is the true God of creation, incomparable to the other gods in the myths of the ancient Near East. God's creation did not come from cosmic warfare; the description of God's destruction of chaos in creation is just to demonstrate that "the Lord is God; there is no other besides him" (Deut 4:35).

123. Achtemeier, "Person and Deed," 175.

The description of Jesus' calming the storm (4:35-41) also has similarities with the story of Jonah (Jonah 1:1-16). Cope suggests parallel elements: "(1) departure by boat; (2) a violent storm at sea; (3) a sleeping main character; (4) badly frightened sailors; (5) a miraculous stilling related to the main character; (6) a marveling response by sailors."[124] Verbal agreement also appears between the two stories: "we are about to perish" (ἀπόλλυμι Mark 4:38; cf. "so that we do not die," μὴ ἀπολώμεθα, Jonah 1:6, 14; 3:9, LXX); "to cease" (κοπάζω, Mark 4:39; Jonah 1:11, 12, LXX); "They feared with great awe" (ἐφοβήθησαν φόβον μέγαν, Mark 4:41; cf. ἐφοβήθησαν . . . φόβῳ μεγάλῳ, Jonah 1:16).[125] Of these parallels, the most striking similar feature is the sleeping of Jonah and Jesus in the midst of the storms.

In spite of their similarities, the differences between these stories are also apparent. First, though both Jesus and Jonah were asleep in a boat in the midst of the furious sea, their roles were not the same when their fearful companions woke them. Jonah is regarded as a victim, but Jesus is the victor over the threatening sea; Jonah must pray for God's help against the stormy sea, but Jesus demonstrates his own power to control the chaos-sea, something only God can do.[126] Mark's portrayal of Jesus here is more in line with God's role in the earlier story than with Jonah's.

Second, though both Jesus and Jonah are seen sleeping on a roaring sea, "the sleeping of Jesus is part of his likeness with God."[127] The image of God's sleeping is related to needy people's ardent desire for him to hear them. Those in a predicament cry out to God to awaken, to arise, and to help them: "Awake, O LORD! Why do you sleep? Rouse yourself, do not cast us off forever!" (Ps 44:23; cf. 35:23; 59:4)."[128] In response to the cries of his disciples, Jesus, like the God of the Israelites, delivers them from the threat of the roaring sea, manifesting his sovereignty by rebuking it. In addition, while Jonah's sleeping as he flees by ship is associated with his rejection of the mission God ordered,[129] Jesus' sleeping is a sign of his "Souveränität und Sicherheit" (sovereignty and security) in the face of a life-threatening situation.[130]

Third, Jonah's story has no reference to the activity of ἐπιτιμάω, which plays a key role in disclosing the main theme of Jesus' stilling of the storm.

---

124. Cope, *Matthew*, 96.
125. Marcus, *Mark 1-8*, 337.
126. France, *Gospel of Mark*, 223-24.
127. Marcus, *Mark 1-8*, 338.
128. Marcus, *Mark 1-8*, 338.
129. Guelich, *Mark 1-8:26*, 266.
130. Gnilka, *Markus*, 195.

While the violent sea with a great storm in Jonah has the theological significance of "divine punishment" because of Jonah's disobedience to God's commandment,[131] the windswept sea in Mark represents not divine judgment but a chaotic force threatening the people of God. The thrust of Mark's story is to demonstrate that Jesus is the Savior who can deliver his people from danger and the Lord of the universe who can subjugate the chaos-sea by rebuking it. In Jonah, however, we cannot discover such implications in the story itself.

Though the main theme and imagery of Jesus' calming the sea came from the exodus story, Jonah's story (1:1–16) also serves as background for Jesus' story.[132] Images from Jonah's story and the exodus story are combined in Mark's narrative. According to Marcus, "conflation of the OT texts is familiar from postbiblical Judaism, especially from the Dead Sea Scrolls, and is common in Mark (see 1:11; 12:36; 14:24, 27, 62)."[133] Mark's narrative shows not only a conflation of OT passages but also a tapestry of OT images.[134] Jesus' calming the roaring sea may allude to both Jonah's story and the exodus story, presenting a mosaic of images: Jesus' sleeping during the voyage may echo the imagery of Jonah's sleeping, and Jesus' calming the roaring sea by his rebuke and the delivering his disciples may reflect the victory at the sea in the exodus story. The images in Jonah's story (e.g., sleeping, a violent storm) may be used to reinforce Jesus' greatness by contrast with Jonah's disobedience. Nevertheless, the main theme and imagery in Mark's account of Jesus' calming the roaring sea are derived from the exodus story. Despite many similarities with Jonah 1, Jesus' story focuses on his rebuke of the violent sea, which demonstrates his sovereignty over the universe. Mark's story is molded mainly by the frame of the exodus story, while Jonah's story functions as a supplement that provides a backdrop for Jesus' seafaring. Here, the sea functions as the medium of combining the images of Jonah's story and the exodus story.

Jesus' calming the storm alludes to the victory at the sea in the exodus story in several ways. First, the "going across" motif plays a role in presenting the main theological purpose of both stories, namely the deliverance of

---

131. Limburg, *Jonah*, 54.

132. Hooker argues that Mark's story has the background of OT passages such as Ps 107:23–32, Jonah 1:1–16, and Exod 14:21–31 (Hooker, *Gospel According to Saint Mark*, 138–39).

133. A typical example of conflation is found in Mark 1:2–3 in which Exod 23:20, Mal 3:1, and Isa 40:3 are conflated. For other instances in the NT, see "Matt 27:9–10; Rom 3:11–18; 9:25–26; 1 Pet 2:6–8" (Marcus, *Mark 1–8*, 147).

134. Another example of a tapestry of OT images in Mark may be suggested in Jesus' walking on the water (6:45–52). This will be discussed in the following section.

God's people.¹³⁵ God's commandment to go across the Rea Sea (Exod 14:20) corresponds to Jesus' order to cross over the Sea of Galilee (Mark 4:35).¹³⁶ As the Israelites who were chased by the Egyptian army and blocked by the sea ultimately crossed the sea safely, the disciples who were threatened by the stormy water finally made a safe crossing. The miraculous redemption took place when the people of God went across the sea.

Second, the "rebuke" of the sea plays a crucial role in disclosing the Christological theme of Mark's narrative and connecting it with the exodus story. As we have seen, the sea in Exod 14 had been reinterpreted as a chaotic force in later OT literature.¹³⁷ The victory over the Egyptian army at the sea came to refer to God's defeat of the power of chaos in a cosmological dimension. The fact that Jesus calmed the roaring sea by his rebuke indicates that the sea is identified with a chaotic force; the sea as chaos is subjugated by Jesus' rebuke. As God revealed himself by showing his sovereignty over the sea in delivering his people, Jesus was manifested as the Lord by demonstrating his control over the sea in order to rescue his disciples.¹³⁸ In this way, Jesus was identified with God and revealed as the universal Savior.

Third, the temporal setting—"when evening came" (ὀψίας γενομένης)—of Mark 4:35¹³⁹ alludes to the similar situation when the Israelites crossed over the Red Sea.¹⁴⁰ In Mark, the boats carrying Jesus and his disciples sailed in the evening and Jesus calmed the sea during the night. In Exodus, God drove the sea back with a strong wind all night (ὅλην τὴν νύκτα, Exod 14:21, LXX) so that the Israelites crossed over the sea and God threw the Egyptian army into confusion at dawn (ἐν τῇ φυλακῇ τῇ ἑωθινῇ,

---

135. All of Jesus' sea miracles in the Gospels have the "going across" motif: Mark 4:35; 6:45; Matt 8:18; 14:22; Luke 8:32; John 6:16. Betz, "Concept of the So-called 'Divine Man,'" 235.

136. Betz, "Concept of the So-called 'Divine Man,'" 236. Betz states that the miracle of the crossing over the Red Sea had been re-enacted in the history of Israel, while a prophet like Moses (cf. Deut 18:15–19) was anticipated. For instance, Joshua parted the Jordan River so that the Israelites may cross over it (Josh 3:14–17); Elijah and Elisha divided the water (2 Kgs 2:8, 14); in Jesus' days, Theudas gave the people the promise that he would separate the Jordan River and make a way for crossing over it (Josephus, *Ant.* 20.92).

137. In relation to the exodus story, post-Pentateuchal literature regarded the sea of the exodus story as chaos (e.g., Ps 74:13; 77:17(16)–21(20); 106:9; Isa 43:16–17; 50:2; 5:9–10).

138. Lane, *Gospel According to Mark*, 176–77.

139. Donahou and Harrington say that the expression ὀψίας γενομένης in the first sea miracle (4:35) functions to foreshadow the second sea miracle (6:47) and to produce the dramatic scene of a dangerous situation, namely the turbulent sea at night (Donahou and Harrington, *Gospel of Mark*, 157).

140. Betz, "Concept of the So-called 'Divine Man,'" 235.

v. 24, LXX) and drowned them. In both stories, the victory over an evil force and the deliverance of the people of God took place during the night.[141]

Fourth, both the disciples and the Israelites showed a lack of faith when faced with the threat of death, reproaching Jesus and Moses. The disciples woke Jesus by asking, "Teacher, don't you care that we are perishing?" (Mark 4:38). In Mark's account the disciples' words have a "rough and indignant" tone; in Matthew and Luke this tone is to some degree reduced.[142] The disciples reproached Jesus for not caring for them (οὐ μέλει σοι) with "a sharp tone of rebuke," demonstrating their lack of faith.[143] In his interpretation of οὐ μέλει σοι, Gundry maintains that "the construction οὐ plus the indicative implies that the disciples do not doubt that Jesus cares. . . . But they show no faith that his care can translate into his saving them from destruction."[144] The disciples' cry is not simply a request for help without a doubt of Jesus' care, but rather a reproach against Jesus, whom they believed to be unconcerned by their dangerous situation. A sentence must not be interpreted in isolation from a passage, but understood in the context of the surrounding passage. If we connect the disciples' cry (v. 38) with Jesus' reproof (v. 40), their cry indicates that they are reproaching Jesus for being careless of their safety. As Guelich properly stats, "as the story now stands, the disciples' cry sets the stage for Jesus' rebuke of their fear and lack of faith in 4:40. Their cry, therefore, does not come as a request but as an expression of despair and anger aimed at their 'Master' (διδάσκαλε) who apparently cared little

---

141. Strictly speaking, ὀψία or ὄψιος (evening) indicate "the period between late afternoon and darkness" ("ὄψιος," BDAG 746). In Mark 4:35-41, though Jesus and his disciples started on a voyage in the evening (v. 35), the storm might have come upon them at deep night. In 6:45-52, when evening came (ὀψίας γενομένης) the boat carrying them was in the midst of the sea (v. 47), but the strong wind was raging against them about the forth watch of the night (περὶ τετάρτην φυλακὴν τῆς νυκτὸς, v. 48), which means at dawn. In the victory at the Red Sea in Exod 14, God drove the sea back with a strong east wind all night (ὅλην τὴν νύκτα, Exod 14:21, LXX) and troubled the Egyptian army at the last watch of the night (ἐν τῇ φυλακῇ τῇ ἑωθινῇ, v. 24, LXX), which indicates the dawn. Though the time setting among the stories is slightly different in terms of evening, all night, and dawn, we can say that the time setting is common in that all the events happened "in the night."

142. Hooker, *Gospel According to Saint Mark*, 139. In Matt 8:25, "Lord, save us! We are perishing!"; in Luke 8:24, "Master, Master, we are perishing."

143. Lane, *Gospel According to Mark*, 176; Edwards, *Gospel According to Mark*, 149.

144. Gundry, *Mark*, 239. Moloney also states that in the interrogative sentence, the negative particle οὐ (not μή) plus the indicative expects a positive answer, and so the disciples' cry implies that they believe Jesus is concerned with their dangerous situation (Moloney, *Gospel of Mark*, 99). Nevertheless, they show a lack of faith in the fear that they will not be saved from the roaring sea.

about them."[145] The disciples indeed doubted their safety in the roaring sea and reproached Jesus' unconcern for their predicament. The theme of the disciples' unbelief appears explicitly when Jesus asks them, "Why are you so afraid? Do you still have no faith?" (4:40).[146]

In Exod 14:10–12, the Israelites, pursued by the Egyptian army and obstructed by the Red Sea, cried out to God for help in fear. This cry was immediately proved as stemming from unbelief when the people complained against Moses due to the threat of death. In spite of experiencing God's miraculous works when they escaped from Egypt, the Israelites still failed to stand in faith. Likewise, the disciples still (οὔπω) do not have belief despite seeing Jesus' earlier miracles.

Finally, the disciples' response to Jesus' epiphany in the middle of the Sea of Galilee is similar to that of the Israelites to God's epiphany in the midst of Red Sea.[147] At the end of both stories, the onlookers feared (φοβέω) after seeing the divine miraculous works (Mark 4:41; Exod 14:31, LXX). However, Mark's use of a cognate accusative in a double expression of fear, ἐφοβήθησαν φόβον (4:41), is the same as that of Jonah 1:10 LXX (ἐφοβήθησαν . . . φόβον) and similar to that of Jonah 1:16 LXX (ἐφοβήθησαν . . . φόβῳ, employing a cognate dative). While the fear in Jonah 1:10 refers to "the sailors' terror of the Lord," the fear in v. 16 indicates "their profound awe before the Lord."[148] In Mark 4:41, the fear (φόβος) is not so much anxiety as a "feeling of reverential awe, a sense of the uncanny."[149] In addition, φόβος, which has a secondary meaning of a "sense of awe in the presence of God," is explicitly related to the "experience of an epiphany."[150] Though Mark's double expression of fear also appears in Jonah, the fear in Mark strongly reflects the exodus story because the fear in both Mark and Exodus was the result of a miraculous epiphany. The Israelites, who saw God's epiphany in the pillar of fire and cloud (Exod 14: 24) and the defeat of the Egyptian army, expressed their fear with awe (v. 31). Likewise, the disciples, who saw

---

145. Guelich, *Mark 1–8:26*, 267. Painter mentions that the disciple's unbelief provides the cause of Jesus' rebuke and instruction: "It is through this act that the weakness of the faith of the disciples is exposed, enabling Jesus to challenge and correct it" (Painter, *Mark's Gospel*, 87).

146. Hooker says that "the narrative is the disciple's failure to understand and believe what is happening in the ministry of Jesus" (Hooker, *Gospel According to Saint Mark*, 140).

147. Betz, "Concept of the So-called 'Divine Man,'" 236.

148. Smith and Page, *Amos, Obadiah, Jonah*, 237.

149. Taylor, *Gospel According to St. Mark*, 277.

150. Guelich, *Mark 1–8:26*, 269.

Jesus' mighty work of calming the sea (Mark 4:39), were filled with fear in reverence (v. 41).

Jesus Walking on the Sea (6:45–52)

In the second sea miracle, Jesus' walking on the water (6:45–52), the sea again functions as an obstacle to the disciples' travels. They were straining at the oars because of an adverse wind that made it difficult for them to reach the opposite side of the Sea of Galilee (6:48). Like the sea in Exodus, the stormy sea in Mark blocked the disciples' path across the sea and threatened their lives.

Many scholars have regarded the thrust of this story as an epiphany of Jesus. According to Dibelius, through the epiphany at the sea, Jesus is proved as a wonder-worker who demonstrates his divine power by walking on the sea.[151] Bultmann argues that the walking on the water is the original motif and the stilling of the storm is added as a secondary feature.[152] Lohmeyer claims that two independent stories, containing the two motifs of Jesus' epiphany and the stilling of the storm, were combined into one in this episode: the inconsistent geographical references in this voyage are evidence that Mark brought together two different stories—the sailing off toward Bethsaida (v. 45) and the arrival of Gennesaret (v. 53).[153] Theissen describes the mixture of epiphany and rescue motifs as a "soteriological epiphany."[154] These motifs are brought together in this episode of Mark: while an epiphany story shows marvelous spectacles, revelatory sayings, or trembling reactions, a rescue story presents an emergency situation, miraculous power, or awestruck reactions.[155]

According to Guelich, though most scholars agree that the motifs of epiphany and rescue appear together in this passage, they had different

---

151. Dibelius, *From Tradition to Gospel*, 94–95.

152. Bultmann, *History of the Synoptic Tradition*, 216.

153. The two conflicting geographical references show the friction in the story, which implies a mixture of the two motifs: "Die Geschichte fügt zwei Motive nicht reibungslos ineinander: Das Wandeln auf dem See und die Stillung des Sturmes [The story does not combine the two motifs without friction: the walking on the sea and the stilling of the storm]" (Lohmeyer, *Das Evangelium des Markus*, 130–32).

154. Theissen, *Miracle Stories*, 97. In the study of Jesus' walking on the sea of the Synoptic Gospels, Heil introduces several Second Temple Jewish writings that contain the episodes of "the sea-walking as a 'sea-rescue' epiphany": T. Naph. 6:1–10; 1QH 3:1–18; 1QH 7:4–5; 1QH 6:22–25 (Heil, *Jesus Walking on the Sea*, 17–30).

155. Theissen, *Miracle Stories*, 94–103.

opinions about the final stage in the progress of combining the two motifs:[156] a development "from a rescue story to an epiphany story,"[157] a development "from an epiphany story to a rescue story,"[158] or simply "a combination of an epiphany and a rescue story."[159] The main framework of this episode comes from a rescue story while an epiphany story serves as an assistant to disclose its central theme. The goal of this story is to show Jesus' deliverance of his people in the furious sea; it is primarily this redemptive power that is manifested by his epiphany.

Before proving my argument, I will discuss the epiphany motif in this episode. There is strong evidence of OT parallels that support an epiphany as the central theme in this sea miracle.[160] The imagery of "walking on the sea" and "passing by" in Mark 6:48 (περιπατῶν ἐπὶ τῆς θαλάσσης; παρελθεῖν) appears using the same words in Job 9:8, 11 (περιπατῶν . . . ἐπὶ θαλάσσης; παρέλθῃ, LXX).[161] Since the ability to walk on the sea is attributed only to God, Jesus is inevitably identified with God when he walks on the sea. In addition, the statement that Jesus was about to pass by (ἤθελεν παρελθεῖν) the disciples is explicitly connected to images of God's "self-revelation" in the OT.[162] According to Heil, "the action of 'passing' (עבר; παρέρχομαι), then, expresses one of the ways in which God appears or comes to men. It signifies the manner by which God makes himself visible and shows himself to human eyes."[163] By "passing by," the glory of God is shown to Moses at

---

156. Guelich, *Mark 1–8:26*, 136.

157. Dibelius, *From Tradition to Gospel*, 100.

158. Gnilka, *Markus*, 267.

159. Lohmeyer, *Das Evangelium Des Markus*, 77.

160. For an exhaustive survey of Jesus' walking on the water and passing by the disciples, see Snoy, "Marc 6:48," 347–63; Fleddermann, "'And He Wanted to Pass by Them' (Mark 6:48c)," 389–95.

161. The similar imagery of God's walking on the sea appears in Ps 77:19; Isa 43:16; Sir 24:5–6; Odes Sol. 39:10. See France, *Gospel of Mark*, 270; Donahue and Harrington, *Gospel of Mark*, 213. According to Stegner, though the imagery of walking on the sea in Job 9:8 explicitly parallels Jesus' walking on the sea, Job's passage serves merely as a supplement for the portrayal of the victory at the sea in Exod 14 (Stegner, "Jesus' Walking on the Water," 222).

162. Edwards, *Gospel According to Mark*, 198. The translation of ἤθελεν has two options, "was about to" or "wanted to." The former rendering is more convincing because this passage emphasizes Jesus' epiphany that is compared with God's epiphany. Donahue and Harrington properly explained it as follows: "Those who favor 'wanted to' interpret this verse as an instance of Jesus' desire for self-concealment in Mark. But this idea is contradicted by the self-revelatory formula of v. 50. Mark stresses rather the epiphany of Jesus, which heightens the subsequent misunderstanding of the disciples" (Donahue and Harrington, *Gospel of Mark*, 213).

163. Heil, *Jesus Walking on the Sea*, 69.

Mount Sinai (παρέλθῃ, Exod 33:22, LXX)[164] and his presence is manifested to Elijah at Mount Horeb (παρελεύσεται, 1 Kgs 19:11, LXX). The theme of epiphany is strengthened by the self-identification expression, "It is I" (ἐγώ εἰμι, Mark 6:50), which is used by God to reveal his identity to Moses at the burning bush (ἐγώ εἰμι ὁ ὤν, Exod 3:14, LXX).[165]

It cannot be denied that the epiphany of Jesus lies at the heart of this sea miracle (Mark 6:45–52). Nevertheless, the miraculous phenomena seen here are not limited to only showing Jesus' epiphany, but also ultimately present his power to rescue the people of God from danger.[166] Jesus' redemption of his disciples at the sea is the main theme of the story, and his epiphany plays an assisting role in delivering this theme. In other words, the rescue motif serves as the framework of the story and the epiphany motif functions as a supplement. This argument can be supported by two aspects: this episode's relationship with the previous sea miracle and its use of imagery from the victory at the sea in the exodus.

To begin, this story (6:45–52) is connected to the previous sea miracle story (4:35–41) in terms of their theme, Jesus as the Savior of God's people and the Lord of the universe.[167] The temporal and spatial settings that convey this theme are similar in the two accounts: both begin "when evening came (ὀψίας γενομένης)" (4:35; 6:47), and both feature the windswept sea as the location of Jesus' deliverance of his disciples. The end of the storm is expressed in exactly the same sentence in the Greek of 4:39 and 6:51 (καὶ ἐκόπασεν ὁ ἄνεμος, "and the wind ceased"), which indicates that the stormy sea represents chaos in both episodes.[168]

In the two sea miracles, Jesus is portrayed as the Savior who redeems the people of God in agony. The main theme of the two episodes is Jesus'

---

164. Heil, *Jesus Walking on the Sea*, 69. Heil suggests three parallels of the epiphanic description between God's revelation to Moses and that of Jesus to his disciples: "He [God] descended, stood there with him, and passed before him" (Exod 33:5–6); "He [Jesus] came to them, walking on the sea, and was going to pass by them" (Mark 6:48).

165. See also the "I am" (ἐγώ εἰμι) passages in Isa 41:4; 43:10–11; 48:12 (Edwards, *Gospel According to Mark*, 198). According to Marcus, "'I am' is also the interpretation of the divine name that God revealed to Moses at the burning (Exod 3:14) and is part of the Ten Commandments that he gave to him on Sinai (Exod 20:2; Deut 5:6)" (Marcus, *Mark 1–8*, 432).

166. With an emphasis on the rescue nature of the epiphany story, Donahue and Harrington define this episode as a "sea rescue epiphany" (Donahue and Harrington, *Gospel of Mark*, 215).

167. Koch argues that the second sea miracle is influenced by the first sea miracle (Koch, *Die Bedeutung der Wundererzählungen*, 105–6).

168. The roaring sea in the second sea miracle also implies chaos in the light of the chaotic force of the sea in the first. In both sea miracles, the chaos-sea ceased (ἐκόπασεν) in response to Jesus' activities of rebuke and epiphany.

deliverance of the disciples from the stormy sea, but the method of redemption differs between the two stories. While the furious sea is calmed by Jesus' rebuke in the first sea miracle, the roaring sea is stilled by his epiphany in the second. Though the means of rescue differ, the images of a rebuke and an epiphany serve to support the same theme of redemption. In addition, Jesus is described as the Lord who reigns over the universe in the two episodes. According to Marcus, "when Jesus quells the power of the sea, strides in triumph across the waves, and announces his presence to the disciples with the sovereign self-identification formula 'I am he' (4:35–41; 6:45–52), he is speaking in and acting out the language of Old Testament divine warrior theophanies, narratives in which Yahweh himself subdues the demonic forces of chaos in a saving, cosmos-creating act of holy war."[169] Jesus thus demonstrates himself to be the Lord of the universe by conquering the chaos-sea.[170]

These two stories are also connected by their use of "question-and-answer." The disciples' question—"Who then is this?" (τίς ἄρα οὗτός ἐστιν; 4:41)—in the first sea miracle is answered by Jesus' proclamation—"It is I" (ἐγώ εἰμι, 6:50)—in the second.[171] Jesus' identity as the Savior and Lord in the first sea miracle is further manifested by his epiphany in the second, which confirms that Jesus has the same power as the God who controls the sea. Though the imagery of Jesus' walking on the sea seems chiefly to present his divine nature in God's likeness, Jesus' epiphany ultimately has the purpose of disclosing his miraculous power to deliver his people, as in the

---

169. Marcus, *Way of the Lord*, 144–45. Marcus claims that in the cosmic nature of the two sea miracles, Jesus is described as a cosmological and eschatological figure who should not be restricted to the title "the Son of David."

170. Watts argues that Isa 43:1–11 serves as a hermeneutical basis to interpret Mark 6:45–52. There appear explicit parallels between Jesus' ἐγώ εἰμι· μὴ φοβεῖσθε in Mark 6:50 and Yahweh's ἐγώ εἰμι, μὴ φοβοῦ in Isa 43:1–11. Yahweh's order not to fear and the promise of his presence in the midst of Israel's passing through the waters are evidently seen in Jesus' command not to be afraid and his presence during the disciples' struggle with the roaring sea. In addition, the images of "testifying as they do to Yahweh's self-declaration, his delivering presence, and protection from the threat of the chaos waters" in Isaiah corresponds to Mark: "Jesus' delivering actions and control over the sea point to the breaking-in, in strength, of Yahweh's kingly reign as he inaugurates the long-awaited NE [New Exodus]." Watts refers to Heil's study of Jesus' walking on the sea in the light of Yahweh's promise of restoration and protection in Isa 43:1–13: "OT background for both the comfort-bringing μὴ φοβεῖσθε and the identifying ἐγώ εἰμι is found in Isa 43:1–13. In the Exodus context of Isa 43:2a Yahweh says, 'When you pass through the waters I will be with you.' Jesus similarly assures his disciples that now he is with them in their distress: 'Take courage, it is I; do not be afraid'" See Watts, *Isaiah's New Exodus and Mark*, 161–62. Refer also to Heil, *Jesus Walking on the Sea*, 59.

171. Boring, *Mark*, 190.

first sea miracle. Both sea miracles agree that Jesus is the Savior and Lord who redeemed his people by subjugating the chaos-sea.

Next, Jesus' walking on the sea (6:45–52) primarily uses the exodus imagery of the victory at the Red Sea as the basic framework of this episode. Above all, the fact that Jesus' epiphany took place on the sea strongly supports the idea that this story was shaped in the mold of the exodus story.[172] In the OT, God's epiphanies to Moses (Exod 33:18–23) and Elijah (1 Kgs 19:11–12) occurred in the mountains. Though the mountains are related to diverse themes, such as "power (Jer 51:25; Dan 2:45), revelation (*Jub.* 1:2–4; 2 *Apoc. Bar.* 13:1), antiquity (Prov 8:25; Job 15:7), eternity (Gen 49:26; Ps 125:1) and pagan religion (Is 14:13; 16:12)," the most significant aspect of the mountain in Jewish literature is its function as "the scene of theophanies."[173] In this episode, however, Jesus' epiphany, which apparently parallels God's epiphany to Moses and Elijah, takes place not on the mountain but on the sea. The purpose of this is to emphasize the rescue theme and recall Israel's past deliverance at the Red Sea: "As the Israelites saw their God in the midst of the deliverance at the sea, so the disciples saw Jesus in delivering them from the windswept sea."[174] The Israelites and the disciples were placed in the same location, expressed in the same phrase: "in the midst of the sea" (ἐν μέσῳ τῆς θαλάσσης, Exod 14:29, LXX; Mark 6:47).

The OT epiphany passages mentioned above are not related to the theme of redemption. Though God reveals himself in his power, identity, glory, and presence in those passages, they do not have a direct connection to the rescue motif: Job 9:8 emphasizes God's power over the sea; Exod 33:18–23 highlights his glory and identity; 1 Kgs 19:11–12 underlines his presence. The story of the victory at the Red Sea in Exod 14 contains not only the rescue motif but also the epiphany motif. Though the images of "walking" and "passing by" do not appear in the account of the victory at the sea, the phrase "the LORD in the pillar of fire and cloud" (κύριος . . . ἐν στύλῳ πυρὸς καὶ νεφέλης, Exod 14:24, LXX) implies "Yahweh's presence."[175] According to Boring, just as God led his people by his presence in the pillar of fire and cloud, Jesus was about to pass by the disciples as a "divine epiphany."[176] God's epiphany in the exodus story is similar to that of Jesus in that he guided his people in the midst of the dangerous situation of the

---

172. According to Stegner, the story of Jesus' walking on the sea "has been molded in the frame of the story of Exodus 14," and is also understood as being in the form of the exodus story in the first century (Stegner, "Jesus' Walking on the Water," 233).

173. Allison, "Mountain and Wilderness," 563.

174. Stegner, "Jesus' Walking on the Water," 227.

175. Durham, *Exodus*, 196.

176. Boring, *Mark*, 190.

sea. The rescue and epiphany motifs appear together in both the victory at the Red Sea and Jesus' walking on the sea, but the main theme of both episodes is the deliverance at the sea, with epiphany serving as a supplement to strengthen the main theme. I do not disregard the significance of the imagery of "walking" and "passing by" in Jesus' second sea miracle, but in Mark's narrative those images were conflated with the exodus image of the victory at the Red Sea.

In order to prove the idea that the sea miracle in Mark 6:45–52 was molded in the frame of the sea miracle in Exod 14, I will now examine the parallelism between Mark 6:45–52 and Exod 14 in terms of their verbal and thematic relationship. First, there are a large number of verbal agreements between the two stories. According to Stegner, "of the 139 Greek words in Mark 6.45–52, as many as 32 may be quoted from Exodus 14."[177] Stegner lists the following parallel words and phrases:[178] the prepositional phrase "over the sea" (ἐπὶ τὴν θάλασσαν: Exod 14:6, LXX; Mark 6:48, 49);[179] "in the mist of the sea" (ἐν μέσῳ τῆς θαλάσσης: Exod 14:16, 29, LXX; Mark 6:47);[180] the repeated use of the Greek "sea" (θάλασσα) instead of "lake" (λίμνη); the verb "to see" (ὁράω: Exod 14:13, 30, 31, LXX; Mark 6:49, 50);[181] the pair of verbs, "to tell" and "to say" (λαλέω and λέγω: Exod 14:1, 12, LXX; Mark 6:50);[182] the verb "fear" (φοβέω: Exod 14:10, LXX; Mark 6:50); the sentence "it is I" (ἐγώ εἰμι, Exod 14:4, 18, LXX; Mark 6:50); the imperative "take heart" in the same person, number, and tense (θαρσεῖτε, Exod 14:13, LXX; Mark 6:50); the verbal root, "to be terrified" (ταράσσω, Exod 14:24, LXX; Mark 6:50);[183] and the words "night" (νύξ, Exod 14:20, 21, LXX; Mark 6:48),

---

177. Stegner also counts the number of verbal agreements with the exception of Markan redactional parts: "If the 41 words ascribed to Markan redactional activity in vv. 45, 51b and 52 are subtracted from the 139 total, 98 Greek words are left. Of these 98, 30 are also found in Exodus 14" (Stegner, "Jesus' Walking on the Water," 220–21).

178. Stegner, "Jesus' Walking on the Water," 217–22. He argues that "the only words in the Greek not found in Exod 14 are 'for,' 'immediately' and 'not'" (Stegner, "Jesus' Walking on the Water," 219).

179. Stegner, "Jesus' Walking on the Water," 217. While ἐπί is accompanied with an accusative in Exod 14:6, "the case is changed to genitive with ἐπί because of the different usage" in Mark 6:48, 49 (ἐπὶ τῆς θαλάσσης).

180. In Exod 14:16, the preposition is not ἐν but εἰς with an accusative (εἰς μέσον τῆς θαλάσσης).

181. Stegner, "Jesus' Walking on the Water," 218. The same root and tense are discovered between Exod 14:30, 31 and Mark 6:49, 50.

182. Stegner, "Jesus' Walking on the Water," 218. Compare ἐλάλησεν κύριος πρὸς Μωυσῆν λέγων (Exod 14:1, LXX) and ὃ ἐλαλήσαμεν πρὸς σὲ ἐν Αἰγύπτῳ λέγοντες (v. 12, LXX) with ὁ δὲ εὐθὺς ἐλάλησεν μετ' αὐτῶν, καὶ λέγει αὐτοῖς (Mark 6:50).

183. In Exod 14:24, the preposition σύν is added to the root ταράσσω.

"heart" (καρδία, Exod 14:4, 5, 8, 17, LXX; Mark 6:52), "land" (γῆ; Exod 14:3, 11, LXX; Mark 6:47), "against" (ἐναντίος, Exod 14:2, 9, LXX; Mark 6:48), and "wind" (ἄνεμος, Exod 14:21, LXX; Mark 6:48, 51).

Second, the most significant parallel between the two stories is their shared theme: the deliverance of the people of God with an epiphany. Both stories focus on the rescue of people in danger. The Egyptian army was pursuing the Israelites with the threat of death, and the Red Sea blocked their escape. God delivered the Israelites by parting the water, and they safely crossed the sea. Likewise, the disciples who wished to reach the opposite side of the Sea of Galilee were endangered by a furious storm. Jesus rescued the disciples when he climbed into the boat with them, and they safely crossed the sea. Further, in both stories deliverance comes with an epiphany. God appeared in the pillar of fire and cloud in the midst of the sea (Exod 14:24) and exterminated the Egyptian army. Similarly, Jesus appeared before the disciples in the midst of the sea (Mark 6:48) and the storm ceased.

Third, the thematic agreement of the two stories is enhanced by their shared location in time and space, namely "at dawn" and "in the midst of the sea." In Exodus, God revealed himself in the pillar of fire and cloud at "the last watch of the night" (ἐν τῇ φυλακῇ τῇ ἑωθινῇ, Exod 14:24, LXX). In Mark, Jesus discloses himself by walking on the sea at "the fourth watch of the night" (τετάρτην φυλακὴν τῆς νυκτός, Mark 6:48). The same Greek word, φυλακή, is used in both verses.[184] Both stories are set "at dawn," which stands for "the time of God's help, because it is the point at which light chases away darkness."[185] Likewise, the sea serves as the spatial setting of both episodes. The Israelites who were chased by the Egyptian army were in danger because the sea blocked their path of escape, and the disciples were in peril because the stormy sea threatened their safe passage. However, "in the midst of the sea" (ἐν μέσῳ τῆς θαλάσσης: Exod 14:16, 29, LXX; Mark 6:47), divine epiphanies delivered both the Israelites and the disciples: God parted the water and defeated the Egyptian army, and Jesus walked on the sea and calmed the storm.

In conclusion, the focal theme of Mark 6:45–52 is Jesus' deliverance of his people, and that the imagery in this passage is drawn from the victory

---

184. The above English translations of Greek are from NIV, which emphasizes the night. RSV renders them "the morning watch" (Exod 14:24) and "early in the morning" (Mark 6:48), stressing the morning. Both translations indicate that the events occurred at dawn.

185. Marcus notes that the symbolic meaning of dawn as "the time of God's help" appears in the OT (e.g., "Exod 14:24; Ps 46:5; 130:6; Isa 17:14"), in Jewish traditions (e.g., "*Joseph and Aseneth* 14:1–2; *Bib. Ant.* 42:3"), and in the NT (e.g., "Mark 16:2") (Marcus, *Mark 1–8*, 423).

at the sea in the exodus story. Though Jesus' epiphany is an important part of this episode, it is molded in the frame of the exodus story and serves as a supplement to reinforce Jesus' identity as the Savior who has the divine nature of God's likeness. Jesus redeemed his disciples from the chaos-sea by manifesting himself as God, the universal Savior who reigns over both nature and the cosmic world.

The Wilderness and the Exodus Imagery

According to Wall, in the history of Israel the wilderness does not simply refer to a geographical place but it also implies "a symbol of the formative events which shaped Israel's covenant relationship with God":

> When we turn to the biblical landscape we find a similar ambivalence with regard to wilderness terrain. The wilderness became a place of transition for the people of Israel as they journeyed from the liberation of Egypt to the promise of Canaan. It was a testing environment, a place of punishment, yet also a place of revelation. Hunger and thirst assailed them, but the giving of Torah was life-bearing. Though they were confused and bewildered, yet it was in the wilderness that the people of Israel claimed their identity as the chosen people of God.[186]

In the wilderness, the Israelites experienced God's gracious guidance and provision, but they also received tests and punishments due to their sin and rebellion. God revealed himself to the Israelites in both these ways, and their identity as the people of God was established in their wilderness wanderings. The wilderness, therefore, has both negative and positive connotations. Leal suggests four possible meanings associated with the wilderness in Scripture: (1) a site with a negative image, featuring the fear, repulsion, or hostility that are associated with sin; (2) the place of the Israelites' encounter with God or angels, where they were tested or entrusted with tasks; (3) the location of God's grace where he revealed himself to the Israelites, who experienced discipline, purification, and transformation; (4) a place where God's good creation is celebrated with honor and reverence.[187] The wilderness motif appears especially in the Pentateuch, the Psalms, the Prophets, Second Temple Jewish literature, and some parts of the NT, and the four attitudes toward the wilderness are present as appropriate to the emphasis of each text. In the present study, I will explore the wilderness motif with

---

186. Wall, "Finding Identity in the Wilderness," 67.
187. Leal, *Wilderness in the Bible*, 63.

a particular focus on God's provision of manna in the exodus story; I will also examine how this location and event had been interpreted in the Pentateuch, later OT writings, Second Temple Jewish literature, and rabbinic writings.[188] In doing so, I will investigate the theological significance of the wilderness that serves as the setting of Jesus' feeding of the crowds.

The historical description of the exodus from Egypt that records the Israelites' journey in the wilderness after their crossing of the Red Sea and before their arrival at Mount Sinai (Exod 15:22—17:7) presents a pattern of wilderness wanderings consisting of three elements: "grumbling," "God's gracious provision in response to that grumbling," and "God's testing of his people."[189] In response to the Israelites' grumbling against the bitter water at Marah, God made it sweet to drink and then tested them with a decree and a law (15:22–27). The pattern of grumbling, provision, and testing continues in the following episodes—manna and quail (16:1–36) and water from the rock at Rephidim (17:1–7). The Israelites consistently complained and sinned against God, but despite their grumbling God steadily took care of them by providing water and bread by his grace. According to Talmon, from a theological perspective the wilderness wanderings are characterized by "two seemingly opposite and yet complementary phenomena": God's infinite "beneficence," paternal "forbearance," and "love" on the one hand, and Israel's "doubt," "apostasy," and "rebellious behavior" on the other.[190] In particular, the episode of the provision of manna in the wilderness (16:1–36) explicitly discloses the two opposing features of God's grace and the Israelites' sin. The Israelites were tested by God. They grumbled about the lack of food, saying that it was better to die by the Lord's hand in Egypt where they sat by the pots of meat and ate bread until they were full than to starve to death in the desert (v. 3). Despite their complaint, God told Moses that he would rain down bread from heaven (v. 5). However, the people were limited to gathering only enough manna for each day, and this instruction served as a test for them.

In the provision of manna in the wilderness, the Israelites saw the "glory" (כָּבוֹד) of the LORD" (16:7, 10). Though the term "glory" in verbal form ("to gain glory, honor"; 14:4, 7, 18) appears earlier, this is the first appearance of the phrase "glory of the LORD" in the OT. This phrase has

---

188. For a study of the manna tradition in the OT, the Palestinian Targums, and the NT, refer to Malina, *Palestinian Manna Tradition*.

189. Enns, *Exodus*, 330. Though the journey from the Red Sea to the Mount Sinai is depicted in Exod 15:22–18:27, the pattern of grumbling, provision, and testing appears explicitly in 15:22–17:7. Exodus 17:8–16 notes the battle against Amalekites and 18:1–27 delineates Jethro's visitation to Moses and his wise advice.

190. Talmon, "מִדְבָּר *midbār*; עֲרָבָה *ʿărābâ*," 8:105.

the significance of a "designation for the actual presence of God"—it is "the language of theophany."[191] At the grumbling of the Israelites, the glory of the Lord was disclosed in order to tell them of his will; God's intervention was accomplished by convincing them of his glory (16:10).[192] When they looked toward the wilderness, the "glory of the LORD" appeared there in the cloud. The wilderness, therefore, serves as "the place of the greatest theophany."[193] In the event of manna and quail, the wilderness predominantly appears as the place where God confers his gracious provision—despite the Israelites' grumbling—and reveals himself to them.

Mauser argues that the images of the wilderness in the Pentateuch are upgraded to a cosmic dimension in the Psalms and the Prophets. While the wilderness in the Pentateuch serves merely as a "foil" for disclosing the contrast between God's grace and the Israelites' rebellion, the wilderness in the Psalms and the Prophets is filled with symbolic and cosmic characteristics.[194] The wilderness motifs were amplified with diverse perspectives in the post-Pentateuchal literature.[195]

First, the wilderness is portrayed as the state of chaos, which will be transformed into a fertile land by God's grace. "To dwell in the desert means, indeed, to dwell in the land of curse, in a condition which is outside the merciful power of God, who turned the wilderness into fertile land."[196] According to Talmon, מִדְבָּר (the wilderness) and תְּהוֹם (the deep) can be employed "synonymously" in "*parallelismus membrorum*": the pairing of מִדְבָּר and תְּהֹמוֹת in Ps 78:15 ("He split rocks open in the wilderness [מִדְבָּר], and gave them drink abundantly as from the deep [תְּהֹמוֹת]") and Isa 63:13 ("Who led them through the deep [תְּהֹמוֹת]? Like a horse in the desert [מִדְבָּר], they did not stumble") illustrate this idea.[197] Like the deep (תְּהוֹם), the wilderness (מִדְבָּר) connotes a chaotic state.

---

191. Meyers, *Exodus*, 131. Durham states that "the evening experience is then specified as the provision of meat, the morning revelation as the provision of bread in abundance" (Durham, *Exodus*, 220).

192. Weinfeld, "כָּבוֹד *kāḇôḏ*," 7:34.

193. Durham, *Exodus*, 220.

194. Mauser, *Christ in the Wilderness*, 36–37. In many parts of my study of the wilderness, I am indebted to Mauser's *Christ in the Wilderness*.

195. Talmon also notes that "in the Pentateuch, the semantic field "wilderness" always refers to the thing itself, to a 'reality,' not an image," but in the post-Pentateuchal literature, the wilderness began to be expressed in various images" (Talmon, "מִדְבָּר *miḏbār*; עֲרָבָה *ʿrāḇâ*," 8:114).

196. Mauser, *Christ in the Wilderness*, 37, 44.

197. Talmon explains their synonymity in "*parallelismus membrorum*" from the usage of ancient Near Eastern literature, such as the Egyptian Book of the Dead (175:2), Babylonian-Assyrian mythology, and Ugaritic myth (Talmon, "מִדְבָּר *miḏbār*; עֲרָבָה

Psalm 77:14-20 echoes the song of Moses and Miriam in Exod 15:1-18, showing that "God's way through the sea leading his people like a flock corresponds to and enacts the mastery of the chaotic waters."[198] In Ps 77, the deep (תְּהֹמוֹת) (v. 16[17]) is mentioned with an "unmistakable allusion to the desert wanderings" (v. 20[21]).[199]

> The waters saw you, O God,
> the waters saw you and they were afraid;
> the very deep (תְּהֹמוֹת) trembled (v. 16[17]).
> You lead your people like a flock
> by the hand of Moses and Aaron (v. 20[21]).

In Ps 29, the glory of God is disclosed all over the universe: in heaven, earth, sea, and wilderness.[200] Here, the mighty waters (מַיִם רַבִּים, v. 3) appear together with the wilderness (מִדְבָּר, v. 8).[201] The mighty waters, symbolizing the chaotic force,[202] are ruled by God's thunderous voice: "The voice of the LORD is over the waters; the God of glory thunders, the LORD thunders over the mighty waters" (v. 3).[203] Likewise, the wilderness is shaken by his voice: "The voice of the LORD shakes the wilderness; the LORD shakes the wilderness of Kadesh" (v. 8).[204] The sentence "shakes the wilderness" may be translated as "makes the wilderness tremble (in fear)"; the verb חיל ("to writhe" or "to make tremble") is employed with this meaning in "Ps 96:9; 97:4; 114:7."[205] Dahood argues that מִדְבָּר refers not only to the desert but

---

ʿarāḇâ," 8:114-15).

198. Mays, *Psalms*, 253.

199. Talmon, "מִדְבָּר *midbār*; עֲרָבָה ʿarāḇâ," 8:114-15. The image of God's guidance of the Israelites in the Pentateuch is expanded here with the image of shepherd and flock. See Hossfeld and Zenger, *Psalms 2*, 280.

200. Psalm 29 praises the glory of God by emphasizing his sovereignty over all his creation, "sky, sea, land, and wilderness." VanGemeren, *Psalms*, 294.

201. Talmon, "מִדְבָּר *midbār*; עֲרָבָה ʿarāḇâ," 8:114-15.

202. Tate, *Psalms 51-100*, 247.

203. According to VanGemeren, the mighty waters (v. 3) that imply the destructive force are subjugated by God: "The direct reference to Yahweh as the glorious El may contain a polemic allusion to the superiority of Yahweh over Baal. Yahweh rules sovereignly over the 'mighty waters.' The Mediterranean Sea was known to the psalmist as a mighty force, whose powerful waves could cause great destruction. But the Lord is sovereign over the terrible forces of the sea (cf. 93:3-4)" (VanGemeren, *Psalms*, 294).

204. VanGemeren, *Psalms*, 295. Though in v. 8 many scholars attempted to identify the location of the "Desert of Kadesh" with Sinai or Orontes, VanGemeren argues that it refers to "the desert region in general," implying that "Yahweh rules over everything, including the vast desert regions."

205. Anderson, *Book of Psalms 1-72*, 237.

also to "land without permanent settlements."²⁰⁶ According to Mauser, the wilderness as the chaotic force is doomed to be destroyed by God when he intervenes to deliver his people.

> The miracle of the Red Sea is in this tradition seen as an embodiment of Yahweh's powers over chaos. It seems, therefore, permissible to interpret the concept of the wilderness in the same categories. The wilderness is one of the powers of chaos which is defeated by Yahweh when he arises to intervene for his people. The desert tradition of Israel is thus given cosmic significance.²⁰⁷

Psalm 68:7(8)–10(11) alludes to the exodus story by combining the historical events with cosmic images. In v. 6(7), the wilderness is described as an arid wasteland inhabited by rebellious people: "the rebellious live in a parched land." This image implies the condition of "the absence of God or his favor" and further indicates "the chaos on which God imposes order."²⁰⁸ However, God marched through the wilderness leading the Israelites and gave them rain in abundance.²⁰⁹ In spite of their rebellion, God provided for them by his goodness (טוֹבָה), making it possible to turn the wilderness into fertile ground.

> When you went out before your people, O God,
> when you marched through the wilderness, *Selah*
> the earth shook,
> the heavens poured down rain,
> at the presence of God, the God of Sinai
>   at the presence of God, the God of Israel.
> You gave abundant rain, O God;
>   you restored your inheritance, when it was weary.
> Your flock found a dwelling in it;
>   in your goodness (טוֹבָה), O God, you provided for the needy.
> (Ps 68:7[8]–10[11])

---

206. Dahood, *Psalms I*, 178.

207. Mauser, *Christ in the Wilderness*, 44.

208. The image of the chaos of the wilderness is well illustrated in the expression, "trackless wastes (וּתֹהוּ)" (or "pathless desert") in Ps 107:40, where God pours contempt on the princes and makes them wander. If the waters are regarded as the "wet chaos," the wilderness is considered as the "dry chaos." See Leal, *Wilderness in the Bible*, 80–81.

209. Anderson notes that some exegetes regards rain as an allusion to the miraculous event of providing the manna and the quails in the desert (Anderson, *Book of Psalms 1–72*, 487–88). See also Vogt, "Regen in Fülle," 395–61.

According to Stock, this passage is compared with the event of crossing the Red Sea in the exodus: "Just as Yahweh crushed the head of the Dragon when Israel passed through the Sea of Reeds, so he subdues the wild, chaotic powers of the wilderness, turns the desert into verdant pastures, as he guides and sustains his people in the wilderness."[210] In a cosmic dimension, the wilderness as the deserted and cursed land is regarded as chaos, and God's goodness changes it into fertile land by giving rain in abundance. The chaotic force of the desert is defeated by God as his grace turns it into green, blooming, and watery ground.

In Isa 40:3, the transformation of the wilderness is explicit, and its purpose is to make a way for the Lord: "A voice of one calling: 'In the wilderness prepare the way of the LORD, make straight in the desert a highway for our God.'" Antithetic phrases describe how obstacles to the Lord's journey through the wilderness will be transformed into good ground for an easy traveling—valleys shall be raised, mountains and hills will be made low, and the uneven or rough ground will be leveled (v. 4).[211] Furthermore, the wilderness in 41:17–20[212] is turned into fertile land, which implies "the conversion of the desert into paradise."[213]

> The poor and needy seek water,
> but there is none;
> their tongues are parched with thirst.
> But I the LORD will answer them;
> I, the God of Israel, will not forsake them.
> I will open rivers on barren heights,
>   and springs in the midst of the valleys.
> I will make the wilderness into a pool of water,
>   and the dry land springs of water.
> I will put in the wilderness
>   the cedar and the acacia, the myrtle and the olive.
> I will set pines in the wasteland

---

210. Stock, *Way in the Wilderness*, 60.

211. Mauser, *Christ in the Wilderness*, 51.

212. The imagery of the transformation of the wilderness into fertile land appears earlier in Isaiah in various ways. According to Goldingay, "Isa. 32 envisages wilderness turned into garden and garden into forest, and goes on to picture wilderness and garden characterized by judgment and justice, and thus by well-being, quietness and trust (forest again becoming a negative image in vv. 19–20). Isaiah 35:1–2, 6b–7 pictures the desert blossoming and rejoicing with the splendour of Lebanon and Carmel (forest and garden) and envisages streams of water bursting out in the wilderness, sand becoming wetland, thirsty ground becoming springs of water." Goldingay, *Message of Isaiah 40–55*, 123–24.

213. Propp, *Water in the Wilderness*, 102.

> the fir and the cypress together,
> so that all may see and know,
>   may consider and understand,
> that the hand of the LORD has done this,
>   that the Holy One of Israel created (בָּרָא) it. (Isa 41:17–20)

Pao argues that "the Exodus tradition of provision in the desert (41:17–20; 43:19) becomes a promise in which Yahweh will 'make her wilderness like Eden' (51:3)."[214] As the first exodus events had been reinterpreted in the light of creative events, God's promise to do new things is related to his creative works in the new exodus.[215] The cursed wilderness in the first exodus is transformed into the blessed land in the new exodus, a place where the poor and needy are given abundant water by God's creative works.

In Isa 43:16–20, the original and the new exodus appear explicitly together, and the images and functions of the sea (the waters) and the wilderness in the original are transformed in the new.[216]

> Thus says the LORD,
> who makes a way through the sea,
> a path through the mighty waters,
> who brings out chariot and horse,
> the army and the power,
> and they lie down, they cannot rise,
>   they are extinguished, quenched like a wick:
> Do not remember the former things,
>   or consider the things of old.
> See, I am doing a new thing;

---

214. Pao, *Acts and the Isaianic New Exodus*, 56.

215. Pao, *Acts and the Isaianic New Exodus*, 56. According to Harner, three themes are interrelated to each other in Isaiah 40–55: "creation faith, the Exodus tradition, and the expectation of the imminent restoration." Harner emphasizes the role of creation faith, in which the Israelites understand who Yahweh is. Since creation faith is based on the assertion of Yahweh's "sovereignty over history," the expectation of Israel's deliverance is strongly connected with his creative work. "It may indeed be true that the Israelites first came to know Yahweh as Lord of history, and their belief in him as Creator was never divorced from this primary context of meaning. But for II Isaiah creation faith, although still 'subordinate,' becomes so important that it can serve as the basis for his belief in Yahweh's imminent redemption of Israel, and so in its turn it gives new vitality to salvation faith." Harner, "Creation Faith in Deutero-Isaiah," 299, 305–6.

216. According to Lim, the victory at the Red Sea, in which a way was made through the sea, functions as "the supreme paradigmatic cosmic, historical, creative, and redemptive act" for the Israelites. When this event is applied to the exilic generation in Isaiah, it refers to the "liberation from a foreign oppressor, deliverance for the purpose of worship, entry into a good land, and an act of divine warfare." Lim, "'Way of the Lord,'" 143.

> now, it springs forth; do you not perceive it?
> I will make a way in the wilderness
>   and streams in the desert.
> The wild animals will honor me,
>   the jackals and the owls,
> because I give water in the wilderness,
>   and streams in the desert,
> to give drink to my chosen people. (Isa 43:16–20)

In the historical description of the victory at the Red Sea (vv. 16–17), a way was made through the sea and the waters served to destroy the Egyptian army. In Isaiah's vision of a new thing (vv. 19–20), however, a way will be made in the wilderness and water will flow to give drink to God's chosen people. The wilderness where false belief and rebellion occurred and unclean beasts lived is transformed into a place where streams flow and the people of God may reside, being supplied with drinking water.[217] In the new exodus, a way is made not through the sea, but in the wilderness, and water serves not as a threatening tool for destruction, but as God's gracious provision for preserving life. According to Matthews, it is significant that the way and the supply of water will be made in the wilderness at the same time: making a way recalls the crossing of the Red Sea, and the provision for the Israelites' needs recollects the wilderness wanderings.[218] The two events of the victory at the Red Sea and the provision during the wilderness wanderings in the original exodus are here conflated into one event in the new exodus.[219] The wilderness becomes the cosmological and eschatological location where the new way is opened and the new world full of life is created with the provision of water. The wilderness in Isaiah is transformed into the blessed land with the expectation of the new exodus.

Second, the wilderness is portrayed as the place where God guides his people as the shepherd of Israel. According to Talmon, "in late prophetic literature and in some psalms, the notion of God as father (Dt. 32:6, 18, 19), protector, and caretaker of his people (Ex. 19:4; Dt. 32:10f.; also vv. 4, 15, 18, 30, 31), which has its roots in the period of wilderness wanderings, is fused with the image of God as 'Israel's shepherd.'"[220]

In Ps 78(77):52, the Israelites are compared to sheep (צֹאן; πρόβατα, LXX) or a flock (עֵדֶר; ποίμνιον, LXX) led by God:[221] "Then he led out his

---

217. Oswalt, *Isaiah*, 491.
218. Mathews, *Defending Zion*, 125.
219. Mathews, *Defending Zion*, 125.
220. Talmon, "מִדְבָּר *miḏbār*; עֲרָבָה *ᵃrāḇâ*," 8:115.
221. "Flock" and its synonyms are frequently employed to describe Israel

people like sheep, and guided them in the wilderness like a flock." The image of God as a shepherd expresses his guidance and care for the Israelites, who are like sheep during their wilderness wanderings.

Isaiah 40:11 also presents God as a shepherd (כְּרֹעֶה; ὡς ποιμὴν, LXX) who will feed and lead his flock (עֶדְרוֹ; ποίμνιον, LXX): "He will feed his flock as a shepherd: he will gather the lambs in his arms, and carry them in his bosom, and gently lead the mother sheep."[222] In vv. 10, 11, two images of God appear simultaneously in the metaphor of arm (זְרוֹעַ)—military warrior and shepherd. On the one hand, God's arm is used to defeat his enemies and secure his reign over the world; on the other hand, it is employed to gather his people with tender and gentle guidance. The two different uses of the arm are intended to show "the two complementary sides of God's nature": He is the one who both fights for and cares for those who depend on him.[223]

Third, the wilderness is the eschatological gathering and feeding place of God's people. The prophets developed a new concept of the wilderness from an eschatological perspective: "the expectation of a new time which Israel will have to spend in the wilderness."[224] They sought for an "eschatological ideal" consisting of "a return to the religious and social conditions" of the wilderness period:[225] "nor shall you ever build a house, or sow seed; nor shall you plant a vineyard, or even own one; but you must always live in tents, that you may live a long time in the land where you reside" (Jer 35:7). According to Mauser, Hosea was the first prophet who mentioned a desert period in Israel's future.[226] Since Israel, described metaphorically as an unfaithful wife, committed sins, Yahweh threatened to "make her like a desert, and turn her into a parched land" (Hos 2:3[5]). Israel should be exiled from her fertile land and placed in the desert, but in spite of Israel's sinfulness, Hosea had a vision of the "renewal of hope" on the basis of Yahweh's faithfulness.[227] In the wilderness, Yahweh will tenderly call Israel

---

metaphorically. Anderson, *Book of Psalms 73-150*, 573.

222. The LXX Greek shepherd (ποιμήν) and sheep (πρόβατον) in Ps 78(77):52 and Isa 40:11 are also used in Mark 6:34 to describe the crowd "like sheep without a shepherd" (ὡς πρόβατα μὴ ἔχοντα ποιμένα).

223. Oswalt, *Book of Isaiah*, 55.

224. Mauser, *Christ in the Wilderness*, 45.

225. Talmon, "מִדְבָּר *miḏbār*; עֲרָבָה *ʿraḇâ*," 8:107–8. Mauser says that the Hebrew שׁוּב (to return) has the eschatological significance of renewal of Israel's sonship: "The word שׁוּב does not denote basically the freedom of the human will to make an ethical decision in turning to God, but it points to a certain status in which alone Israel's filial relationship to God can be renewed and which God, through his judgment, will reestablish in the future—the status of Israel in the wilderness" (Mauser, *Christ in the Wilderness*, 48).

226. Mauser, *Christ in the Wilderness*, 45.

227. Mauser, *Christ in the Wilderness*, 45.

again, and she will be restored: "Therefore, I will now allure her, and bring her into the wilderness, and speak tenderly to her" (Hos 2:14[16]). The call to the wilderness selects the theme of devastation from previous verses (e.g., vv. 3, 12) and changes it into a way of restoration.[228] Garrett says that "later prophets developed this idea too: the wilderness is not only a place of deprivation but is also a place of renewal and innocence (see Jer 2:2; 31:2; Ezek 20:10–38)."[229] In Hosea, the renewal of the relationship between God and Israel in the wilderness may recall the covenantal relationship that God formed with Israel at Mount Sinai in the exodus.[230] The covenant metaphor is used in the background of the wilderness, where Israel's new beginning in relationship with God may be established.[231] The return to the wilderness is therefore "a return to the grace of God,"[232] implying the restoration of Israel's original relationship with God, namely "the genuine status as the sonship to God."[233]

Isaiah also called the Israelites to the wilderness; he who proclaimed the new exodus commanded them to prepare the way of the Lord (Isa 40:3, 4). It is in the wilderness that they should prepare the way, for it is in the wilderness that they will see the return of the Lord. Eschatologically, then, the wilderness is the place where the people of God should gather and prepare themselves to see and meet him. These prophetic announcements affected rabbinic literature and the members of the Qumran community who lived and purified themselves in the wilderness in expectation of the Messiah's arrival.[234]

The eschatological expectation of the new exodus arose vigorously in Second Temple Jewish literature and rabbinic writings that envisioned the

---

228. Garrett, *Hosea, Joel*, 88.

229. Garrett, *Hosea, Joel*, 88. Mays also says that "'[w]ilderness' is more than a place; it is a time and situation in which the pristine relation between God and people was untarnished and Israel depended utterly on Yahweh" (Mays, *Hosea*, 44).

230. Stuart, *Hosea-Jonah*, 53; Dearman, *Book of Hosea*, 121; Mays, *Hosea*, 44.

231. Dearman explains the new formation of Israel's identity in the wilderness as follows: "With his [Hosea] reference to the wilderness, he is not finished with the marriage/covenant metaphor. As the place of covenant making and divine guidance, where Israel needed to depend totally on the covenant Lord, the wilderness is also the place of marital beginnings. *Wooing* Israel, *speaking to her heart*, and *bringing her to the wilderness* are ways to reprise the national identity as a second bridal period." Dearman, *Book of Hosea*, 121.

232. Mauser, *Christ in the Wilderness*, 46.

233. Stock, *Way in the Wilderness*, 61.

234. Mauser, *Christ in the Wilderness*, 61.

messianic age[235] unfolding in the wilderness.[236] Above all, it was a popular expectation among the Jews that the blessings of the manna provision would resume in the messianic age and the Messiah would feed his people in the wilderness. In 2 Bar. 29:8, manna is expected to rain again with "eschatological hope":[237] "And it will happen at that time that the treasury of manna will come down again from on high, and they will eat of it in those years because these are they who will have arrived at the consummation of time."[238]

Mauser notes that the expectation of the messianic age can be traced in the rabbinic writings: "the tendency to fashion the period of salvation after the pattern of the first exodus is not only discernible in the connexion with the Messianic hope; it also leads to the assumption that the great miracles

235. The term "messianic" may be largely understood in two ways: It narrowly refers to "the expected Davidic savior of Israel" and broadly to "an eschatological age of God's intervention in creation and history" (Noll, "Qumran and Paul," 782). The messianic expectation in early Judaism took diverse forms. Some anticipated a particular Messianic figure like David (e.g., Ps. Sol. 17). Some Qumranites looked for two messianic figures—one is related to priesthood and the other to kingship (e.g., 1QS 9:11). Others expected a prophet like Moses (e.g., 4QTest). Still others hoped for "the coming of a messianic age in general without focusing on a particular messianic figure" (Witherington, "John the Baptist," 384). Here, one needs to distinguish between "messianic" and "eschatological." While the term "eschatological" generally implies the state of "a radical and lasting change" performed by God or his agents, the term "messianic" focuses on a figure as a redeemer, who will transform this age and provide the new world. See Jonge, "Messiah," 4:778; Juel, "Messiah," 889–90. Messiah means "anointed one." When Israel had her own kingdom, kings and high priests were anointed. In this period, "Messiah" did not have any eschatological connotation. However, when Israel lost their kingdom in the Second Temple period, they expected the anointed one who would reestablish the kingship. In this sense, "Messiah" has an eschatological implication. See Collins, "Messiah, Jewish," 4:59. In general, the messianic age refers to "the era that will be inaugurated by God's decisive intervention in human history, in order to establish his eternal kingdom under the Messiah." It is "characterised by righteousness, justice and peace, by the outpouring of the Holy Spirit and by the restoration and renewal of God's people and of creation" (Manser et al., Dictionary of Bible Themes, 600).

236. Mauser, Christ in the Wilderness, 53–61. Stock, Way in the Wilderness, 62–63; Kittel, "ἔρημος, ἐρημία, ἐρημόω, ἐρήμωσις," 2:658–59. In the Greco-Roman period, some Jews, especially Qumranites, withdrew themselves to the wilderness for purification in order to prepare the messianic age. In popular eschatology, redemption would begin in the wilderness and the Messiah would be shown there ("Matt 24:26; Acts 21:38; Ant. 20.167; J.W. 2.259–63; 7.437–38" [Jones, "Wilderness," 5:851]). According to Allison, "a return to the wilderness and a Second Exodus would herald the messianic age." In addition, the blessings of the messianic age would be poured out in the wilderness (e.g., messianic banquet: 1QSa 2:11–22). Allison, "Mountain and Wilderness," 565.

237. France, Gospel of Mark, 262.

238. In this monograph, the English translation of the Old Testament Pseudepigrapha is taken from Charlesworth, Old Testament Pseudepigrapha.

during the sojourn in the desert would be repeated in the last days."[239] The typology of Moses and the Messiah as the redeemer is used frequently and expressed in various ways: "As the first redeemer (Moses), so the final redeemer (the Messiah)."[240] One of the typological parallels between Moses and Messiah is the provision of manna: the Messiah would give the eschatological blessing of manna as Moses provided manna in the wilderness.[241] There are several rabbinic mentions of this manna provision:

> As the first Redeemer causes manna to descend, so shall also the last Redeemer cause manna to descend. (*Qoheleth Rabba* on Eccl 1:9)
>
> For whom has it [i.e., the manna] now been prepared? For the righteous in the age that is coming: everyone who believeth is worthy and eateth of it. (*Tanhuma*, b^ešallaḥ 21)
>
> You shall not find it [i.e., manna] in this age, but ye shall find it in the age that is coming. (*Mekilta* on Exod 16:25)[242]

Chapman claims that Jesus' feeding miracles in Mark 6:31–44 and 8:1–10 refer to the blessing of manna in the messianic age.[243] Jesus' feeding miracles served as the ground of Peter's confession of Jesus as the Messiah (8:29) because Peter saw the messianic mission of providing manna in Jesus' miraculous feeding of the crowd with bread in the wilderness.[244] If we connect 8:21 with vv. 27–29 by omitting vv. 22–26, Peter's answer (confession)

---

239. Mauser, *Christ in the Wilderness*, 55.

240. Jeremias illustrates various typological connections between Moses and Messiah as follows: "In this precise form the typology of Moses and the Messiah is first found in Qoh. r., 1, 28 on 1:9: 'R. Berekia (c. 350) said in the name of R. Jiçchaq (II, c. 300): As the first redeemer, so the last redeemer. As it is said of the first redeemer: And Moses took his wife and his sons and had them ride on an ass (Exod 4:20), so the last redeemer, for it is said: Lowly and riding on an ass (Zech 9:9). As the first redeemer caused manna to come down, for it is said: Lo, I cause bread to rain down upon you from heaven (Exod 16:4), so the last redeemer will cause manna to come down, for it is said: White bread will lie on the earth (Ps 72:16 Midr.). As the first redeemer caused the well to spring forth (Num 20:11), so the last redeemer will cause water to spring forth, for it is said: And a fountain will break forth out of the house of Yahweh (Joel 3:18).'" Jeremias, "Μωυσῆς," 4:860.

241. France says that the provision of manna in the wilderness would be repeated in the messianic age according to the eschatological expectation (France, *Gospel of Mark*, 262).

242. Cranfield suggests these three references to the manna provision in rabbinic writings. The English translation is taken from him (Cranfield, *Mark*, 222).

243. Chapman, *Orphan Gospel*, 55–61.

244. Chapman, *Orphan Gospel*, 57–58.

in v. 29 can be related to Jesus' question in v. 21: Jesus asks, "Do you still not understand [about the meaning of the feedings in the desert]?" (v. 21); Peter answers, "[I understand] You are the Christ" (v. 29).[245] This assumption is problematic, however, because Jesus' question is a rebuke and lament for the disciples' incomprehension and hardened hearts; it is not an actual question. It is difficult to find definite evidence that Peter's confession was inspired by his experience of Jesus' feeding miracles. Nevertheless, Peter also had in mind the popular expectation of a Messiah who would provide the blessings of manna, and that his confession following the two feeding miracles might possibly reflect Jewish messianic expectations.[246]

There was also a belief among the Jews that the Messiah would "arise in the wilderness and gather his people."[247] As Moses led the Israelites in the desert, the Messiah would guide his people into the wilderness.[248] This belief and expectation inspired revolutionary messianic movements in the wilderness,[249] and Josephus criticized messianic pretenders who rebelled in the desert as follows:[250]

> And now did the madness of the *Sicarii*, like a disease, reach as far as the cities of Cyrene; For one Jonathan, a vile person, and by trade a weaver, came thither and prevailed with no small number of the poorer sort to give ear to him; he also led them into the desert, upon promising them that he would show them signs and apparitions. (Josephus, *J.W.* 7.437–438)[251]

Acts 21:38 also mentions a revolt that was stirred up by the Egyptians who led four thousand terrorists out into the wilderness. In Matt 24:26, the wilderness is cited as the place where the Messiah is expected to appear:

---

245. Chapman, *Orphan Gospel*, 59–60.

246. The fact that the feeding miracles are placed before Peter's confession has the intention of showing Jesus' identity as the eschatological Messiah who feeds his people as God fed the Israelites in the wilderness. In the Gospel of John, the crowd tried to make Jesus a king by force after he performed a feeding miracle (6:1–15). Therefore, the feeding miracles in the wilderness are explicitly related to the mission of the Messiah. In addition, the fact that Jesus' feeding took place in the wilderness (ἔρημος) evidently alludes to the manna provision of the exodus, so that Mark describes Jesus as the Messiah like Moses. Jeremias argues that "it is presupposed that this miracle will be expected of the Messiah" (Jeremias, "Μωυσῆς," 4:862).

247. Mauser, *Christ in the Wilderness*, 56.

248. Jeremias, "Μωυσῆς," 4:860.

249. Kittel, "ἔρημος, ἐρημία, ἐρημόω, ἐρήμωσις," 2:658–59.

250. Mauser, *Christ in the Wilderness*, 57–58.

251. In this monograph, the English translation of the Works of Josephus is taken from Josephus, *Works of Josephus*, translated by Whiston.

"So, if they say to you, 'Behold, he is in the wilderness,' do not go out."[252] As Mauser says, "the call to the wilderness is nothing less than synonymous with the claim of Messiahship."[253]

In the Qumran community, the wilderness was the place where the "penitents of the desert" (שבי המדבר [šābê hammiḏbār]: "those who return from the wilderness," 4QpPs^a 3:1) withdrew from the city, gathered together, and settled in the wilderness to prepare the way of the Lord according to the prophet's calling in Isa 40:3.[254] The Qumran community understood the preparation of the way of the Lord in the wilderness as the second period of wilderness life would begin the last deliverance of God's people.[255]

> And when these exist as a community in Israel in compliance with these arrangements they are to be segregated from within the dwelling of the men of sin to walk to the desert in order to open there His path. As it is written: «In the desert, prepare the way of ****, straighten in the steppe a roadway for our God." This is the study of the law which he commanded through the hand of Moses, in order to act in compliance with all that has been revealed from age to age, and according to what the prophets have revealed through his holy spirit.[256] (1QS 8:12-16)

The Qumran community's communal structure reflects Moses's grouping of the Israelites as instructed by his father-in-law Jethro (Exod 18:21, 25; Num 31:14; Deut 1:15). Following Moses, they subdivided community members into thousands, hundreds, fifties, and tens, and they regarded such groupings as an "eschatological model for their sectarian life (1 QS 2:21-23; CD 13:1; 1 QM 4:1-5:17; 1QSa 1:14-15, 28-29)"[257]: "In the third place all the people shall enter the Rule, one after another, in thousands, hundreds, fifties and tens, so that all the children of Israel may know their standing in God's Community in conformity with the eternal plan" (1QS 2:21-23). This practice recollects the Israelites' wilderness wanderings in the exodus.

---

252. Kittel, "ἔρημος, ἐρημία, ἐρημόω, ἐρήμωσις," 2:658-59.

253. Mauser, *Christ in the Wilderness*, 58.

254. Talmon, "מִדְבָּר *miḏbār*; עֲרָבָה *ʿrāḇâ*," 8:118.

255. Mauser, *Christ in the Wilderness*, 60.

256. In this monograph, the English translation of the Qumran texts is taken from Martínez, *Dead Sea Scrolls Translated*, translated by Watson.

257. The fact that Jesus ordered the disciples to have the crowd sit down in groups of hundreds and fifties recalls the wilderness experience led by Moses in the exodus. Guelich, *Mark 1-8:26*, 341; Gnilka, *Markus*, 260-61.

In addition, the community members who lived as the people of the new covenant in the wilderness would participate in the messianic banquet.[258]

> This is the assembly of famous men, [those summoned to] the gathering of the community council, when [God] begets the Messiah with them. . . .. And [when] they gather at the table of community [or to drink] the new wine, and the table of community is prepared [and] the new wine [is mixed] for drinking, [no-one should stretch out] his hand to the first-fruit of the bread and of the [new wine] before the priest, for [he is the one who bl]esses the first-fruit of bread and of the new wine [and stretches out] his hand towards the bread before them. Afterwards, the Messiah of Israel shall stretch out his hand towards the bread. [And afterwards, shall] bless all the congregation of the community, each [one according to] his dignity. (1QSa 2:11–22)

The Qumran community, then, gathered together in the wilderness according to the prophetic announcement, prepared themselves as the true people of a new covenant, and participated in a messianic banquet. They saw the wilderness as the place where the eschatological drama would unfold in the messianic age.

The Wilderness as the Setting of the New Exodus in Jesus' Feeding Miracles (Mark 6:31–44 and 8:1–10)

We have now explored the use of wilderness imagery in relation to the exodus story in the OT, Second Temple Jewish literature, and rabbinic writings. In the historical description of the exodus, the wilderness is the place where God's gracious provision was given to the Israelites in spite of their grumbling. Though the Israelites were tested by God in the desert, they witnessed the glory of the Lord in the same place. In post-Pentateuchal and Second Temple Jewish literature, the wilderness is interpreted from cosmic and eschatological perspectives. First, it is regarded as a place of chaos that will be transformed by God's grace into a fertile land full of vitality and a flat road

---

258. Guelich, *Mark 1–8:26*, 341. Though the term "messianic banquet" is not found in the biblical writings, it may be used to explain the "imagery in which eschatological salvation is portrayed as a grand banquet, whether or not the Messiah is specifically mentioned." Because the people suffer from hunger and the paucity of food, eschatological salvation is naturally expected in the image of a great banquet where the people are fully satisfied with a plentiful supply of food. See Boring, "Messianic Banquet," 4:66. For a detailed discussion of the messianic banquet in the Bible and extra-biblical literature, see also Smith, "Messianic Banquet," 4:788–91.

for the way of the Lord. Second, it is the place where God leads his people as the shepherd of Israel. Third, it is the place where the people of God will be gathered for the eschatological restoration of their intimate relationship with God and fed with the blessing of manna in the messianic age.

Jesus' feeding miracles in Mark 6:31-44 and 8:1-10 reflect the manna event in the exodus — the wilderness setting of these episodes supports this interpretation. Before discussing the theological significance of the wilderness in the two feeding miracle stories, we need to understand why Mark includes two such similar feeding stories in his narrative. Two reasons for this may be suggested, one related to Mark's rhetorical technique and the other to his geographical description. The first reason is that Mark develops and emphasizes the themes of Jesus' greatness and the disciples' incomprehension by employing his favorite literary device, repetition.[259] The disciples' ignorance, seen in their failure to understand the first feeding miracle (6:52), is further developed through Mark's emphasis on their unbelief in the account of the second feeding miracle, after which Jesus rebukes them for their hardness of hearts and failure to recognize the meaning of the loaves (8:13-21).[260] Through this repetition, Jesus' greatness in performing the two feeding miracles is mentioned twice (vv. 19-20).

The second reason for Mark's inclusion of both feeding miracles is that Mark is able to depict Jesus as the Savior who feeds not only the Jews but also the Gentiles by arranging the two feeding episodes in two different locales.[261] The feeding of the five thousand (6:31-44) took place in Jewish territory, while the feeding of the four thousand (8:1-10) occurred in Gentile territory. This geographical difference implies that the two feeding miracles are intended to show that Jesus fed the Jews in one episode and the Gentiles in the other.[262] Mark's narrative develops through repetition, but also through variations of characters, settings, and plot.[263] In the case of the two feeding miracles, the main variation is geographical and serves to demonstrate that Jesus is the Savior of both the Jews and the Gentiles.

In this section, I will examine how the feeding miracles are related to the manna event of the exodus in terms of their spatial setting in the

---

259. For the functions of repetition, see Williams, *Other Followers of Jesus*, 52-55.

260. Boring, *Mark*, 219.

261. In chapter 3, I discussed Mark's geographical description of Jesus' missional itinerary in terms of two cycles, one for the Jews and the other for the Gentiles.

262. Boring says that "in this section [Mark 8:1-10] Mark is also developing the theme of the transition of the gospel from its Jewish origins to the Gentile context of his own time and place, with 'bread' and 'feeding'/'eating' as key symbols of this transition (cf. 6:31, 36, 41, 44, 52; 7:2-5, 28; 8:1, 4-6, 14-21)" (Boring, *Mark*, 219).

263. Williams, *Other Followers of Jesus*, 53.

wilderness, and how the wilderness setting discloses the theological theme of the feeding miracles in the light of the new exodus. Because the two feedings of the five thousand and the four thousand are so similar in their characters, events, and settings—with the exception of several differences, especially in the Jewish and Gentile characteristics of each episode—rather than considering them separately I will investigate the two feeding miracles together to discover the theological significance of the wilderness setting.

To begin, Jesus' feeding miracles took place in the wilderness (ἔρημος), which corresponds to the location of the manna provision in the exodus. In the first feeding miracle (6:31–44), five thousand people ate their fill following Jesus' multiplication of five loaves and two fishes.[264] Before this miracle, the disciples reported on the mission to the Galilean villages (v. 30) that Jesus had ordered them to carry out. In his mission commandment to the

---

264. As regards multiplication of food, Jesus' feeding miracles are in some ways similar to Elisha's feeding miracle in 2 Kgs 4:42–44. Marcus suggests parallels in "the vocabulary and sequence of events" between Jesus' feeding of the five thousand and Elisha's feeding miracle as follows (Marcus, *Mark 1–8*, 415–16):

Elisha takes bread and ears of grain	Jesus takes bread and fish
Elisha commands: "Give to the men, that they may eat"	Jesus commands: "Give them something to eat"
Servant asks skeptically how he is to feed a hundred men	Disciples ask skeptically how they are to feed the crowd
Elisha repeats the command	Jesus commands disciples to sit the people down
Servant sets food before the people	Disciples distribute food to the people
The people eat and food is left over	The people eat and food is left over

France argues that "Mark had the story in mind, since not only is the situation of a hungry crowd and lack of food similar, but also the narrative focuses on the same motifs, the command to the servant/disciples to feed the crowd, their surprised question in response, the satisfying of hunger, and the food left over at the end" (France, *Gospel of Mark*, 262). Donahue and Harrington notes "the ratio of those fed" by Elijah and Jesus: while Elisha fed the one hundred with twenty loaves (five per loaf), Jesus fed the five thousand with five loaves (one thousand per loaf) (Donahue and Harrington, *Gospel of Mark*, 207). Jesus' feeding miracle was far greater than that of Elisha. According to Guelich (*Mark 1–8:26*, 344), Jesus' huge miracle shows that "a 'greater than Elisha' is here." Boring also claims that Jesus' feeding miracle demonstrates that he is "not only 'more than a prophet' (Matt 11:9); as the eschatological prophet he is *much* more" (Boring, *Mark*, 185). Jesus' feeding miracles may echo Elisha's feeding miracle in its content and order and Mark might have known Elisha's story and had it in mind. As Hooker says, however, despite their similarities, "the most important background to the Markan narrative is the story of God's provision of manna for Israel in the wilderness (cf. Exodus 16; Numbers 11)" (Hooker, *Gospel According to Saint Mark*, 164). The provision of manna in the wilderness in the exodus story functions as the main frame for Jesus' feeding story, while Elisha's feeding story plays a supplementary role.

disciples (vv. 7–11), Jesus gave them instructions to take nothing but a staff and sandals—items that are actually prohibited in the parallel accounts in Matt 10:10 and Luke 9:3.[265] This difference may indicate that Mark followed a tradition, independent of Matthew and Luke, which reflected the exodus tradition.[266] In Exod 12:11, the Israelites were commanded to be ready for the escape from Egypt before the day of the Passover, "with your cloak tucked into your belt,[267] your sandals on your feet, and your staff in your hand." The similarity in the commands for preparation in Exodus and Mark demonstrates that "the missionary instruction to the disciples is given in accordance with the instruction given to Israel at the outset of her wanderings

265. Diverse options have been suggested to solve this synoptic problem. Power explains the different usages of the staff (ῥάβδος) which may cause the discrepancy among the synoptic Gospels, like this: whereas the staff allowed in Mark refers to the stick that is used as the tool to help walking and shepherding, the rod forbidden in Matthew and Luke refers to the club that is employed to protect the enemy by shepherds. See Power, "Staff of the Apostles," 241–66. According to Johnson, the fact that the rules of carrying the necessities for mission work are more rigorous in Matthew and Luke than in Mark may indicates that Matthew and Luke reflect the original form whereas the Markan reading is corrupt (Johnson, *Commentary on the Gospel According to St. Mark*, 116). Bultmann claims that Mark as a Hellenistic evangelist may weaken the primitive and strict Palestinian rules in order to facilitate the mission work in the Greco-Roman world (Bultmann, *History of the Synoptic Tradition*, 145). These arguments, however, are too hypothetical, not suggesting solid evidence. Carson renders the injunction in Matt 10:9–10 "μὴ κτήσησθε . . . ῥάβδον" as "Do not procure . . . a staff," supposing that the disciples must not procure a new staff and sandals: while the verb αἴρω in Mark 6:8 means "taking," κτάομαι in Matt 10:9 implies "procuring." He attempts to harmonize the difference between Matthew and Mark in that Matthew's instruction not to procure a staff means not to acquire a new staff, but just to use what they already possessed. See Carson, "Matthew," 8:245. However, his argument seems to be inconsistent. If it is true, for instance, a bag that the disciples already possessed may be carried in the mission journey in Matthew, but it is not allowed in Mark. When the verb κτάομαι is applied to other items in mission necessities, there arises a problem. In addition, Luke 9:3 uses the same verb αἴρω as Mark 6:8, but the rules to the personal possessions in mission journeys are same with Matt 10:10. No clear explanation is easily made. See France, *Gospel of Mark*, 248–49; Stein, *Mark*, 293.

Though it is difficult to harmonize the different rules about possessing various items in missional journey in Synoptic Gospels, Mark 6:8–9 evidently reflects the situation of the Israelites' flight from Egypt (Exod 12:11). Mauser emphasizes the significance of the similarities between Mark 6:8, 9 and Exod 12:11 (Mauser, *Christ in the Wilderness*, 133). According to Osborne, "many have connected Mark's allowing staff and sandals with Exod 12:11, where the Israelites on the eve of the exodus are told to eat the Passover in haste, with staff in hand and sandals on the feet. In this way the mission may be seen as a new exodus" (Osborne, *Matthew*, 379). In Jesus' mission commandment (6:8, 9), Mark portrays the disciples' mission journey in the light of a new exodus.

266. Mauser, *Christ in the Wilderness*, 133.

267. This is the paraphrased translation of NIV. A more literal translation of αἱ ὀσφύες ὑμῶν περιεζωσμέναι (LXX) is "your loins girded" (RSV).

through the desert."²⁶⁸ The four necessities for the journey are identical in Exodus and Mark: a staff, a belt, a tunic, and sandals²⁶⁹ (Exod 12:11; Mark 6:8, 9). These clothing items recollect the urgency and anticipation of the exodus.²⁷⁰ According to Marcus, "if these Exodus parallels are deliberate . . . Mark probably wishes to imply that the disciples' missionary journey will be a participation in the new exodus inaugurated by Jesus."²⁷¹ The mission commandment in Mark corresponds to the instruction at the outset of the exodus, which implies the beginning of the wilderness wanderings. The disciples' mission journey may then allude to the wilderness life. The disciples' mission report in 6:30 serves as the connection between Jesus' sending out the disciples (vv. 6b–13) and his feeding of the five thousand (vv. 31–44), and both episodes highlight the wilderness motif of the exodus: the preparedness for the wilderness lifestyle and the provision of food in the wilderness.

Next, in the two feeding episodes as in the exodus story, the wilderness is also the place where the people complained and were tested. The Israelites complained about their hunger in the wilderness (Exod 16:2–3), showing their lack of faith; the disciples who asked Jesus to dismiss the crowd showed a similar response of grumbling and unbelief.²⁷² According to Lane, the disciples and the crowd who followed Jesus are "representative of Israel" in the wilderness.²⁷³ In the feeding of the five thousand, the disciples asked Jesus to send the crowd away to get some food in the neighboring country and villages because "this is a deserted place" (Mark 6:35–36). In response to Jesus' order to the disciples to give the crowd something to eat, they complained

---

268. Mauser, *Christ in the Wilderness*, 133.

269. Edwards, *Gospel According to Mark*, 180. Though the belt and the tunic are not clearly stated in the words of Exod 12:11 LXX, they are supposed in the description of the Israelites' dressing for the flight from Egypt. See also Boring, *Mark*, 175. Marcus parallels "no money in the belt" (Mark 6:8) with "loins girded" (Exod 12:11) as a similar image and "single tunic" (Mark 6:9) with "single garment" (Deut 8:4; 29:5) (Marcus, *Mark 1–8*, 388–10). Comparing the rules for carrying necessities in mission journeys between Cynics and Exodus, Marcus supposes that Mark may follow the Exodus tradition. As in Mark, Cynic philosophers did not possess bread, bag, and two cloaks during their journey, but in contrast to Mark, sandals were permitted to the Cynics.

270. Edwards, *Gospel According to Mark*, 180. Mauser also argues that "the injunction to the disciples to carry neither bread nor bag, which is simply the bread container, can consequently be understood in analogy to the wilderness situation of Israel. As Israel was fed in the desert with manna which she could not herself provide, so the disciples are to be kept alive with nourishment for which they do not have to take thought themselves" (Mauser, *Christ in the Wilderness*, 133–34).

271. Marcus, *Mark 1–8*, 389.

272. Grassi, *Loaves and Fishes*, 14.

273. Lane, *Gospel According to Mark*, 226.

about how they would need to go and buy two hundred denarii worth of bread to feed them (v. 37). In the feeding of the four thousand, the disciples questioned Jesus' compassion on the starvation of the crowd: "How can one feed these people with bread here 'in the desert'?" (8:4). In both episodes, the wilderness is described as a place where no food can be supplied. The disciples' comments connote skepticism regarding the possibility of feeding people in the wilderness.[274]

Though the "testing" of the disciples is not explicitly stated in Mark's feeding episodes as it is in John,[275] Jesus' order to the disciples is meant to test their faith. Even after experiencing the feeding of the five thousand, the disciples show skepticism about where they could get enough bread to feed the four thousand in the desert. In a boat during the final sea-crossing (8:13–21), Jesus rebuked them for their hardened hearts and failure to recognize the instruction from the two feeding miracles (vv. 17–21). In the wilderness, Jesus tested the disciples' understanding of who he is and what he had done for them.

Finally and most notably in the two feeding miracles, the wilderness has a cosmological and eschatological significance that reflects the new exodus in several aspects. First, the wilderness is the place where Jesus gathers his people and gives them rest. This has eschatological implications.[276] Jesus told the disciples who took a mission journey to withdraw to a deserted place to rest (6:31); this is consistent with the repeated theme of God's promise to give rest to his people in the wilderness tradition.[277] According to Lane, "it was the literal rest of the wilderness generation led by Moses and Joshua which became the type of the final rest promised to the people of God in a second exodus in the preaching of Isaiah and Jeremiah."[278] By inviting the disciples to the wilderness, Jesus provided the promised rest in the wilderness.[279] In addition, the eschatological rest in the wilderness

---

274. Guelich claims that the disciples' complaint in the first feeding is concerned with "*how* they could afford" the food, whereas their skepticism in the second feeding is related to "*where* one could get" it (Guelich, *Mark 1–8:26*, 404).

275. In John 6:6, Jesus' asking Philip where he should buy bread for the people to eat is intended to "test" him.

276. Lane, *Gospel According to Mark*, 225.

277. Mauser, *Christ in the Wilderness*, 135. He enumerates several verses in the OT and the NT, which reflect the promise of rest in the wilderness tradition (Deut 3:20; 12:9f.; 25:19; Josh 1:13, 15; 21:44; Ps 95:7–11; Isa 63:14; Jer 31:12; Heb 3:7—4:13). See Mauser, *Christ in the Wilderness*, 33, 41, 73–74.

278. Two passages about the expectation of rest are suggested in the prophetic writings: "Isa 63:14 (in the context of 63:10–14) and Jer 31:2 (in the context of 30:23–31:6)." Lane, *Gospel According to Mark*, 225; Mauser, *Christ in the Wilderness*, 135.

279. Lane, *Gospel According to Mark*, 225.

was fulfilled with "the communion of a meal," which Jesus prepared for his people in the wilderness by multiplying bread.[280]

Second, the wilderness is transformed into green pasture full of vitality.[281] The wilderness is no more a place where no provisions can be supplied. As previously discussed, the wilderness is transformed from a deserted and cursed land into a fertile land in the new exodus. In the Psalms and the Prophets, God's goodness changes the wilderness into verdant pastures in which flocks dwell with abundant rain (e.g., Ps 68:7[8]–10[11]). The wilderness will be turned into a paradise like Eden (e.g., Isa 51:3). In Mark 6:39, the "green grass" (χλωρός χόρτος) in the desert reflects the transformation of the wilderness to be full of "refreshment, life, and joy."[282] The wilderness becomes an eschatological place where the Messiah holds a huge banquet for his people. Mark's vivid description of the green grass also implies that the miracle of feeding the five thousand took place during the spring, the season when the grass grows.[283] The green grass associates this feeding miracle with the spring festival of the Passover; this connection is made explicit in John 6:4. As Marcus notes, the green grass reflects the imagery of the Passover or the exodus: "Blooming grass, like the Passover/exodus typology in general, points forward to an expected eschatological recapitulation of the exodus events."[284]

Third, the wilderness is the place where a shepherd leads and feeds his sheep.[285] In the wilderness, a shepherd shows his faithfulness to his sheep by leading, protecting, feeding, and caring for them. Mark's portrayal of blooming grass covering the wilderness indicates that the wilderness becomes a lush pasture where the shepherd can provide food for his sheep.[286] The true shepherd leads his sheep into green pastures (Ps 23:2) and cares for them there; the imagery of the wilderness as verdant pasture evokes the shepherd motif. Jesus is regarded as a shepherd in that he had compassion on the crowd when he saw their wretched condition, "like sheep without a shepherd" (Mark 6:34).[287]

---

280. Mauser, *Christ in the Wilderness*, 135.

281. Mauser, *Christ in the Wilderness*, 136–37.

282. Mauser, *Christ in the Wilderness*, 136.

283. France, *Gospel of Mark*, 267.

284. Marcus, *Mark 1–8*, 408. Gnilka examines the parallel image of the green grass in the wilderness from Isa 35:1–2 and 2 Bar. 29:5–8 (Gnilka, *Markus*, 260).

285. Lane, *Gospel According to Mark*, 229.

286. Erlangen, "Die beiden Erzählungen von der Speisung," 10–22.

287. Quoting Zech 13:7, Mark 14:27 identifies Jesus as the shepherd who would be stricken: "Jesus said to them, 'You will all become deserters; for it is written, "I will strike the shepherd, and the sheep will be scattered."'" See Boring, *Mark*, 394. The shepherd

In the OT, God is presented as a shepherd who guides, cares for, and feeds his flock (e.g., Isa 40:11),[288] and the Israelites are described as sheep in the wilderness wanderings (e.g., Ps 78(77):52).[289] The expression of the crowd's pathetic situation, "like sheep without a shepherd" (ὡς πρόβατα μὴ ἔχοντα ποιμένα), is "the metaphor for lack of care and leadership" in the OT.[290] In Num 27:17, Moses asked God to appoint a leader to replace him and guide the Israelites so that they would not be "like sheep without a shepherd" (ὡσεὶ πρόβατα οἷς οὐκ ἔστιν ποιμήν, LXX) in the wilderness.[291] In Ezek 34:5–6, when the appointed leaders failed in faith, the people of God were scattered like sheep because there was no shepherd (διεσπάρη τὰ πρόβατά μου διὰ τὸ μὴ εἶναι ποιμένας, LXX). Both of these passages are associated with the wilderness motif.[292] In response to Moses's prayer, God

---

(Jesus) will be smitten and the sheep (the disciples) will be dispersed. In the following verse (v. 28; cf. 16:7), however, Jesus promises that after his resurrection he will go to Galilee where the disciples (the scattered sheep) will be gathered again. In this sense, Moloney says, "As with great compassion he looked upon the great throng of sheep without a shepherd beside the sea of Galilee [in the wilderness] (6:34, 39, 42), he will deal similarly with his scattered disciples" (Moloney, *Gospel of Mark*, 288). According to Marcus, Zech 9–14 has the image of a shepherd and sheep, which presents not only the destruction of Israel and her worthless leaders, but also the Lord's care for her. For instance, in 10:6–12, the Lord dispersed the people in his rage, but he would gather them again in his compassion. Likewise, Mark 14:28 ("I will go before you to Galilee"; cf. "There you will see him [Jesus]" in 16:7) foreshadows that Jesus will shepherd his disciples by re-gathering them to Galilee: "a new beginning in which Jesus will return to the place [Galilee] where his career started and display the same compassion for lost sheep that marked his ministry there (see 6:34)." See Marcus, *Mark 8–16*, 972. In his narrative, Mark (e.g., 6:34; 14:27, 28) explicitly portrays Jesus as the shepherd who has compassion on his people and will gather, lead, and care for them.

288. Watts argues that Mark's portrayal of Jesus as a shepherd and the disciples and the crowd as sheep corresponds to the imagery of Yahweh as a shepherd and his people as sheep in Isaiah. "The sheep/shepherd imagery is highly developed in the Isaianic NE [New Exodus]" (e.g., 40:1–11), and "Yahweh's compassion" and "his provision for his people" in Isaiah serve as the motif of Jesus' feeding miracles in Mark. See Watts, *Isaiah's New Exodus and Mark*, 197.

289. In Ps 78(77) and Ezek 34, the motifs of Yahweh's and David's shepherding of his people in the exodus/new-exodus imagery are seen together. See Watts, "Mark," 160.

290. France, *Gospel of Mark*, 265.

291. In 1 Kgs 22:17, Micaiah predicted the defeat of Ahab's army, saying that all Israel will scatter "like sheep without a shepherd" (ὡς ποίμνιον ᾧ οὐκ ἔστιν ποιμήν, LXX). The expression "like sheep without a shepherd" is similar between Num 17:27 and 1 Kgs 22: 17. Though the Greek "shepherd" (ποιμήν) is the same between the two verses, "sheep" is different: while the former uses πρόβατον, the latter employs ποίμνιον. Mark 6:34 adopts the vocabulary πρόβατον. Therefore, Mark's expression seems to follow Num 17:27. In Ezek 34:5–6, the Greek words for sheep and shepherd are also the same as in Mark 6:34. For a detailed discussion, see Watts, "Mark," 158–61.

292. Lane, *Gospel According to Mark*, 226.

appointed Joshua, whose Greek name is "Jesus" (Ἰησοῦς) in the LXX, as the one to lead the Israelites out and bring them through the wilderness (Num 27:15-18). In Ezek 34, God promised to set up a true shepherd, "my servant David," who would feed the Israelites (v. 23) and make a covenant of peace allowing them to live safely in the wilderness (v. 25).[293] Against the background of these OT passages, Lane argues that Mark 6:34 portrays Jesus as "the one appointed by God to be the leader of the people in their exodus into the wilderness."[294] In his compassion to the starving crowd, Jesus is manifested as the "promised eschatological shepherd"[295] who provides for his sheep in the wilderness.

Fourth, the people of God are arranged by groups in the wilderness. Jesus ordered the disciples to make the crowds who gathered around him sit down in groups of hundreds and fifties in the wilderness (6:39-40). According to Marcus, since "the declining order of number is unusual (contra e.g., 4:8, 20)," the grouping numbers may have a historical background.[296] This grouping recalls the arrangement of the Israelites in Mosaic camps by thousands, hundreds, fifties, and tens in the wilderness (Exod 18:21, 25). In addition, the fact that the camps are associated with the officials of the twelve tribes in Deut 1:15 may possibly be connected to the twelve baskets full of broken pieces of bread and fish (Mark 6:43).[297] Mark's usage of the number may thus be interpreted in the light of the exodus typology.[298]

---

293. In Ezek 34:25, God promised to get rid of wild beasts in the wilderness so that the Israelites may live there, which implies the transformation of the wilderness into paradise (cf. Isa 35:9). See Mauser, *Christ in the Wilderness*, 37.

294. Lane, *Gospel According to Mark*, 226. Jesus is described as the shepherd who has both images of a "Mosaic figure" and the "Davidic Messiah." Marcus, however, argues that this passage connects the shepherd imagery more strongly to the image of Moses. Though the "sheep without a shepherd" phrase is not restricted to Moses, it reflects "Moses's words in Num 27:17, and in moving from an allusion to Moses to a reference to Jesus' teaching, Mark is probably drawing on a Jewish tradition that sees the Torah, the teaching of Moses, as the divine response to the dilemma of the shepherdless sheep of Israel." See Marcus, *Mark 1-8*, 406. Stein also argues that "the christological nature of this saying [Mark 6:34] may be especially apparent in Num 27:16-17, where Moses's request for someone to lead Israel is answered in Joshua (Num 27:18-23)" (Stein, *Mark*, 313).However, it is difficult to determine which figure (Yahweh, Moses, or David) the shepherd imagery of Mark 6:34 refers to. Though Jesus is here portrayed in the context of Num 27:17 focusing on the wretchedness and wandering of sheep due to the absence of a shepherd in the wilderness, Jesus' miraculous feeding of the crowd ultimately refers to God's provision for his people as a shepherd feeds his sheep (Isa 40:11).

295. Guelich, *Mark 1-8:26*, 340.

296. Marcus, *Mark 1-8*, 408.

297. Marcus, *Mark 1-8*, 408.

298. Marcus, *Mark 1-8*, 408.

The Qumran community also followed the model of Moses's grouping of the Israelites in the wilderness to form the organizational configuration of their community in order to show that they were the true Israel corresponding to the Israel of the exodus. The members of the Qumran community were grouped in thousands, hundreds, fifties, and tens (1QS 2:21–22; 1QSa 1:14–15; CD 13:1; 1QM 4:1—5:17).[299] These people who thought of themselves as living in the last days while waiting for the Messiah(s) structured their community in preparation for eschatological events.[300] In Mark 6:39–40, then, the groupings of hundreds and fifties in the wilderness may imply that the crowd around Jesus stands for the eschatological community.[301] The crowd as the eschatological community therefore becomes "the recipient of the Messianic grace" and the people are blessed by Jesus' miraculous provision in the wilderness where the new exodus is realized.[302]

Finally, the wilderness is the gathering and feeding place where the messianic banquet will be spread. All the crowds reclined (ἀνακλῖναι/ ἀνέπεσαν) in groups (συμπόσια συμπόσια/πρασιαὶ πρασιαί) on the green grass of the wilderness (6:39–40). The Greek words ἀνακλίνω and ἀναπίπτω (to recline) express the posture taken by ancient people at a meal.[303] In the Greco-Roman sphere, the guests of a banquet generally reclined on couches; in the Jewish world, however, the reclining posture at a meal is related to the Passover.[304] Marcus notes that the mention of reclining on the grass may

299. Donahue and Harrington, *Gospel of Mark*, 206.

300. Collins, *Mark*, 325.

301. Collins, *Mark*, 325.

302. Mauser, *Christ in the Wilderness*, 137.

303. "ἀνακλίνω" and "ἀναπίπτω," BDAG 65, 70.

304. Marcus, *Mark 1–8*, 407. Jesus and his disciples reclined (ἀνάκειμαι) at the table when they ate the Passover meal (14:18). "Despite Exod 12:11, which stipulates that the Passover sacrifice should be eaten in haste and readiness to depart, later Jews stretched the Passover meal, or seder, into a banquet in which the exodus from Egypt was recounted in a leisurely manner and participants reclined as a sign of their status as free people" (Marcus, *Mark 8–16*, 949). In the rabbinic writings, the diner generally "*sat down* (Heb. *yašab*, Aram. *yeteb*)" in the days of Jesus (e.g., "j. Ber. 7:11c.48: *yšbw w'kle*; j. Ber. 8.11d.57 [cf. 50]: *hyh ywšb w' wkl bšbt*; the same in Aramaic texts b. Sanh. 38a: *ytbw bs' dt'* ; j. Ber. 7.11b.62 and [verbally identical] 11c.42: *hww jtbyn 'klyn*; further Ber. 6.6; b. Ber. 41b"). Before the table custom of sitting down in Palestine, the ancient Israelites "squatted on the floor" at meals (e.g., "1 Sam. 20.5, 24f.; cf. further Gen. 27.19; Ex. 32.6 [=1 Cor. 10.7]; Judg. 19.6; 1 Kings 13.20; Prov. 23.1; Ecclus 31.12, 18, etc."). Therefore, reclining at the table was done at special meals. "Wherever the gospels speak of reclining at meals they mean either a meal in the open (the feeding of the multitudes), or a party (Mark 12.39 par.; 14.3 par.; Luke 7.36, 37, 49; 11.37; 14.15; John 12.2), or a feast (Mark 2.15 par. especially Luke 5.29), or a royal banquet (Mark 6.26 par.), or a wedding feast (Matt. 22.10, 11; Luke 14.8, 10), or the feast of the salvation time (Matt. 8.11; Luke 13.29, cf. 16.23)." Jesus and his disciples would not surely have reclined at the

be "part of the Passover typology."³⁰⁵ The imagery of the Passover meal not only reminded the people of the exodus from Egypt, but also made them anticipate the eschatological messianic banquet.³⁰⁶ In these Greek words, France discovers the image of the "messianic banquet":

> These terms are especially associated with the Graeco-Roman style of reclining at table. In a Jewish context, where meals were generally taken seated, these terms would normally indicates a more formal "banquet" setting, following the Graeco-Roman style, rather than an ordinary meal. While at an open-air picnic sitting at table was in any case out of the question, it is possible that by using such terms Mark intends to hint that, while it was hardly a formal occasion and the fare was basic, there was an air of festivity about it which made it, at least with hindsight, a foreshadowing of the messianic banquet.³⁰⁷

The Greek συμπόσιον literally means "drinking-party," but is better interpreted as "banquet."³⁰⁸ The use of this word implies that "the meal hosted by Jesus is a kind of banquet."³⁰⁹ The literal sense of the Greek πρασιά is "garden plot" or "garden bed,"³¹⁰ and this word is not elsewhere employed to describe people.³¹¹ However, Mark used the distributive repetition, πρασιαὶ πρασιαί,³¹² to describe the groups of the people by contrasting them with the green grass.³¹³ This expression gives "a remarkable visual impression of the scene, with men lined up in groups like plots of vegetables on the green

---

table when they ate at ordinary meals. However, the fact that they reclined at the table at the Passover meal implies that "it was a *ritual duty* to recline at the table as a symbol of freedom, also, as it is expressly stated, for 'the poorest man in Israel.'" See Jeremias, *Eucharistic Words of Jesus*, 48–49. In the light of the custom of "reclining at the table at the Passover meal," the crowd's "reclining" on the green grass of the wilderness in Jesus' feeding alludes to the Passover, which furthermore refers to a messianic banquet. Though the ancient Israelites ate bread in haste for the escape from Egypt, the crowd of Jesus reclined on the green grass while enjoying a messianic banquet.

305. Marcus, *Mark 1–8*, 407.
306. Grassi, *Loaves and Fishes*, 19.
307. France, *Gospel of Mark*, 267.
308. "συμπόσιον," BDAG 959.
309. Collins, *Mark*, 324.
310. "πρασιά," BDAG 860.
311. France, *Gospel of Mark*, 267.
312. Marcus notes that "the distributive expression is a Semitic idiom" (Marcus, *Mark 1–8*, 407).
313. "πρασιά," BDAG 860.

grass."³¹⁴ These Greek words not only recall God's provision for the Israelites in the wilderness but also anticipate the eschatological moment when the people of God will be gathered into community in the last days.³¹⁵ The eschatological banquet of the messianic age will be held in the transformed wilderness full of vitality.

Military images can also be found in the feeding episodes. In the OT, the metaphor of "the sheep without a shepherd" is especially related to the request for the military leadership, as when Moses asked God to appoint a leader to replace him for the upcoming campaigns (Num 27:17).³¹⁶ The groupings of "thousands, hundreds, fifties, and tens" were generally made for military units.³¹⁷ In Mark, Jesus saw the crowd as "sheep without a shepherd" (6:34) and ordered them to sit down in groups of hundreds and fifties (v. 40). In addition, the references to many people's movement of "coming and going" (v. 31) and Jesus' "arriving ahead of them" (v. 33) may indicate "the wilderness commotion" with "messianic fever."³¹⁸ These images depict Jesus as the militant-messianic warrior.

I do not believe, however, that Jesus' feeding miracles were performed in the context of military campaigns.³¹⁹ Rather, in both feeding episodes, the miracles are primarily the results of Jesus' compassion (σπλαγχνίζομαι, 6:34; 8:2) on the crowds who suffer from hunger. Jesus is here described as "the Messiah in whom the divine mercy is present."³²⁰ The crowds are fed with abundant food in the fullness of Jesus' grace. As Gnilka notes, the eschatological people of God are not summoned to prepare for warfare, but invited as the banqueters in Jesus' table fellowship (*Tischgemeinschaft*).³²¹ In the wilderness, therefore, Jesus gathered the crowds to have table fellowship, and true communion between Jesus and his people is accomplished in the messianic banquet.³²²

314. France, *Gospel of Mark*, 267.

315. Guelich, *Mark 1–8:26*, 341.

316. Budd, *Numbers*, 308.

317. However, the divisions in Exod 18:21, 25 are used for civilian groupings. See Stuart, *Exodus*, 418.

318. Edwards, *Gospel According to Mark*, 194. See also Brandon's argument that Jesus was a Zealot sympathizer (Brandon, *Jesus and the Zealots*, 221–83).

319. Edwards claims that Jesus will not be a "militant-messianic shepherd of the sheep." "His model as host of the wilderness banquet is not that of Barabbas, a Zealot chieftain, but that of Moses." See Edwards, *Gospel According to Mark*, 195.

320. Köster, "σπλάγχνον, σπλαγχνίζομαι, εὔσπλαγχνος, πολύσπλαγχνος, ἄσπλαγχνος," 7:554.

321. Gnilka, *Markus*, 261.

322. Refer to the practice of table fellowship as the messianic banquet in the Qumran

Conclusion

The exodus story was passed down for generations and deeply stamped on the memories of the Israelites. This story served not only as the basis for establishing their identity, but also as the ground for anticipating their future deliverance and restoration. In Mark's narrative, Jesus' ministry reflects the exodus events, and spatial arrangement and description allude to exodus images. The most important events in the exodus may be the victory at the Red Sea, the provision of manna and quail in the wilderness, and the giving of the Law at Mount Sinai. The sea, the wilderness, and the mountain function as the main settings of the crucial events of the exodus; they are also employed as the settings of Jesus' ministry in Mark's narrative. Before entering Jerusalem, Jesus performed his ministry for the kingdom of God in and around Galilee. He also attempted to take a missional journey beyond Galilee by crossing over the Sea of Galilee. At this point, the significant events disclosing Jesus' identity occurred against the background of spaces—the sea, the wilderness, and the mountain—that recall the exodus story. These events include Jesus' calming and walking on the sea (4:35-41; 6:45-52), his feeding of the five thousand and the four thousand in the wilderness (6:31-44; 8:1-10), and his transfiguration on the mountain (9:2-8). Not only are the contents of these events connected to the exodus events that occurred in the same spaces, but also the sequence of the spaces (the sea, the wilderness, and the mountain) is the same as in the exodus.

In the present study, I focused on Jesus' later ministry in and beyond Galilee (4:35—8:21). This section is divided according to a frame that reflects the exodus story: a first cycle of sea and desert miracles (4:35—6:44), a second cycle of sea and desert miracles (6:45—8:10), and a conclusion (8:11-21). The two sea miracles in Mark correspond to the victory at the sea in the exodus; the two feeding miracles in the wilderness are paralleled with the manna event in the desert. The sea-desert twin motifs are found frequently in the OT.[323] Psalm 78, a historical poem recounting the exodus events, shows particularly strong similarities in pattern (order) and other parallels with Mark 4:35—8:21.[324] The sea-desert twin motifs and the use of spatial settings play a significant role in revealing the similarities between these two passages. Psalm 78 consists of an introduction (vv. 1-11), two

---

Community (e.g., 1QSa 2:11-22).

323. E.g., Ps 78:13-25; 106:9; 107:23-31; Isa 40:12; 41:18; 51:10. See Kee, *Community of the New Age*, 112.

324. Earlier in this chapter, I examined the intertextual relationship (or innerbiblical allusions) between Ps 78(77):12-32 and Mark 4:35—8:21 in relation to pattern (order), settings, verbal agreements, and theme.

recitals (vv. 12–39; 40–64), and two sequels (vv. 33–39; 65–72). The first recital (vv. 12–32) begins with the victory at the sea, ends with the manna provision, and is followed by a conclusion denouncing Israel's unbelief. Likewise, Mark's two cycles (4:35—6:44; 6:45—8:10) begin with the sea miracles, end with the feeding miracles, and are followed by a concluding lament over the disciples' incomprehension and hardened hearts (8:11–21).

In the OT and Second Temple Jewish literature, the sea and the wilderness were interpreted in cosmological and eschatological dimensions. The sea, a physical obstacle blocking the Israelites' escape from the Egyptian army, was understood at another level as chaos that should be destroyed by God. God rebuked (גָּעַר, ἐπετίμησεν, Ps 106(105):9 and LXX; גְּעָרָה, ἀπειλή, Isa 50:2 and LXX) the sea and delivered the Israelites from the chaotic force of the sea; he also destroyed the Egyptian army to deliver the Israelites in the midst of the sea (ἐν μέσῳ τῆς θαλάσσης, Exod 14:29, LXX) and revealed himself in the pillar of fire and cloud. God's epiphany is expressed in the imagery of "walking on the sea" and "passing by" a person (παρέλθῃ, Exod 33:22, LXX; παρελεύσεται, 1 Kgs 19:11, LXX; περιπατῶν ... ἐπὶ θαλάσσης; παρέλθῃ; Job 9:8, 11, LXX). At the sea, then, God delivered his people by conquering the chaotic force and revealing himself in his power and majesty.

The two sea miracles in Mark (4:35–41; 6:45–52) reflect the exodus story, with the sea serving as a spatial setting that recollects God's victory at the sea. In the first sea miracle, Jesus rebuked (ἐπετίμησεν, 4:39) the storm-tossed sea and calmed it. In the second sea miracle, he appeared to the struggling disciples in the midst of the sea (ἐν μέσῳ τῆς θαλάσσης, 6:4), walking on the sea and passing by them (περιπατῶν ἐπὶ τῆς θαλάσσης ... παρελθεῖν, 6:48) while making the roaring sea cease. In these two episodes, the chaos-sea was subjugated and calmed by Jesus' rebuke and epiphany, and the disciples were safely delivered. The main thrust of these sea miracles is the redemption of God's people, through which Jesus is demonstrated as the universal Savior who has the power to control the chaos-sea. Mark's use of exodus imagery highlights the cosmological and eschatological significance of Jesus' redemptive work, which ultimately manifests his sovereignty over the universe.

The wilderness has a special meaning to the Israelites, for they were formed as the people of God in the wilderness wanderings of the exodus. The wilderness, like the sea, has cosmological and eschatological implications in the OT, Second Temple Jewish literature, and rabbinic writings. The wilderness stands for a place of chaos that will be transformed into the blessed land by God's grace. It is also the eschatological place where God leads his people as a shepherd who feeds and cares for them. Messianic expectation arose in the wilderness, where the eschatological banquet will be spread for the people of God in the messianic age.

The two feeding miracles (6:31–44; 8:1–10) echo the exodus story, and the wilderness functions as a spatial setting that recalls the manna event in the exodus. Like the Israelites in the desert, the disciples complained about the lack of food in the wilderness, concerned about how they could feed the crowds. Jesus responded by miraculously multiplying bread to feed the crowds in the wilderness. Here, the wilderness is the place where the eschatological blessing of the manna was accomplished in the light of the new exodus and the messianic banquet was spread in anticipation of the ultimate banquet at the end of time. Jesus called his disciples into the wilderness and gave them rest (6:31). Green grass (χλωρός χόρτος, v. 39) sprouted, implying the transformation of the wilderness. Jesus had compassion on the crowds because they were like sheep without a shepherd (v. 34) and arranged them to sit down in groups of hundreds and fifties (v. 40). All these details contribute to Mark's picture of Jesus as the eschatological shepherd who held the messianic banquet in the wilderness where he shared table fellowship with his people. In the feeding miracles, the wilderness serves as the place where Jesus was manifested as the Messiah who cared for his people as the eschatological shepherd and fed them with the messianic banquet.

In the sea and the desert miracles, Jesus "as the bearer of sovereign authority granted to him on behalf of the new covenant" redeemed and fed his people in "the eschatological re-enactment of the Exodus."[325] Jesus delivered his people at the sea and fed them in the wilderness, just as God did in the exodus. In the twice-repeated rescues and feedings, Jesus is manifested as the eschatological Savior who will redeem all the people, not only the Jews but also the Gentiles, and the universal Lord who will reign over cosmic forces.

---

325. Kee, *Community of the New Age*, 112.

chapter 5
Conclusion

Summary

In NT scholarship, the study of space has been underrepresented in comparison with the study of time. While Jesus' life and ministry have been intensively explored in terms of eschatology—i.e., with *time* significance—*space* has tended to be treated as simply a given room or inactive backdrop where events took place. Interest in the space where Jesus ministered has, however, gradually increased, and space has received greater attention from sociological and literary perspectives. In particular, spatial investigations into the social circumstances of Galilee, the place of origin of Jesus' missional movement, have begun to attract serious scholarly attention. The important functions of space in literature are also becoming better recognized: spatial settings serve not only to generate atmosphere but also to disclose the purposes and themes of narratives. The inclusion of spatial analysis in textual study will provide a fresh hermeneutical lens through which to interpret the NT literature.

In this study, I have employed spatial analysis to explore Jesus' missional movement in Mark 4:35—8:21. I distinguished between three kinds of space—"social," "geographical," and "allusive"—and examined the purposes and significance of Jesus' ministry in the light of each kind of space.

In chapter 1, I began by introducing the issues and questions raised by Markan spatial description, then explained the methodological approaches that I would employ to analyze each kind of space in Mark 4:35—8:21. Many scholars have regarded Mark's geographical description as inaccurate and vague and his geographical arrangement of Jesus' ministry as clumsy.

If we carefully examine Markan space, however, we can see that his spatial presentation was exquisitely shaped through the use of rhetorical devices to disclose his theological purposes.

I suggested three methodological approaches appropriate to the examination of three kinds of spaces. First, the theories of territoriality and representational space were introduced as tools for the study of social space. In light of these theories, Mark's spatial presentation of Jesus' itinerary in and beyond Galilee has the purpose of revealing Jesus' lordship over the territories where he traveled. Jesus' missional journey through both Jewish territory and Gentile territory implies that he is the lord not only of the Jews but also of the Gentiles. In addition, the exploration of Mark's representation of Galilean social environments discloses his theological or ideological views. By studying the dialectic relationship between spatial practice (the experienced) and representational space (the imagined), we can see how Mark understood Galilean society and expressed its social circumstances in his own narrative world.

Second, I considered geographical space through the use of a narrative approach to analyze the structure of Mark 4:35—8:21, focusing on settings that consist of time, space, and social circumstances and on the use of rhetorical devices. The spatial settings, which change according to Jesus' geographical movement, play a key role in forming the structure of this section, and the geographical movement is arranged according to Markan rhetorical devices. The narrative structure, based on geographical space, thus provides the hermeneutical framework of this section, which may disclose Mark's theological purpose.

Third, I introduced the concept of intertextuality and used allusion as a methodological approach to the study of allusive space. The places where Jesus ministered do not simply refer to physical locations; they also have historical, symbolic, ideological, or theological implications. Space serves to evoke memories of Israel's past or anticipations of her future. This study examined allusion to gain insight into how the sea and the wilderness reflect historical events of the exodus and the cosmological and eschatological implications of those events as they had been reinterpreted and represented in the OT and Second Temple Jewish literature. These implications function to reveal the significance of Jesus' sea and feeding miracles in the light of the new exodus.

In chapter 2, I considered the social space of Galilee. To begin, I surveyed a number of studies on the relationship between Galilee and Jerusalem. I do not accept the argument that Galilee and Jerusalem had a relationship of rivalry or conflict, because scholars have not discovered any traditional or material evidence that such conflict actually existed. There is also no evidence that Mark describes clashes between them, though he does portray Galilee and Jerusalem in different colors. Rather, as Freyne suggests, Jesus' geographical movement presents the "restoration of geography."[1] In his Galilean ministry, Jesus broke the ethnic boundaries between the Jews and the Gentiles; in his Jerusalem ministry, he established the new identity of the true people of God. Mark 4:35—8:21 portrays Jesus' missional journey into Jewish territory and Gentile territory, which destroyed ethnic barriers, accomplished the universal gathering of people around Jesus regardless of their ethnicity, and indicated that Jesus is the Savior of both the Jews and the Gentiles.

Next, I examined three features of Mark's narrative representation of the social space of Galilee. First, Galileans, though under the influence of a Jewish religious ethos, were open to a new order and values that differed from those of the temple and Jerusalem. Second, Galilean society contained complaints against the authority of Jerusalem; even as Jesus taught ideas and performed miracles that were opposed by the religious leaders of Jerusalem, Galileans welcomed Jesus, crediting him with "a new teaching with authority" (1:27). Third, Galilee is portrayed as the central place to which people from every direction could come to find Jesus and from which Jesus could go in every direction to meet them. In short, Mark describes Galilee as fertile ground for the development and success of Jesus' missional movement.

In chapter 3, I explored geographical space, focusing on the narrative structure of 4:35—8:21. Mark arranges the episodes of Jesus' ministry according to Jesus' geographical movement: the overall and explicit structure of Mark's narrative is Galilee (1:1—8:21); Journey to Jerusalem (8:22—10:52); Jerusalem (11:1—16:8). Mark 4:35—8:21 presents Jesus' missional movement in and beyond Galilee, in a cyclic pattern. The section consists of two cycles (4:35—6:44; 6:45—8:10) and a conclusion (8:11–21). The two cycles, divided according to Jesus' geographical movement, exhibit a repetitive pattern in their arrangement of Jesus' geographical movement from sea (4:35-41; 6:45-52), to land (5:1—6:30; 6:53—7:37), to wilderness (6:31-44; 8:1-10). The similarity between parallel episodes in the two cycles extends to their similar spatial settings: sea miracles at the sea; exorcisms, healings, and sayings on the land; feeding miracles in the wilderness. Geographical space, therefore, plays a significant role in forming the structure of this cyclic pattern. In each cycle, Jesus begins his journey with a voyage from west to east—during which he delivers his disciples at the sea—and he ends by feeding the crowd at the wilderness. Each cycle also includes an overland journey, during which Jesus exorcizes demons, heals the sick,

---

1. Freyne, "Geography of Restoration," 289–311.

and gives instructions relating to mission. While the first cycle focuses on Jesus' mission in Jewish territory, the second cycle focuses on his mission in Gentile territory; taken together, they indicate that Jesus is the Savior not only of the Jews, but also of the Gentiles.

Mark 8:11–21, which serves as the conclusion of the two cycles, includes boat and bread motifs. In particular, the discussion about bread between Jesus and his disciples on the sea (8:13–21) is related to the earlier sea and feeding miracles. Just as a way motif serves as the central axis of 8:22—10:52, a boat motif plays a key role in the structural framework of 4:35—8:21. The two sea miracles (4:35–41; 6:45–52) are connected to Jesus' discussion with his disciples on the sea (8:13–21) in that all these episodes take place in a boat. In addition, the disciples' incomprehension becomes worse with each boat episode: Jesus reproaches the disciples' lack of faith in 4:35; the disciples mistake Jesus for a ghost in 6:49; and in 8:17 Jesus rebukes the disciples for their ignorance about the meaning of bread despite their having experienced two feeding miracles. Jesus' twofold reproach—"Do you still not perceive or understand? Are your hearts hardened?"—in 8:17 is connected to the two previous sea miracles: the first rebuke is related to the disciples' question in the first sea miracle ("Who then is this?" [4:41]), and the second charge is related to the disciples' ignorance in the second sea miracle ("for their hearts were hardened" [6:52]). Jesus' discussion with his disciples on the sea (8:13–21) is also connected to the two feeding miracles (6:31–44; 8:1–10) by the bread motif, in that Jesus reminded the disciples of the meaning of bread by referring directly to the two feeding miracles (from the five loaves, five thousand were fed and twelve basketfuls of pieces were gathered [8:19]; and from the seven loaves, four thousand were fed and seven basketfuls of pieces were gathered [8:20]).

The themes of Christology and discipleship are combined and interrelated in Mark 4:35—8:21, but that this section may emphasize Christology more than discipleship. The disciples' fearful rhetorical question about Jesus' identity at the beginning of this section ("Who then is this?" [4:41]) is answered by Jesus' rebuking rhetorical question to the disciples at the end of the section ("Do you still not understand?" [8:21]). Though Jesus' rebuking question emphasizes the disciples' incomprehension, it inversely highlights Jesus' greatness. By asking this question, Jesus was able to remind his disciples of the miraculous works he had performed in feeding the four and five thousand people in the wilderness. Despite the disciples' incomprehension, Jesus consistently shows them who he is by performing mighty works. In the way-motif section on Jesus' journey to Jerusalem (8:22—10:52), Jesus reveals his identity to the disciples through a discussion or sayings in three passion predictions (8:31; 9:31; 10:33–34). Likewise, in this boat-motif section (4:35—8:21), Jesus discloses his identity to the disciples through miraculous works (e.g., the sea and feeding miracles).

In chapter 4, I examined allusive space, which may evoke memories of Israel's history. Space does not simply refer to a human field of activity—it also connotes historical traces, symbolic meanings, and ideological or theological significance. In Mark's narrative, for instance, the sea, the wilderness, and the mountain contain historical, symbolic, and ideological or theological implications, which may reflect the history of Israel. I argued that the sea and wilderness settings of Jesus' sea and feeding miracles (4:35–41; 6:31–44; 6:45–52; 8:1–10) serve to remind us of the exodus events that took place at the sea and in the wilderness. To begin, I examined structural parallelism between Mark 4:35—8:21 and Ps 78:12–32. The sea-desert twin motifs appear frequently in the Psalms and Isaiah.[2] Psalm 78:12–32, a historical poem describing the exodus events, provides particularly strong structural parallelism with Mark 4:35—6:44 and 6:45—8:10, in that the sea and the wilderness serve to frame the beginning and end in the passage. Just as God begins by delivering the Israelites during a sea-crossing and ends by feeding them with manna in the wilderness in Ps 78:12–32, Jesus begins with rescuing his disciples at the sea during a sea-crossing it and ends by feeding the crowd in the wilderness in Mark 4:35—6:44 and 6:45—8:10. Thematic parallelism is also evident, for just as the Israelites failed to stand in belief despite experiencing God's mighty works, the disciples do not understand who Jesus is despite seeing Jesus' miraculous works.

Next, I investigated how Jesus' sea and feeding miracles allude to the victory at the sea and the provision of manna in the wilderness during the exodus by tracing the spatial images and implications of the sea and the wilderness in the OT and Second Temple Jewish literature. The sea, which was an impediment and threat to the Israelites as they were chased by the Egyptian army, had been subject to cosmological and eschatological reinterpretations. The sea took on the imagery of cosmic chaos, which must be destroyed and ruled by God's mighty power. The song of Moses and Miriam (Exod 15:1-21) praises God for destroying the Egyptian army in the sea, using his mighty power to control the chaos-waters and manifesting his universal sovereignty over both earthly nations and cosmic forces. Several Psalms (e.g., 66:6; 74:13; 77:17–21; 78:13) celebrate the mighty power God revealed by dividing the sea and letting the Israelites pass through the waters. The sea (the waters) feared and trembled before God's presence, implying the complete subjugation of the chaos-waters under God's rule. Psalm

---

2. For instance, the sea-desert twin motifs appear in Ps 78:13–25; 106:9; 107:23–31 and in Isa 40:12; 41:18; 51:10. See Kee, *Community of the New Age*, 112.

106:9 (105:9 LXX) uses the Greek verb ἐπιτιμάω ("rebuke") to demonstrate God's control over the chaos-waters; this verb is similarly employed in Mark 4:39 when Jesus calms the wind-swept sea.

In Isaiah (e.g., 43:16–17; 50:2; 51:9–10; 63:12), God's victory over the Egyptian army at the sea is suggested as grounds for faith and anticipation of the Israelites' future redemption from Babylon. Isaiah's eschatological vision of the new exodus is based on God's past redemptive acts in the exodus from Egypt. Here too, the sea (the waters) is depicted as a chaotic force that must destroyed by God's power and God accomplishes his redemptive works by controlling the chaos-waters, thus manifesting his sovereignty over the universe. The cosmological and eschatological implications of the sea (the waters) in the exodus imagery ultimately elevate God's redemptive works into the universal dimension.

In Jesus' sea miracles, the sea reflects the exodus imagery. The storm-tossed sea is not only a threat to the disciples' lives but also a chaotic force to be rebuked by Jesus. In the two sea miracles, Jesus calmed the roaring sea by rebuking and walking on it, allowing his disciples to safely cross the sea. Jesus demonstrates his identity as the universal Savior by controlling and subjugating the chaos-sea. Jesus' redemptive works at the sea, which allude to the victory at the sea in the exodus, may be interpreted as a new exodus with cosmological and eschatological significance.

The wilderness is a special place in the history of Israel, for the Israelites established their identity as the people of God in the wilderness wanderings of the exodus. In the wilderness, God revealed himself to the Israelites by graciously providing for them or by punishing them for their sins. Though the Israelites constantly grumbled and sinned against God, he did not forsake them but consistently showed them his mercy and gracious care, particularly through his daily provision of manna and quail in the wilderness. In the OT and Second Temple Jewish literature, the wilderness is associated with diverse images and implications: it is portrayed as a state of chaos that by God's grace will be transformed into fertile land or a flat road for his coming (e.g., Ps 68:7–10; Isa 40:3; 41:17–20; 43:16–20), as a place where God cares for his people as the shepherd of Israel (e.g., Ps 78:52; Isa 40:11), and as a place of eschatological gathering and feeding at the banquet in the messianic age (e.g., 2 Bar. 29:8; 1QS 8:12–16; 1QSa 2:11–22).

Jesus' feeding miracles in Mark 6:31–44 and 8:1–10 allude to the manna event in the exodus, and the wilderness plays a key role in establishing this connection. Like the Israelites in the exodus, the disciples complained about the impossibility of finding food in the wilderness (8:4), but Jesus miraculously fed the crowd by multiplying bread. In the feeding miracles the wilderness not only serves as a prompt to recall the manna event but also carries cosmological and eschatological implications. The wilderness is depicted as the place where "green grass" (χλωρός χόρτος, 6:39) grows, which implies a transformed wilderness full of vitality. It is the place where Jesus the shepherd compassionately (6:34) guides and cares for his people and the place where Jesus gathers and feeds his people with a messianic banquet (6:39, 40). The grouping of hundreds and fifties and the expression "reclining (ἀνακλῖναι/ἀνέπεσαν) in groups (συμπόσια συμπόσια/πρασιαὶ πρασιαὶ)" recall not only the arrangement of the Israelites in the exodus, but also the image of the eschatological messianic banquet.

The sea and wilderness in Jesus' sea and feeding miracles serve as spatial backgrounds alluding to the exodus events in the past. These places also have cosmological and eschatological implications suggesting that Jesus' miracles are understood as the new exodus. In this way, Markan spatial allusions lead us to interpret Jesus' ministry in the light of the new exodus.

To conclude, exploring Mark's narrative on the basis of spatial analysis will provide a fresh hermeneutical framework for interpreting Jesus' life and ministry. Mark's narrative presentation of space is closely related to his understanding of Jesus' works—consequently, Markan spatial presentation reveals Mark's theological purposes. In Mark 4:35—8:21, Jesus' missional movement may be interpreted in terms of social space, where Galilee provided good soil for the growth of Jesus' missional ministry; in terms of geographical space, where the cyclic pattern of Jesus' travels present his missions both to the Jews and the Gentiles; and in terms of allusive space, where Jesus' missional works are interpreted in the light of the new exodus. In Markan spatial presentation, therefore, Jesus is depicted as the Savior of both the Jews and the Gentiles, and his missional ministry is portrayed as the new exodus.

Theological Implications

The main concern of this study has been to discover the theological themes of Mark 4:35—8:21 through a spatial analysis of Mark's narrative. This study of Markan spatial presentation may contribute to Markan scholarship by providing a fresh hermeneutical lens for the interpretation of Mark's narrative. This type of spatial analysis can also be used to explore other biblical writings.

First, the investigation of Mark's presentation of space plays an important role in disclosing his perspective on the world (social space) around him. Space is not simply described *per se*, but is instead "represented"

CONCLUSION 239

according to one's own view of the world. Mark selected and arranged the spaces, all of which centered on Jesus, in his own way. Mark also understood and described Jesus' spatial practices from a theological perspective (e.g., Jerusalem vs. Galilee or cities vs. villages). The study of how Mark understood Jesus' spatial practices and represented them in the narrative world serves to illuminate Mark's theological themes.

Second, this study is significant in its interpretation of Markan geographical space in the dimension of "narrative space"—that is, its exploration of Mark's geographical presentation in light of his literary techniques. Jesus' geographical movement in Mark's narrative must be examined not simply by tracing his itinerary, but also by investigating Mark's rhetorical devices. Though structural analyses based on the assumption of pre-Markan sources regard Mark's geographical description as inaccurate or vague, this study emphasizes the significance of geography in the narrative, arguing that Mark's portrayal of geography is not only correct but also intentionally theological. Mark's arrangement of Jesus' geographical movement is a key to constructing the narrative structure of Mark 4:35—8:21, in which Mark's theological themes may be disclosed. In order to show that Jesus is the Savior not only of the Jews but also of the Gentiles, Mark arranges Jesus' geographical movement in a cyclic pattern, traveling between Jewish and Gentile territories. A study of the pattern of spatial (geographical) changes therefore helps the reader to grasp the author's intentions and theological themes.

Third, the exploration of the connotative meanings of space may enrich our understanding of Mark's narrative. Space contains historical traces, symbolic meanings, and ideological or theological significance, and Mark projected these spatial implications into his narrative. Because biblical writings are closely related to past events and earlier biblical writings, Mark also reflects historical events and earlier biblical texts. In this sense, Markan space may allude to OT events and literature. This study illustrated the use of the sea and the wilderness as allusive spaces that recollect the cosmological and eschatological significance of exodus events, thereby demonstrating that Jesus' ministry in these spaces can be interpreted as a new exodus. The exploration of spatial allusions may therefore provide a fresh interpretive tool to advance our understanding of Mark's narrative and other biblical texts.

Finally, this study's integrative examination of social, geographical, and allusive space may lead us to a more comprehensive understanding of Mark's narrative. The Gospel of Mark is not only a historical record of Jesus' life, ministry, death, and resurrection, but also a literary work written in Mark's own literary style. Both the historical and the literary characteristics of Mark's narrative advance his theological themes. We need to understand the historical, literary, and theological aspects of Mark's work, and Markan space must be examined in an integrative way. This study carried out the spatial analysis of Mark's narrative using multi-dimensional approaches and presented the theological themes of Mark 4:35—8:21 from diverse angles.

The scholarly community needs to pay more attention to space in interpreting biblical literature, and this study has demonstrated how Mark 4:35—8:21 can be understood through spatial analysis. To gain a comprehensive understanding of a text, I looked at three categories of space—social, geographical, and allusive. The type of spatial analysis used in the present study should not be limited to the text I focused on, but should be applied to the other sections of Mark's narrative as well (e.g., 1:1—4:34; 8:22—10:52; and 11:1—16:8). Furthermore, this approach can be employed to analyze the spatial presentations of the other Synoptic Gospels and John, which exhibit both similarities and differences in their approaches to spatial presentation. In doing so, we can discover the individual and unique theological theme of each Gospel. These methods of spatial analysis can ultimately be used to interpret many other biblical writings and discover their theological themes. I hope the study of spatial presentation may lead us to a deeper and more fruitful understanding of the biblical writings.

Bibliography

Abrams, Meyer Howard, and Geoffrey Galt Harpham. *A Glossary of Literary Terms*. 9th ed. Boston: Wadsworth Cengage Learning, 2009.

Achtemeier, Paul J. "Person and Deed: Jesus and the Storm-Tossed Sea." *Int* 16 (1962) 169–76.

———. "Toward the Isolation of Pre-Markan Miracle Catenae." *JBL* 89 (1970) 265–91.

Albert, Pietersma, and Wright Benjamin G., eds. *A New English Translation of the Septuagint*. New York: Oxford University Press, 2007.

Allen, Leslie C. *Psalms 101–150*. Rev. ed. Word Biblical Commentary 21. Nashville: Thomas Nelson, 2002.

Allison, D. C., Jr. "Mountain and Wilderness." In *DJG* 563–65.

Alt, Albrecht. "Galiläische Problome." In *Kleine Schriften Zur Geschichte Des Volkes Israel II*, by Albrecht Alt, 363–435. München: C.H. Beck, 1953.

Alter, Robert. *The Art of Biblical Narrative*. Rev. ed. New York: Basic, 2011.

Anderson, A. A. *The Book of Psalms 1–72, 73–150*. New Century Bible. Grand Rapids: Eerdmans, 1972.

Anderson, Bernhard W. *Creation Versus Chaos: The Reinterpretation of Mythical Symbolism in the Bible*. Philadelphia: Fortress, 1987.

———. "Exodus Typology in Second Isaiah." In *Israel's Prophetic Heritage; Essays in Honor of James Muilenburg*, edited by Bernhard W. Anderson and Walter Harrelson, 177–95. New York: Harper & Brothers, 1962.

———. *Understanding the Old Testament*. 3d ed. Englewood Cliffs, NJ: Prentice-Hall, 1975.

Baarlink, Heinrich. *Anfängliches Evangelium: Ein Beitrag zur näheren Bestimmung der theologischen Motive im Markusevangelium*. Kampen: Kok, 1977.

Baker, David L. *Two Testaments, One Bible: The Theological Relationship Between the Old and New Testaments*. 3d ed. Downers Grove, IL: InterVarsity, 2010.

Baker, David W. "The Wind and the Waves: Biblical Theology in Protology and Eschatology." *ATJ* 34 (2002) 13–37.

Baltzer, Klaus. *Deutero-Isaiah: A Commentary on Isaiah 40–55*. Translated by Klaus Kohl. Hermeneia–A Critical and Historical Commentary on the Bible. Minneapolis: Fortress, 2001.

Barnwell, William H. *Our Story according to St. Mark*. Minneapolis: Winston, 1982.

Barr, James. "The Synchronic, the Diachronic, and the Historical: A Triangular Relationship?" In *Synchronic or Diachronic?: A Debate on Method in Old Testament Exegesis*, edited by Johannes C. de Moor, 1–14. Leiden: Brill, 1995.

Barthes, Roland. "Theory of the Text." In *Untying the Text: A Post-Structuralist Reader*, edited by Robert Young, 31–47. Boston: Routledge & Kegan Paul, 1981.
Bartholomew, Craig. "Introduction." In *"Behind" the Text: History and Biblical Interpretation*, edited by Craig Bartholomew, et al., 1–16. Scripture and Hermeneutics Series 4. Grand Rapids: Zondervan, 2003.
Bauer, David R. *The Structure of Matthew's Gospel: A Study in Literary Design*. JSNTSup 31. Sheffield: Almond, 1988.
Bauer, Walter. "Jesus der Galiläer." In *Festgabe für Adolf Jülicher zum 70. Geburtstag, 26. Januar 1927*, edited by Rudolf Bultmann, 16–34. Tübingen: J. C. B. Mohr, 1927.
———, et al. *Greek-English Lexicon of the New Testament and Other Early Christian Literature*. 3rd ed. Chicago: University of Chicago Press, 2000.
Beal, Timothy K. "Glossary." In *Reading Between Texts: Intertextuality and the Hebrew Bible*, edited by Danna Nolan Fewell, 21–24. Louisville: Westminster John Knox, 1992.
———. "Ideology and Intertextuality: Surplus of Meaning and Controlling the Means of Production." In *Reading Between Texts: Intertextuality and the Hebrew Bible*, edited by Danna Nolan Fewell, 27–39. Louisville: Westminster John Knox, 1992.
Beale, G. K., and D. A. Carson. "Introduction." In *Commentary on the New Testament Use of the Old Testament*, edited by G. K. Beale and D. A. Carson, 111–249. Grand Rapids: Baker Academic, 2007.
Berlin, Adele. *Poetics and Interpretation of Biblical Narrative*. Sheffield: Almond, 1983.
Bertram, Georg. "Der hellenismus in der Urheimat des Evangeliums." *AR* (1935) 265–81.
Best, Ernest. "Discipleship in Mark: Mark 8:22–10:52." *SJT* 23 (1970) 323–37.
———. *Following Jesus: Discipleship in the Gospel of Mark*. JSNTSup 4. Sheffield: JSOT Press, 1981.
———. *The Temptation and the Passion: The Markan Soteriology*. SNTSMS 2. Cambridge: Cambridge University Press, 1965.
Betz, Otto. "The Concept of the So-called 'Divine Man' in Mark's Christology." In *Studies in New Testament and Early Christian Literature: Essays in Honor of Allen P. Wikgren*, edited by David Edward Aune, 229–40. NovTSup 33. Leiden: Brill, 1972.
Bland, D. S. "Endangering the Reader's Neck: Background Description in the Novel." In *The Theory of the Novel*, edited by Philip Stevick, 313–31. New York: Free Press, 1967.
Blass, Friedrich, et al. *A Greek Grammar of the New Testament and Other Early Christian Literature*. Translated by Robert W. Funk. Chicago: University of Chicago Press, 1961.
Boring, M. Eugene. *Mark: A Commentary*. New Testament Library. Louisville: Westminster John Knox, 2006.
———. "Messianic Banquet." In *NIDB* 4:66–67.
Botterweck, G. J., and H. Ringgren, eds. *Theological Dictionary of the Old Testament*. Translated by J. T. Willis, et al. 15 vols. Grand Rapids: Eerdmans, 1974.
Bowman, John. *The Gospel of Mark: The New Christian Jewish Passover Haggadah*. Studia post-Biblica 8. Leiden: Brill, 1965.
Brandon, S. G. F. *Jesus and the Zealots: A Study of the Political Factor in Primitive Christianity*. New York: Scribner's Sons, 1967.
Brooks, James. *Mark*. The New American Commentary 23. Nashville: Broadman, 1991.

Brower, Kent E. "Review of Eric C. Stewart, *Gathered around Jesus: An Alternative Spatial Practice in the Gospel of Mark*." *JSNT* 33 (2011) 56-57.

Bruckner, James K. *Exodus*. New International Biblical Commentary on the Old Testament. Peabody: Hendrickson, 2008.

Brunson, Andrew C. *Psalm 118 in the Gospel of John: An Intertextual Study on the New Exodus Pattern in the Theology of John*. WUNT 2/158. Mohr Siebeck, 2003.

Buchanan, George Wesley. *Introduction to Intertextuality*. Lewiston: Mellen Biblical, 1994.

Buchholz, Sabine, and Manfred Jahn. "Space in Narrative." In *Routledge Encyclopedia of Narrative Theory*, edited by David Herman, et al., 551-55. London: Routledge, 2005.

Budd, Philip J. *Numbers*. Word Biblical Commentary 5. Waco, TX: Word, 1984.

Bultmann, Rudolf. *The History of the Synoptic Tradition*. Translated by John Marsh. 2nd ed. New York: Harper & Row, 1968.

Campbell, Antony F. "Psalm 78: A Contribution to the Theology of Tenth-Century Israel." *CBQ* 41 (1979) 51-79.

Carson, D. A. "Matthew" in *Matthew-Luke*, edited by Frank E. Gaebelein. Vol. 8. The Expositor's Bible Commentary. Grand Rapids: Zondervan, 1984.

―――, and Douglas J. Moo. *An Introduction to the New Testament*. 2nd ed. Grand Rapids: Zondervan, 2005.

Catchpole, David R. "The 'Triumphal' Entry." In *Jesus and the Politics of His Day*, edited by Ernst Bammel and C. F. D. Moule, 319-34. Cambridge: Cambridge University Press, 1984.

Chapman, Dean W. "Locating the Gospel of Mark: A Model of Agrarian Biography." *BTB* 25 (1995) 24-36.

―――. *The Orphan Gospel: Mark's Perspective on Jesus*. Sheffield: JSOT Press, 1993.

Charlesworth, James H., ed. *The Old Testament Pseudepigrapha*. 2 vols. New York: Doubleday, 1983.

Chatman, Seymour. *Story and Discourse: Narrative Structure in Fiction and Film*. Ithaca: Cornell University Press, 1978.

Clayton, Jay, and Eric Rothstein, eds. *Influence and Intertextuality in Literary History*. Madison: University of Wisconsin Press, 1991.

Clifford, Richard J. "The Exodus in the Christian Bible: The Case for 'Figural' Reading." *TS* 63 (2002) 345-61.

―――. *Fair Spoken and Persuading: An Interpretation of Second Isaiah*. New York: Paulist, 1984.

―――. "In Zion and David a New Beginning: An Interpretation of Psalm 78." In *Traditions in Transformation: Turning Points in Biblical Faith*, edited by Baruch Halpern and Jon D. Levenson, 121-41. Winona Lake, IN: Eisenbrauns, 1981.

Coats, George W. *Rebellion in the Wilderness: The Murmuring Motif in the Wilderness, Traditions of the Old Testament*. Nashville: Abingdon, 1968.

Collins, Adela Yarbro. *Mark: A Commentary*, edited by Harold W. Attridge. Hermeneia–A Critical and Historical Commentary on the Bible. Minneapolis: Fortress, 2007.

Collins, John J. "Messiah, Jewish." In *NIDB* 4:59-66.

Cope, O. Lamar. *Matthew: A Scribe Trained for the Kingdom of Heaven*. CBQMS 5. Washington: Catholic Biblical Association of America, 1976.

Cranfield, C. E. B. *The Gospel according to Saint Mark: An Introduction and Commentary*. Cambridge: Cambridge University Press, 1959.

Culler, Jonathan D. *The Pursuit of Signs: Semiotics, Literature, Deconstruction*. Ithaca: Cornell University Press, 1981.

Cullmann, Oscar. *Christ and Time: The Primitive Christian Conception of Time and History*. Translated by Floyd V. Filson. Rev. ed. Philadelphia: Westminster, 1964.

Curtis, Adrian H. W. "The 'Subjugation of the Waters' Motif in the Psalms, Imagery or Polemic?" *JSS* 23 (1978) 245–56.

Dahood, Mitchell J. *Psalms I:1–50*. Anchor Bible 16. Garden City: Doubleday, 1965.

Dalman, Gustaf. *Sacred Sites and Ways: Studies in the Topography of the Gospels*. Translated by Paul P. Levertoff. London: Society for Promoting Christian Knowledge, 1935.

Danker, F. W. "Mark 8:3." *JBL* 82 (1963) 215–16.

Daube, David. *The New Testament and Rabbinic Judaism*. JLCRS 2. New York: Arno, 1973.

Davies, William David. *The Gospel and the Land: Early Christianity and Jewish Territorial Doctrine*. Berkeley: University of California Press, 1974.

Dearman, J. Andrew. *The Book of Hosea*. New International Commentary on the Old Testament. Grand Rapids: Eerdmans, 2010.

Derrett, J. Duncan M. *The Making of Mark: The Scriptural Bases of the Earliest Gospel*. 2 vols. Shipston-on-Stour: Drinkwater, 1985.

Derrida, Jacques. *Dissemination*. Translated by Barbara Johnson. Chicago: University of Chicago Press, 1981.

———. "Living On: Border Lines." In *Deconstruction and Criticism*, edited by Harold Bloom, et al., 75–176. Translated by James Hulbert. New York: Continuum, 1979.

DeSilva, David Arthur. *An Introduction to the New Testament: Contexts, Methods & Ministry Formation*. Downers Grove, IL: InterVarsity, 2004.

Dewey, Joanna. "The Literary Structure of the Controversy Stories in Mark 2:1–3:6." In *The Interpretation of Mark*, edited by William R. Telford, 141–51. Philadelphia: Fortress, 1985.

———. "Mark as Interwoven Tapestry: Forecasts and Echoes for a Listening Audience." *CBQ* 53 (1991) 221–36.

———. *Markan Public Debate: Literary Technique, Concentric Structure, and Theology in Mark 2:1–3:6*. SBLDS 48. Chico: Scholars, 1980.

Dibelius, Martin. *From Tradition to Gospel*. Translated by Bertram Lee Woolf. 2nd ed. New York: Scribner's Sons, 1935.

Dodd, C. H. *The Parables of the Kingdom*. Rev. ed. New York: Scribner, 1961.

Donahue, John R., and Daniel Harrington. *The Gospel of Mark*. Sacra Pagina Series 2. Collegeville: Liturgical, 2002.

Dozeman, Thomas B. *Commentary on Exodus*. Eerdmans Critical Commentary. Grand Rapids: Eerdmans, 2009.

Draisma, Sipke, ed. *Intertextuality in Biblical Writings: Essays in Honour of Bas Van Iersel*. Kampen: J. H. Kok, 1989.

Durham, John I. *Exodus*. Word Biblical Commentary 3. Waco, TX: Word, 1987.

Edwards, James R. *The Gospel according to Mark*. Pillar New Testament Commentary. Grand Rapids: Eerdmans, 2002.

Eissfeldt, Otto. *The Old Testament: An Introduction, Including the Apocrypha and Pseudepigrapha, and Also the Works of Similar Type from Qumran: The History*

of the Formation of the Old Testament. Translated by Peter R. Ackroyd. Oxford: Blackwell, 1965.
Elliott-Binns, Leonard Elliott. *Galilean Christianity*. Studies in Biblical Theology. Chicago: Alec R. Allenson, 1956.
Enns, Peter. *Exodus*. The NIV Application Commentary. Grand Rapids: Zondervan, 2000.
Erlangen, Gerhard Friedrich. "Die beiden Erzählungen von der Speisung in Mark 6:31–44; 8:1–9." *Theologische Zeitschrift* 20 (1964) 10–22.
Evans, Craig A. "Listening for Echoes of Interpreted Scripture." In *Paul and the Scriptures of Israel*, edited by Craig A. Evans and James A. Sanders, 47–51. JSNTSup 83. Sheffield: JSOT Press, 1993.
———. *Mark 8:27–16:20*. Word Biblical Commentary 34B. Nashville: Thomas Nelson, 2001.
Farrer, Austin. *A Study in St. Mark*. Westminster: Dacre, 1951.
Ferguson, Sinclair B., et al., eds. *New Dictionary of Theology*. Leicester: InterVarsity, 1988.
Fishbane, Michael. *Biblical Interpretation in Ancient Israel*. Oxford: Clarendon, 1985.
———. "Inner Biblical Exegesis: Types and Strategies of Interpretation in Ancient Israel." In *Midrash and Literature*, edited by Geoffrey H. Hartman and Sanford Budick, 19–37. New Haven: Yale University Press, 1986.
Fisher, Fred L. "New and Greater Exodus: The Exodus Pattern in the New Testament." *SwJT* 20 (1977) 69–79.
Fleddermann, Harry. "'And He Wanted to Pass by Them' (Mark 6:48c)." *CBQ* 45 (1983) 389–95.
Fowler, Robert M. *Let the Reader Understand: Reader-Response Criticism and the Gospel of Mark*. Minneapolis: Fortress, 1991.
———. *Loaves and Fishes: The Function of the Feeding Stories in the Gospel of Mark*. SBLDS 54. Chico, CA: Scholars, 1981.
France, R. T. *The Gospel of Mark: A Commentary on the Greek Text*. New International Greek Testament Commentary. Grand Rapids: Eerdmans, 2002.
Freedman, David Noel, ed. *Anchor Bible Dictionary*. 6 vols. New York: Doubleday, 1992.
———, et al., eds. *Eerdmans Dictionary of the Bible*. Grand Rapids: Eerdmans, 2000.
Freyne, Seán. "Galilean Religion of the First Century CE against its Social Background." *PIBA* 5 (1981) 98–114.
———. *Galilee from Alexander the Great to Hadrian, 323 BCE to 135 CE: A Study of Second Temple Judaism*. Wilmington & Notre Dame: Michael Glazier & University of Notre Dame Press, 1980.
———. *Galilee, Jesus, and the Gospels: Literary Approaches and Historical Investigations*. Philadelphia: Fortress, 1988.
———. "Galilee-Jerusalem Relations according to Josephus's Life." *NTS* 33 (1987) 600–9.
———. "The Geography of Restoration: Galilee-Jerusalem Relations in Early Jewish and Christian Experience." *NTS* 47 (2001) 289–311.
———. "Jesus and the Urban Culture of Galilee." In *Text and Contexts: Biblical Texts in Their Textual and Situational Contexts: Essays in Honor of Lars Hartman*, edited by T. Fornberg and D. Hellholm, 75–121. Oslo: Scandinavian University Press, 1995.
———. "Urban-Rural Relations in the Light of the Literary Sources." In *Galilee and Gospel: Collected Essays*, 45–58. WUNT 125. Tübingen: Mohr Siebeck, 2000.

Garland, David E. *Mark*. The NIV Application Commentary Series. Grand Rapids: Zondervan, 1996.
Garrett, Duane A. *Hosea, Joel*. The New American Commentary 19A. Nashville: Broadman & Holman, 1997.
Geddert, Timothy J. "The Use of Psalms in Mark." *BT* 1 (2009) 109-24.
Genette, Gérard. *Narrative Discourse: An Essay in Method*. Translated by Jane E. Lewin. Ithaca: Cornell University Press, 1980.
Gibson, Jeffrey. "Jesus' Refusal to Produce a 'Sign' (Mk 8:11-13)." *JSNT* 38 (1990) 37-66.
Gnilka, Joachim. *Das Evangelium Nach Markus: Mk 1-8:26*. 5th ed. Evangelisch-Katholischer Kommentar zum Neuen Testament. Zürich: Benziger Verlag, 1998.
Goldingay, John. *The Message of Isaiah 40-55: A Literary-Theological Commentary*. London: T&T Clark, 2005.
———. *Psalms 42-89*. Baker Commentary on the Old Testament Wisdom and Psalms. Grand Rapids: Baker Academic, 2007.
———. *Psalms 90-150*. Baker Commentary on the Old Testament Wisdom and Psalms. Grand Rapids: Baker Academic, 2008.
Goppelt, Leonhard. *Typos, the Typological Interpretation of the Old Testament in the New*. Translated by Donald H. Madvig. Grand Rapids: Eerdmans, 1982.
Grassi, Joseph A. *Loaves and Fishes: The Gospel Feeding Narratives*. Collegeville: Liturgical, 1991.
Greenstein, Edward L. "Mixing Memory and Design: Reading Psalm 78." *Proof* (1990) 197-218.
Grundmann, Walter. *Jesus der Galiläer und das Judentum*. Leipzig: Verlag Georg Wigand, 1940.
Guelich, Robert A. *Mark 1-8:26*. Word Biblical Commentary 34A. Nashville: Thomas Nelson, 1989.
Gundry, Robert H. *Mark: A Commentary on His Apology for the Cross*. Grand Rapids: Eerdmans, 1993.
Gunkel, Hermann. *Die Psalmen*. 4th ed. Handkommentar zum Alten Testament 2/2. Göttingen: Vandenhoeck & Ruprecht, 1929.
———. *Schöpfung Und Chaos in Urzeit Und Endzeit: Eine Religionsgeschichtliche Untersuchung Über Gen 1 Und Ap Joh 12*. Göttingen: Vandenhoeck und Ruprecht, 1895.
Gunther, Müller. "Erzählzeit und erzählte Zeit." In *Festschrift für Paul Kluckhohn und Hermann Schneider gewidmet zu ihrem 60*, 195-212. Tübingen: J. C. B. Mohr, 1948.
Haenchen, Ernst. *Der Weg Jesu: Eine Erklärung des Markus-Evangeliums und der kanonischen Parallelen*. Berlin: Töpelmann, 1966.
Hamilton, Victor P. *The Book of Genesis: Chapters 1-17*. New International Commentary of the Old Testament. Grand Rapids: Eerdmans, 1990.
Harner, Philip B. "Creation Faith in Deutero-Isaiah." *VT* 17 (1967) 298-306.
Harvey, David. *The Condition of Postmodernity: An Enquiry into the Origins of Cultural Change*. Oxford: Blackwell, 1990.
Harvey, Julien. "La typologie de l'Exode dans les Psaumes." *ScEccl* 15 (1963) 383-405.
Hatina, Thomas R. *In Search of a Context: The Function of Scripture in Mark's Narrative*. JSNTSup 232. London: Sheffield Academic, 2002.
Hawthorne, Gerald F., et al., eds. *Dictionary of Paul and His Letters*. Downers Grove, IL: InterVarsity, 1993.

Hays, Richard B. *Echoes of Scripture in the Letters of Paul*. New Haven: Yale University Press, 1989.
Healy, Mary. *The Gospel of Mark*. Catholic Commentary on Sacred Scripture. Grand Rapids: Baker Academic, 2008.
Hedrick, Charles W. "What Is a Gospel: Geography, Time and Narrative Structure." *PRSt* 10 (1983) 255–68.
Heidel, Alexander. *The Babylonian Genesis; The Story of the Creation*. 2nd ed. Chicago: University of Chicago Press, 1951.
Heil, John Paul. *Jesus Walking on the Sea: Meaning and Gospel Functions of Matt 14:22–23, Mark 6:45–52, and John 6:15b–21*. AnBib 87. Rome: Biblical Institute, 1981.
Henderson, Suzanne Watts. *Christology and Discipleship in the Gospel of Mark*. SNTSMS 135. Cambridge: Cambridge University Press, 2006.
Hobbs, E. C. "The Gospel of Mark and the Exodus." PhD diss., University of Chicago, 1958.
Homan, Michael M. "Bethsaida." In *EDB* 174.
Hooker, Morna D. *The Gospel according to Saint Mark*. Black's New Testament Commentaries. Peabody: Hendrickson, 1991.
———. "Isaiah in Mark's Gospel." In *Isaiah in the New Testament*, edited by Steve Moyise and Maarten J. J. Menken, 35–49. London: T&T Clark, 2005.
———. "Mark." In *It Is Written: Scripture Citing Scripture: Essays in Honour of Barnabas Lindars, SSF*, 220–30. Cambridge: Cambridge University Press, 1988.
Horsley, Richard A. *Archaeology, History, and Society in Galilee: The Social Context of Jesus and the Rabbis*. Valley Forge: Trinity International, 1996.
———. *Galilee: History, Politics, People*. Valley Forge: Trinity International, 1995.
Hossfeld, Frank-Lothar, and Erich Zenger. *Psalms 2: A Commentary on Psalms 51–100*. Translated by Linda M. Maloney. Hermeneia–A Critical and Historical Commentary on the Bible. Minneapolis: Fortress, 2005.
Iverson, Kelly R. *Gentiles in the Gospel of Mark: Even the Dogs Under the Table Eat the Children's Crumbs*. LNTS 339. London: T&T Clark, 2007.
Jenkins, Luke H. "A Marcan Doublet: Mark Vi. 31–vii. 37, and Viii. 1–26." In *Studies in History and Religion: Presented to Dr. H. Wheeler Robinson, MA, on His Seventieth Birthday*, edited by Ernest A. Payne, 87–111. London: Lutterworth, 1942.
Jeremias, Joachim. *The Eucharistic Words of Jesus*. Translated by Norman Perrin. New Testament Library. London: SCM, 1966.
———. "Μωυσῆς." In *TDNT* 4:848–73.
Johnson, Earl S., Jr. "Mark 10:46–52: Blind Bartimaeus." *CBQ* 40 (1978) 191–204.
Johnson, S. E. *A Commentary on the Gospel according to St. Mark*. Harper's New Testament Commentaries. New York: Harper, 1960.
Johnston, James A. "Mark 2:1–3:6 and the Sequence of Isaiah's New Exodus in Isaiah 57:14–58:14." PhD diss., Trinity Evangelical Divinity School, 2008.
Johnston, R. J. *A Question of Place: Exploring the Practice of Human Geography*. Oxford: Blackwell, 1991.
Jones, Brian C. "Wilderness." In *NIDB* 5:848–52.
Jonge, Marinus de. "Messiah." In *ABD* 4:777–88.
Josephus, Flavius. "The Wars of the Jews." In *The Works of Josephus: Complete and Unabridged*, translated by William Whiston, 543–772. Peabody: Hendrickson, 1987.
Juel, Donald. "Messiah." In *EDB* 889–90.

Kakkanattu, Joy Philip. *God's Enduring Love in the Book of Hosea: A Synchronic and Diachronic Analysis of Hosea 11:1–11*. Forschungen zum Alten Testament 2. Reihe 14. Tübingen: Mohr Siebeck, 2006.

Katzenstein, H. J. "Tyre." In *ABD* 6:686–90.

Keck, Leander E. "Mark 3:7–12 and Mark's Christology." *JBL* 84 (1965) 341–48.

Kee, Howard Clark. *Community of the New Age: Studies in Mark's Gospel*. Philadelphia: Westminster, 1977.

———. "Review of Werner Kelber, *The Kingdom in Mark: A New Place and a New Time*." *JR* 56 (1976) 122–23.

———. "The Terminology of Mark's Exorcism Stories." *NTS* 14 (1968) 232–46.

Keener, Craig S. *The Gospel of Matthew: A Socio-Rhetorical Commentary*. Grand Rapids: Eerdmans, 2009.

Keesmaat, Sylvia C. "Exodus and the Intertextual Transformation of Tradition in Romans 8:14–30." *JSNT* 54 (1994) 29–56.

Kelber, Werner H. *The Kingdom in Mark: A New Place and a New Time*. Philadelphia: Fortress, 1974.

———. *Mark's Story of Jesus*. Philadelphia: Fortress, 1979.

———. *The Oral and the Written Gospel: The Hermeneutics of Speaking and Writing in the Synoptic Tradition, Mark, Paul, and Q*. Philadelphia: Fortress, 1983.

Kittel, Gisela. "'Wer Ist Der?' Markus 4:35–41." In *Jesus Christus als die Mitte der Schrift: Studien zur Hermeneutik des Evangeliums*, edited by Christof Landmesser, et al., 517–42. BZNW 86. Berlin: de Gruyter, 1997.

———. "ἔρημος, ἐρημία, ἐρημόω, ἐρήμωσις." In *TDNT* 2:657–60.

———, and G. Friedrich, eds. *Theological Dictionary of the New Testament*. Translated by G. W. Bromiley. 10 vols. Grand Rapids: Eerdmans, 1964–1976.

Koch, Dietrich Alex. *Die Bedeutung der Wundererzählungen für die Christologie des Markusevangeliums*. BZNW 42. Berlin: de Gruyter, 1975.

Kort, Wesley A. *Narrative Elements and Religious Meanings*. Philadelphia: Fortress, 1975.

Köster, H. "σπλάγχνον, σπλαγχνίζομαι, εὔσπλαγχνος, πολύσπλαγχνος, ἄσπλαγχνος." In *TDNT* 7:548–59.

Kraus, Hans-Joachim. *Psalms 60–150*. Translated by Hilton C. Oswald. Minneapolis: Fortress, 1993.

Kristeva, Julia. *Desire in Language: A Semiotic Approach to Literature and Art*. Edited by Leon S. Roudiez. Translated by Thomas Gora, et al. New York: Columbia University Press, 1980.

———. *Revolution in Poetic Language*. Translated by M. Waller. New York: Columbia University Press, 1984.

Kroeger, Catherine C. "Women in Greco-Roman World and Judaism." In *DNTB* 1276–80.

Kuhn, Heinz-Wolfgang. *Ältere Sammlungen im Markusevangelium*. SUNW 8. Göttingen, Germany: Vandenhoeck & Ruprecht, 1971.

Kümmel, Werner Georg. *Introduction to the New Testament*. Translated by Howard Clark Kee. Rev. ed. Nashville: Abingdon, 1975.

———. *Promise and Fulfilment: The Eschatological Message of Jesus*. 3d and rev. ed. SBT 23. London: SCM, 1961.

Kurz, William S. "Intertextual Use of Sirach 48:1–16 in Plotting Luke-Acts." In *The Gospels and the Scriptures of Israel*, edited by Craig A. Evans and William Richard Stegner, 308–24. JSNTSup 104. Sheffield: Sheffield Academic, 1994.

Lampe, G. W. H., and K. J. Woollcombe. *Essays on Typology*. SBT 22. Naperville: Alec R. Allenson, 1957.

Lane, William L. *The Gospel according to Mark: The English Text with Introduction, Exposition, and Notes*. New International Commentary on the New Testament. Grand Rapids: Eerdmans, 1974.

Lang, Friedrich Gustav. "'Über Sidon mitten ins Gebiet der Dekapolis' Geographie Und Theologie in Markus 7:31." *ZDPV* 94 (1978) 145–60.

Leal, Robert Barry. *Wilderness in the Bible: Toward a Theology of Wilderness*. New York: Peter Lang, 2004.

Lefebvre, Henri. *The Production of Space*. Translated by Donald Nicholson-Smith. Oxford: Blackwell, 1991.

Lenski, Gerhard. *Power and Privilege: A Theory of Social Stratification*. New York: McGraw, 1966.

Leonard, Jeffery M. "Identifying Inner-Biblical Allusions: Psalm 78 as a Test Case." *JBL* 127 (2008) 241–65.

Lévi-Strauss, Claude. "The Structural Study of Myth." *JAF* 68 (1955) 428–44.

Lightfoot, Robert Henry. *Locality and Doctrine in the Gospels*. The Bampton Lectures. New York: Harper and Brothers, 1938.

Lim, Bo H. "The 'Way of the Lord' in the Book of Isaiah." PhD diss., Trinity Evangelical Divinity School, 2006.

Limburg, James. *Jonah: A Commentary*. Old Testament Library. Louisville: Westminster John Knox, 1993.

Lohmeyer, Ernst. *Das Evangelium des Markus*. 17th ed. KEK. Göttingen: Vandenhoeck & Ruprecht, 1967.

———. *Galiläa und Jerusalem*. FRLANT 4. Göttingen: Vandenhoeck & Ruprecht, 1936.

Loos, Hendrik van der. *The Miracles of Jesus*. NovTSup 9. Leiden: Brill, 1968.

Lührmann, Dieter. *Das Markusevangelium*. HNT. Tübingen: Mohr Siebeck, 1987.

———. "Die Pharisäer und die Schriftgelehrten im Markusevangelium." *ZNW* 78 (1987) 169–85.

Malbon, Elizabeth Struthers. "Echoes and Foreshadowings in Mark 4–8: Reading and Rereading." *JBL* 112 (1993) 211–30.

———. "Galilee and Jerusalem: History and Literature in Marcan Interpretation." *CBQ* 44 (1982) 242–55.

———. *Hearing Mark: A Listener's Guide*. Harrisburg: Trinity International, 2002.

———. "The Jesus of Mark and the Sea of Galilee." *JBL* 103 (1984) 363–77.

———. "Narrative Criticism: How Does the Story Mean?" In *Mark & Method: New Approaches in Biblical Studies*, edited by Janice Capel Anderson and Stephen D. Moore, 29–57. 2nd ed. Minneapolis: Fortress, 1992.

———. *Narrative Space and Mythic Meaning in Mark*. San Francisco: Harper & Row, 1986.

Malina, Bruce J. "Christ and Time: Swiss or Mediterranean?" *CBQ* 51 (1989) 1–31.

———. *The Palestinian Manna Tradition: The Manna Tradition in the Palestinian Targums and Its Relationship to the New Testament Writings*. Leiden: Brill, 1968.

Manser, Martin, et al., eds. *Dictionary of Bible Themes: The Accessible and Comprehensive Tool for Topical Studies*. Grand Rapids: Zondervan, 1999.

Marcus, Joel. *Mark 1-8: A New Translation with Introduction and Commentary*. Anchor Bible 27. New York: Doubleday, 2000.

———. *Mark 8-16: A New Translation with Introduction and Commentary*. Anchor Bible 27A. New Haven: Yale University Press, 2009.

———. *The Way of the Lord: Christological Exegesis of the Old Testament in the Gospel of Mark*. Louisville: Westminster John Knox, 1992.

Martin, William C. "An Exegesis of Isaiah 51:9–11." *ResQ* 9 (1966) 151–59.

Martínez, Florentino García, ed. *The Dead Sea Scrolls Translated: The Qumran Texts in English*. Translated by Wilfred G. E. Watson. 2nd ed. Leiden: Brill, 1996.

Marxsen, Willi. *Mark the Evangelist: Studies on the Redaction History of the Gospel*. Translated by James Boyce, et al. Nashville: Abingdon, 1969.

Mason, Steve. "Pharisees." In *EDB* 1043–44.

Matera, Frank J. "The Incomprehension of the Disciples and Peter's Confession (Mark 6:14–8:30)." *Bib* 70 (1989) 153–72.

Mathews, Claire R. *Defending Zion: Edom's Desolation and Jacob's Restoration (Isaiah 34–35) in Context*. BZAW 236. New York: de Gruyter, 1995.

Mathews, K. A. *Genesis 1–11:26*. The New American Commentary 1A. Nashville: Broadman & Holman, 1996.

Mathewson, David. "New Exodus as a Background for 'The Sea Was No More' in Revelation 21:1c." *TJ* 24 (2003) 243–58.

Mauser, Ulrich W. *Christ in the Wilderness: The Wilderness Theme in the Second Gospel and Its Basis in the Biblical Tradition*. SBT 39. London: SCM, 1963.

Mays, James L. *Hosea: A Commentary*. The Old Testament Library. Philadelphia: Westminster, 1969.

———. *Psalms*. Interpretation: A Bible Commentary for Teaching and Preaching. Louisville: John Knox, 1994.

McKnight, Scot, and Joel B. Green, eds. *Dictionary of Jesus and the Gospels*. Downers Grove, IL: InterVarsity, 1992.

Meier, John P. *A Marginal Jew: Rethinking the Historical Jesus: Companions and Competitors*. Vol. 3. 1st ed. Anchor Bible Reference Library. New York: Doubleday, 1991.

Meyer, Eduard. *Ursprung und Anfänge des Christentums*. Stuttgart and Berlin: J. G. Cotta, 1921.

Meyers, Carol L. *Exodus*. New Cambridge Bible Commentary. Cambridge: Cambridge University Press, 2005.

Meyers, Eric M. "Jesus and His Galilean Context." In *Archaeology and the Galilee: Texts and Contexts in the Graeco-Roman and Byzantine Periods*, edited by Douglas R. Edwards and C. Thomas McCollough, 57–66. Atlanta: Scholars, 1997.

Moloney, Francis J. *The Gospel of Mark: A Commentary*. Grand Rapids: Baker Academic, 2002.

Moore, Stephen D. *Poststructuralism and the New Testament: Derrida and Foucault at the Foot of the Cross*. Minneapolis: Fortress, 1994.

Mowery, Robert L. "Pharisees and Scribes, Galilee and Jerusalem." *ZNW* 80 (1989) 266–68.

Moxnes, Halvor. "The Construction of Galilee as a Place for the Historical Jesus—Part I." *BTB* 31 (2001) 26–37.

———. "The Construction of Galilee as a Place for the Historical Jesus—Part II." *BTB* 31 (2001) 64–77.
Moyise, Steve. "Intertextuality and the Study of the Old Testament in the New Testament." In *The Old Testament in the New Testament: Essays in Honour of J. L. North*, edited by Steve Moyise, 14–41. JSNTSup 189. Sheffield: Sheffield Academic, 2000.
Neirynck, Frans. "Duality in Mark." *ETL* 47 (1971) 394–463.
———. *Duality in Mark: Contributions to the Study of the Markan Redaction*. Leuven: Leuven University Press, 1972.
———. "Duplicate Expressions in the Gospel of Mark." *ETL* 48 (1972) 150–209.
———. "L'Évangile de Marc: Á Propos D'un Noveau Commentaire." *ETL* 53 (1977) 153–81.
Neusner, Jacob. *First-Century Judaism in Crisis; Yohanan Ben Zakkai and the Renaissance of Torah*. Nashville: Abingdon, 1975.
Nineham, D. E. *The Gospel of St. Mark*. Baltimore: Penguin, 1963.
Ninow, Friedbert. "Typology." In *EDB* 1341.
Nixon, R. E. *The Exodus in the New Testament*. Tyndale New Testament Lecture. London: Tyndale, 1963.
Noll, S. F. "Qumran and Paul." In *DPL* 777–83.
O'Day, Gail R. "Jeremiah 9:22–23 and 1 Corinthians 1:26–31: A Study in Intertextuality." *JBL* 109 (1990) 259–67.
Oepke, Albrecht. "γυνή." In *TDNT* 1:776–89.
Osborne, Grant R. *The Hermeneutical Spiral: A Comprehensive Introduction to Biblical Interpretation*. 2nd ed. Downers Grove, IL: InterVarsity, 2006.
———. *Matthew*. Zondervan Exegetical Commentary on the New Testament. Grand Rapids: Zondervan, 2010.
———. "Redaction Criticism." In *New Testament Criticism and Interpretation*, edited by David Alan Black and David S. Dockery, 199–224. Grand Rapids: Zondervan, 1991.
Oswalt, John N. *The Book of Isaiah: Chapters 40–66*. New International Commentary of the Old Testament. Grand Rapids: Eerdmans, 1998.
———. *Isaiah*. The NIV Application Commentary. Grand Rapids: Zondervan, 2003.
Otzen, Benedikt, et al. *Myths in the Old Testament*. Translated by Frederick Cryer. London: SCM, 1980.
Overman, Andrew. "Jesus of Galilee and the Historical Peasant." In *Archaeology and the Galilee: Texts and Contexts in the Graeco-Roman and Byzantine Periods*, edited by Douglas R. Edwards and C. Thomas McCollough, 67–73. Atlanta: Scholars, 1997.
Paffenroth, Kim. "Scribes." In *EDB* 1173.
Painter, John. *Mark's Gospel: Worlds in Conflict*. London: Routledge, 1997.
Pao, David W. *Acts and the Isaianic New Exodus*. WUNT 2/130. Tübingen: Mohr Siebeck, 2000.
Patterson, Richard D. "Victory at Sea: Prose and Poetry in Exodus 14–15." *BSac* 161 (2004) 42–54.
Perkins, Larry. "Kingdom, Messianic Authority and the Re-Constituting of God's People: Tracing the Function of Exodus Material in Mark's Narrative." In *Biblical Interpretation in Early Christian Gospels, Volume 1: The Gospel of Mark*, edited by Thomas R. Hatina, 100–15. LNTS 304. London: T&T Clark, 2006.

Perrin, Norman. *The New Testament, an Introduction: Proclamation and Parenesis, Myth and History.* New York: Harcourt Brace Jovanovich, 1974.
Pesch, Rudolf. *Das Markusevangelium 1. Teilband: Einleitung und Kommentar zu Kap. 1:1–8:26.* 2nd ed. Herders theologischer Kommentar zum Neuen Testament. Freiburg, Germany: Herder, 1977.
———. *Naherwartungen: Tradition und Redaktion in Mark 13.* Dusseldorf: Patmos-Verlag, 1968.
Petersen, Norman R. "The Composition of Mark 4:1–8:26." *HTR* 73 (1980) 185–217.
———. *Literary Criticism for New Testament Critics.* Philadelphia: Fortress, 1978.
Pfister, Manfred. "Konzepte der Intertextualität." In *Intertextualität: Formen, Funktionen, anglistische Fallstudien,* edited by Broich Ulich and Manfred Pfister, 1–30. Tübingen: Niemeyer, 1985.
Phelan, John E. "Rhetoric and Meaning in Mark 6:30–8:10." PhD diss., Northwestern University, 1985.
Piaget, Jean, and Bärbel Inhelder. *The Child's Conception of Space.* Translated by F. J. Langdon and J. L. Lunzer. London: Routledge and Kegan Paul, 1956.
Pickup, Martin. "Matthew's and Mark's Pharisees." In *In Quest of the Historical Pharisees,* edited by Jacob Neusner and Bruce D. Chilton, 67–112. Waco, TX: Baylor University Press, 2007.
Piper, Otto A. "Unchanging Promises: Exodus in the New Testament." *Int* 11 (1957) 3–22.
Porter, Stanley E. "The Use of the Old Testament in the New Testament: A Brief Comment on Method and Terminology." In *Early Christian Interpretation of the Scriptures of Israel: Investigations and Proposals,* edited by Craig A. Evans and James A. Sanders, 79–96. Sheffield: Sheffield Academic, 1997.
———, and Craig A. Evans, eds. *Dictionary of New Testament Background: A Compendium of Contemporary Biblical Scholarship.* Downers Grove, IL: InterVarsity, 2000.
Powell, Mark Allan. *What Is Narrative Criticism?* Guides to Biblical Scholarship. Minneapolis: Fortress, 1990.
Power, Edmond. "The Staff of the Apostles: A Problem in Gospel Harmony." *Bib* 4 (1923) 241–66.
Propp, William H. C. *Exodus 1–18: A New Translation with Introduction and Commentary.* Anchor Bible 2. New York: Doubleday, 1999.
———. *Water in the Wilderness: A Biblical Motif and Its Mythological Background.* HSM 40. Atlanta: Scholars, 1987.
Rad, Gerhard von. *Genesis: A Commentary.* Rev. ed. Philadelphia: Westminster, 1972.
Rawlinson, A. E. J. *St. Mark.* Westminster Commentaries. London: Methuen, 1925.
Reid, Daniel G., ed. *The IVP Dictionary of the New Testament: A One-Volume Compendium of Contemporary Biblical Scholarship.* Downers Grove, IL: InterVarsity, 2004.
Rengstorf, K. H. "σημεῖον." In *TDNT* 7:200–61.
Resseguie, James L. *Narrative Criticism of the New Testament: An Introduction.* Grand Rapids: Baker Academic, 2005.
Rey-Coquais, Jean-Paul. "Decapolis." In *ABD* 2:116–21.
Reymond, Philippe. *L'eau, sa vie, et sa signification dans l'Ancien Testament.* VTSup 6. Leiden: Brill, 1958.

Rhoads, David, et al. *Mark as Story: An Introduction to the Narrative of a Gospel.* 2nd ed. Minneapolis: Augsburg Fortress, 1999.

Rhoads, David. "Narrative Criticism and the Gospel of Mark." *JAAR* 50 (1982) 411–34.

———. "Narrative Criticism of the New Testament." In *Method and Meaning: Essays on New Testament Interpretation in Honor of Harold W. Attridge*, edited by Andrew B. McGowan and Kent Harold Richards, 107–24. Atlanta: Society of Biblical Literature, 2011.

———. *Reading Mark: Engaging the Gospel.* Minneapolis: Fortress, 2004.

———. "Social Criticism." In *Mark & Method: New Approaches in Biblical Studies*, edited by Janice Capel Anderson and Stephen D. Moore, 145–79. 2nd ed. Minneapolis: Fortress, 1992.

Riches, John K. *Conflicting Mythologies: Identity Formation in the Gospels of Mark and Matthew.* Studies of the New Testament and Its World. Edinburgh: T&T Clark, 2000.

Ringgren, L. "יָם, *yām*." In *TDOT* 6:87–98.

Robbins, Vernon K. *Exploring the Texture of Texts: A Guide to Socio-Rhetorical Interpretation.* Harrisburg: Trinity International, 1996.

Rosner, Brian S. *Paul, Scripture, and Ethics: A Study of 1 Corinthians 5–7.* Grand Rapids: Baker, 1999.

Sack, Robert David. "Human Territoriality: A Theory." *AAAG* 73 (1983) 55–74.

———. *Human Territoriality: Its Theory and History.* Cambridge: Cambridge University Press, 1986.

Sakenfeld, Katharine Doob, ed. *The New Interpreter's Dictionary of the Bible.* 5 vols. Nashville: Abingdon, 2006–2009.

Saldarini, Anthony J. "Pharisees." In *ABD* 5:289–303.

———. "Political and Social Roles of the Pharisees and Scribes in Galilee." In *SBL Seminar Papers*, 200–9. Vol. 27. Atlanta: Scholars, 1988.

———. "Scribes." In *ABD* 5:1012–16.

Sawicki, Marianne. "Spatial Management of Gender and Labor in Greco-Roman Galilee." In *Archaeology and the Galilee: Texts and Contexts in the Graeco-Roman and Byzantine Periods*, edited by Douglas R. Edwards and C. Thomas McCollough, 7–28. Atlanta: Scholars, 1997.

Schmid, Josef. *Das Evangelium nach Markus.* 2nd ed. Regensburger Neues Testament 2. Regensburg: F. Pustet, 1950.

Schmidt, Daryl D. *The Gospel of Mark: With Introduction, Notes, and Original Text.* Sonoma, CA: Polebridge, 1991.

Schneck, Richard. *Isaiah in the Gospel of Mark I–VIII.* Vallejo, CA: BIBAL, 1994.

Scholer, D. M. "Women I: Gospels." In *IVPDNT* 1095–102.

Schreiber, Johannes. *Theologie des Vertrauens: Eine redaktionsgeschichtliche Untersuchung des Markusevangeliums.* Hamburg: Furche-Verlag, 1967.

Seely, David Rolph. "The Image of the Hand of God in the Exodus Traditions." PhD diss., University of Michigan, 1990.

Sherwin-White, A. N. *Roman Society and Roman Law in the New Testament.* Grand Rapids: Baker, 1963.

Smalley, Stephen S. "Redaction Criticism." In *New Testament Interpretation: Essays on Principles and Methods*, edited by I. Howard Marshall, 181–95. Grand Rapids: Eerdmans, 1977.

Smith, Billy K., and Franklin S. Page. *Amos, Obadiah, Jonah*. The New American Commentary 19B. Nashville: Broadman & Holman, 1995.
Smith, Dennis E. "Messianic Banquet." In *ABD* 4:788–91.
Smith, Gary V. *Isaiah 40–66*. The New American Commentary 15B. Nashville: Broadman & Holman, 2009.
Smith, Stephen H. "Bethsaida via Gennesaret: The Enigma of the Sea-Crossing in Mark 6:45–53." *Bib* 77 (1996) 349–74.
———. *A Lion with Wings: A Narrative-Critical Approach to Mark's Gospel*. Sheffield: Sheffield Academic, 1996.
Snoy, Thierry. "Marc 6:48: '. . . et il voulait les dépasser': proposition pour la solution d'une énigme." In Évangile Selon Marc, edited by M. Sabbe, 347–63. BETL 34. Louvain: Louvain University Press, 1973.
Soden, Hermann von. "Das Interesse des apostolischen Zeitalters an der evangelischen Geschichte." In *Theologische abhandlungen. Carl von Weisäcker zu seinem siebzigsten geburstage, 11. December 1892*, 111–69. Freiburg: Mohr Siebeck, 1892.
Sommer, Benjamin D. *A Prophet Reads Scripture: Allusion in Isaiah 40–66*. Stanford: Stanford University Press, 1998.
Stanley, Christopher D. *Paul and the Language of Scripture: Citation Technique in the Pauline Epistles and Contemporary Literature*. Cambridge: Cambridge University Press, 1992.
Stegner, William Richard. "Jesus' Walking on the Water: Mark 6:45–52." In *Gospels and the Scriptures of Israel*, edited by Craig A. Evans and W. Richard Stegner, 212–34. JSNTSup 104. Sheffield: Sheffield Academic, 1994.
Stein, Robert H. "Interpreting the Synoptic Gospels." In *Interpreting the New Testament: Essays on Methods and Issues*, edited by D. A. Black and D. S. Dockery, 336–56. Nashville: Broadman & Holman, 2001.
———. *Mark*. Baker Exegetical Commentary on the New Testament. Grand Rapids: Baker Academic, 2008.
Stemberger, Günter. "Galilee–Land of Salvation?" In *The Gospel and the Land: Early Christianity and Jewish Territorial Doctrine*, edited by W. D. Davies, 409–38. Berkeley: University of California Press, 1974.
Stewart, Eric C. *Gathered around Jesus: An Alternative Spatial Practice in the Gospel of Mark*. Eugene, OR: Cascade, 2009.
Stock, Augustine. *The Way in the Wilderness: Exodus, Wilderness, and Moses Themes in Old Testament and New*. Collegeville: Liturgical, 1969.
Storey, David. *Territory: The Claiming of Space*. 2nd ed. New York: Routledge, 2012.
Strack, Hermann Leberecht, and Paul Billerbeck. *Kommentar zum Neuen Testament aus Talmud und Midrasch*. 6 vols. München: Beck, 1922.
Stuart, Douglas K. *Exodus*. The New American Commentary 2. Nashville: Broadman & Holman, 2006.
———. *Hosea-Jonah*. Word Biblical Commentary 31. Waco, TX: Word, 1987.
Suhl, Alfred. *Die Funktion der alttestamentlichen Zitate Und Anspielungen im Markusevangelium*. Gütersloher: Gütersoher Verlagshaus G. Mohn, 1965.
Swartley, Willard M. *Israel's Scripture Traditions and the Synoptic Gospels: Story Shaping Story*. Peabody: Hendrickson, 1994.
———. "A Study in Markan Structure: The Influence of Israel's Holy History upon the Structure of the Gospel of Mark." PhD diss., Princeton Theological Seminary, 1973.

Talmon, S. "מִדְבָּר midbār; עֲרָבָה 'arābâ." In *TDOT* 8:87–118.
Tannehill, Robert C. "Disciples in Mark: The Function of a Narrative Role." *JR* 57 (1977) 386–405.
Tate, Marvin E. *Psalms 51–100*. Word Biblical Commentary 20. Nashville: Thomas Nelson, 1990.
Taylor, Vincent. *The Gospel according to St. Mark*. 2nd ed. London: Macmillan, 1966.
Teugels, Lieve M. *Bible and Midrash: The Story of "The Wooing of Rebekah" (Gen 24)*. CBET 35. Leuven: Peeters, 2004.
Theissen, Gerd. *The Gospels in Context: Social and Political History in the Synoptic Tradition*. Translated by Linda M. Maloney. Minneapolis: Fortress, 1991.
———. *The Miracle Stories of the Early Christian Tradition*. Translated by Francis McDonagh. Philadelphia: Fortress, 1983.
Thiselton, Anthony C. "Hermeneutics." In *NDT* 293–97.
Thompson, Michael. *Clothed with Christ: The Example and Teaching of Jesus in Romans 12:1–15:13*. JSNTSup 59. Sheffield: JSOT Press, 1991.
Tilley, Christopher. *A Phenomenology of Landscape: Places, Paths, and Monuments*. Oxford: Berg, 1994.
Treier, Daniel J. "Typology." In *DTIB* 823–27.
Trocmé, Etienne. *The Formation of the Gospel according to Mark*. Translated by Pamela Gaughan. Philadelphia: Westminster, 1975.
Tromp, Nicholas J. *Primitive Conceptions of Death and the Nether World in the Old Testament*. BibOr 21. Rome: Pontifical Biblical Institute, 1969.
Tsumura, David Toshio. *The Earth and the Waters in Genesis 1 and 2: A Linguistic Investigation*. JSOTSup 83. Sheffield: JSOT Press, 1989.
Twelftree, Graham H. *Jesus the Miracle Worker: A Historical & Theological Study*. Downers Grove, IL: InterVarsity, 1999.
———. "Scribes." In *DNTB* 1086–89.
Tyson, Joseph B. "Blindness of the Disciples in Mark." *JBL* 80 (1961) 261–68.
VanGemeren, Willem A. *Psalms*. Edited by Tremper Longman III and David E. Garland. Vol. 5. Rev. ed. The Expositor's Bible Commentary. Grand Rapids: Zondervan, 2008.
Vanhoozer, Kevin J. *Is There a Meaning in This Text?: The Bible, the Reader, and the Morality of Literary Knowledge*. Grand Rapids: Zondervan, 1998.
———, et al., eds. *Dictionary for Theological Interpretation of the Bible*. Grand Rapids: Baker Academic, 2005.
Van Oyen, Geert. *The Interpretation of the Feeding Miracles in the Gospel of Mark*. CBRA 4. Brussel: Koninklijke Vlaamse Academie van België, 1999.
Vermès, Géza. *Jesus the Jew: A Historian's Reading of the Gospels*. New York: Macmillan, 1973.
Vogt, Ernst. "Regen in Fülle (Psalm 68:10–11)." *Bib* 46 (1965) 359–61.
Volkmar, Gustav. *Marcus und die Synopse der Evangelien nach dem urkundlichen Text und das geschichtliche vom Leben Jesu*. Zürich: Verlag von Caesar Schmidt, 1869.
Vorster, Willem S. "Intertextuality and Redaktionsgeschichte." In *Intertextuality in Biblical Writings: Essays in Honour of Bas Van Iersel*, edited by Sipke Draisma, 15–26. Kampen: J. H. Kok, 1989.
Wall, Lynne. "Finding Identity in the Wilderness." In *Wilderness: Essays in Honour of Frances Young*, edited by R. S Sugirtharajah, 66–77. LNTS 295. London: T&T Clark International, 2005.

Walton, John H. *Genesis*. The NIV Application Commentary. Grand Rapids: Zondervan, 2001.

Watts, Rikki E. *Isaiah's New Exodus and Mark*. WUNT 2/88. Tübingen: Mohr Siebeck, 1997.

———. "Mark." In *Commentary on the New Testament Use of the Old Testament*, edited by G. K. Beale and D. A. Carson, 111–249. Grand Rapids: Baker Academic, 2007.

Weeden, Theodore J. "The Heresy That Necessitated Mark's Gospel." In *The Interpretation of Mark*, edited by William Telford, 64–77. Philadelphia: Fortress, 1985.

———. *Mark-Traditions in Conflict*. Philadelphia: Fortress, 1971.

Wefald, Eric K. "The Separate Gentile Mission in Mark: A Narrative Explanation of Markan Geography, the Two Feeding Accounts and Exorcisms." *JSNT* 60 (1995) 3–26.

Weinfeld, M. "כָּבוֹד kābôḏ." In *TDOT* 7:22–38.

Weiser, Artur. *The Psalms: A Commentary*. Old Testament Library. Philadelphia: Westminster, 1962.

Weiss, Johannes. *Das älteste Evangelium: ein Beitrag zum Verständnis des Markus-Evangeliums und der ältesten evangelischen Überlieferung*. Göttingen: Vandenhoeck und Ruprecht, 1903.

Weizsäcker, Carl. *Untersuchungen über die evangelische Geschichte: Ihre Quellen und den Gang ihrer Entwicklung*. Tübingen and Leipzig: Mohr Siebeck, 1864.

Wellhausen, Julius. *Das Evangelium Marci*. Berlin: G. Reimer, 1903.

Wenham, Gordon J. *Genesis 1–15*. Word Biblical Commentary 1. Nashville: Thomas Nelson, 1987.

Wieder, Naphtali. *The Judean Scrolls and Karaism*. London: East and West Library, 1962.

Williams, Joel F. *Other Followers of Jesus: Minor Characters as Major Figures in Mark's Gospel*. JSNTSup 102. Sheffield: JSOT Press, 1994.

Williamson, Lamar, Jr. *Mark*. Interpretation: A Bible Commentary for Teaching and Preaching. Louisville: Westminster John Knox, 2009.

Witherington, Ben, III. *The Gospel of Mark: A Socio-Rhetorical Commentary*. Grand Rapids: Eerdmans, 2001.

———. "John the Baptist." In *DJG* 383–91.

Woodroof, Timothy. "The Church as Boat in Mark: Building a Seaworthy Church." *ResQ* 39 (1997) 231–49.

Wrede, William. *The Messianic Secret*. Translated by J. C. G. Greig. Cambridge: James Clarke, 1971. Originally published as *Das Messiasgeheimnis in den Evangelien; Zugleich ein Beitrag zum Verständnis des Markusevangeliums*. Göttingen: Vandenhoeck & Ruprecht, 1901.

Younger, K. Lawson, Jr. "The Deportations of the Israelites." *JBL* 117 (1998) 201–27.

Author Index

Abrams, Meyer Howard, 23, 33, 147
Achtemeier, Paul J., 8, 111–15, 121, 127–28, 184, 190
Allen, Leslie C., 180
Allison, D. C., Jr., 200, 213
Alt, Albrecht, 80
Alter, Robert, 38
Anderson, A. A., 206-7, 211
Anderson, Bernhard W., 162, 177, 181

Baarlink, Heinrich, 129
Baker, David L., 42
Baker, David W., 176
Baltzer, Klaus, 184
Barnwell, William H., 103
Barr, James, 71
Barthes, Roland, 43–44
Bartholomew, Craig, 10–12
Bauer, David R., 35
Bauer, Walter, 80
Beal, Timothy K., 43–45
Beale, G. K., 48–50
Berlin, Adele, 20
Bertram, Georg, 80
Best, Ernest, 103, 135–36, 157
Betz, Otto, 193, 195
Billerbeck, Paul, 60
Bland, D. S., 2–3
Boring, M. Eugene, 97–98, 134–35, 148, 155, 199–200, 217–19, 221, 223
Bowman, John, 9, 102
Brandon, S. G. F., 228
Brooks, James, 132, 139
Brower, Kent E., 77

Bruckner, James K., 179
Brunson, Andrew C., 43–44, 49, 51, 53, 55, 165
Buchanan, George Wesley, 46
Buchholz, Sabine, 31–32
Budd, Philip J., 228
Bultmann, Rudolf, 196, 220

Campbell, Antony F., 166
Carson, D. A., 48–50, 108, 220
Catchpole, David R., 157
Chapman, Dean W., 4–5, 15–16, 187, 214–15
Chatman, Seymour, 20–21, 31–32, 35
Clifford, Richard J., 162, 165–67, 169–70, 186
Coats, George W., 166
Collins, Adela Yarbro, 91, 129–30, 133, 135, 172, 189, 226–27
Collins, John J., 213
Cope, O. Lamar., 191
Cranfield, C. E. B., 4, 140, 214
Culler, Jonathan D., 45
Cullmann, Oscar, 28–29
Curtis, Adrian H. W., 180–81

Dahood, Mitchell J., 206–7
Dalman, Gustaf, 139–40
Danker, F. W., 142
Daube, David, 67
Davies, William David, 59–60
Dearman, J. Andrew, 212
Derrett, J. Duncan M., 9
Derrida, Jacques, 43
DeSilva, David Arthur, 10

Dewey, Joanna, 6, 30–31, 35–40, 51, 71–73, 146–47, 161
Dibelius, Martin, 196–97
Dodd, C. H., 66
Donahue, John R., 25, 85, 91–92, 106, 133, 141, 144, 150, 172, 174, 197–98, 219
Dozeman, Thomas B., 179
Draisma, Sipke, 44
Durham, John I., 178–79, 205

Edwards, James R., 29, 38, 115, 119, 138, 140, 151–52, 188, 190, 194, 198, 228
Eissfeldt, Otto, 165
Elliott-Binns, Leonard Elliott, 6, 60–61
Enns, Peter, 204
Erlangen, Gerhard Friedrich, 223
Evans, Craig A., 42, 52, 132

Farrer, Austin, 9, 102
Fishbane, Michael, 49, 53
Fisher, Fred L., 9, 162
Fleddermann, Harry, 197
Fowler, Robert M., 37, 101–3, 106–8, 110, 114, 121–22, 128, 156
France, R. T., 29, 66–67, 84, 91–95, 97, 106–7, 119, 135, 139, 148, 152, 154, 188, 191, 197, 213–14, 219–20, 223–24, 227–28
Freyne, Seán, 6, 60, 70, 73–75, 79–87, 91–93, 95–96, 98–99, 234

Garland, David E., 172
Garrett, Duane A., 212
Geddert, Timothy J., 171
Genette, Gérard, 25–28, 32
Gibson, Jeffrey, 154
Gnilka, Joachim, 191, 197, 216, 223, 228
Goldingay, John, 166, 179–81, 183, 185, 208
Goppelt, Leonhard, 42
Grassi, Joseph A., 221, 227
Greenstein, Edward L., 174
Grundmann, Walter, 80

Guelich, Robert A., 29, 66, 91, 106–7, 109, 114–15, 132, 139–40, 142, 154, 172, 191, 194–97, 216–17, 219, 222, 225, 228
Gundry, Robert H., 4, 107, 109, 114–15, 141, 157–58, 194
Gunkel, Hermann, 165, 176
Gunther, Müller, 26

Haenchen, Ernst, 64, 103
Hamilton, Victor P., 177
Harner, Philip B., 209
Harpham, Geoffrey Galt, 23, 33, 147
Harrington, Daniel, 25, 85, 91–92, 106, 133, 135–36, 141, 144, 148, 150, 172, 174, 189, 193, 197–98, 219, 226
Harvey, David, 13, 16
Harvey, Julien, 169
Hatina, Thomas R., 9, 10
Hays, Richard B., 44, 50, 52–54
Healy, Mary, 132
Hedrick, Charles W., 120, 131
Heidel, Alexander, 177
Heil, John Paul, 196–99
Henderson, Suzanne Watts, 157
Hobbs, E. C., 9
Homan, Michael M., 94
Hooker, Morna D., 9, 38, 67, 114–15, 132–33, 135, 157–58, 171–72, 192, 194–95, 219
Horsley, Richard A., 81, 86
Hossfeld, Frank-Lothar, 165, 169–71, 180, 206

Inhelder, Bärbel, 14
Iverson, Kelly R., 124, 142

Jahn, Manfred, 31–32
Jenkins, Luke H., 4, 8, 103, 105–8, 127–28
Jeremias, Joachim, 214–15, 227
Johnson, Earl S., Jr., 134
Johnson, S. E., 220
Johnston, James A., 9
Johnston, R. J., 13
Jones, Brian C., 213
Jonge, Marinus de, 213

Josephus, Flavius, 82, 88–89, 94, 97, 152, 193, 215
Juel, Donald, 213

Kakkanattu, Joy Philip, 71
Katzenstein, H. J., 139
Keck, Leander E., 108–10
Kee, Howard Clark, 55, 67–68, 163–64, 182–83, 189–90, 229, 231, 236
Keener, Craig S., 81
Keesmaat, Sylvia C., 51–52
Kelber, Werner H., 6, 59, 65–69, 119, 121, 124, 126, 129, 131, 157, 160
Kittel, Gisela, 189, 213, 215–16
Koch, Dietrich Alex, 189, 213, 215–16
Kort, Wesley A., 23
Köster, H., 228
Kraus, Hans-Joachim, 165–69
Kristeva, Julia, 43–44
Kroeger, Catherine C., 152
Kuhn, Heinz-Wolfgang, 8, 102, 109–10
Kümmel, Werner Georg, 8, 66–67, 121, 130
Kurz, William S., 46

Lampe, G. W. H., 42
Lane, William L., 67, 92, 94, 103, 106, 119, 139, 140, 154, 221–22, 225
Lang, Friedrich Gustav, 102, 140
Leal, Robert Barry, 203, 207
Lefebvre, Henri, 2, 13, 16–18
Lenski, Gerhard, 88
Leonard, Jeffery M., 53–54
Lévi-Strauss, Claude, 6, 68
Lightfoot, Robert Henry, 6, 59
Lim, Bo H., 209
Limburg, James, 197
Lohmeyer, Ernst, 6, 59, 63–64, 102, 196–97
Loos, Hendrik van der, 189
Lührmann, Dieter, 89, 132

Malbon, Elizabeth Struthers, 3, 5, 6, 8, 20–21, 25, 30, 35–36, 39, 55, 58–59, 65, 68–71, 98–99, 114, 122, 124, 126, 129, 132–33, 137, 149, 155–58, 187
Malina, Bruce J., 29, 204
Marcus, Joel, 9, 25, 28, 110, 114, 134, 154, 173, 190–92, 198–99, 202, 219, 221, 223–27
Martin, William C., 184–86
Marxsen, Willi, 6, 8, 59, 62–65, 102, 120–21
Mason, Steve, 88
Matera, Frank J., 157
Mathews, Claire R., 210
Mathews, K. A., 176–77
Mathewson, David, 176
Mauser, Ulrich W., 205, 207–8, 211–16, 220–23, 225–26
Mays, James L., 165–66, 170, 206, 212
Meier, John P., 91–92
Meyer, Eduard, 8, 103
Meyers, Carol L., 205
Meyers, Eric M., 87
Michie, Donald, 6, 30–31, 36–38, 51, 71–73, 146–47, 161
Moloney, Francis J., 194, 224
Moore, Stephen D., 44–45
Mowery, Robert L., 89
Moxnes, Halvor, 2, 86–87, 95–96, 100
Moyise, Steve, 44–46
Neirynck, Frans, 110, 113, 128
Neusner, Jacob, 91
Nineham, D. E., 4
Ninow, Friedbert, 42
Nixon, R. E., 9, 164
Noll, S. F., 213

O'Day, Gail R., 47
Oepke, Albrecht, 151–52
Osborne, Grant R., 8, 10–11, 19–21, 25, 42, 46–48, 52–54, 71, 137, 220
Oswalt, John N., 185, 210, 221
Overman, Andrew, 87

Paffenroth, Kim, 90
Page, Franklin S., 195
Painter, John, 195
Pao, David W., 11, 182–84, 186, 209
Patterson, Richard D., 169

Perkins, Larry, 9
Perrin, Norman, 103
Pesch, Rudolf, 8, 102-3, 107-10, 127-28
Petersen, Norman R., 8, 34, 102, 116-20, 125, 128-29, 132-33, 137, 143, 156
Pfister, Manfred, 45
Phelan, John E., 8, 122, 153
Piaget, Jean, 14
Pickup, Martin, 89
Piper, Otto A., 9, 161-62, 164-65
Porter, Stanley E., 43, 51, 53
Powell, Mark Allan, 5, 11, 20-22, 24, 30, 34-35, 147
Power, Edmond, 220
Propp, William H. C., 54, 179, 208

Rad, Gerhard von, 177
Rawlinson, A. E. J., 3
Rengstorf, K. H., 119
Resseguie, James L., 23, 36-37
Rey-Coquais, Jean-Paul, 144
Reymond, Philippe, 176-78
Rhoads, David, 2, 5, 9, 21-23, 30-31, 33-34, 36-40, 51, 71-73, 99, 146-47, 161-62
Riches, John K., 31
Ringgren, L., 177, 179-81
Robbins, Vernon K., 12
Rosner, Brian S., 47-48

Sack, Robert David, 2, 13-15
Saldarini, Anthony J., 88-90
Sawicki, Marianne, 96
Schmid, Josef, 8, 103, 107
Schmidt, Daryl D., 111
Schneck, Richard, 9
Scholer, D. M., 151-52
Schreiber, Johannes, 115
Seely, David Rolph, 184
Sherwin-White, A. N., 93-94
Smalley, Stephen S., 136-37
Smith, Billy K., 195
Smith, Dennis E., 217
Smith, Gary V., 182-83
Smith, Stephen H., 3, 9, 23-28, 114, 161-62

Snoy, Thierry, 113, 197
Soden, Hermann von, 8, 102
Sommer, Benjamin D., 46
Stanley, Christopher D., 51
Stegner, William Richard, 178, 197, 200-201
Stein, Robert H., 25, 115, 119, 132, 135, 141, 172, 220, 225
Stemberger, Günter, 61, 63-65
Stewart, Eric C., 1, 4, 58-60, 70, 76-77, 79, 96
Stock, Augustine, 208, 212-13
Storey, David, 13
Strack, Hermann Leberecht, 60
Stuart, Douglas K., 212, 228
Suhl, Alfred, 9
Swartley, Willard M., 9, 173

Talmon, S., 204-5, 210
Tannehill, Robert C., 157
Tate, Marvin E., 166, 170, 180, 206
Taylor, Vincent, 103, 195
Teugels, Lieve M., 38
Theissen, Gerd, 4, 196
Thiselton, Anthony C., 10, 42
Thompson, Michael, 50-51, 53-55
Tilley, Christopher, 13, 17-18
Treier, Daniel J., 42
Trocmé, Etienne, 157
Tromp, Nicholas J., 178
Tsumura, David Toshio, 177
Twelftree, Graham H., 91, 188
Tyson, Joseph B., 156-57

VanGemeren, Willem A., 167, 181, 206
Vanhoozer, Kevin J., 44-45
Van Oyen, Geert, 8, 102
Vermès, Géza, 91
Vogt, Ernst, 207
Volkmar, Gustav, 102-3
Vorster, Willem S., 45, 47-48, 50

Wall, Lynne, 203
Walton, John H., 176-77
Watts, Rikki E., 9, 172-75, 179, 183, 190, 199, 224
Weeden, Theodore J., 157

Wefald, Eric K., 84, 124, 129, 150, 154
Weinfeld, M., 205
Weiser, Artur, 170
Weiss, Johannes, 103
Weizsäcker, Carl, 8, 102
Wellhausen, Julius, 103
Wenham, Gordon J., 176–77
Wieder, Naphtali, 60
Williams, Joel F., 37, 133, 135–36, 145–46, 150, 218

Williamson, Lamar, Jr., 134
Witherington, Ben, III, 40, 129, 213
Woodroof, Timothy, 131–32
Woollcombe, K. J., 42
Wrede, William, 3, 101

Younger, K. Lawson, 80

Zenger, Erich, 165, 169–71, 180, 206

www.ingramcontent.com/pod-product-compliance
Ingram Content Group UK Ltd.
Pitfield, Milton Keynes, MK11 3LW, UK
UKHW022000220326
11408UKWH00003B/402